THE LOST HISTORY OF TENNESSEE WHISKEY

HEROES, VILLAINS, AND LEGENDS FROM A WHISKEY STORY TIME FORGOT

DREW HANNUSH

Copyright © 2023 by Drew Hannush

The Lost History of Tennessee Whiskey

All rights reserved. No part of this publication may be reproduced, distributed or transmitted in any form or by any means, including photocopying, recording, or other electronic or mechanical methods, without the prior written permission of the publisher, except in the case of brief quotations embodied in critical reviews and certain other noncommercial uses permitted by copyright law. Whiskey Lore is a trademark of Travel Fuels Life, LLC.

Neither the author nor the publisher assume any responsibility or liability whatsoever on behalf of the consumer or reader of this material.

Any website links are being provided as a convenience (including pass-through links) and for informational purposes only; the website owners are alone responsible for the accuracy, legality of their content. Contact the external site for information regarding its content.

The content in this book is intended for educational purposes.

First Edition 2023, Published by Travel Fuels Life, LLC (dba Whiskey Lore)

Cover Photos by Drew Hannush

ISBN: 978-1-7348651-6-5
Kindle ISBN: 978-1-7348651-7-2

Audiobook available at whiskey-lore.com/audio

Dedication

To my dad for the stories and giving me a love for history; to my mom for helping me look into the hearts of people; and to Alan and Colleen for the unfailing support.

Also Cal for inspiring me and changing my perspective on life. Your courage, grace, and ability to rise above makes you legendary.

Contents

PREFACE	VII
PART ONE: HISTORY	1
1. BEFORE TENNESSEE WHISKY	3
2. THE FIRST DISTILLERS	11
3. PLANTING THE SEED	19
4. THE FUGITIVE	27
5. A REMARKABLE LIFE	41
6. OLD HICKORY	55
7. THE WILD FRONTIER	69
PART TWO: LOST DISTILLERS	83
8. BIRTH OF AN INDUSTRY	85
9. WHAT MADE IT LINCOLN?	95
10. DEMON ALCOHOL	107
11. TROUBLE BREWING	121
12. WHISKY REBELLION	133
13. THE HEARTBEAT OF OLD LINCOLN	147
14. AGAINST ALL ODDS	163
15. THE GOLDEN AGE OF OLD ROBERTSON	177
16. TIGHTENING THE GRIP	189

17.	MEN OF MYSTERY	199
18.	WATERFORD WANDERER	213
19.	THE REVENOOR	229
20.	WOMEN OF MYSTERY	245
21.	THE SHOT THAT KILLED WHISKY	257
22.	OL' DAN IS DEAD	279
23.	THE BOSS AND MEMPHIS	295
24.	LAST RITES	317
25.	A DIFFERENT KIND OF PROHIBITION	329
PART THREE: REVIVAL		345
26.	HOW DRY I AM?	347
27.	NOT SO FAST!	361
28.	AND THEN THERE WERE TWO	375
29.	PLAYED TO PERFECTION	391
30.	BLAZING A NEW TRAIL	401
EPILOGUE: FINDING HISTORY		427
ACKNOWLEDGEMENTS		433
BIBLIOGRAPHY		437
ENDNOTES		441
INDEX AND COMMUNITY		481

PREFACE

What is Tennessee whiskey?

If you asked me that question in 2018, I would have said Jack Daniel's and George Dickel. If you asked me what makes those different from Bourbon, I couldn't have told you.

If you asked me what Bourbon is, I would say: American whiskey distilled in Kentucky, using limestone-filtered water. Naming brands would be easy; there are hundreds.

The lack of awareness of the differences between Bourbon and Tennessee whiskey is no accident.

Since Prohibition, Kentucky has produced millions of gallons of Bourbon and spent millions of dollars promoting it. When historians talk about American whiskey, they talk about it from a Kentucky Bourbon perspective. Kentucky Bourbon is so dominant, distillery tours have to remind you that Bourbon is a distinctive product of the United States, not just Kentucky.

As for Tennessee whiskey, it was several years after Prohibition before Jack Daniel's became the first brand to return. It took another two decades before George Dickel returned, and the full return of Tennessee whiskey is a recent occurrence. It's not a surprise I didn't realize the spirit had a history.

So, when I decided to learn about American whiskey, naturally my instinct was to go to Kentucky. As I plotted out my personal whiskey education tour, I put 17 Kentucky distilleries on my schedule. The only reason I put Jack Daniel's and George Dickel on my agenda was because Tennessee was on the way home.

The Kentucky tour was great! I enjoyed the whiskey tastings and learning what made each distillery's process unique. But what really stood out were all the stories, history, and lore. And it wasn't just the history of the distillery––most tour guides paid homage to the evolution of Bourbon as well. Obviously, whiskey-loving Kentuckians are born with Bourbon pride.

When I crossed into Tennessee and got down to George Dickel, I enjoyed the tour but the history confused me. From what I was hearing, it was possible George Dickel never saw his own distillery. They weren't even sure if the bronze bust outside was an accurate representation of him. And they said very little about the legacy of Tennessee whiskey.

Then I headed off to Lynchburg and the Jack Daniel Distillery. From a distillery history standpoint, it was the exact opposite of George Dickel. There was so much history and lore, and the small-town distillery feel was so charming, it became my favorite tour of the entire trip. However, it was all Jack Daniel's history with no focus on the state. I left with the impression that these were the only two professional whiskey distilleries in the state's history.

Because of this, when it came time for me to expand my whiskey knowledge, I didn't give Tennessee a second thought. Instead, I headed off to Scotland. There were so many brilliant stories there, I returned home and launched my whiskey storytelling podcast *Whiskey Lore Stories*. This led to another Kentucky trip. From that came my book, *Whiskey Lore's Travel Guide to Experiencing Kentucky Bourbon*.

Again, Tennessee was nowhere in my plans. Ireland was my next destination. I had my plans all set for April 2020. Of course, the pandemic put an end to that plan. Like everyone else, I sat and waited to renew my life's journey.

Finding Tennessee

With my Kentucky book launched and no way to get overseas, I started thinking more about Tennessee. Over the winter, I heard the names of a couple of other brands of Tennessee whiskey beyond Jack and George. I did a Google Maps search and, to my surprise, found 20 additional distilleries I didn't know existed.

I plotted out a trip across the state with 19 distilleries on a ten-day schedule. I started in the eastern part of the state at Tennessee Hills Distillery. Built into a pre-Civil War era salt house, I learned about the building and the historic town of Jonesborough while talking to Stephen, the owner. But we didn't cover the state's distilling history.

Then I went to Lost State Distillery in Bristol, where I toured, and learned about their charcoal mellowing process and their history. Then I asked about their whiskey "Shelby's Reserve" and where it got its name from. Apparently, Evan Shelby made whiskey in the area in the 1770s and held the distinction of being Tennessee's first distiller.

This was just the information I was looking for. But for the rest of the journey, I struggled to find anything beyond each distillery's own recent history. Still, there was a comfort in the coziness of those Tennessee distilleries. I was meeting founders and distillers, something I didn't experience in Kentucky. I felt like I was watching an industry re-emerge. But re-emerging from what?

Then, I caught an episode of Jack Daniel's *Around the Barrel* podcast. The guest was Jack Daniel's historian Nelson Eddy. I didn't even realize a position like "distillery historian" existed. The host Lucas was focusing on the history of Jack Daniel's bottle shape, but it was a side conversation that really drew me in. Nelson talked about a shootout in the streets of Nashville that led to Tennessee Prohibition, ten years before the rest of the country.

It piqued my curiosity. I decided it was time to interview founders who seemed to have a sense of Tennessee's distilling past. My first visit was with Andy Nelson of Nelson's Green Brier in Nashville. He told me how he and his brother stumbled upon the story of their ancestor Charles Nelson, who was the largest distiller in the state in the 19th century. The next day I was in Lynchburg having a fascinating conversation with Nelson Eddy about the Nashville shootout, Jack Daniel's lore, and the distillery's first master distiller, Nearest Green.

I couldn't get enough. Over the next two years, I dug into the story of Tennessee Prohibition and the Lincoln County Process, and tried to understand the story of George Dickel. I found other characters like the wholesaler-turned-distiller J.W. Kelly. And I was finding the more recent history fascinating, too. For the longest time, only three counties in the state were open to distilling. Chattanooga Distillery had to fight to get the laws changed so they could distill in their own hometown. But everything I was learning, I was learning on my own. There were no comprehensive books on Tennessee whiskey history.

I thought about writing a book myself, but a history book is a large undertaking that requires deep research. I continued to collect bits and pieces of information, but turned my attention to writing a Tennessee distillery travel guide instead.

During a trip to Company Distilling at Thompson Station, in the fall of 2022, I met the distillery's founder, Heath Clark. Heath is someone I long wanted to talk to. His desire to open a distillery led him to draft legislation that ignited the current Tennessee whiskey boom. I asked him about those early days and told him about my Tennessee whiskey history book project. When I told him I had put that project on ice to work on the travel book, he urged me to press forward with the history book. In that instant, I committed all of my energies to this project.

My travel habits changed immediately. Instead of traveling to distilleries, I was heading to local, state, and national archives. Newspapers became my friend as I looked for contemporary accounts of distillers and distilleries. I began shaping chapters, which quickly expanded from ten to 30. The more I dug in, the more I found Tennessee whiskey's past to be rich with stories. And what I was learning wasn't just shaping Tennessee whiskey's history. It was reshaping my understanding of American whiskey history.

It has been a long journey of rabbit holes and revisions. I prepared over 600 pages of notes for this book. Deciding which stories to cut was a difficult process. I decided to avoid lore and only include stories supported by facts. The resulting work is the most complete picture of the area's amazing 250 year distilling history produced to date. I hope it is as enlightening for you as the research material was for me.

Just keep a few things in mind while you read:

Prepare to have your knowledge of whiskey history challenged in this work. As I mentioned before, much of America's whiskey history comes from a Kentucky Bourbon perspective. It also relies too heavily on Scots-Irish and Whiskey Rebellion narratives. As you read this book, new heroes, villains and legends will emerge. It won't be long before you realize, Tennessee played a bigger role in the early days of distilling than history has led you to believe.

Know that the modern rules of Tennessee whiskey only came about in 2013. These are similar to Bourbon's rules, with the additional step of charcoal mellowing. This leads to the conclusion Tennessee whiskey is simply an altered version of Bourbon: A mindset that has caused Tennessee's distilling legacy to be minimized. As you will learn, in the 19th century, Tennessee and Kentucky were strong competitors. Competitors look for an edge. It's time to let go of modern rules and assumptions and learn how Tennessee's whiskey and distillers set themselves apart.

Also, don't be too concerned with firsts. Marketing departments are obsessed with saying something is "the first" or "the best." Early distillers were just doing a chore. They didn't care if they were first, so few records exist of their activities, and most of their processes evolved over time. Meanwhile, "the best" is a matter of taste. While marketing departments are the reason products become known, they are also a barrier to learning the genuine history of the spirit. As you will discover, 19th-century marketing is filled with fables. Some of those fables have survived into the modern age because they were the easiest records to access. In researching this book, know that I approached every marketer's claim with the skepticism they deserve. And while I fall into the trap of firsts occasionally, I have done my best to avoid those claims.

Another thing to keep in mind is the relationship between personal titles, distillery names, and the people actually doing the work. Ask a current master distiller what they do day in and day out, and it might surprise you to find they don't really distill. Some are ambassadors, some are production directors, and, in small- to medium-sized distilleries, they may take a more hand-on approach. It was the same in the past. We assume that because they named a distillery after an individual, that means he did the distilling. In reality, Tennessee and Kentucky whiskeys were just as likely distilled by enslaved workers as by the man whose name adorned the business. And before whiskey became an industry, distilling was a hearth skill usually performed by women. Yet we rarely mention their names in whiskey history. It is a problem that any historian worth their salt would love to see remedied. But if those distillers weren't documented then, it is hard to document them now. So, as you read these pages, remember the forgotten souls that were the glue that held this industry together and helped it grow.

And know too that the early part of this book will focus heavily on the state's history and tavern culture. To understand distillers, we have to understand the spirit of the state they live in and the culture and obstacles they faced. Distillers will weave in and out early on, but will become a primary focus as the book progresses. Occasionally, we will take an unexpected turn into a seemingly unrelated story. Trust me, the story will add value to your knowledge of Tennessee whiskey or whiskey in general.

Just one more thing. Don't get confused by the alternate spellings of whiskey. Before the 20th century, the spelling of the word was a matter of taste. The Scottish have been one of the few cultures to remain faithful to a single spelling for almost 300 years. In Tennessee, prior to Prohibition, an overwhelming majority of writers spelled the word "whisky." I will continue that tradition, unless a brand consistently spells it whiskey. With any Prohibition or post-Prohibition "whiskey" I will use the "e" unless a brand like George Dickel spells it the old way.

Now, it is time to dive into Tennessee whiskey history. Enjoy the journey. By the end, I think you will agree that Tennessee whiskey history is fascinating and has been hidden for far too long.

PART ONE: HISTORY

BIRTH OF TENNESSEE AND ITS WHISKY

Chapter 1

BEFORE TENNESSEE WHISKY

The Friends' Goodwill

It was a journey unlike any they could imagine. Fifty-two men, women, and children huddled together, dreaming of an American promised land.

Their ship, the *Friends' Goodwill*, was a small but sturdy vessel. Yet, as they left the picturesque Irish quay of Larne Harbour in County Antrim, they quickly realized it was unsuitable for their needs. But these were desperate times and the *Goodwill*'s passengers felt an undying need to escape from a land that had never quite embraced them.

It was a feeling shared by a growing number of people known as the Ulster-Scots. To them, life in Ireland had become unbearable and those fifty-two souls who sailed that May morning in 1717 represented the inception of their great escape. By the end of the century, over a quarter of a million Ulster-Scots followed in the *Goodwill*'s path.

The ship was stocked with an ample supply of food, water, and supplies for a normal two and a half month journey. But the passengers quickly learned the North Atlantic had its own timetable. Days into their journey, they encountered an incredible storm. Slipping deeper and deeper into the grip of angry waves, they held on for dear life. Most were unprepared for the vicious temper of the sea. Many fell ill, turning the *Goodwill* into a torture chamber of grief and sickness.

To make matters worse, the storms kept pulling the small craft back toward European shores.

As one month passed into two, a quiet desperation set in. They were only halfway to their destination. Food stocks were low and the captain limited rations to mere crumbs. Days into their second month, a glorious cry drifted down from the crow's nest. "Ship ahead!" A merchant ship traveling east had wandered into their path. When the captain of the vessel saw the wretched state of the *Goodwill*'s passengers, he provided additional rations.

As the days and weeks passed, the passengers tried catching dolphins and sharks to stretch their meager food supplies. Some questioned whether they would ever see America.

After four torturous months at sea, the crew and passengers alike gave a mighty sigh at the words "land ho." Boston Harbor must have looked like paradise on Earth; the hunger disappeared and faint rays of hope grew bright. As the feet of those Ulster-Scots kissed the ground, they gave a prayer to the heavens that this new land would be different.

The Ulster-Scots

The migration to America wasn't the first journey for the Ulster-Scots. As their name suggests, they were once residents of the borderlands of Scotland and England. Presbyterians by faith and hardscrabble farmers by labor, King Henry VIII planted them in Ireland to subdue the Gaelic lords and Catholics. Subsequent kings and queens also used this plantation system to populate the island with people more subservient to the crown. While the Catholics remained, the Gaelic lords gave up their lands during the Flight of the Earls in 1607, allowing the plantation system to expand exponentially in the northern Irish province of Ulster.

As their numbers increased, kings and queens saw the Ulster Presbyterians as a threat to the Church of England. When King William III died in 1702, his successor Queen Anne placed major restrictions on the Ulster-Scots. Using the

Test Act, she forced Catholic and Presbyterian ministers to take the sacrament of the Church of England. If they refused, they lost their rights to perform weddings and funerals.

Then plantation rack rents rose to an unmanageable level, making Presbyterian farmers all but enslaved to their landlords. When a severe drought hit the land in the early 1710s, the poorest among them had to decide: Did they want to be enslaved as renters in Ireland or deal with temporary indentured servitude as payment for passage to America? For most, the choice was simple.

The Journey to the Land of the Cherokee

The first groups of Ulster-Scots (who initially became known as the Scotch-Irish in America) were welcomed by Royal Governor Samuel Shute of the Massachusetts and New Hampshire provinces. He thought the hearty Scotch-Irish made an excellent frontier buffer against the aggressions of the tribes and the French in Canada.

His encouragement led to more boats arriving from Ulster during the summer of 1718. Two of the boats held the congregation of Rev. James MacGregor, who settled in Nutfield, New Hampshire, established a community, and changed the town's name to Londonderry to honor their homeland. The town was then used as a staging point for Scotch-Irish migration up to Nova Scotia and south to Pennsylvania.

The first wave of Pennsylvania-bound Scotch-Irish found a friendly advocate in an Ulsterman and Quaker named James Logan. Holding the post as provincial secretary, he felt their bravery and thirst for freedom would be a godsend on the increasingly violent frontier, and he provided them with lands west of Philadelphia. But their defensiveness and rowdy behavior didn't sit well with the area's pacifist Quakers. So many moved deeper into the western frontier.

Isolated living was well suited to the Scotch-Irish. The oppression of the Crown had taught them self-sufficiency. They worshiped and taught their children in private the same way they had when Queen Anne stripped their rights.

They were wary of outsiders and felt more comfortable among their kin and close friends. But as they settled out west, they earned a reputation as squatters, building cabins on other people's land grants.

From the 1720s through the 1760s, wave after wave of Ulster-Scots boarded ships in Larne, Derry, Belfast, and Portrush arriving at the ports of Philadelphia, Charleston, Baltimore, and New York. Most of the immigrants moved beyond the coastal cities into the valleys just east of the Allegheny Mountains.

But, contrary to popular belief, the Scotch-Irish didn't immediately migrate into the Appalachian Mountains. The music, dancing, food, and whisky they would bring to Tennessee and Kentucky would have to wait as King George III closed off these lands to English settlers through a royal proclamation. These vast hunting grounds were to be preserved for the Cherokee, Chickasaw, Shawnee, and other indigenous tribes.

Carolina, Not Tennessee

To learn about Tennessee's early settlers and distillers, it's important to understand how the state came into being.

Upon arriving in the New World, the English claimed the lands of the Cherokee, Chickasaw, Shawnee and other tribes as part of Virginia Colony. After the English Civil War and subsequent fall of Oliver Cromwell, eight noblemen helped King Charles II take the throne. As a thank you, the king partitioned Virginia Colony and rewarded them with titles in the newly formed Province of Carolina. They split the colony first at the 36th parallel, then eventually at 36°30' with the Carolina-Virginia border running to the Pacific Ocean.[1] Eventually, they divided Carolina into north and south. The future State of Tennessee started as part of North Carolina.

The early settlers in Carolina never strayed far from the eastern seaboard. Any movement required numbers, as the Tuscarora, Cherokee and others fought back against the usurping of their lands by European settlers. This changed in the 1740s when land speculators realized the potential value of the western frontier.

Three men led the exploration and surveying movement of this era––Christopher Gist of the Ohio Company, James Patton of the New River Company, and Dr. Thomas Walker of the Loyal Land Company. Gist surveyed the Ohio River between the Forks of the Ohio near modern-day Pittsburgh and the Falls of the Ohio at modern-day Louisville. Patton and Walker pushed west into Virginia and down to the North Carolina border.

When Gist built a fort near the Forks of the Ohio, he drew the ire of the French, who had claimed that area for themselves. The heightened tensions led to the French and Indian War. This brought a halt to English land speculation on the dangerous frontier as the Iroquois Confederacy or Six Nations sided with the French.

One of the few nations that seemed open to an alliance with the British was the Cherokee, thanks to the diplomatic work of Chief Attakullakulla. Known as Little Carpenter, the chief bonded with the English from the start. They even invited him to England in the 1730s to see the Old World. Chief Attakullakulla was charismatic, witty, and charming––the only thing he lacked was height. And while his English was a little rough, it was sufficient for the purpose.

When an alliance was formed, the British offered to protect the Cherokee and built several forts throughout the Carolinas for this purpose. One of these outposts was Fort Loudoun, just west of the Appalachian Mountains in Overhill Cherokee territory––part of modern-day Tennessee.

But the relationship between the Cherokee and British soured. The Cherokee felt the British were using their warriors for fodder. If a battle went awry, the Cherokee were the first to be blamed, and after battling they had to traverse long distances home without compensation. This led to frustrated warriors pillaging British settlements on their way home.

On one such trip through Virginia, Cherokee warriors helped themselves to unattended horses in a field. Angry settlers attacked the warriors and killed thirty men.[2] When the surviving warriors returned home, they staged a series of retaliatory raids against the colonists. A group of twenty-four Cherokee leaders went to Charleston (then known as Charles Town) to calm the simmering storm.

South Carolina's Royal Governor rewarded them with a trip in shackles to Fort Prince George. They remained prisoners in the Upstate South Carolina stockade indefinitely.

Ever the peacemaker, Chief Attakullakulla's plan was to lobby for their release. But his rival, Chief Oconostota, arrived first with a dozen warriors or more. Luring the fort's commanding officer, Lt. Richard Coytmore, out of the gates, the Cherokee killed him. Another soldier was killed inside the fort by the prisoners who had concealed tomahawks and knives during their captivity. Seeking revenge, the British soldiers inside the fort retaliated by killing all twenty-four Cherokee prisoners.[3]

In turn this led to the Anglo-Cherokee War erupting amid the French and Indian War, during which isolated Fort Loudoun became a target and the Cherokee put it under siege. After several months of running through their supplies, the British capitulated in August 1760. Three days after the British soldiers and their families evacuated the fort and set out for Fort Prince George in South Carolina, the Cherokee attacked. Twenty-four men, women, and children were killed. The rest were ransomed over the following few months.[4]

At the conclusion of these two frontier wars, King George III had seen enough. The wars had drained parliament's coffers and public sentiment in Britain was turning negative. To keep the peace, the king's Royal Proclamation Act of 1763 drew an imaginary border to the east of the Appalachian and Allegheny Mountains, creating an Indian reserve in the west. The Crown prohibited British subjects from settling beyond the line until treaties opened them up, putting the future of the State of Tennessee and Tennessee distilling on hold.

Taking the Overhill Lands

If there was a staging ground for pioneer exploration into what became Tennessee and Kentucky, it was along the banks of the Yadkin River in North Carolina. This was the home of three influential pioneers: Christopher Gist, Richard Henderson, and a longhunter named Daniel Boone.

Born in Reading, Pennsylvania in 1734 to parents of English and Welsh ancestry, Daniel Boone's hunger and passion for hunting was clear from an early age. At 16, his family moved to the Yadkin River Valley in North Carolina, where Daniel took hunting trips into the eastern slopes of the mountains. Eventually, he made his way into the Overhill region, scouting along the Watauga River in what is now Tennessee.

The 26-year-old frontiersman left his mark on a tree near the Tennessee creek that now carries his name. His message? "D Boon cilled a bar 1760." This remembrance of a slaying of what was likely a black bear marks the beginning of the decade-long golden age of the longhunter. These hardened frontiersmen traveled deep into the western Indian reserve, quietly surveying while waiting for the king's promised treaties. This exploration was mostly peaceful, although it did eventually build animosity with the tribes.

In the lands of the Great Lakes to the north, the proclamation line was doing little to curb violence. An Ottawa chief named Pontiac continued to fight the invading English settlers. This led Great Britain into negotiations with the leaders of the Six Nations of the Iroquois. The British wanted to redraw the proclamation line to stop the violence, and the Iroquois wanted the British to stop encroaching on their land. An agreement was reached in October 1768 and the Treaty of Fort Stanwix was signed in New York. The British gained ground in Pennsylvania and down through the territory of Kentucky and points to the east of the Tennessee River. Yet no one thought to include the Cherokee or Shawnee in these negotiations. Without notice, the treaty took away much of their fertile hunting ground.

Meanwhile, Attakullakulla and the Cherokee were in South Carolina negotiating a much less aggressive change to the line. Signed one month after the New York accord, the Treaty of Hard Labour provided more land for colonists to settle, though it still kept them east of the Appalachian Mountains.[5] The confusion between the two agreements gave opportunistic land grabbers a chance to take advantage of the situation. The era of the pioneer had begun and settlers and distilling would soon follow.

Chapter 2

THE FIRST DISTILLERS

In the search for the origins of Tennessee whisky, few would think to look in Ben Franklin's *Pennsylvania Gazette*. But page six of the June 28, 1770 edition holds a clue to the inception point of Tennessee distilling.

In the last column was an advertisement that read, "To be SOLD by the SUBSCRIBER, living in Frederick county, Maryland, the following tracts of LAND..."[6]

Some have made the claim that the author is Tennessee's first distiller. His name: Evan Shelby, Jr.

The Enterprising Welshman

Born in Tregaron, Wales in 1720, Evan Shelby, Jr. was the second son of Evan and Catherine Davis Shelby. Encouraged by the opportunities offered by the New World, the Shelbys packed up everything they owned and moved to America. They began their new lives in Lancaster County, Pennsylvania, but eventually settled in Frederick County, Maryland.

Evan Jr. was in his early teens when the family purchased their Maryland farm. He spent his first few years helping his father on the farm and improving his hunting skills on his own. At 25, he married Letitia Cox, the daughter of a nearby plantation owner.

Evan, who would eventually attain the rank of Brigadier General in the American Army, started his military career far from the glory of battle, working as a road builder in the British Army. His leadership abilities impressed his superiors, and he was soon at the head of a group of rangers. When soldiers first met him, he looked the part of a scrapper. Short and muscle bound, his love and tolerance for spirits had him drinking other men under the table. But he never let it keep him from peak performance on a mission, and it never stole his ambition. His sharp focus endeared him to his superiors, as did his competence, and his ability to inspire his men. He rose to the rank of captain during the French and Indian War and commanded an advanced scouting team at the battle of Fort Duquesne near modern-day Pittsburgh.

After the war, Evan tried his hand at several occupations. He acquired lands, tended to his farm, raised and sold cattle, and opened a mercantile. But his first love was the fur trade, so he found two partners and jumped in with both feet. His company developed relationships with trading posts around the Great Lakes. But the timing was poor. Chief Pontiac of the Ottawa tribe was waging war on settlers throughout the area. With danger all around and no one to trade with, their business quickly dried up. His partners lost everything and moved to Canada to avoid paying their debts. Evan was left to sell his lands to keep himself out of debtor's prison. If not for the land grants he received for his military service, he might have lost it all. With the loss of his primary income, he took a post as justice of the peace and began to rebuild his life.

By the late 1760s, he grew tired of the struggles in Maryland and was eager to find a new home in the south, initially purchasing a few hundred acres in Rowan County, North Carolina. Then when he learned of the treaties of Fort Stanwix and Hard Labour, his interest shifted. The land west of the Appalachian Mountains had long been prized for the promise it held. Without hesitation, he placed an ad in the *Pennsylvania Gazette*, and took off with his wife Leddie for southwest Virginia.

Watauga and Holston

The Shelbys weren't the first Europeans to settle in the Cherokee Overhill region. The earliest settler, as the legend goes, was a Virginian named William Bean. A friend of Daniel Boone's, he joined the longhunter on some of his scouting expeditions through the Watauga River Valley. By the end of the 1760s, he built a cabin and moved his family to the banks of Boone's Creek.

Boone would introduce another early settler, Wake County resident James Robertson, to the region. While traveling to Kentucky Country with Boone, Robertson became enamored with the Watauga River Valley. He purchased a piece of land, planted corn, and went back east to fetch his wife Charlotte. James Robertson became an important early settler, with his ability to speak the Cherokee language, his leadership skills, and his pioneering spirit.

What Robertson didn't do, however, was distill his corn into whisky. This is because he and his wife were pious teetotallers. It is possible they distilled alcohol for their own medicinal use, but not for sale or trade.

Another more adventurous settler moved far west of the Watauga settlement. John Carter, a bold Tidewater Virginian, saw the benefits of opening up a trading post along the Holston River. He encouraged his business partner, William Parker, to get in on the scheme and set up shop on the west bank of the Holston in 1770, near modern day Rogersville, Tennessee. The Holston was a well-traveled river connecting eastern markets with the endless hunting grounds of the south and west. River traffic, vigorous trade with the Cherokee, and new settlers to the area made the trading post a success. Soon it expanded into a well stocked mercantile. But a move this deep into tribal lands was risky, and a friendly local tribesman warned Carter that an attack on his store might be imminent. Ignoring the warning, his business was ransacked. Instead of rebuilding, Carter left the business to his partner and moved east to the Watauga settlement.

The Mercantile at Shelby Station

John Carter wasn't the only one to see value in the Holston River. In December 1770, Evan Shelby, his wife Leddie, and part of his family drove cattle from Maryland to Southwest Virginia, using the river as a guide. Evan was so impressed with the area he began looking for property. But then, bad news came from Maryland. Leddie's father, David Cox, had died. Evan took his wife back north and the couple spent the next year settling the family's affairs in Maryland.

But Evan never forgot Southwest Virginia. His plan was to establish a large mercantile to supply both settlers and travelers heading into Kentucky country. He convinced both his extended family and his good friend Isaac Baker to move south.

He chose a large plot of land known as Sapling Grove. Located to the east of the Cumberland Gap along the North Carolina-Virginia border, it perfectly fit Evan's plans. He paid a fellow military man, Captain Anthony Bledsoe, to erect a store there. Evan went back to Maryland to complete the sale of his land holdings and put in orders for goods from suppliers back east to stock his new store. Then he and Isaac Baker officially purchased Sapling Grove in November 1773.[7] His friend took the northern half, while Evan took the southern half, including the building for his store and access to a creek.

The move to Sapling Grove was an inspired one. It wasn't long before Evan's store became a magnet for settlers in the Watauga River Valley and the newly populated Nolichucky River Valley. James Robertson, William Bean, and even John Carter and his son Landon were frequent shoppers. The first stop for newcomers like Virginian Valentine Sevier and his son John was Evan Shelby's store. It was part welcome center, gathering spot, and news outpost, as well as a store for supplies. Eventually a stockade surrounded the mercantile store, making it an area of protection as well. Known as Fort Shelby, it became a staging point for military battles and trips into Kentucky country, just as Evan had hoped. It became a favorite stop for longhunters and land surveyors like Daniel Boone and Richard Henderson.

The store's popularity was due, in great measure, to its plentiful supply of the essentials of life. There were sacks of salt, sugar by bulk or in loaves, and bags of tea (they were still British citizens, after all). Chocolate, consumed as a beverage, was sold, and spices were also stocked, though they were beyond the budget of most settlers. There were perishable items like salted pork and beef brought from Evan's farm and eggs supplied by local farmers looking for store credit. Items like vegetables and fruits were rarely in stock because of spoilage and as most settlers foraged or had gardens of their own.

But there was more than just food on the shelves. Settlers could find shoes, homespun, socks, clothing, and sewing supplies like needles and thread, scissors and buttons. Cooking pots, knives, forks, spoons, cups and dishes were all available, too. From time to time fancy dresses or hats might arrive from Philadelphia, London or Paris. There were also lifesaving tools--flintlocks and gunpowder to protect against intruders and for hunting needs. Shoes and saddles were available for horses to make sure transportation was reliable

As for alcohol, Evan stocked plenty of it. But rather than whisky, his primary spirit was rum. In fact, one of the first invoices from Evan's store at Shelby Station was a purchase of two quarts of rum by none other than Daniel Boone himself.[8] He also became a supplier to the Continental Army, providing spirits for the soldier's daily rations.

Where's the Whisky?

There are several factors that cause the mind to drift to whisky as the preferred spirit choice of settlers west of the Alleghenies.

The first is the belief the Scots-Irish (who were known as Scotch-Irish until the end of the 19th century) are the reason there is distilling in Tennessee. However, there are more English and Welsh names associated with Tennessee's early distilling than there are Scots-Irish.

Next is the myth that Tennessee distillers came to the area to escape taxation after the Whiskey Rebellion. In reality, Evan Shelby was selling locally distilled spirits over two decades before the Whiskey Rebellion.

The third factor is Kentucky's dominance over the story of American spirits. With the Bourbon style of whiskey referred to as "America's Spirit," it's easy to forget that early Americans actually preferred rum.

The other way a Bourbon-first attitude messes with the mind is through its late arrival as a spirit. The earliest Kentucky distillers on record started after the Revolutionary War. Evan sold his spirits before the Boston Tea Party, an event that led to the Revolution. When rum became scarce during the war, George Washington began including rye whisky in the soldiers' rations. This move was a real turning point for American tastes, earning whisky a patriotic vibe.

Another reason whisky wasn't a featured part of the store's inventory comes down to the frontier barter system. Life for these settlers wasn't easy, and actual cash was scarce. In order to get supplies from the local store, like food, salt, and other necessities, they would trade items like eggs, tobacco, pelts, or distilled spirits. In the 1770s, rum's popularity made it more valuable in trade.

But this raises another question. Where did these inland pioneers get the sugar and molasses needed for distilling rum?

This question assumes that all rum is a product of West Indies molasses and sugarcane. In New England, before the war, a lot of it was. And while Evan Shelby could secure stocks of these types of goods, they were too expensive for most of the Overhill distillers. So instead of island rum, distillers made continental rum from local sources.

The most widely available source to Overhill distillers was the sugar maple tree. Sugar maples are an excellent source of wood sugars; eight gallons of sap make a pound of sugar. You could distill the syrup or you could make the sugar first and then distill that. While it didn't bring the profits island rum did, continental rum was still more valuable than corn whisky.

The First

For a shining example of how hard it is to find firsts in whisky history, look no further than Evan Shelby, Jr. While his life on the frontier is one of the most well documented, thanks to the preservation of the Shelby Family Papers at the Library of Congress, there are still many reasons to question his standing as Tennessee's first distiller.

Scholars have long used 1770 as the date of his arrival to the area. It's a case that should be strengthened by his decision to move to the region with the treaties that broke the Royal Proclamation Line in 1768. However, when he and his family made their first trek to the area in December 1770, it was likely some miles north of Sapling Grove, closer to the Holston River. The earliest he arrived at Sapling Grove was sometime in 1772, giving other distillers the opportunity to get the jump on his first claim.

Then there is the question of what defines the first distiller. Does this mean the first person to fire up a still, the first person to barter spirits, or the first person to sell their spirits for profit? With Evan Williams, historians suggest he is Kentucky's first "commercial" distiller. They specify "commercial" because it would be impossible to confirm the first person who fired up a still. After all, distilling was a chore like slopping hogs or tilling a field.

Another issue is the realigning and establishing of borders. A 1783 distillery in Louisville would have been in Virginia, not Kentucky. Kentucky didn't exist as a state until 1792. And the same problem exists for Evan Shelby. Tennessee didn't become a state until July 1796, two years after his death. Then there is the additional problem of an area known as Squabble State. Until 1779, Evan believed he lived in Virginia, not North Carolina (the future Tennessee). In fact, he fought as a colonel in the Virginia militia. This only changed when Governor Thomas Jefferson had the border of Virginia and North Carolina resurveyed to stop the squabbling. The new survey split Sapling Grove in half, with Evan's southern property lying in North Carolina and Isaac Baker's northern half in Virginia.

Having a popular mercantile like Shelby Station is another reason some historians consider him the first. Many future grocers rectified spirits. But if Shelby Station is considered on this point, John Carter's store on the Holston predates Shelby by three years. John Carter's son Landon, who was a pre-teen in those days, eventually became a distiller. Is it possible that he learned the craft from his father? Is John Carter the real first distiller? If the inventory taken from his will is any indication, he probably wasn't. Not a single piece of distilling equipment is mentioned.

Then there is the question: how do we know if Evan Shelby ever distilled? Yes, he had a mercantile, a gristmill, and a large farm with cattle. Everything points to distilling. Yet, the first reference to distilling is an order for whisky in 1780. The document shows a transaction with a distiller named Peirce Wall. It states that Evan agreed to provide rye meal and malt to Peirce. In return, the distiller was allowed to keep a fifth of the rye whisky he made while returning the rest to Evan as part of the transaction.[9] That doesn't make Evan sound like a distiller. It makes him sound like a good businessman who contracted others to distill. Yet his son Isaac went on to own a distillery in Kentucky. So was Isaac the distiller at Sapling Grove? Or perhaps it was a hired hand, or an enslaved person.

We may never know. And it's just as well. Whether Evan Shelby was the first or wasn't doesn't really matter. The records of his store and his life at Sapling Grove give us a glimpse into frontier life we rarely get. Those records give us a sense of whisky's true importance on the frontier, a focus on more than just corn whisky in early Tennessee distilling, and proof that whisky came to the area long before the Whiskey Rebellion. And that is enough to make him special in the history of Tennessee distilling and Tennessee whiskey.

Chapter 3

PLANTING THE SEED

Kana'ti and Selu

The warmth of the sun; the days of carefree joy. To the children of Kana'ti and Selu, life was simple, and no cares troubled their minds. They felt protected and never wanted for anything.

There was comfort in their daily routines. Each morning, Kana'ti went off alone, returning shortly after with a deer, wild bird or other game ready to be prepared for a meal. While he was gone, Selu would head to the small shack at the edge of the homesite and emerge with a bounty of corn in her basket. The afternoon passed with Selu pounding the corn into meal for making bread, while Kana'ti skinned and prepared the meat. In the afternoon, the children would play by the river and come home to a wonderful meal. At night they would lay their heads down, their bellies contented.

Into this peaceful existence entered a boy from the wild. All alone, he asked to join them for a few days and Kana'ti and Selu welcomed him into their home. Filled with curiosity, the boy asked many questions. Mostly he was preoccupied with the source of the food they were eating. Where was Kana'ti finding these animals and what was in that shack that enabled Selu to provide so much corn? Quietly, he asked two of the older boys if they would help him discover their parents' secrets.

The next morning, the boys huddled together, waiting for Kana'ti to go off on his walk. They followed far behind, so as not to be detected. As he walked toward the swamp, the three boys took a position on a nearby hill. Suddenly Kana'ti stopped, pulled a reed, and started assembling something. It was an arrow. As he walked up the mountainside, the boys followed closely behind. When he reached the top, Kana'ti approached a large stone that appeared to be blocking a cave. With little effort, Kana'ti moved the stone just enough that a deer escaped. Kana'ti pushed the rock back, reached for his weapon, and killed the deer. Then he threw his prize over his shoulders and walked down the mountain. The three boys were quite pleased with themselves for learning Kana'ti's great secret.

Days later, the wild boy convinced the two older boys they should try to kill a deer just like Kana'ti. They hurried down to the swamp, assembled their own weapons, and ran up the hill to the cave. But the stone wasn't as easy to move as they thought. It took every bit of the boys' energy to get it dislodged. When it moved, it rolled back several feet. Wild animals suddenly ran through the boys, knocking them to the ground. They sat there in dumbfounded amazement. So many birds filled the sky the sun grew dark. So many animals thundered out of the cave that the ground shook. Back home, Kana'ti felt a burning inside his skin as he watched the sunlight grow dim and felt the Earth shake. Not seeing the boys around, he knew what had happened and the anger inside him rose. He went off to find them.

Somehow, the boys returned home without crossing Kana'ti's path. They were hungry, so they went to find Selu. But there was no meat for them to eat. So Selu said she would prepare a special meal. Then the wild boy said, "let's go spy on her when she goes to that shack and discover her secret for gathering corn." When she walked to the shack, the boys took turns looking inside through a crack in the mortar. It was the wild boy's turn to watch when Selu began vigorously rubbing her belly. His jaw dropped as he watched ears of corn falling from the ceiling into her basket. With a look of fear in his eyes, he turned to the boys, saying, "It's witchcraft!" He warned the others not to eat of those stocks of corn. Then he told them, "she is a witch, she must be killed!" The boys looked stunned, but reluctantly agreed.

Just then, Selu came up behind them and let them know she had overheard their conversation. She told them that if they killed her, they would have to plant and gather their own corn. Then in a calm voice she said, "to produce the first grains, drag my lifeless body over the ground in a circle and my blood would provide the corn you need." When the wild boy gave the children a determined glance, they attacked and killed Selu.

Just then an angry Kana'ti returned. Seeing what the boys had done, he looked at them sternly and said, "from this point forward, I can no longer help you. You will have to make your own bows and arrows and hunt for the wild beasts in the wilderness on your own."

In the years that followed, a great tribe formed. To survive, its members moved from place to place, tilling the land, planting corn, and hunting wild beasts just as Kana'ti and Selu told them. But the days of peace and comfort were gone and life would never be so easy again.[10]

The Story of Corn

There are three elements required to start making modern day Tennessee whiskey--water, yeast, and a grain mixture made up of at least 51% corn. The rest of the grain formula, referred to as the mashbill, may also include wheat, rye, and other flavoring grains to enhance the personality of the spirit. Barley is used to assist the conversion of starch into fermentable sugars for the yeast to feed on. But of all the grains used in making Tennessee whiskey, corn is the most dominant.

Yet most of us take the existence of corn for granted. In American society, corn is used to make everything from meals to fuel additives to sugar substitutes. For most people, imagining the United States without corn is like imagining whiskey without the alcohol. After all, when the pilgrims arrived, they enjoyed a bounty of corn thanks to their native hosts. It seems like an everyday part of the North American landscape.

However, corn is not a native grain of the United States. It came from points south, although the specific location is still being argued over by archaeobotanists. Unlike other germinating plants, neither flint nor dent corn seed themselves. This forces human interaction for the grain to spread. This is where the Cherokee origin story of Kana'ti and Selu comes in. It emphasizes the importance of corn, the need for planting and harvesting, and the need for spreading the seed. In fact, the Cherokee word for corn is "selu" in honor of the corn mother, whose blood and body gave life to the tribe. The Cherokee belief that corn equalled survival is a big reason the grain is here today.

Early European settlers didn't know what to make of corn at first. Corn was a generic name for raw grains in the old country, so they referred to it as maize or Indian corn instead. While less respected than other grains, corn's reliability was undeniable. When settlers wanted to claim land, they planted corn to show ownership and to prevent squatters. As the pioneers moved west, corn became insurance as farmers tested the soil and climate conditions for other grains. It fed the family, the enslaved population, and fattened hogs and livestock.

For distillers, the soft starches of dent corn made it perfect for making whisky. As more farmers adopted it, the grain flourished across Tennessee and Kentucky. Eventually, it became synonymous with Bourbon and Tennessee whisky. So it begs the question, why is the connection between corn, the tribes, and whisky not talked about?

It comes down to the deplorable way European explorers and settlers used whisky as a weapon against the tribes. Starting with the Canadian fur trade, French explorers realized they could get the upper hand in trade negotiations if they dished out firewater to the natives. Unprepared for this highly intoxicating unaged spirit, the natives consumed the spirit too fast. When they realized they were being swindled by the traders, the inebriated tribesmen turned violent. The few ruthless traders who escaped the tomahawk used the violence to propagandize the "drunken Indian" stereotype.

In 1701, the Pennsylvania Assembly tried to curb the weaponizing of spirits by prohibiting the sale of rum to the tribes. In 1745, the Georgia colony attempted a similar measure during the Augusta Conference. Then, in 1802, Chief Little Turtle of the Miami Nation lobbied the federal government to pass the Indian Nonintercourse Act.[11] It gave the president power to restrain the trade of alcoholic spirits to tribe members. Presidents seldom used this power and, like most prohibitory laws, there was no enforcement.

Modern historians are now expanding research beyond the settlers' perspective. Perhaps a more universal focus will help repair the relationship between corn, the tribes, and whisky.

The Three Stars

From its beginning, Tennessee has stood as one of the strongest agricultural states in the nation. For its distillers, this has allowed a great measure of self-sufficiency. The state contains all the natural resources prized in American spirits—pure limestone-filtered water, ample amounts of grain, and a plentiful wood supply.

Look deeper and you will find a diversity of agriculture in each region that defines the character of spirits created from one end of the state to the other. Tennessee's state flag symbolizes this diversity with its red backdrop, blue circle, and three white stars. The stars represent the three distinct regions of Tennessee, known as the Grand Divisions: East, Middle, and West.

East Tennessee is prime growing land for whisky-related grains like wheat, corn, oats, and, to a lesser degree, rye. There is a plentiful supply of sugar maple trees, perfect for making sugar shine, rum, and charcoal for the whisky mellowing process. There are also plenty of apple, pear, and peach trees that provide ample fruit for brandy. The mountainous nature of the area perfectly suited the private nature of the Scotch-Irish.

Middle Tennessee is the most diverse region in the state. At its heart is the Central Basin, surrounded by a landform known as the Highland Rim. Mountains and hills in the east give way to pseudo planes and then rolling hills and rougher terrain as you get closer to the Tennessee River. Corn, barley, rye, and oats have always grown well in Middle Tennessee. Fruit trees allowed for various types of brandy production. Lumberjacks sourced enough oak to feed a growing coopering industry. And those with more level ground or tired soil grew tobacco and cotton. The farm sizes in Middle Tennessee ranged from single family farms to larger plantation-style affairs.

West Tennessee was a late bloomer and most of its land and farms in the early years mimicked the Antebellum plantations of the deeper south. Cotton became the lifeblood of the region. While corn and other hearty grains grow in West Tennessee, it has never held significant advantages for distilling. Instead, its strength comes from its access to the Mississippi River. Coopers thrived in Memphis, thanks to the delivery of oak from the Ozark Mountains. It also became a connection for wholesalers sending whisky down the river or receiving whisky from Kentucky, Pennsylvania, and Ohio. There was little need for distilling in an area rich with imports.

While the soil and climate had a significant influence on how these regions developed, the shape of the state was another.

Drive north to south on Interstate 65 today, and as long as you don't hit Nashville traffic (which means you're probably driving at two in the morning) you can easily glide through the state in under two hours. But if you travel along I-81 to I-40 from Bristol to Memphis, you're easily looking at a 7 ½ hour drive, without hitting that same Nashville traffic.

In the pioneer era, a trip from Bristol to Memphis on horseback, in a covered wagon, or by boat was a rare occurrence and would take over a week. So, in reality, pioneers in East Tennessee were as unlikely to meet someone from Memphis as they were someone from Philadelphia. Completion of the railroad and introduction of the telegraph had minimal effect. The first real union in the state came from the biannual gathering of the General Assembly in the state capital of Knoxville and later Nashville. The blue circle surrounding the three stars in the state flag represents the eventual unification of the state. But even in this modern era, some of the cultural differences between the regions are still palatable.

The eastern part of the state has always stayed true to its more individualistic attitude regarding spirits. The moonshine culture still thrives there. In Middle

Tennessee, larger distilleries feed commerce and keep the tax dollars rolling into the state. Out west, distilleries are few and the most successful are on the "mighty Mississippi." These distinctions were true in the 18th and 19th centuries and even Prohibition couldn't completely remove these distinct regional personalities.

Yet there is still only one Tennessee, and the red background in the state flag represents that binding spirit.

But for the whisky fan, that red could represent something else. The grain that grows in plentiful supply from the Appalachians to the Mississippi. And the one grain that Tennessee whisky can't do without––corn.

Thank you, Selu.

Chapter 4

THE FUGITIVE

Stump's Run Massacre

In a little jailhouse, on the fringes of civilization, two murderers sat awaiting judgment. To the people of Carlisle, there was little doubt of their guilt. This meant the only thing left to decide was, would they face justice in this little frontier town or would they travel to Philadelphia?

Of the two killers, few knew about the one named Jim Ironcutter. But there was no mistaking his partner in crime. It was none other than Hans Frederick Stump, the founder of Fredericktown.

Their foul deed was eerily similar to the kind perpetrated by a local vigilante group called the Paxton Boys. When Chief Pontiac fought his rebellion, the colonial government left the area settlers unprotected. This spun the Paxtons into a murderous rampage. In their minds, the royal governor was failing to protect the frontier, so they had to take matters into their own hands. But their punishments were random and brutal. Wanting to send a message, they murdered every man, woman, and child in the nearby Conestoga tribe. This shocked and disgusted the pacifist Quakers, who saw no justification in the attack. The Conestogas were a peaceful tribe and there was no evidence they had taken part in Pontiac's War.[12]

Now, just as the community was settling back down, Stump, a family man, tavern owner, and a regional town founder, had opened old wounds.

To make matters worse, not only had he admitted openly to the killing, he was bragging about it. It was his boastfulness that landed both him and his servant in jail.

In Stump's description of the events, the trouble started on a bitter January night in 1768 when six drunken Indians were hammering down rum at his public house. When they demanded more, he was afraid "that they intended to do him some Mischief."[13] To get them out of their wits, he fed them rum until they all passed out. He beat all six to death with the heavy handle of a tomahawk. Then he scalped them and took their limp bodies down to the creek. Breaking the ice, he disposed of them in the creek to hide the evidence of his crime.

The next morning, he relayed the entire story to his indentured servant, a German immigrant named John Ironcutter. He wanted the man to follow him up to the homes of the Indians at Middle Creek. He was sure the other family members would want to retaliate when they discovered the six were missing after visiting Stump's. When Stump and Ironcutter reached the cabin, all they found were the three wives of the men they had murdered and an infant. The two men attacked and killed all four and burned the cabin with their victims' lifeless bodies inside.

The next day, Stump was at George Gabriel's gristmill on Penn's Creek, bragging about the events of the last two days. One of Gabriel's customers, William Blyth, was appalled by the murder and came to Gabriel's to hear the story for himself. He immediately rode to Philadelphia to alert the Provincial Council.

The Provincial Governor John Penn immediately put a 200 pound sterling bounty on the heads of Stump and Ironcutter. Word quickly spread, and the governor dispatched Captain William Patterson from Fort Augusta to arrest the two men. But bringing Stump and Ironcutter in was no simple task. It took nineteen men to subdue them and bring them to the jail in Carlisle, Pennsylvania.[14] Details of what became known as Stump's Run Massacre and the Indian-killer Frederick Stump quickly traveled up and down the Susquehanna River.

Days after his capture, Stump was laying back on his cot, wondering if they were measuring a rope for his hanging. Then an unusual number of horses' hooves created a clamor outside. Just then, a knock on the door startled the jailer; two slightly unkempt gentlemen walked in through the door and asked him for a shot of whisky. As the jailer's arm went to retrieve a jug, several more men came in the door brandishing cutlasses and pistols. This sudden swarm of vigilantes threatened to kill him if he got in their way. They made their way to the dungeon with axes, a sledge, and a crowbar. Outside, sixty more men rode in on horseback and encircled the modest jail. After a few minutes' work Stump and Ironcutter were freed from their cell and whisked out the door. The sheriff, who was away having his breakfast in a nearby tavern, could only frown as a group of sixty vigilantes rode by with his prisoners.

It looked like the work of the Paxtons. Authorities relayed messages throughout Paxton Township, hoping someone might turn the fugitives in.[15] The story of the massacre would reach all the way to Fort Stanwix and almost upset the treaty negotiations going on there. But all agreed, rum was an evil thing.

As for the outlaws, Hans Frederick Stump and John Ironcutter, they remained fugitives from justice and disappeared into Pennsylvania lore.

The Republic

Further to the south, 1768 was a year of frustration for the Overhill Cherokee. They had just seen their great hunting grounds taken away in the treaties of Fort Stanwix and Hard Labour. And no one was certain where the real borders were. So, in October 1770, another treaty was called for, this time at Lochaber Plantation, South Carolina. There, Chief Attakullakulla regained some of the lost Overhill lands for the Cherokee. As part of the treaty, they brought in a Virginia politician and surveyor named John Donelson to resurvey the lines.

The new boundaries established by the Donelson survey didn't please the settlers in the Watauga and Nolichucky river regions. Suddenly they were squatters on Cherokee land. The Crown informed John Carter, Valentine and John Sevier, James Robertson, and William Bean that they would have to leave. John

Carter knew the only way they could keep their homes was to create their own government and negotiate independently with the Cherokee.

The result was the short-lived Watauga Association, a semiautonomous pseudo republic. It was a treasonous act that was ignored by the authorities, who were busy with the Sons of Liberty and their tea party in Boston. James Robertson used his skills as an interpreter and helped the Wataugans negotiate a ten-year land lease with the Cherokee.

Then war broke out between the British and the colonists. Immediately, Virginia and North Carolina declared themselves free of the Crown's authority. Wanting to be part of the new nation, the Wataugans declared themselves the Washington District and asked Virginia to annex them. While they waited for a response, they formed a "committee of safety" to provide for their defense. Virginia had no interest in the territory, so they entered North Carolina as Washington County. But, to the dismay of the Cherokee, North Carolina wouldn't recognize the Wataugans' ten-year lease.

Angered by this betrayal, Dragging Canoe, the son of Chief Attakullakulla, went on the attack. He coordinated simultaneous attacks against settlers in the Watauga and Nolichucky river valleys, and a fort on the Holston called Eaton's Station. With the rebels of Washington County siding with the Americans, Dragging Canoe hoped to gain the support of the British in his war. But the Battle of Island Flats at Eaton's Station saw the defeat of the Cherokee. Dragging Canoe left the battlefield severely wounded.[16] He swore he'd never forget that day, nor the destruction of Cherokee villages by the militia in the days that followed. His mission from that day forward was to make the settlers' lives a living hell.

The Overmountain Men

While Thomas Jefferson's Declaration of Independence set the terms for America's separation from the Crown, his settling of the Squabble State affair may have changed the course of the American Revolution itself.

In the north, the British and Americans were fighting to a stalemate. With more loyalist sympathies in the south, the British changed strategies and laid siege to Charleston, South Carolina.

Jefferson's 1779 redrawing of the North Carolina-Virginia line placed Shelby Station south of the line. This not only changed Tennessee whisky history, it gave a much-needed boost to America's forces. Evan Shelby's son, Colonel Isaac Shelby, gave up his Virginia commission and became part of North Carolina's force.

From the time he hit the battlefield, Colonel Shelby showed his abilities as a leader, heading several brilliant tactical victories. His victories, sometimes in the face of overwhelming odds, gave hope to the American troops in South Carolina. But just as he was preparing for a showdown with the equally brilliant Major Patrick Ferguson, disaster struck at Camden. The continental's primary force in the south collapsed under General Horatio Gates, and they abandoned the field. The devastating defeat sent Colonel Shelby back to Shelby's Station to regroup.

Major Ferguson was well aware of Shelby's successes and the reputation of the Scotch-Irish fighters living in Washington County. To keep them out of the fight, he sent a furloughed prisoner to Shelby's Station with a message––stay home, or face the destruction of your homes and community.

It was Ferguson's biggest mistake of the war. Angered by the threat, Colonel Shelby rode to Sycamore Shoals near modern-day Elizabethtown to meet with another young leader, John Sevier. They planned their attack, met up with General Charles McDowell, and they made their way to Kings Mountain in South Carolina to face Ferguson's forces.

Referred to as the Overmountain Men, Shelby and Sevier's forces fought the British tree to tree, guerilla warfare style. Seasoned in battles with the Cherokee, their forces slowly made their way up the mountain until they reached Major Ferguson. The outstanding leader met his demise after being shot off his horse. It was a decisive victory for the American troops. The Overmountain Men had turned the tide of the war. The only thing left was a march across North Carolina up to Yorktown, Virginia, where the French fleet and George Washington's troops accepted the British surrender.

A New Beginning

Not long before the Battle of Kings Mountain, James Robertson and John Donelson were making plans to settle further inland. The area of interest was a little French outpost called Salt Lick. The two men struck a deal with land speculator Richard Henderson to settle on what is now the site of modern day Nashville.

Robertson's job was to put together a group of hardened men, lead them to the bluffs along the Cumberland River, and prepare the land for settlers. John Donelson was to take a larger contingent that would include women, children, the enslaved, and all of their belongings along a water route. Robertson's path had the benefit of Daniel Boone's Wilderness Road, while Donelson had a more treacherous path. He would have to survive Dragging Canoe's tribal villages, the rough waters of Muscle Shoals, and a long ride up the Tennessee River.

When Captain Amos Eaton heard the plan, he was intrigued. He gathered up eight families and made a plan to follow Robertson's group down the Wilderness Road to French Lick.

One of the family patriarchs coming along with Eaton made him a little uncomfortable. The stocky, short-haired scraper was a braggart who could spin a tall tale. Captain Eaton wasn't sure what he could believe. The man talked of being part of South Carolina's St. Paul's Parish Militia, headed by the legendary Swamp Fox, Lieutenant Colonel Francis Marion. While under Marion's command he said he had snuck up on five British officers playing cards and killed them with his rifle. For his trouble he was sent to a prison in St. Augustine, but he bribed a guard and escaped. And boasted that he was invincible when it came to the Indians. The man said the only reason he had brought his family to Watauga was because the British had burned his gristmill and distillery in Augusta, Georgia.[17] He was hoping to get a new start on the frontier. Because the man had a sweet wife and well-mannered children, Captain Eaton saw no harm in having them along. And if half of what this man said was true, he'd be a great ally in case of attacks by the Cherokee or Shawnee.

But, days into the trip, two men decided to get under the braggart's skin and told him they had put a spell on his gun. This sent the man into a rage. He picked up the gun, cocked it, and pointed it in their direction. With a sneer in his voice he told them he'd kill any man who messed with his weapon. He appeared to have every intention of killing the men on the spot, but others talked him out of the rash act. As the trip progressed, the man went back to telling his stories. One that seemed unreal was when the man started bragging about killing a handful of Indians in his tavern, along with their families. He said he was a fugitive from Pennsylvania colony.[18]

He called himself Hans Frederick Stump. Was he truly the fugitive as he claimed?

As Captain Eaton's party neared the bluffs at French Lick, Stump saw the perfect piece of land by a creek. He could envision a beautiful little tavern and a gristmill along its banks. He thanked Captain Eaton, pitched his tent and prepared to make a new home for his family.

It was Christmas Eve 1779 and the start of a new life on the frontier. The future was a great unknown.[19]

Establishing the New Frontier

It was a bone-chilling day when James Robertson and his men finally arrived at the bluffs at Salt Lick. The temperature was so low that the Cumberland River had frozen over, creating the perfect ice bridge for the weary travelers to cross. With John Donelson's flotilla of families on the way, efforts to build a protective stockage began posthaste. They named it Fort Nashborough, after General Francis Nash who died at the Battle of Germantown near Philadelphia. The fort was truly isolated and in dangerous territory. The closest tenuous settlements in the region were far to the north and east.

One of those settlements was Evan Shelby's friend Anthony Bledsoe. Anthony and his brother Isaac had set up a camp near fertile hunting ground thirty miles to the northeast and dubbed it Bledsoe's Lick.

Another was a Scotsman, Thomas Kilgore. One of the more colorful characters in the early days of Middle Tennessee, he came to the area in 1775 as a longhunter. During the trip, he became enamored with the areas around the Red River and Sulphur Fork Creek. It was a fertile hunting ground and had plenty of natural resources for a permanent settlement. He bookmarked it in his mind, then he and his mates finished their hunting and returned home back east with a nice collection of furs and pelts. Then in spring of 1778, he headed west by himself. He stopped off at Bledsoe's Lick, met Anthony and Isaac, then made his way to the Middle Fork of the Red River. There he found a cave where he could safely hide from hostiles. He planted corn and used rivers and creeks when he traveled, hoping to keep Chickasaw trackers off his scent. When the harvest came, he grabbed some of the corn and walked five-hundred miles back east and staked his claim with the North Carolina government. Even at 68 years old, Thomas Kilgore had boundless energy and a rich pioneering spirit. He convinced his wife Lydia Ann and some neighbors there was a better life to be had out west. Kilgore Station joined Bledsoe Station as one of only two English-speaking outposts in the area until Robertson's arrival further south.[20]

But there was someone else in the area, even before them: A French-Canadian fur trapper named Jacques-Timothe Boucher, Sieur de Montbrun. The English simply called him Timothy Demonbreun. Timothy was the reason other settlers referred to the area around the bluffs as French Lick. It earned the name Salt Lick thanks to the rich mineral deposits that drew thousands of bison to the area. Holding the high ground overlooking the Cumberland River, it had a strategic position that made spotting intruders much easier. Only the west lacked good sightlines. Demonbreun liked the company of Robertson's men and assimilated quickly with the community upon their arrival.

The one thing the area didn't have was a legal framework. James Robertson took the lead in setting up a local government; making revisions to the rules of the old Watauga Republic, the Cumberland Compact became the law of the settlement. It called for the building of satellite forts or "stations" to give points of protection around the area for the settlers, and called for the election of judges and defined frontier justice. In total, 256 men signed the document, including the Bledsoes, John Donelson, James Robertson, future sheriff and tavern owner John Boyd, Frederick Stump, and Stump's son Jacob.[21]

Those who established homesteads received some welcomed news from the North Carolina Legislature. To reward them for their bravery, each man that arrived before July 1, 1780 was to receive a 640-acre pre-emptive land grant. It would take almost six years for Stump to secure it. But it eventually served the purpose of legitimizing the homes of Kilgore, Bledsoe, Stump, Donelson, Eaton, Robertson, and all the others who helped establish Fort Nashborough.[22]

The Gristmill and Tavern at White's Creek

Within weeks, the Stumps made substantial progress in the construction of their new home five miles north of Fort Nashborough. Built of red cedar logs, it was quite impressive for the newly minted frontier. Even though the state did not yet officially sanction it as a tavern, that didn't stop the Stumps from hosting guests.

Meanwhile, they were also hard at work building a gristmill on what became known as White's Creek. For pioneers, a gristmill meant an area was open for business. The gristmill was a center of commerce, where local farmers brought their grains to be ground into productive grist, cornmeal, and flour. It allowed Stump to mill his own corn, wheat, rye, oats, and barley for his new distillery. But it also meant he could profit from milling other farmers' grains.

Early frontier mills came in a variety of sizes. If only a small creek was available, farmers built simple shacks with a tub mill inside. Rather than having a big vertical waterwheel, these smaller operations had a mini wooden horizontal wheel inside a tub. The force of water turned the wheel and thus the millstone.

Another type of mill was the horse mill. In this setup, the miller hitched a horse or donkey to a sweep. The animal's power combined with torque to turn the millstone.

Creekside water mills like Stump's were the most valuable to a community. As long as the water source was dependable, the mill could operate most of the year. With his sizable farm, it is a good bet that Frederick Stump's water-wheel-driven gristmill looked more like the picturesque larger mills we think of today. He was a man who loved cutting-edge equipment, and no price was too great to bear for efficiency.

The Return of Dragging Canoe

Growth was slow for the Stumps, however. The fear of Chickasaw and Cherokee attacks kept new people away from Fort Nashborough and Eaton's Station. Dragging Canoe had kept his promise to make life a living hell for the settlers. His new branch of Chickamauga Cherokee took a creative approach to keeping the pioneers unsettled. Knowing his warriors couldn't match the gun and manpower at Fort Nashborough or the smaller stations, Dragging Canoe's men instead staked out the woods and attacked settlers traveling between the stations, and those hunting and foraging for food.

Ten months after their arrival, the threat came close to home for the Stumps. Frederick's son Jacob and his cousin Jonathan Gais learned that a party of natives stole two horses from Eaton's Station. They decided to see if they could steal them back. As they made their way down Wells Creek, about a half mile from the station, they spotted the men they thought had stolen the horses. They shot and killed two and were chased by the others. Soon more warriors came out of the woods. The two settlers ran for their lives back toward the stockade. When shots rang out, John felt the sting of a bullet pierce his leg, then another and another. The warriors were in hot pursuit. As he got closer to the fort, he saw the friendly guns pointing down between the spikes of the stockade at Eaton's Station. Emboldened, he turned and fired, killing one of his pursuers. That was enough to stop the sound of racing feet behind him. Confident Jacob was just behind him, John whipped around to see where the warriors were. They were gone. And there was Jacob, lying fifty yards behind him in a lifeless heap.[23]

Other more distant outposts were becoming unsettled as well. In the early days of settlement, the only thing Thomas Kilgore had to worry about at Kilgore Station was his wife Lydia's famous temper. It was said that in his longhunting days, Thomas used to have to throw his hat in the door before entering to see if she was in a good mood. If the hat didn't fly back out, he could enter.[24] However, the local Chickasaw tribe had eventually grown tired of his fort's presence and attacks on foragers became too much. For a time, Kilgore Station sat empty, its inhabitants seeking shelter elsewhere.

Bledsoe's Lick also came under attack by a group of Chickasaw raiders, during which Anthony Bledsoe himself was a casualty. The raid almost put an end to the little settlement and its inhabitants sought temporary shelter at nearby Mansker's Station.[25]

Even Fort Nashborough eventually saw an attack. Dragging Canoe wanted to see if he could weaken the fort by drawing its soldiers out and isolating them. The ruse started when two Cherokee warriors fired at the fort and then ran into the woods. In response, James Robertson gathered twenty men. They saddled up, and he led them out of the fort to chase down the attackers. From the stockade, James' wife Charlotte watched her husband ride away and was horrified to see a group of Indian warriors coming toward the fort, ready to fight. The Battle of the Bluffs was on. Within minutes, James and the rest of his soldiers were off their horses and taking casualties. When they tried to retreat, more of Dragging Canoe's Chickamauga warriors appeared from out of the woods behind the fort, blocking the entrance. Seeing her husband surrounded, Charlotte bravely opened the gates and set the dogs loose. With the canines jumping on the attacking warriors, it created enough of a diversion for Robertson and his men to get back inside the fort, though not without sustaining a disheartening loss of five dead and two wounded soldiers.[26]

From that day forward, attacks by the Chickamauga Cherokee, Creeks, and Chickasaws became a daily concern for the settlers of the area. The price of those 640 acres was high for many. Out of the original 256 signers of the Cumberland Compact, nearly one-third were killed in battles with Dragging Canoe and his allies by 1784.[27]

The Father and Old Man Stump

Dragging Canoe or no Dragging Canoe, there were two old men who were not about to be dissuaded from establishing their distilling operations.

Thomas Kilgore eventually established his gristmill and was one of the first in the area to distill. The date of his first distilling remains a mystery, but it would have been in the late 1780s, when he was in his seventies. The spunky old Scotsman would eventually reach the ripe old age of 108.[28]

Frederick Stump, no spring chicken himself, continued the work of building his distillery and gristmill without the help of his son Jacob. Stump mostly went about his business unmolested. But he would face a challenge from the man appointed by the North Carolina Legislature to head the newly formed government.

Pious as ever, the emergence of the liquor trade did not thrill James Robertson. If he had his way, Frederick Stump's dream of whisky distilling would never have found its way to the region. When North Carolina established Davidson County's court system in 1783, Robertson used the Acts of the Assembly to set the tone for whisky production and consumption in the region. Under the guise of preserving grain due to a recent shortage, in 1785, he outlawed whisky distillation within the entire county.[29] Stump ignored the decree.

Soon things turned in Stump's favor. Liquor was arriving from out of town and the higher prices were causing too much money to leave the community. To solve the issue, Robertson added a tariff on imported liquor. The unintended consequence? Robertson's tariff was a boon for Stumps' spirits.

Eventually, the liquor trade won out. Once a road opened between Clinch Mountain in the east and Nashville, the influx of new settlers brought a demand for taverns. Frederick eventually applied for his own tavern license from the State of North Carolina and received it in 1789.[30]

By this point, Stump was becoming a local tycoon, accumulating land with the wealth he generated from the tavern, mill, and distillery, and renting his other properties in return for grain. When he purchased one of the first cotton gins in the area, he increased his enslaved workforce.[31]

Stump might have thought his operation was big enough to keep local tribes away, but on October 10, 1792, a local tribe successfully burned down his distillery causing him a loss of $1,250.[32] By this point, Old Man Stump was so well off he simply replaced it with a much larger distillery.

As a youth, Stump was a braggart and a violent man. In many ways, he was a man of his times. Was he the fugitive Hans Frederick Stump? The evidence suggests it. But whoever he was before Tennessee, when it comes to his distilling operation, one thing is sure. He wasn't Tennessee's first distiller, but in the early days, he was its wealthiest.

Chapter 5

A REMARKABLE LIFE

The Tavern

In the days before Tennessee statehood, after the mercantile, few things held as much importance to locals and travelers alike as the tavern. The first tavern in a community would become a gathering spot for local news, trade negotiations, picking up mail from back east, and downing food and drinks. For travelers, the tavern was an oasis after a long ride through wild and hostile territory.

Taverns, or ordinaries as some old timers called them, came in all shapes and sizes. The typical tavern was log-cabin style and had two floors. The downstairs featured a bar, tables, and chairs, while the upstairs had rooms for accommodation. Outside, taverns provided stables with supplies to shoe, feed, and water horses. Sometimes, the horses had better accommodations than their owners, as overbooked taverns placed two strangers in a cot.

Men dominated the tavern culture. If a woman was in a tavern, she was the owner, the server, or a prostitute. If it was a large tavern, they would keep proper ladies in a separate room, away from the rowdy men.

The food in a tavern was hearty, but with few options; you ate whatever the cook prepared. Pork, beef, potatoes, and cornbread were in abundance in the territory and found their way onto many a tavern table. Drinks were limited to the basics, and the heavy Scotch-Irish influence on the frontier meant those taverns sold more whisky than beer. Hard spirits like rum, brandy, and whisky arrived in barrels, with the liquor transferred to jugs, pitchers, or bottles for easy access. Some taverns had their own stills and made their own liquor, but most brought spirits in from local farms or purchased them from the same sources as the local mercantile.

As towns grew larger and larger across the frontier, the number of taverns increased. This gave travelers a choice of accommodations and locals an opportunity to segregate into their own cliques. Nashville had several taverns. Few had official names——most taverns were identified by the object painted on the sign outside. Three of Nashville's most prominent public houses included the Bell Tavern, the Red Heifer, and The Cross Keys. If the owner was well known and respected or if they became synonymous with a tavern, their first or last name would become affixed to the name of the business, for example, Stump's Tavern or the House of Laudner.

In Nashville, two of the most popular early tavern owners were John "King" Boyd and Bob Renfro. King Boyd ran a respectable house, but there was always an undercurrent of rowdiness bubbling beneath the surface. Its owner was the strong yet reserved type. In contrast, Bob brought a wit and charm to his establishment.

Both men were talented storytellers, and had survived the harrowing journey of John Donelson's flotilla. But this is where the similarity in experiences ended. Boyd kept his stories to the building of Fort Nashborough. Bob's stories were extraordinarily rich, featuring moments of near impossibility. Travelers usually left unconvinced, but the locals knew Bob's stories to be true.

He talked of the horrors of the Battle Creek Massacre, where several Renfros lost their lives. He detailed historic legal cases he'd won against all odds. And he raved about the local government and business community that helped him live out his dream of owning a tavern.

Bob's life was truly remarkable. In fact, he is one of the most compelling figures in the history of early Middle Tennessee.

Yet, no one knows where he was born, when he died, or where he is buried. And sadly, neither Bob nor anyone who ever heard him weave his stories thought to write the details down for posterity. Yet the few public records that remain are enough to show a man who overcame incredible obstacles to live life on his own terms.

The Renfros

For those that made their way to the bluffs at Salt Lick with the Robertson and Eaton excursions, it was a tense journey without incident. For Bob and the Renfros, the journey south with the Donelson flotilla hadn't been so easy.

Led by Captain John Donelson's aptly named ship *The Adventure*, the Renfros, Boyds, Stuarts, and several other families prepared to sail their own vessels through the heart of Dragging Canoe's Chickamauga villages. All hoped the sheer size of the floating caravan would dissuade any violent attacks along the way. The boats were filled with human cargo and all the necessities of life needed on the wild frontier.

The Renfros were one of the largest contingents of the flotilla. They had several boats filled with scores of men, women, children, and the enslaved. They hoped to find the perfect spot to establish a new community, close to the Salt Lick settlement.

Christmas 1779 was just a couple of days away when the great flotilla took off from Fort Patrick Henry down the Holston River. What a sight it must have been.

The plan was to meet up with another flotilla under the leadership of Captain Blackmore before heading down the Tennessee River. But the plans went awry almost immediately. The falls near Reedy Creek and the harsh winter weather bogged the party down for almost two months. And just as soon as they were moving again, John "King" Boyd's family boat beached at the Pool Valley Shoal. For two days they sat, waiting for the waters to rise to continue the journey. Days later, the Henry family boat sank as they met the more aggressive waters of the French Broad. They needed all hands to raise the craft and save the family's belongings.

When they finally reached the Clinch River, Captain Blackmore's flotilla was patiently waiting. If they were looking for strength in numbers, the added companions were a godsend. The flotilla increased to 40 vessels, including scows, canoes, and hollowed-out tree trunks called pirogues. But it was early March, and they were barely on the way to their destination. And worse yet, the danger was still in front of them.

Then the unexpected happened. Several members of the Stuart family came down with smallpox. To prevent a major outbreak, they placed the sick in a single boat that sailed far off to the rear of the main body.

Ironically, the first good fortune for the flotilla came in the form of a cold and windy storm. Just as they were passing the first of the Chickamauga Cherokee villages, they noticed its inhabitants were nowhere to be seen. The weather apparently sent them inland, away from the river.

But the next day, they came upon another village. Here the Cherokee waved at the boats, inviting them ashore. An advanced canoe was sent to see if the villagers had peaceful intentions. Just then, Archy Coody, a man of mixed race, jumped in a canoe with several other Cherokee and warned the men in the approaching canoe of the dark intentions of the people on shore. They heeded the warning and the flotilla continued down the river. As the bulk of the boats passed by, a large group of Cherokee wearing red and black paint came running out of the woods, whooping a war cry. They jumped in canoes and gave chase, but the large group of boats moved swiftly with the current to safety.

But the poor Stuart family in the trailing boat caught the full vengeance of the angry Chickamauga. A swarm of warriors quickly overwhelmed the boat's inhabitants. Bob and the rest of the Renfros could hear the shrieks and the screams of the terrified Stuarts, but they were too far away to provide any help. Some died painful deaths on the boat, while the Chickamauga took others prisoner. That village would pay a heavy price for the warrior's deeds, with a smallpox epidemic ravaging it, killing scores of Cherokee.

The Donelson group met village after village and several attacks over the next seven days. Then they had to face their next obstacle, the whirlpools and intense currents at Muscle Shoals. The flotilla survived intact, but there were some desperate moments.

The rest of the journey was long, but not as intense. Still, when the group met the aggressive waters at the mouth of the Cumberland River, several families stuck to the Ohio and Mississippi rivers. Some settled in Natchez while others went up into Illinois country. The group that remained included the Renfros, the Boyds, and the inhabitants of *The Adventure*, including Donelson's daughter Rachel, her husband Lewis Robards, and James Robertson's wife Charlotte. They waited out the heavy currents for a few more days before finally making their way down the Cumberland.

As the group reached the Red River, the modern-day site of Clarksville, the Renfros found the home they desired and bid the Donelson flotilla safe travels.[33] Exhausted from Chickamauga attacks, the family decided their best plan was to set up a stockade further inland.

But the dozens of souls at Renfro Station underestimated how intense life on the frontier could be. The fifty miles between them and Fort Nashborough exposed them to fierce attacks by the Chickasaw and Choctaw. Within two months, the Shawnees began deliberately targeting individuals who wandered away from Renfro Station. Several more attacks finally drove the families to realize their position was untenable.[34]

Like their far off neighbors at Bledsoe Station, the Renfros abandoned their new home for the safety of a larger community. They sent word down to Donelson and Robertson as they needed help with moving their large family to Fort Nashborough. It would be Bob's first opportunity to see the bluffs and the town that would change his life.

The Red Heifer and the Drifter

For the hardened frontier man, the place to gather to let off some steam was John "King" Boyd's Red Heifer. In the early days of Nashville, not long after the founders laid out the streets, Boyd's Spring Street establishment became the place to be.

Its proprietor was a family man at heart. He rarely let whisky pass his lips and took no guff. He could be stoic and stiff, but at other times he let his guard down and could be a little rebellious. The Heifer was a respectable place, meaning John never let a woman darken its doors. That would have been scandalous. Yet he had no problem providing his friends with a little whisky on the Sabbath.

This laxity could have led him to the local jail if James Robertson had found out. But John thought, what harm would a little tipple do to a thirsty customer? So, to get around the watchful eyes of the authorities and keep his patrons happy, he would hide a vial of whisky on a leather string outside the Heifer's backdoor. He demanded no money for this offering, but a shilling usually found its way into John's pocket at one point or another.

But it wasn't just the practice of supplying liquor on Sunday that had John skirting the local laws. Colonel Robertson had just lowered the boom on his distillation ban, so John had to keep his still hidden far from sight. And since the colonel would never visit a tavern, the best hiding place was in the back room of the Red Heifer.

Many a tavern served whisky, but John's provided some of the best juice in the area, thanks to one of his patrons, Sam Martin. Sam had a fondness for wine and for blending whisky. He loved going to the Heifer because he thought John's spirit was of superior quality. After a few magic blends, he soon became part of the decor in the stillroom as an unofficial assistant to the tavern owner.

But, to many, Sam Martin was a man with several flaws: he was a braggart, he seemed to be full of mischief, and he was excessively thrifty, usually at John's expense. The focus on these so-called faults eventually led to one of the biggest scandals in the early days of Nashville.

It seems Sam never paid for the liquor he consumed. Yet he always had the means. He carried with him a large Spanish milled dollar and two silver shillings. Since continental bills had lost much of their value, a Spanish milled dollar was like gold, especially in a barter economy. Yet, despite the jingling in his pocket, he never once offered money to John. Most felt Sam thought it was his right to have free samples since he was lending his skills to John. And John never called him to task for the pilfering.

Then there was the problem with Sam's excessively private nature. As a signer of the Cumberland Compact, he could have been a leader in the community. Instead, he kept to himself. But what set off the rumor mill was the time he went hunting with old Ike Johnson. When the two were captured by Creek warriors. Ike escaped, but he said Sam refused to leave. Then the Creeks ransacked Kilgore's Station, forcing old Thomas and Lydia Kilgore to abandon their home. A year later, Sam returned to Nashville with two fine fresh horses and silver spurs. Suspicions arose that he got the horses by helping the Creeks with their attack on Kilgore's Station, but evidence never surfaced.

Then, one fateful day, Sam walked into the Heifer with his friend, Russell Gower. The two men were sitting at a corner table watching John Boyd talk to two boys that had brought bottles into the tavern. They laid their money down on a barrelhead and John drew them some whisky from a barrel behind the bar. When the two boys ran off, John immediately headed into the back to check on the progress of a run of "red-eye." While going about his duties, John turned and through the doorway saw Russell putting something in his mouth. Then he saw Martin taking a drink of what looked like water and struggling to get it down. It was highly suspicious because everyone knew water wasn't something that usually passed Sam's lips.

When John walked back into the tavern, Sam and Russell were gone and so was the money the boys left on the barrelhead. John started kicking scenarios around in his head. He had owed Sam some money for work he had done––did Sam abscond with the money to level the balance sheet? And what had Russell put down his gullet?

Sam had been a daily visitor to the Heifer, but in his absence all the rumors around him started filling John's mind. He began discussing his theories with the customers about how the pair stole the money. Sam said it shocked him to see how fast and fierce this slander spread throughout the little Nashville community and out to the countryside.

A duel was the way to cure slander back in that day, but Sam took his grievance to court. He wanted payment for what John owed him, and he wanted to be compensated for the damage to his reputation. The court record showed:

> *"Sam Martin complains... Boyd on or about the third of March, 1785, at Nashville, in this county, did then and there, spitfully and maliciously scandalize the sd Martin by speaking slanderous words of him... By which the sd Martin saith he is damaged to the value of One Thousand Pounds; and therefore he brings this suit, and so f orth"*

But the case never came to trial. Once again, Sam Martin disappeared from Nashville--this time, never to be heard from again. Had he returned to the Creeks with his Spanish-milled dollar and John Boyd's pocket change?

After the excitement died down and the distilling season ended, it was time to take the now empty barrel of spirits to the backroom. When it was rolled on its side, a funny noise protruded from its bowels. Several men picked up the barrel and shook it until the musical sound of rolling coinage rang out from the floor. When the men returned the barrel to its proper position, all drew their glances to the objects that had dislodged from within the barrel. There before their eyes were several shillings and Sam Martin's Spanish-milled dollar.[35]

Against All Odds

As Bob sat nervously before the judge at the Davidson County Courthouse, he must have thought he was in the middle of a dream. It had been fourteen years since the harrowing journey from Fort Patrick Henry and so much had happened since then. He remembered the day he arrived at Fort Nashborough. What a relief to see friendly faces after the series of events he witnessed on the trip south from Renfro Station. And now, here he was, awaiting word on whether the court would grant him permission to open his very own tavern within the town limits. He had the perfect spot picked out, just south of the Public Square. There would be plenty of foot traffic and he would be far enough away from Lardner Clark's and the Red Heifer to earn his own clientele. He started to wondered much harder his path to tavern ownership was than theirs. Suddenly, the voice of the judge broke the string of thoughts dancing in his head.

It was January 16, 1794, a historic day as it turned out. When the judge's gavel fell, Nashville saw something it had never seen before and wouldn't see again for over half a century. The court ruled that "a certain Negro called Bobb in the town of Nashville be permitted to sell Liquor and Victuals."[36]

The surprising part isn't just that a Black man could own a tavern in Nashville during this era, but that Bob was also an enslaved man. At the time, an enslaved person couldn't even purchase alcohol, let alone sell it.[37] So how did it happen?

The answer isn't known. It takes a lot of speculation, as Bob's life between 1792 and 1801 is well documented but confusing. The first time he shows up in the record is when Josiah Love, John Renfro and Olive Shaw, the widow of Joseph Renfro, sell his services to John Mays. Olive and Joseph were members of the Donelson flotilla that settled at Renfro Station near modern day Clarksville. When the situation at the fort became untenable, two groups left the fort on their way to Fort Nashborough. When one group arrived near Sycamore Creek, they were attacked by Chickasaw and Choctaw and Joseph, Bob's enslaver, and the husband of Olive, lost his life. It became known as the Battle Creek Massacre. Bob was with Olive and the other group. They were told of Joseph's fate by his group's only survivor.[38] Now on August 8, 1792, Bob was with John Mays—or was he? In April of the following year, the Davidson County Court began documenting a dispute between Robert Nelson and Josiah Love over an enslaved man named Bob. Nelson wanted to take Bob, but Josiah filed an injunction with the court to stop it. In financial straits, Josiah sold Bob's rights to Elijah Robertson on August 17th, 1793. But then, the court dissolved the injunction and, with Bob being Love's only valuable asset, the court sold his services on the courthouse steps. His rights were sold by the court to an attorney named Robert Searcy.[39] Now Bob's rights were in the hands of two men. And yet, somehow during this time he was given the right to seek ownership of his own tavern. Credit for that likely belongs to Elijah Robertson, James Robertson's brother.

For a year, Bob would run his tavern, not knowing his fate or the man who gained his rights. Whichever way the court decision went, Bob's tavern hung in the balance.

In the end, the court decided that since the sheriff sold Bob's rights before he officially received word of the injunction, the courthouse sale stood.[40] What a relief it must have been for Bob when he was given the full support of Robert Searcy to run his tavern.

Bob apparently had an excellent reputation around town for how he handled his business. But it almost all came crashing down the day a local schoolmaster, Anderson Lavender, walked into the tavern. While the two were chatting, Anderson felt Bob had insulted him and he lunged across the bar, threatening to kill Bob. When patrons called the authorities, contemporary standards would suggest the man in cuffs would be Bob. Instead, it was the schoolmaster that was hauled off to jail. When the case went to court, a new member of the judiciary, Andrew Jackson, heard the case. Anderson pleaded not guilty, but as the trial progressed, the jury could not reach a verdict. Finally, the prosecutor dropped the case and Andersen was made to pay the cost of the court.[41] Even though no justice was served, it was a nod to Bob's standing in the community that the authorities arrested the white man in the entanglement.

As a new century dawned, things were changing for Bob. In 1801, his former competition, the Red Heifer, shut down after John "King" Boyd took the job of sheriff of Davidson County. Apparently, the town didn't hold his trade on the Sabbath against him. Then Bob approached Robert Searcy about the possibility of purchasing his freedom. Over the years, he had been saving every dime he could, hoping for the opportunity. To his great relief, Searcy agreed, and he released Bob from his enslavement. When the community heard Bob had been set free, they went one step further. Fifty-three prominent Davidson County citizens signed a petition to the General Assembly requesting Bob's full emancipation, "giving him all the privileges that is usual to persons in a similar situation." Signers included Robert Searcy, Sheriff John Boyd, and several other merchants, attorneys, judges, and tavern owners.[42]

On November 10, 1801, the long journey for this enslaved man came to an end. A joint act by the Fourth General Assembly of the State of Tennessee was placed in the public record:

> *BE IT ENACTED BY THE GENERAL ASSEMBLY OF THE STATE OF TENNESSEE, That the said negro man, Bob, shall be, and he is hereby emancipated and forever set free, to all intents and purposes whatever, and shall in future be known by the name of Robert Renfro.*

Speaker of the House William Dickson and Speaker of the Senate James White added their names to the document, and with that, history was made.[43] At long last, his future was his own. He celebrated by purchasing a lot on Main Street, where he established a new house of entertainments and boarding house for the "accommodation of gentlemen."[44]

Soon after, Robert began advertising his establishment in the paper, telling one and all that he charged fair rates for genteel boarders at the sign of the eagle.[45] He also sublet space to a man named Samuel Hutchinson, a tailor and ladies habit maker from Baltimore who had moved his business to Nashville.[46]

As for court cases, Robert would find himself in front of a judge several times. Such was the life of the owner of a house of entertainment. Frederick Stump also found himself in front of Andrew Jackson's court several times.

After twelve strong years as a free man and eighteen years as a tavern owner, Robert decided it was time to upgrade his business. Now known as The Cross-keys, he advertised his grandiose plans in the newspaper:

> *"Additional buildings are contemplated which shall be bountifully supplied with every kind of provender that can be furnished in the vicinity of Nashville, an attentive ostler will continually be kept, and every attention shall be paid to the well feeding, curing and watering of horses which is regularly attended to three times in the day, good cooks are provided and his table shall be furnished with every luxury and dainty which Nashville market can afford, a sober, steady & accommodating Bar-keeper is procured, & every other pre-requisite necessary to render guests comfortable, and what will very much contribute to their quiet, is his old and uniform custom of not entertaining any dissipated or disorderly guests, which will not be departed from, & for bill of cost, or terms of boarding cheaper I believe than any other place, ($5 per week for man and horse,) he tenders his grateful thanks to the public for their former custom, and hopes for a continuation of their favours which will be thankfully acknowledged by ROBERT RENFRO."*[47]

But in December 1812, his stables went up in flames after a spark turned into a fire that roared through the dry hay. The fire soon consumed his stables and the adjoining stables.[48] But, quick on his feet, Robert immediately found a nearby stable, made an agreement with the owner and began boarding his visitors' horses there. Within weeks, he erected new stables. It was a stroke of luck that his tavern was spared the destruction.[49]

However, a year later, on March 11, 1814, the entire town of Nashville faced a devastating fire and Robert's Cross-keys Tavern was a casualty. Again, he moved quickly to reestablish the business in a new place. He rented a stone tavern down the street and instructed his friends and customers to visit him there.[50] It was a smaller establishment, but maybe easier for Robert to handle with his advancing age.

Yet what happened after this is a complete mystery. Robert's last entry in the records is a request for someone to lease property he owned on College Street. He was willing to make a ten-year lease, but he was never again mentioned in the records. There's no death date, no gravesite, no knowledge of any next of kin. His name has been lost to the ages.

Robert Renfro was a remarkable man who lived a remarkable life. Imagine the privilege of being a fly on the wall of that tavern. The stories Robert could tell.

Chapter 6

OLD HICKORY

Done in by a Need for Whisky

A little town east of the mountains was alive with chatter, and gossip was everywhere. A hero from the Battle of Kings Mountain was a prisoner of the state and being transported to Morganton, North Carolina, to await trial.

It was none other than General John Sevier. The charge was treason against the state of North Carolina. And, as the legend goes, the authorities had captured him while he was trying to buy whisky and rum at Jonesborough general store. How had things gone so wrong for the general?

The problems started when the continental government put forth the Ordinance Act of 1785. Thomas Jefferson, looking for a way to ease Congress' war debts, suggested creating territories out of the state owned lands west of the Appalachian Mountains. He hoped the sales would raise money sufficient for Congress' needs. Inspired by the idea, North Carolina ceded the Overhill region and beyond to the federal government for the creation of a new territory. But the disorganized U.S. Congress wasn't in a hurry to react.

Abandoned and left to fend for themselves, former North Carolina citizens west of the Appalachians needed a solution, and fast! They were facing battles with the Chickamauga with no official military force in place. Following the death of his father John, Landon Carter reached out to General John Sevier. The two worked together to bring the citizens of Greene, Washington, and Sullivan counties together for a conference. The solution presented was to organize a new state, the State of Frankland.

But just as Sevier and Carter set plans in motion, the State of North Carolina repealed their cession bill. To protect the area, they offered General Sevier a position at the head of the Washington County militia. Sevier hedged, then reluctantly rolled ahead with the plans for the new state, with the shortened name of Franklin.

After the establishment of a state constitution, the First General Assembly voted in Sevier as the state's first governor. Governor Sevier immediately sent William Cocke to Washington to lobby Congress for their blessing. But the area was now serving two masters. And North Carolina Governor Alexander Martin wasn't happy about the breakaway region. He offered to let the citizens of Franklin back into North Carolina without the payment of past taxes. Sevier wouldn't budge. Governor Martin appointed Colonel John Tipton to protect the three North Carolina county governments.

The message on statehood from Congress was no, although a few members voted in favor of it. Then Sevier reached out to Benjamin Franklin, hoping the old statesman would be so overwhelmed by the honor of having a state named after him that he might lobby Congress. But the answer wasn't quite what Sevier had hoped for.

> *"His Excellency Governor Sevier.*
> *I am sensible of the honor which your Excellency and your council thereby do me, but being in Europe when your State was formed, I am too little acquainted with the circumstances, to be able to offer you [any assistance] that may be of importance..."*
> *- Benjamin Franklin 1787 June 30"*[51]

To pressure Sevier, the governor ordered the sheriff to seize the general's enslaved workers to cover unpaid taxes. Knowing they were being held at Colonel

Tipton's farm, an angry Sevier raised a posse of over a hundred men. They marched on Tipton's farm and the Battle of Franklin commenced. Ten minutes later, General Sevier was in retreat.

This is when he made his way to the general store to buy some whisky. He likely needed it. But the visit turned into a scuffle and someone told Tipton of his presence. Soon enough he found himself confined to a jail cell on the eastern side of the mountains in North Carolina.

He wasn't there for long, however. Someone forgot to secure his cell, and General Sevier escaped. The sheriff, William Morrison, had fought with the general at the Battle of Kings Mountain. Some charged collusion, but the sheriff only shrugged his shoulders.

What happened next is one of the strangest twists of fortune in American history. With Sevier's term as governor over and no one voted into his place, the State of Franklin collapsed. General Sevier, now a fugitive from the law, was leading troops against the Cherokee. With his hero status, he ran for and won a seat in the North Carolina General Assembly as senator for Greene County. The General Assembly reviewed the charges against him. They deemed his early opposition to the State of Franklin as reason enough to exonerate him. The last act on the matter was a pardon by North Carolina Governor Alexander Martin.

During his term in the Senate, Sevier voted to ratify the U.S. Constitution. He also voted for the ceding of North Carolina's lands west of the Appalachian Mountains. The federal government would accept the territory and renamed it the Territory South of the River Ohio. John Sevier, whose fighting spirit was never in doubt, was appointed Brigadier General of its militia. But the icing on the cake was when the one-time fugitive became the first governor of the State of Tennessee.

To say early Tennessee leaders had some rough edges would be an understatement. In fact, one of Tennessee's best-known founders almost found himself in a duel with John Sevier. But then Andy Jackson was never afraid of paces at dawn.

Jackson was a troubled man, knee deep in flaws. But if he was in your corner, he was the best friend you could have. There were times he appeared to be Robert

Renfro's guardian angel in court. Yet he was an enslaver who said he found the slave trade unappealing. He adopted and raised a little Creek Indian boy as his own, after the boy's mother died during a battle; yet he ignored a Supreme Court ruling and ordered the removal of eastern tribes to areas west of the Mississippi. The burden of the deadly Trail of Tears falls at Jackson's feet. As president, he was the last to leave the country debt free, but he almost broke it to do so. He was the hero of New Orleans and a patriot. But also aided and abetted a suspected traitor, Aaron Burr, the man who killed Alexander Hamilton in a duel.

In fact, the only things you could count on with the politician, general, and one time distiller Andrew Jackson, were his passions for land speculation, his feisty temper, his distaste for the British, and his undying love for John Donelson's daughter Rachel.

Statesman, Fighter, Lawyer, Grocer

American prospects looked weak after the fall of Charleston. The victory set the British Redcoats free to ravage inland South Carolina with the help of loyalist support. The man in charge of the march was British Lieutenant Colonel Banastre Tarleton, and the cocksure officer saw little resistance on his march to North Carolina. That all changed when he reached the Waxhaws region, just south of the border.

Tarleton's opposition came from two inexperienced regiments of Virginia Continentals led by Virginia Colonel Abraham Buford. When the outmanned Redcoats engaged, their skills turned the tide quickly and all seemed lost for the patriots. Accounts differ, but it was said Buford ordered the raising of a white flag. Apparently Tarleton didn't see the flag because he was trapped under his dead horse. The result was chaos, with the Americans laying down their weapons and the British fighting on, with Tarleton's account suggesting they were avenging their fallen leader. At the end of the battle, Tarleton's loyalist troops captured, killed, or wounded three quarters of Buford's force. The Americans blamed

Tarleton for the carnage, suggesting he told his men to give no quarter--meaning no prisoners were to be taken and the wounded killed.

The Battle of Waxhaws became useful propaganda and a rallying cry for Americans. Even the Overmountain Men yelled, "Buford's revenge" and "remember Tarleton's quarter," as they made their way up Kings Mountain.

Soldiers that survived Waxhaws were taken to the nearest makeshift hospital, a little white church in the woods. It was there that a 13-year-old Andrew Jackson and his brothers Hugh and Robert helped their mother Elizabeth attend to the wounded. That day, Jackson's disdain for the British was born.

Jackson's mother was a patriot who insisted that her son's help fight for the American cause. Andrew's brother Hugh was the only one old enough to fight, but he died of heat exhaustion while encamped with General Davie's forces near Charleston. Robert and Andrew served as scouts until the British captured them; while being detained Andrew received a scar on his face from a British soldier's sword when he refused to polish the Redcoat's boots. Not long after, the two boys came down with smallpox. Andrew recovered, but Robert passed away. Then, Andrew's mother Elizabeth went to help the sick and dying on a British prison ship in Charleston Harbor. While there, she contracted cholera and died. With his father long since dead, Andrew became an orphan.

At the war's conclusion, Andrew moved to Salisbury, North Carolina, to be mentored by local attorney Spruce Macay. While living at a nearby tavern, Andrew earned a reputation as a notorious partier. A local resident said, "Andrew Jackson was the most roaring, rollicking, game-cocking, horse-racing, card-playing, mischievous fellow that ever lived in Salisbury." He drew further ire when he invited a group of prostitutes to his dance school's Christmas ball. When he gained entrance to the bar, Andrew took off for Jonesborough in the State of Franklin, where his first official act as an attorney was to put his name to the failed petition for separation from North Carolina.[52]

Looking to further his legal career, he accepted a position as a public prosecutor in the newly formed Mero District of North Carolina in November 1788. The Mero government seat was in Nashville.

Here, Andrew boarded with John Donelson's widow, Rachel Stockley-Donelson. She had run a boarding house out of her home since her husband's mysterious killing during a trip to Kentucky two years earlier. Here, Andrew met the couple's daughter, Rachel Donelson-Robards. He was instantly smitten--but Rachel was married. Her husband, Lewis Robards, had traveled with the Donelson flotilla years before. But Robards' interest in Rachel was waning. Still, he wasn't about to let this man move in on his territory, and so he let Andrew know of his displeasure. At the urging of his bunkmate and best friend John Overton, Andrew moved out of the house.

But Robards became an absentee husband and eventually sent a letter to his mother-in-law asking her to take Rachel back. Andrew and Rachel thought the message was clear--Lewis was abandoning his wife. Two years later, feeling they were free of Robards, Andrew and Rachel were married, even though Robards hadn't granted a divorce. It would be a scar on the couple's reputation for the rest of their lives. The two would remarry after Robards eventually granted a divorce.

It was May 1794 and, thanks to treaties, it brought the end of the wars with Cherokee, Shawnee, Chickasaw, and Creeks. With territories opening up, Andrew Jackson and John Overton went into a land speculation partnership.

The following year, Andrew opened a general store in Nashville with his brother-in-law, Samuel Donelson. One of the products he offered was whisky, as evidenced by a letter Andrew wrote to one of his customers, George Neville.

> *"Sir, I expect to set out for Philadelphia Shortly. Wish you to Come up and bring with you the patent of the Land you promised. The wiskey is ready for you and I hope you will come and take it away. I trust you will not disappoint me as I have been obliged to pay one hundred Dollars Cash for the Whiskey, and will be obliged to pay your order on me in Cash, as I could not procure the pork in the store."*
> *- Andrew Jackson (March 17, 1796)*[53]

Where he sourced the whisky is unknown. And apparently the store failed, as he ended his partnership with Samuel Donelson by June 1796.

While Andrew was wheeling and dealing whisky, the Territory South of the River Ohio was preparing to become a state. Fifty-five delegates met in Knoxville in the Spring of 1796. Andrew Jackson joined William Blount, James Robertson, William Cocke, and William Fort at the convention.

Two pieces of lore come out of this convention. One suggests that Robertson County farmer distiller William Fort wrote the final document.[54] The other gives credit to Andrew Jackson for suggesting Tennessee as the name of the state.

Congress approved the inclusion of Tennessee as the sixteenth state in the Union and set the borders of the modern state. However, the Cherokee and Chickasaw still reserved much of the land to the south and west of Nashville. Andrew Jackson became the state's first U.S. congressional representative.

When he returned to Rachel in Nashville, Representative Jackson purchased a new home called Hunters Hill. He saw it as a suitable place for farming and distilling. Eventually, he also wanted to get back into the mercantile business. But first he had to make his way to Washington, D.C.

The origin of Andrew's interest in whisky is unknown. Perhaps his time selling the spirit at the Jackson-Donelson mercantile inspired him. Or maybe his good friend John Overton suggested it. President Washington had appointed Overton as Supervisor of the Revenue for the District of Tennessee--a job that showed Overton just how popular and lucrative distilling was in the brand new state of Tennessee.

Hamilton's Excise

Before March 1791, American distilling had been a tax-free endeavor for farmers across the country. No one thought twice about setting up a still in the barn or even in the kitchen. But when Secretary of the Treasury Alexander Hamilton began looking for ways to fund the government, he saw a tax on whisky distillation as the best method.

The stories of how excise taxes in Britain had helped to industrialize the craft fascinated Hamilton. He wanted to see America develop as an industrial power, so he crafted rules that enticed budding industrialists to join the trade. The secretary knew large-scale producers could bring hefty profits and tax revenue into the Treasury.

But not everyone would benefit from Hamilton's scheme. The ones he hurt the most were the farmers who bartered with whisky and used distillation to eke out a profit from their yearly harvest. One of Hamilton's rules was that the tax had to be paid in cash. Farmers were more than willing to pay their fair share, but they couldn't because they were cash poor.[55]

This led to uprisings in Western Pennsylvania that would become known as the Whiskey Rebellion. No tax collector was safe. Not even a distiller and tax collector like General John Neville escaped unscathed. It was the burning of his home, Bower Hill, that brought Alexander Hamilton and the military into Pittsburgh. It was that show of force that eventually led the insurrectionists to disband.

The popular myth is the Whiskey Rebellion sent distillers south into Kentucky and Tennessee to avoid the tax. But most of these farmers were too poor to leave their land grants and simple farms for points unknown. It didn't matter, anyway. If they went to Tennessee, John Overton's collectors were there, ready to knock on the stillhouse door.

The records Overton kept give a glimpse into the size and scope of distilling in Tennessee. One year after the Whiskey Rebellion, Overton's records show that over 46,000 gallons of spirits were distilled in Tennessee.

In those records, we find some familiar names. Frederick Stump's freshly rebuilt White's Creek distillery featured two stills. John "King" Boyd's Red Heifer had one registered still. Landon Carter, John Carter's son, had two registered stills. Thomas Kilgore and William Fort were two of almost two dozen distillers around the Red River and Sulphur Fork Creek in Robertson County.

One notable name that is missing is that of Brigadier General Evan Shelby, who died a couple of years before the excise law went into effect. But his son Isaac, the hero of Kings Mountain and Governor of Kentucky, continued the tradition in his new home state.

Even though there wasn't a distillers rebellion in 18th century Tennessee, the tax was not easy to collect. Overton wrote several letters to Philadelphia, asking Hamilton for assistance with collection of the tax. He also wrote to Tennessee farmers imploring them to get caught up with their payments.

The Hunters Hill Distillery

One person Overton didn't have to chase, at first at least, was his good friend Andrew Jackson. The distillery he was building at Hunters Hill was behind schedule, thanks to his term as a congressman in Washington, his law practice, his new general store, and his farm. Things were further delayed when Senator William Cocke stepped down from his post and the General Assembly appointed Jackson to take his place as a U.S. Senator. Finally, in 1798, ex-Senator Jackson came home to Nashville, taking a seat in the Tennessee Superior Court as a jurist. He finally had time to focus on Hunters Hill.

Within months, Jackson's two stills were humming away. Correspondence during that time shows corn whisky as Jackson's principal product. But like George Washington's distillery at Mount Vernon in Virginia, Hunters Hill distilled rye whiskey as well. George Deaderick of Stones River, apparently a high rye fan, wrote Jackson saying he'd "be very thankful to have one Barrel of at least one third Rye."[56]

But distilling at Hunters Hill abruptly came to a halt in June 1799 when the sound of evening crickets were drowned out by shouts and a distinct crackling noise. The stillhouse was ablaze, sparked by what no one could say. Enslaved workers and family members brought buckets to the scene, but the heat and flames were too much. The roof beams gave way, and the entire structure caved in. It sounded like a Fourth of July festival when several barrels filled with 300 gallons of whisky exploded.

The next morning, Jackson surveyed the damage and deemed the loss total. Orders kept coming in, but there was no way to fill them. As if losing the distillery wasn't enough, Overton's collector had shown up to count the stills and collect the $53.19 due in duties (around $1,400 today). Jackson disputed the charge. The whisky was gone--why should he have to pay tax on it? But six months later, a persistent assessor was back again, requesting payment.[57]

A frustrated Jackson sought to dispute the charge officially. He went down to Nashville and stood before the Justice of the Peace, Thomas Hutchings, and gave an accounting of the damage. He pointed out his inability to distill with the damaged equipment. Judge Jackson signed his name to it and used it as evidence as he pleaded his case to congress. All he asked was that they circumvent the authority of the Secretary of the Treasury. He finished his letter saying that "he could not believe that the United States would draw Money from the misfortunes of her Citizens."[58]

But in the end, they did. Jackson's petition was referred to the Committee of Claims, who rejected it on February 12, 1803. What really stuck in Jackson's craw was the fact Thomas Jefferson had repealed all of Alexander Hamilton's excise taxes seven months earlier. The whisky tax that employed John Overton and fed the Whiskey Rebellion was gone, but Jackson was still on the hook for his lost whisky. He begrudgingly paid the tax.

Feeding the Chain

With Jackson temporarily out of business, it left the celebration over the demise of the tax to Frederick Stump. Now in his eighties, he was running a farm, tavern, and distillery, while making profits off the other plantations he owned around Middle Tennessee. With no tax, he turned grain into duty-free whisky. Stump raked in the profits.

To the east of town, Hunters Hill was awash with activity and Jackson wasn't about to let his distillery misfortunes get the better of him. In February 1802 he entered into a new partnership, Jackson and Watson & Company, with his neighbor Thomas Watson, and Rachel's nephew, John Hutchings. The plan was to open two distilleries, one at Hunters Hill and another on Watson's farm. They also planned to add cotton gins, one to Jackson's farm and the other to Hutchings. The products created from these enterprises would feed a chain of general stores. One was at Hunters Hill, another at Watson's farm, plus a store in Gallatin, and another in Lebanon, Tennessee.[59]

The rebuilding of Jackson's distillery was the first thing on the agenda. He wanted to do things right, so he hired an experienced distiller and contracted a professional, William Irby, to set up his stills. Some of the milled corn came from Jackson's estate, and he ordered in bushels of corn and rye to supplement his supply while he waited for harvest. He also ordered four barrels of tight cooperage, plus 370 gallons of whisky as a starter for the stores.[60]

Meanwhile, Jackson was commissioned as a Major General in the Tennessee militia and used the post to supply the troops at a garrison near Muscle Shoals with daily rations, including whisky. But Thomas Watson wouldn't see any of it. He wanted out of the business by 1803.[61] Watson's store was emptied, with the products going to Hunters Hill. Jackson continued business in Davidson County under the name Andrew Jackson & Co.

But it wasn't long before Jackson grew tired of the distilling business. There were better profits to be had in cotton. He sold Hunters Hill in 1804 and bought the adjoining property. He had a log cabin built and dubbed the land The Hermitage.

When he closed up the Hunters Hill store, Jackson sent the goods down to the store at the encampment near Muscle Shoals. Then he negotiated a sale of the Gallatin store to his friend James Winchester. He wanted to consolidate and put all of his focus on building a single entertainment complex at nearby Clover Bottom. There he would feature a race track, tavern, stables, outhouses, and a general store.

As for whisky, he took a temperance pledge with a friend John Verell in January 1806. The first man to take a drink would be required to buy the other a complete tailored suit of clothes.[62] It's hard to say how long the general avoided booze. He was definitely fond of it and believed strongly in its medicinal properties.

But his lack of drinking didn't keep him out of trouble. Jackson was sensitive about his wife Rachel's honor, especially surrounding her first marriage to Jackson. When he caught wind that Charles Dickinson, a man Robert Renfro once sued for breach of contract, had trampled Rachel's honor, Jackson confronted him. But Dickinson cooled down the fiery Jackson by suggesting he was drunk at the time he made the derogatory comments and wasn't sure he'd said them. Jackson accepted the apology.

Then, a race was planned at Clover Bottom between Jackson's prized horse, Truxton, and Dickinson's father-in-law Joseph Erwin's horse, Ploughboy. Jackson had purchased Truxton from his temperance partner John Verell. Jackson and Erwin had arranged that if Ploughboy couldn't race, a compensation of $800 would be paid in the forfeit to Jackson. When Ploughboy came up lame, Jackson requested the money and, after some negotiations, Erwin paid.

The trouble started when one of Jackson's friends enhanced the story, putting Joe Erwin in a terrible light. Soon Thomas Swann, a friend of Dickinson's, stepped into the fray and began a war of words with Jackson in Thomas Eastin's *Impartial Review and Cumberland Repository*. When Swann saw Jackson at Winn's Tavern, he moved toward him. Jackson became incensed with the accuser's brashness, pulled out his cane and began rapping him on the head repeatedly. After that incident, exchanges grew darker and more public. But it was a quote by Dickinson in Eastin's paper that sent Jackson over the top. Dickinson called him a "worthless scoundrel, a poltroon and a coward." Jackson wrote Dickinson back and said Charles owed the "satisfaction due [to him] for the insults offered."[63]

Since duels were illegal in Tennessee, the two met across the border in Adairville, Kentucky on May 30, 1806. Dickinson was renowned for his accuracy with a gun, and it seemed Jackson's fate was sealed. Jackson's second was John Overton's older brother, Thomas. Overton suggested maybe they should let Dickinson fire first, which confused and concerned Jackson, but Overton suggested a strategy to get his rival to miss. It all hinged on whether Overton could win the coin toss for his man.

When he did, the two men stepped their paces and turned to face each other. Overton looked at Jackson as Dickinson stood at the ready, gun at his side. Jackson was stiff but resolute. Still looking at Jackson, Overton said, "Gentleman, are we ready?" The two men agreed they were. As Dickinson waited for the visual cue of Overton turning his head to acknowledge his agreement, Overton quickly yelled out, "fire!" Dickinson flinched, and shot. The bullet hit Jackson in the chest, but it wasn't fatal. Now it was Jackson's turn. Dickinson braced as Jackson raised his pistol. The gun went half cocked. Yet, inexplicably, Jackson was permitted to fix his gun. When he leveled the gun a second time, the shot rang out, and Dickinson buckled and crumpled in a heap. He would live for only a few moments. Jackson had met his mark and Dickinson would slowly bleed to death.[64]

The bullet in Jackson's chest was aimed at his heart, but only succeeded in breaking a couple of ribs. But the bullet was too close to his heart for surgeons to remove, and so he kept that symbol of the fatal duel for the rest of his life. Jackson's popularity suffered in Tennessee for the next couple of years. His famous misfire became fodder for the newspapers. Rarely did combatants get a second shot after a misfire. Why he was allowed a second shot remains a mystery for the ages.

For the next few years, it was a time of warfare for Jackson. There were no further whisky transactions in his correspondence. Instead, Jackson took the lead in the Creek Wars in Mississippi Territory as part of the Tennessee Militia. When the War of 1812 raged across the northeast, Jackson was commissioned as a general in the United States Army. He became a national hero when word spread of his lopsided victory against the British at New Orleans. His elevated status with the populace helped him win the nation's highest office in 1828. And his association with whisky would live on, with his face and nickname Old Hickory being used for several whisky brands years in the future.

Looking back on Jackson's military career, during his few years on the battlefield, he was joined by one of the most unlikely of officers. The former fugitive, Frederick Stump. At 90 years old, the U.S. Army commissioned him Captain of the Cavalry, under the command of Colonel John Coffee. Even at his advanced age, he was a fierce fighter.[65]

After the war, Stump returned to White's Creek to settle down. His wife Anna had passed away in 1804 from a painful illness,[66] and Frederick's sons had moved off to run successful businesses of their own. Emotionally alone, he began a relationship with a barmaid at Old Stump's Tavern. Catherine Gingery was a Pennsylvania girl some 70 years his junior. The two were married and when he passed away some years later, he left her a house by the creek that she lived in until she passed away at 96.[67]

It was a wild and crazy end to the saga of Frederick Stump.

Chapter 7

THE WILD FRONTIER

To his many friends and well-wishers in the state of Tennessee, the words cut like a dagger to the heart. The state's favorite son was dead. For the town of Memphis, it seemed almost impossible to imagine. Just weeks before, on that last glorious night before he crossed the Mississippi for points west, the streets and pubs had been filled with people, sharing drinks and toasting their hero. He seemed invincible. But the morning news, detailing the fierce battle on the Texas frontier, said differently.

> "The storming lasted less than an hour. The end of David Crockett of Tennessee, the great hunter of the west, was as glorious as his career through life had been useful. He and his companions were found surrounded by piles of assailants, whom they had immolated on the altar of Texas' liberties. The countenance of Crockett was unchanged; he had in death that freshness of hue, which his exercise of pursuing the beasts of the forest and the prairie had imparted to him."[68]

Newspapers across the nation would search for clues as to what happened at the little Spanish mission called The Alamo. The anguish of the writers was palpable. The man they had so depended on for humorous or cutting daily headlines was gone and oh, how they lamented losing him. But he had died as he lived, fighting for what he believed in, and no one could fault him for that.

There are few people who painted as vivid a picture of the frontiersman as David Crockett. From humble beginnings, he became a legendary bear hunter. He stood up as a Tennessee volunteer. He tried his hand at distilling whisky and, when tragedy ended that career, he turned misfortune into a legendary career in politics. Crockett was a master of sarcasm and never held back his disdain for his opposition, yet they had to respect him; he was the voice of the common man. It has to be said, no book about Tennessee would be complete without the dynamic and homespun legend of Davy Crockett.

The Rise of the King

Born in 1786 near Limestone Creek in the State of Franklin (or North Carolina, if you prefer), David Crockett came of age in a world of strife and financial instability.

His grandparents, David and Elizabeth, brought the family from Maryland to the Watauga River region at the start of the American Revolution. David's father John and two of his brothers went off to fight for the American cause. But they left the family exposed to Dragging Canoe's war on the settlements. The Chickamauga killed his grandparents in one of the raids, while taking two of his uncles hostage.

After his father and two uncles returned from the Battle of Kings Mountain, they struggled to get the family back on their feet. David's father John went to work for the local government while his mother Rebecca took care of their growing family.

When David was born, the family was in the middle of several moves. Trying to find a lasting occupation, John built a gristmill on Cove Creek with a partner, Thomas Gilbreath. But when flood waters came dangerously close to wiping out the business, John looked for a new enterprise on higher ground.

This led the family to Morristown, where John Crockett leased land from a Quaker named John Canady. The property was on the main road between Abingdon, Virginia, and the territorial capital of Knoxville. David's father thought it was the perfect location for a tavern. Unfortunately, the travelers he attracted were of meager means, which kept the family finances in a sorry state.

Desperate to get out of debt, John was ready to grab at any option he could. When a Dutchman named Jacob Siler stopped to rest at the Crockett's tavern, he asked if John's twelve-year-old son David could help drive his cattle up to Natural Bridge, Virginia. To David's surprise, his father willingly indentured him to this stranger for $6 ($200 today).

When David finished the 250-mile journey, Siler didn't want to let him go. Homesick and feeling like a prisoner, he planned his escape, and when he spotted one of the tavern's patrons riding south, David asked the man for a ride.

Upon returning home, his father told him he had enrolled the boy in a nearby school. For David, it was his first chance to learn to read and write. But his growing wild streak took over, and he ended up brawling with another student. Worried the schoolmaster would take a switch to him, he started playing hooky day after day, and talked his brothers into covering for his truancy. Noticing the boy's absence, the schoolmaster contacted John and asked about David's whereabouts. Unaware of the visit, David walked into the tavern to find his father angry and full of whisky. After berating David, he ran after him with a hickory stick. Knowing he could easily confuse his drunken father, as he crossed a hill, he ducked behind some bushes and watched as his father ran by. Scared at what might happen if he returned home, he ran away.

For the next few months, David drove cattle and helped with farming chores anywhere he could. Looking for a skilled trade, he spent eighteen months apprenticing for a Virginia hatter named Elijah Griffith. But when Griffith became insolvent, he left David with nothing. Now sixteen, he decided it was time to make peace with his father and headed home. When he arrived in Morristown, he went to see his brothers to take the temperature of the situation. When his sister recognized him, she ran over, threw her arms around him and said, "here, here is my lost brother!" She hadn't seen him for three years and no one in the family knew whether he was dead or alive. When his father saw him, he hugged David and instantly forgot all past indiscretions.

Yet for the elder Crockett, financially, nothing had changed. After David took a part-time job with John Canady, he found out his father owed the man a $40 debt. So David worked off the debt before accepting any money for himself. When he settled the debt, David brought the note home and gave it to his father. John panicked, thinking old man Canady had sent his son home to demand payment. When David told him he had settled the debt, John burst into tears.

By this point in his life, David was filled with life experiences, but still couldn't read or write. When he became infatuated with a girl, he was heartbroken when she turned down his affections and he was sure it was because of his lack of education. So when John Canady offered to have his son provide David with some schooling, he jumped at the chance. With his brain filled with knowledge, he had the confidence to ask his next love interest, Polly Finley, for her hand in marriage. She happily accepted.

It didn't take long for the young couple's family to grow. David would later say he was better at growing a family than growing a fortune. Unable to secure property for his family in East Tennessee, he decided it was time to move west. With the help of Polly's father, the young Crockett family packed their bags and headed to Lincoln County.

The first area they explored was around the east fork of Mulberry Creek, close to modern-day Lynchburg. To feed the family, David hunted deer and small game, but what he really wanted to do was take down a bear––unfortunately, one never crossed his path. After a brief stay, the family crossed the line into Franklin County and settled on Beans Creek.

One day, while at a local tavern, David overheard the locals talking about a massacre far to the south at Fort Mims, in which several people had apparently lost their lives after Creek warriors raided the fort. Remembering the stories of his grandparents, Crockett jumped at the chance to get into the fight. He volunteered as a scout with Francis Jones' Company of Mounted Riflemen, under the command of Colonel John Coffee. But David saw little action and never made it near Fort Mims.

After his enlistment was up, he went back to Beans Creek to settle down. But the War of 1812 pulled him back in. Reenlisting, he became a member of the Tennessee Mounted Gunmen under the command of Captain John Cowan. But again, he saw little action and spent most of his time hunting and foraging for food for the unit.

When David returned home, his bride Polly took ill and passed away. The heartbroken frontiersman buried her near their home at Beans Creek. Knowing he needed help with his three young children, he began courting another young widower, Elizabeth Patton. Her husband had died in the recent conflict and she had two kids of her own. The pair were quickly married. While it was a marriage of convenience, it was Elizabeth's steady hand that played an important role in the next stage of David's life.

When David went on a hunting trip out west, he camped around land recently opened for settlement on Shoal Creek in Lawrence County. It seemed like the perfect place to set up a milling operation, similar to what his father had when he was a little boy. He made plans to move from Beans Creek immediately.

Crockett put every penny he had into the endeavor. After all, this was to be his legacy. On top of his own investment, he borrowed over $3,000 (the equivalent of $77,000 today). When completed, he had a powder mill, gristmill, and a large distillery with two copper pot stills, all situated on Shoal Creek.

Now officially a businessman, he decided it was time to inch into politics. He took the position of commissioner with the newly formed Lawrence County and helped survey its borders.

But David thought he could do more. He saw the plight of the rural poor and thought the General Assembly was too preoccupied with other matters to pay attention to their needs. In 1821, he stepped down from his job as county commissioner, made a bid for a seat in the Tennessee General Assembly, and won.

But the day he took his seat in the assembly, then meeting in Murfreesboro, he received some devastating news. When they said it was about his business, he half expected them to say the powder mill had blown sky high. It was worse. A storm had washed all three of his buildings away after Shoal Creek turned into a raging river. The debris in the water broke his millstone in two. He said, it "just made a complete mash of me." His wife, Elizabeth, stayed stoic throughout the entire ordeal. David said she was the reason he didn't do something drastic or deceitful to recover from the tragedy. Instead of complaining, her strength and understanding helped him realize he could muster the will to start over again.

He never rebuilt the distillery or mills. Some say David didn't make all the creditors whole. And while the situation may have ended the dreams of lesser men, David saw it as a sign.

The Tennessee General Assembly was just the beginning for the frontiersman. He had bigger plans in mind. Yet when his quirky country sensibilities landed in a seat in the U.S. Congress, no one in Washington was quite sure how to take him. Was he a country bumpkin or a man of substance? It didn't take long for his quick wit and well-reasoned opinions to endear him to his colleagues.

To his friends who knew him from the early days, he would always be David. But the rest of the world would get to know and love him as either Colonel Crockett, or simply Davy.

Bell's Tavern

At the same time David Crockett was building his distillery at Shoal Creek, another famous Tennessean was negotiating to secure the western part of the state for new settlement. Signed by General Andrew Jackson, Kentucky's ex-Governor Isaac Shelby, and the Chickasaw, the 1818 Treaty of Tuscaloosa opened the remaining areas of Kentucky and Tennessee to settlement. History remembers it as the Jackson Purchase.[69]

According to lore, this wasn't the only impact General Jackson had on the future of West Tennessee. Before the founding of Memphis on May 22, 1819,[70] the story goes that three men that owned the land sat down to enjoy drinks at the Bell Tavern to draw out plans for the town. Those men were General Jackson, Judge John Overton, and General James Winchester.[71]

Many take the story at face value. Historians dispute it. So is it history or is it lore?

It is true that Jackson, Overton, and Winchester owned all the land that became the town of Memphis. It was one of the earliest and riskiest purchases made by the land speculation company owned by Jackson and Overton. This 5,000-acre land grant on the bluffs overlooking the Mississippi River was once the property of John Rice. Normally, it would be a valuable piece of property. But because it sat in the heart of prized Chickasaw tribal lands, it had to be left alone. And it didn't look like it was going to open anytime soon.[72]

This led Jackson to offload half his land to the Winchester family in 1797. Eventually James Winchester bought out his other family members and became sole owner of that quarter of the property.[73] Jackson's idea of investing that money elsewhere was inspired. The land sat idle for over two decades before settlement was possible, thanks to the Jackson Purchase.

When it finally opened up, it's easy to imagine Jackson, Winchester, and Overton were champing at the bit to make this long-held land purchase profitable. But Jackson would sell half of his remaining portion to General Winchester in December 1818;[74] and he handed power of attorney for his remaining land to his partner, Judge Overton. If Jackson was interested in Memphis, he didn't show it in his actions.

Where did the story come from?

Some of it may have developed from a post Civil War article in the *Memphis Daily Appeal*. The author describes the condition and construction of the historic tavern. Then matter-of-factly, they reveal the famous event and its participants:

> *"This decaying wooden structure, like most houses built here in the earlier years of the century, was rejected upon cedar posts instead of foundation stones. To these the weatherboarding of two low stories is nailed. The structure, thirty feet square, is not more than twenty in height. There is not a vestige of paint remaining on the exterior*

> walls and within there are six narrow rooms unplastered, with low ceilings. The old mantelpieces bear the imprint of many bootheels. In fact, tradition designates the track of Andrew Jackson on the mantle of the little chamber which he was wont to occupy. It was in this contracted apartment that Jackson, Judge Overton and Gen. Winchester planned the city..."[75]

To further the validity of Jackson's presence at the tavern, a long-time resident of the town, Mrs. Whittier, tells of dining at the tavern at the same time General Jackson was there. The combination of the author's recollections and the elderly woman's account make the meeting seem plausible. The author finishes the article with an admonishment of the city's youth for not knowing this important piece of history. He suggests they should pay more attention to the words of people like Mrs. Whittier.[76]

But there are parts of her story that don't jibe with history. She tells of her arrival in the area in 1811 with her husband Squire Grace, who she says served with the first high court of the area as a judge.[77] This would be hard to do when Tennessee didn't have a government established in the area until almost a decade after their arrival. It also would have required them to be squatters in a dangerous land.

This is a great example of why details in newspapers can't always be taken at face value. Some journalists are prone to relying too heavily on their own memory or oral tradition when writing their articles. Bias or the need to prove a thesis also leads to questionable research. The problem is compounded when poorly researched stories from one paper are rewritten in another newspaper, or syndication plants the same inaccuracies in papers across the nation. This renders the old "use two sources to verify facts" moot. Poor research has led to many of the fables people believe in today. A researcher must always tap into their inner skepticism.

This article is also an example of why oral tradition is hard to trust. Two main issues develop when counting on a human to get the story right: The fallibility of memory and the brain's close connection with the heart.

The first issue goes without saying. Few people have a photographic memory, and memories morph and erode with time. Events once clearly defined mix with other memories and slowly become obscured. Omitting critical details thanks to forgotten memories can change the whole direction or impact of a story. And the more someone passes a story around, or the more distant it gets from the event, the less reliable it becomes.

It is possible that Mrs. Whittier's memories are correct, but just out of time. When hearing the 1811 date, if the reporter knew his history, he should have asked how long after her arrival it was before what Tennesseans called "the big shake." A poor memory for dates can be cured by relating smaller events to major events. The big shake was an earthquake in 1811 along the Mississippi that was felt as far away as Canada. She couldn't have missed it.

But if memory is the enemy of clear detail, then the connection between the head and heart is where oral tradition really gets into trouble. A desire to create winners and losers leads to stories being told with important elements either elevated or omitted. Passing one story through multiple people results in multiple stories as each person picks out the elements they find most interesting, entertaining, or easily told. Plus, people love to embellish to make a story bigger than it really is. And sometimes, to make a point, the storyteller will purposefully twist the story in a convenient direction.

This is not to say that all oral tradition is untrustworthy. Nor is it to say all contemporary writings are free from these same issues. In writing history, all things need to be examined with a critical eye.

The tone and opinions of the author are all over this newspaper story. He seems bent on moralizing about the lost respect for history and all that happened before the Civil War. He also sells us the idea of Mrs. Whittier as an unimpeachable source. After all, her husband was a public official. This credibility leads the reader to take the information at face value. This is the fastest way to a new piece of lore.

Another issue for researchers is historical speculation. In writing the history of a particular event, historians will try to bridge two ideas to reach logical conclusions. This creates a need to fill in details where none exists. It is almost impossible not to do, particularly if the historian wants to move the narrative forward, prove their own thesis, or make the story entertaining. But like playing craps or baccarat, the chances of success are mixed.

In the case of Jackson's presence at the Bell Tavern, some historians have concluded it never happened because the general never stepped foot in Memphis. But between May 18 and May 22, when Memphis was founded, there appear to be gaps in Jackson's writings. So it's not out of the question that he made a trip out west from his home in Nashville.

It could be speculated that since there are no known contemporary newspaper accounts of a meeting with Jackson involved, that it never took place--especially with such famous people involved.

But there is an even bigger piece of evidence that makes the historic meeting at the Bell Tavern on the Chickasaw Bluffs implausible. The problem is that there is no record of a Bell Tavern existing in the area in 1819.

So that begs the question, does the story have the right Bell Tavern? The bell was a popular symbol for taverns, going all the way back to England. And in Tennessee there were no less than five Bell Taverns around the state in 1819, in Nashville, Franklin, Rogersville, Greeneville, and near Jackson in Huntingdon. It seems the only place there wasn't one was in Memphis–at least not yet.

The reality is, there probably was a meeting, but it wasn't at the Bell Tavern and it didn't include Old Hickory. The evidence lies in the March 29, 1819 edition of Clarksville's Tennessee Weekly Chronicle. John Overton and James Winchester placed a notice of their intention to meet at the home of Paddy Meagher. If the meeting took place, it's a good bet drinks were served, as Paddy was running an ordinary prior to the Memphis City and Shelby County governments being set up—but it wasn't the Bell. Bell Tavern wasn't built until at least five years after the meeting. It's likely the connection with the Bell came out of the fact Paddy was its first proprietor.[78] The association of Winchester and Overton at Paddy's ordinary, and the later association of Paddy running the Bell likely infused over time.

It's a story that shows the fallibility of memory and the problem of newspapers and historians documenting lore.

Hell and Texas

If there's one thing Colonel Davy Crockett made loud and clear to his friends in Tennessee, it was that he was no fan of Old Hickory. While Crockett did support Jackson as a Tennessean in his first run for the presidency, he didn't make that mistake twice. He stood in opposition to Jacksonian policies and candidates for the rest of his life. In fact, as a member of the U.S. Congress, Rep. Crockett would stand alone in the Tennessee delegation when he voted against Jackson's Indian Removal Act of 1830. It would gain him the praises of Cherokee leader John Ross, but cost him his seat in the next election.

Davy's constituents eventually forgave him, and he won another term in Congress. While there, he wrote his autobiography, with the assistance of Kentucky Congressman Thomas Chilton. He also used his gift of sarcasm to write a biography for Andrew Jackson's hard-drinking vice president called *The Life of Martin Van Buren*. The *Baltimore Patriot* panned it saying, "The colonel, though a literary man of great eminence and success, is yet, as the world very well knows, wholly unsophisticated."[79]

Davy knew his chances of returning to office for another term were thin. After he officially lost the election, he packed his bags and headed west. It seems that an old friend, former Tennessee Governor Sam Houston, was in a battle for Texas independence and Davy wanted a break from politics. His name had been bandied about as a presidential candidate, but he deferred that to Martin Van Buren, reasoning that there had been a president from the south for too long. Let a northerner have a turn, so the country would be ready for another southerner in the future.[80] It sounded like Davy had every intention of coming back to Washington.

On his way to Texas, he stopped off in Memphis to say goodbye to old friends. It wasn't his first visit to the area. Back in 1823, he almost lost his life on the Obion River when he captained a flatboat loaded down with barrel staves on a journey to Memphis. As the boat entered the Mississippi River, Davy was taking a nap in the cabin. A mouthful of water rudely interrupted his snoring. The boat hit a fallen tree and split in two. Davy made it out the door just in time and was rescued. The only problem was that, in the rush to get to shore, he forgot to put on his britches.[81]

On another visit, he was enjoying the drinking experience at a Memphis tavern when he made a bet. He wanted to show everyone he could jump farther into the river, make the biggest splash, and stay the driest. Colonel Eppy White took him up on the bet. At 300 pounds, Davy realized he wouldn't stand a chance against the colonel in the water displacement game. He backed out of the bet but honored his agreement in buying the whisky. It's said Davy threw the "biggest drunk" Memphis had ever seen.[82]

On this last visit to Memphis, before heading off to Texas and his destiny, he stopped off to do some equal-opportunity drinking around town. First, he went to McCool's pub, where he was greeted by the sound of cheers and huzzahs. It was a festive afternoon of drinking with memories filling the room. As one observer, Colonel W. T. Avery, recalled, before he could leave, the crowd demanded a speech. Standing on a counter, Davy got the crowd riled up with his typical humor. He finished the speech by saying "I told the voters that if they would elect me I would serve them to the best of my ability, but if they did not, they might go to hell and I would go to Texas. I am on my way now." He was a man of his word. As he left, he made a quick stop by the Union Hotel to say goodbye to friends. Then he made his way down to the ferry landing.

Colonel Crockett was just as you would picture, wearing "his veritable coon-skin cap and hunting shirt, bearing upon his shoulder his ever faithful rifle," said one observer. He saluted his friends, stepped upon the little ferry flatboat, and turned to the pilot and gave a nod. The flat boat slowly made its way down the Wolf River into the Mississippi. The few that stood there watched the entire journey, seeing Davy all the way to the Arkansas docks before he disappeared into the horizon.[83]

When Davy reached Nacogdoches, Texas, he delivered the same speech he'd given at McCool's pub.[84] He followed up by signing an oath with the Provisional Government of Texas with some 65 other men. From there, they sent him out to the Alamo Mission in San Antonio. And the rest, as they say, is history.

PART TWO: LOST DISTILLERS

FIRST GOLDEN AGE OF TENNESSEE WHISKY

Chapter 8

BIRTH OF AN INDUSTRY

It was the dawn of a century filled with incredible innovations thanks to the spark set off by the Industrial Revolution in Europe. The ancient techniques of making everything by hand were quickly giving way to steam- and coal-powered machines. These advances massively cut down production time and increased output.

Industrialization caused many Americans to move away from their farms and into cities for work. This meant that, rather than growing the foods their family required, they earned a wage and purchased what they needed, putting a great dependence on the grocer, mercantile, and distribution networks to get essential products into the stores. For the city dweller, the old system of bartering disappeared. Cash was king.

West of the Appalachian Mountains, however, this transformative revolution wouldn't be seen for generations. Knoxville and Nashville remained relatively small. And not only was it difficult for innovative ideas and equipment to reach the distant frontier, there were few places to apply them. Landowners, holding onto 640-acre land grants, were slow to move onto their claims. Each settler had to weigh the benefits of tilling the land versus the risks their families would face against raiding Chickamauga, Creeks, and Chickasaw warriors.

But change came in 1792 when Dragging Canoe died from what was thought to be a heart attack. It appears he died after dancing all night, during a celebration of a newly won alliance with the Muskogee and Choctaw tribes. Without his energy, focus, leadership, and tactical acumen, the tribe was in disarray. The Battle of Fallen Timbers, and the destruction of two Chickamauga villages in August 1794, did the tribe in. They capitulated and signed a treaty at Tellico Blockhouse one month later.

That treaty was like a pistol shot in the air. No longer were settlers timid about moving to the isolated frontier. Finally, they could establish their lands and learn what they could grow. It ushered in the era of the Middle Tennessee farmer distiller.

The Rise of Robertson

One of the first areas beyond Nashville to establish a distilling tradition was along the banks of the Red River and its tributaries, including Sulphur Fork Creek. Just a two-day wagon ride north of the frontier outpost at Fort Nashborough, the area had everything a distiller needed, numerous creeks, iron-free and mineral-rich limestone-filtered water, decent soil for growing crops, oak trees for barrels, fruit trees for brandy, and sugar maple trees for rum and charcoal. The old Scotsman Thomas Kilgore is thought to be the area's first distiller, with the mill he established in the late 1780s.[85]

The next to arrive was a brave and confident Virginian named Benjamin Menees. A second-generation American, Benjamin's father James McNees came to America to escape the plantations of Ireland. He brought his family from County Cavan, Ireland to Lancaster County, Pennsylvania, where Benjamin was born in 1743. Eventually they moved to Amherst County, Virginia, where Benjamin married 15-year-old Ann Wade. The couple had seven children and appeared to be settling into their lives when, in 1780, Benjamin set his sights on the west.[86] The family settled on Spring Creek, a tributary of Sulphur Fork Creek. There Benjamin established a water mill and set up a simple distilling operation using a forty gallon still.[87]

For a decade, Benjamin and his family survived on the tense frontier with few neighbors. But after the treaty at Tellico, Benjamin and his neighbor William

Blount recruited people to the area. They also became delegates to North Carolina's two U.S. Constitution ratifying conventions. William's political ambitions would lead him to the governorship of the Territory South of the River Ohio. When he needed someone to set up a government for Tennessee County (a partial forerunner to Robertson County), he asked Benjamin, who served as a judge and justice of the peace for the county, while earning profits off his distilling.[88]

When he died in 1811, Benjamin's son William Dawson Menees had picked up the craft and established his own mill complete with two stills. In his will, his father Benjamin left him additional land at the mouth of Sulphur Fork Creek to expand his business.[89]

Next to arrive in the region was a farmer distiller and surveyor who was a throwback to the era of the longhunters. Thomas Johnson was born in the Yadkin River Valley and likely grew up hearing stories of local heroes Daniel Boone and Richard Henderson.[90] But the days of the longhunter were long gone, so Thomas tried his hand at land speculation and surveying. The place that most inspired him was the land around Sulphur Fork Creek. He acquired land through grants and cash acquisitions in the late 1780s. As a prolific landowner, Thomas was invited as a delegate to help shape the Tennessee State Constitution in 1796.[91] He celebrated statehood by purchasing another parcel of land at the mouth of Spring Creek off of Sulphur Fork Creek.[92] It is there he established a 131 gallon still, becoming the third-largest distiller in the area. Within five years, he added two more stills to become the largest distiller in Robertson County.

Like the other land-holding farmer distillers in the area, Thomas took an active role in the defense of his community, serving as a colonel in the Robertson County militia. In 1813, he saw action at the Battle of Horseshoe Bend, serving under Old Hickory. It was the last battle in the Creek Wars and Johnson earned honor and recognition for his bravery under fire.[93]

But out of all the early names in Robertson County distilling, none had the influence or staying power of the Pitts and Woodards. Living in the coastal plains of eastern North Carolina, the journey of these two families started after a curious 21-year-old Thomas Woodard acquired a land grant in 1787 along the north side of the Red River.[94] A farmer at heart, he convinced his wife, Elizabeth Pitt, that more fertile lands lay to the west. They gathered their two sons, William and Arthur, and moved six hundred miles due west from Edgecombe County. Their journey through the Appalachian Mountains led them to Beaver Dam Creek, a branch of the Sulphur Fork. After purchasing the land, Thomas established a water mill.[95] When a nearby 640-acre plot became available, he sent word back east to his brother-in-law Arthur Pitt, who secured the land for a very reasonable dollar per acre.[96] Like Thomas, he too established a mill on one of his springs. These patriarchs set the foundation for not one, but two Robertson County distilling legacies.

The Woodards and Pitts weren't the only future distillers to leave Edgecombe County. William Fort moved out west in the early 1790s.[97] William was one of the most successful farmers in Tarboro but was frustrated that poor soil limited his farming almost exclusively to tobacco. The fast growth of the tavern culture in Edgecombe showed him that the future was in corn. He purchased 320 acres at the mouth of Elk Fork Creek on the Red River in 1793. There he set up a mill and the largest still in the area at 263 gallon capacity.[98]

A few years later, another distilling legacy would come out of Edgecombe when John and Martha Draughon moved their four children west to Robertson County.[99] Their son George Elvis Draughon would become one of the most amiable and respected distillers in the county after the Civil War.

With these distillers huddling around the same area, a visitor canoeing down Sulphur Fork Creek in the early 19th century might have thought they'd just died and gone to gristmill and distilling heaven. Every couple hundred feet, another farmer distiller was plying their trade. This drew even more distillers, including Jonathan Derden who moved up from Davidson County in 1796;[100] war veteran Andrew Irwin, who settled in the early 1790s;[101] James Appleton, who purchased land from another recent arrival John Couts in 1797;[102] and John Couts who purchased a hundred acres and a mill from Thomas Woodard to establish his own distilling operation at Beaver Dam Creek.[103]

Eventually, these Robertson County distilling families intermingled. John Couts' granddaughter Tabitha married George E. Draughon. Thomas Johnson's daughter Nancy married John Couts' son William. And other distilling names like Holman, Starks, and Brown would all come out of branches of the Robertson County family tree.

With all of this growth, the last of Overton's records listed 22 Robertson County whisky and brandy distilleries in operation in 1801. While the tastes and smells of these historic brews are lost to time, the old timers were always quick to remind people of the amazing sour mash whiskies that came out of early Robertson County. Distilling was just one of many chores for these early distillers, but they were always proud of what they distilled. And the good name they established would only grow stronger as subsequent generations took over the controls.

The Farm Distillery

While Robertson County's farmer distillers focused on reputation, Frederick Stump's distillery focused on volume. With fourteen satellite plantations feeding grain and profits to the home base, his setup inspired copycats like W. Barrow of The Grove.[104] What Stump and Barrow didn't realize was that their system was the forerunner to the era of distillery first operations, where the farm fed the distillery, rather than distilling being a byproduct of farming.

In terms of grain choices, corn liquor was the most profitable for new distillers. The grain delivered higher yields, lower cost, and was available throughout the state. For the consumer, this meant a lower cost when they were ready to refill their flask or ceramic jugs. Corn whisky quickly distanced itself from its rye rival as the state's dominant style.

But whisky wasn't the only thing being distilled in the early 19th century. Peach and apple brandy distilleries dominated early Tennessee distilling. In the east, the shift from rum to whisky took a curious turn. The poorer families began adding sugar to their corn mash to speed distillation and cut costs. This was the forerunner to sugar shine.

Because of the high interest in distilling, landlords offered turnkey opportunities for new distillers. Acreage was packaged with a small farm, horse or water mill, good springs, and a low-cost log still or fully functioning modern steam distillery already set up for operation. If the farm was excessively large or had a capacity to produce great volumes of alcohol, the landlord might include enslaved workers as part of the lease.

Of course, as with any fast-growth industry, there were swindlers ready to take advantage. One budding entrepreneur, Mr. Harris, was talked into two tracts of land, cattle, hogs, a distillery, and 350 bushels of corn by a con man named Robert Dennon. Paying for the property, sight unseen, Harris lost his total investment when Dennon disappeared into the night without ever showing him the property.[105] Luckily, these were rare cases.

As the era of the farm distillery strengthened over the first two decades of the 19th century, innovation finally made its way to the frontier. Inventor Phares Bernard's patented steam plan found its way into several Middle Tennessee distilleries by 1819.[106] It included a steam still, a steam boiler, and a water-pump system. Tools like these allowed distillers other ways to improve output and profits beyond grain choice.

For those malting their own grain, a much-needed advancement was the revolving kiln. Malting is time-consuming, backbreaking work, and usually very little malted barley is needed to help in conversion. Some distillers resorted to buying malted grain from outside sources, but the kiln helped reduce space constraints and allowed the distiller to cure wheat or malt corn, barley, oats, and rye, all while increasing profits.

All of this technology ushered in another age––that of the salesman. An enterprising pitchman named Thomas Malone posted an advertisement in the Nashville Whig inviting distillers to visit Dr. Newnan's plantation between Franklin and Nashville. There, they could "see the ease, cheapness, and convenience, speed and independence of the wooden distillery, by the application of cast or copper pipes." No doubt Thomas would offer a strong sales pitch during the viewing.[107]

When Joseph Dwyer realized his distillery was just a little more than he could handle, he extolled the virtues and benefits of technology in his *Nashville Banner* ad:

> *"The farm, situated on Little Harpeth, ten miles South of Nashville and eight miles from Franklin in the direct line between both, [consists] of 880 acres, steam and grist mill, and a revolving kiln for curing of wheat or drying of corn, malt, etc. The rapidity of the grinding [furnishes] material for 1 barrel of whiskey per diem, while consumption of fuel never exceeds two cords of ordinary wood. The distillery is capable of producing with the labor of two hands, 5 barrels of whiskey per diem, and being supplied by a never failing spring can be worked throughout the year."*[108]

As the operations became larger and competition grew stronger, it took more than family members and an enslaved workforce to produce the quality and volume that was necessary. This led to outsourcing through word of mouth and through ads. A distillery advert in the *Clarion and Tennessee State Gazette* from 1813 had these needs. "Wanted at distillery near Haysborough five and a half miles from Nashville, a Distiller that can be well recommended, likewise a Cooper to whom liberal wages will be given if early application is made."[109] The emphasis on increased wages for putting in an early application showed how hot the market was getting for this kind of talent.

But not all things were simple to bring in-house, so complementary industries appeared. Reliable gristmills for grinding rye, wheat, barley, and cornmeal increased in number. And in Robertson County, where there was a plentiful supply of trees, a coopering industry developed. Barrel staves were expertly made and tight cooperage prepared for the distiller, so they could focus on what they were producing rather than what they were putting it in. And no longer were distillers dependent on getting their copper pot stills shipped in from Philadelphia. Hynes and Fletcher in Nashville became a dependable source for copper pots from thirty gallons to over three hundred and thirty gallons.[110]

Eventually the use of outside sources allowed some distilleries to become independent of farms. This was validation that the industry was in full swing. But the age of independent distilleries, brands, and marketing were still far off in the future.

The Emergence of the Nashville Market

By the time of Frederick Stump's death in May 1820, whisky production had spread to farms around the developing communities of Franklin, Columbia, and Springfield. Small farmer distillers kept to their local communities, but Nashville was becoming an excellent source of revenue. Its population had tripled between 1810 and 1820.

Around town, taverns with sleeping accommodations and food for boarders were being replaced by liquor, wine, and beer by the drink establishments called tippling houses. While ideal for thirsty patrons, the atmosphere of these establishments was a little more rowdy than in the old taverns. Tippling houses and taverns alike purchased barrels from area distillers, but they also began receiving barrels from Kentucky and Pennsylvania thanks to the open access provided by the Cumberland River. This increased volume of imported whisky, eventually created a demand for grocers and wholesale firms that could handle the logistics of getting liquor into or out of the area.

At the same time, Tennessee whisky was making its way down the Mississippi River on flatboats headed for Natchez, New Orleans, and beyond. The value of this shipped whisky was demonstrated in the higher prices it fetched outside of Nashville. In the 1830s, a gallon of Tennessee whisky cost twice as much in Natchez as it did at home.

By the 1820s, Tennessee had so many distillers littered across the state that it was one of the largest producers in the country. And the farm distilleries provided another advantage for the state. With their protein-rich spent grains being fed to cattle and hogs, Tennessee became one of the largest sources of salted meats in the nation.

There is little doubt that the early success of the state of Tennessee owed a lot to its farmers and distillers. The question was, could they sustain the momentum? Kentucky was a rising star and seemed destined to form a distilling legacy of their own.

Chapter 9

WHAT MADE IT LINCOLN?

Rough and Tumble

Picture a family on the wild frontier, finishing their morning breakfast. Ma wipes her hands on her apron as she picks up Pa's empty plate. Pa tells the children to get their Saturday morning chores done so they can go fishing later that afternoon. He then walks over to his wife and kisses her on the cheek as she finishes cleaning the crockery from the morning meal.

She tells him she needs to take the wagon into Fayetteville to drop off a fresh supply of eggs.

"At the war office?" he asks, with concern in his voice.

No, she wasn't taking eggs to the local recruiting office. The war office was the name affectionately given to the Fayetteville grocery store.[111] In the early 1810s, Lincoln County was on the edge of civilization. And while law existed in the county, its rough and tumble citizenry sometimes handled justice with their own fists. In those days, a trip to the war office might get you more than just a store credit for eggs.

Arnold's grocery in Smithfield wasn't much safer.[112] If you were a young lady heading in to buy some flour or material for a dress, the sound of angry voices meant don't go in. Yet most folks didn't seem to mind. There was little entertainment in the area, so watching a good brawl meant some good local gossip would be on the way. The only things that weren't allowed in an Arnold's brawl were weapons, including teeth.

It seems Lincoln County was the Wild West, before the Wild West. In the 1810s, ramshackle buildings lined Fayetteville's streets and taverns outnumbered churches. In fact, there were five tavern licenses for Fayetteville alone, including one held by Ephraim Parham, the man who donated the land for the town.[113]

And all of this competition kept prices low and patrons coming back. Travelers could secure a shared cot for only six cents. Stabling of horses with plenty of hay and fodder ran at 25 cents a night. Taverns provided a warm meal for 25 cents and an additional 12 cents would refill a half-pint flask with quality whisky or peach brandy. For a treat, West Indies rum was 25 cents. If all you could afford was cheap corn whisky, that was only six cents a half pint.[114]

For those that wanted to stay, the beautiful hills of the Highland Rim made an idyllic setting. The Lincoln County landscape was rich with pastoral farmland. Farmers grew cash crops like corn, wheat, flax, and cotton, and also had vegetable gardens with Irish and sweet potatoes for their families. The Scotsman and Irishman felt right at home with cattle and sheep dotting the fence free hillsides. Larger farms had mules and horses for transportation. Oxen and horses were available for tilling the land. Families lived in modest one- and two-story log cabins, sometimes paired with a barn guarded by a hog pen and chicken coop.

Of course, with animals roaming free, predators lurked. Wolves were a major problem for early settlers. To control the population, the government paid bounties for a wolf's scalp. Regular game, including elk, deer, beaver, squirrels, and racoons provided meat, furs, and pelts.

Lincoln County remained isolated for many years. Sitting on the edge of the untamed Mississippi Territory, the pioneers had to be self-sufficient. Transporting goods to and from Nashville meant a three-day journey by packhorse or wagon. The Elk River gave flatboats access to the Tennessee River, but it wasn't a simple journey. The rough waters of Muscle Shoals and the still-active Choctaw tribe created obstacles.

As for distilling, records are thin. While Robertson County had the advantage of being documented by John Overton's assessors, Lincoln County's distillers didn't arrive until ten years after the excise ended. This leaves the early years of Lincoln County distilling in the hands of oral tradition. Two of the best 19th century sources for this information are books by agricultural historian Joseph Buckner Killebrew and a series of books written in 1886 by the Goodspeed Publishing Company. But while they provide excellent sketches of early distilling in the area, the greater detail has been lost to the ages.

Yet early Lincoln County must have had quite the whisky culture. Goodspeed touts a good number of gristmills and taverns in the area in the second decade of the 19th century. The isolated nature of Lincoln County suggests many of these gristmills had stills or were fed by distilling operations that supplied the taverns.

Area gristmills came in a variety of shapes and sizes. Smaller tub mills dotted the smaller creeks of the county, feeding farmers' private stills. The water mills that lined the Elk River likely fed grain back to several farmer distillers. There were a few horse mills, including three in Petersburg, with the largest operation being run on Joel Yowell's farm.[115] But whether he ran a distillery is unknown. The earliest specific mention of a distillery is James Crawford's. He also ran a sawmill and gristmill. Peter Cunningham and L.P. Myrick built a still-house onto Cunningham's gristmill and sold the spirits at their mercantile.[116]

The most popular area for distilling was along the East Fork of Mulberry Creek. It quickly earned a reputation similar to Sulphur Fork Creek in Robertson County. The first distillery specifically mentioned on East Mulberry Creek was built in 1825 by Samuel Isaacs and John Silvertooth. Isaacs also built a second distillery on his own, south of Lynchburg.[117]

One of the earliest distillers to gain a reputation for the quality of his spirits was Middleton Fanning, Jr.[118]

Born in Elbert County Georgia in 1796, he would arrive in Lincoln with his parents, Middleton Sr. and Delpha Fanning, in the late 1810s. He married 18-year-old Rachel Harper soon after arriving, and the two raised a family while Middleton worked his father's farm. By 1829, he was ready to work his own land and laid down $300 for a 100-acre farm along Dry Creek, near to where it intersected with the Elk River.[119] Middleton became an investor in farmland and grew wealthy through land acquisitions and distilling. He slowly built up the reputation of his distillery for over thirty years. When he died in 1861, his wife held onto the distillery for five more years until she passed. When the property was listed as being up for auction, the local paper promoted that "the BEST DISTILLERY IN THE COUNTY" was on the property.[120] It is unclear whether that was a sales pitch or a fact, but it shows a great appreciation for what Middleton Fanning Jr. had created.

Another name that rose to the top in Lincoln County's early distilling scene was that of William Tolley. Arriving from Mercer, Kentucky in the late 1820s,[121] he formed a business partnership with a native Tennessean, Benjamin Harrison Berry. The team of Tolley and Berry invested heavily in lands around the budding village of Lynchburg and along East Mulberry Creek. Tolley and Berry were instrumental in the early growth of Lynchburg. Beyond distilling, they became original trustees of the Lynchburg Academy.[122] Berry eventually opened his own mercantile, B. H. Berry & Co.; and William established the firm Tolley, Eaton & Park, with one of Lincoln County distilling's great rising stars, Alfred Eaton.

Alfred was born the youngest son of John and Elizabeth Marsh Eaton. He was only three years old when the family moved to Lincoln County in 1812, settling on 60 acres purchased from Thomas Eastland on the East Fork of Mulberry Creek.[123] The record doesn't show John Eaton as a distiller, but his son Alfred became a distilling legend.

When William Tolley brought Alfred into the company, he had no idea his young distiller was about to shape two distilling dynasties. Not only did Alfred teach his own sons how to distill, he taught William's three sons, John Dean, William Polk, and Benjamin Tolley, as well. For the next eight decades, the names Tolley and Eaton became synonymous with Lincoln County whisky, all thanks to Alfred's guiding hand.

John Eaton, Alfred's father, played another role in the future of Lincoln County distilling. In 1836, he sold two prime pieces of land on East Mulberry Creek to a middle-aged farmer from Franklin County who was looking to plant roots in an area.[124] Calaway and Lucinda Daniel would turn the land into a lucrative farming business. And while Calaway wasn't a distiller of note, his son Jasper Newton would be. In fact, Jack would far surpass the legacies of Tolley and Eaton, taking the name Lincoln County around the world.

What's in a Name?

For those who tasted Lincoln or Robertson county whiskies, the quality showed the pride their distillers took in crafting a whisky. But not all whisky in the early 19th century was praiseworthy.

Frontier whisky could range from hot to hot damnation. Taken straight off of the still, some distillers would place the whisky in barrels, but many used jugs or ceramic demijohns of 1 to 16 gallons in size. The vessels were just for temporary storage, rather than aging, so the spirit remained rough. But when barrels of Pennsylvania rye made their way down the Ohio River to the Cumberland, these boat-aged spirits made a powerful impression. In 1808, John Wright, a Franklin, Tennessee merchant, felt the quality was noteworthy enough to advertise it as Old Monongahela Whisky. Giving it a name made it stand out like French Cognac and Spanish Madeira.[125] This was unheard of for an American spirit up to that time. With brand names not yet relevant in the United States, it marked the beginning of an era of selling American whisky by its region. Up to that point, it was simply "corn whisky" or just "whisky."

The next whisky region to earn a reputation was Kentucky's Bourbon County. Like Old Monongahela, Bourbon likely earned its nickname from the barrel's place of origin being branded into the barrelhead. The first known mentions of "Bourbon" and "old Bourbon" appeared on the pages of a Kentucky newspaper as early as May 1, 1821.[126] Tennessee saw its earliest-known regional distinction provided in October 1824, when a merchant named Duke Goodman took out ads in the *Charleston (SC) Daily Courier* selling beer barrels of Old Tennessee Whiskey.[127]

Unfortunately, the *Daily Courier* article doesn't mention a distilling source; nor does it say what that style entails. What makes it notable is that the location was important enough to list. That barrel would have traveled a great distance to reach Charleston, most likely by boat.

Lincoln and Robertson were late bloomers in getting "known" for their whiskies, but eventually they were. But were Monongahela, Bourbon, Robertson, and Lincoln simply origin names? Or was there a distinctive style or process associated with each?

Of all the county names, Bourbon is the only one with an official designation today, thanks to the U.S. Congress.

The only other county name still promoted on the list is Lincoln County, with the charcoal mellowing process being nicknamed the Lincoln County Process. In 2013, the Tennessee General Assembly codified the charcoal mellowing process with House Bill No. 1084 as a requirement for labeling something "Tennessee whiskey."

But that brings up two questions: was the state right to choose the mellowing process as the state style? And during its heyday, was it this process, also known as leaching, the thing that really defined Lincoln County whisky?

To answer these questions, it is good to know what makes charcoal mellowing important to a distiller. And this takes us back to the very origins of whisky.

The Lincoln County Process?

The first time the word whisky shows up in print is in 1715 in *A Book of Scottish Pasquils*. The author quotes a gentleman suggesting, "whiskie [sic] shall put our brains in a rage."[128] Prior to that, the spirit went by the name "water of life," translated into various languages. In Latin, it is *aqua vitae*; in Scandinavian, it is *aquavit*; in French, it is *eau da vie*; in Scottish Gaelic and Irish, it's variations of *usque beatha*; and so on. It was made of whatever grains were available. On its own, it was rough and usually unaged.

To tame the harsh flavor of early *aqua vitae* or whisky popular techniques included adding liberal amounts of water, aromatics, or flavorings. Sometimes it was doctored at the source, but often that process was left to whomever was selling it.

In Tennessee, a commission store run by Joseph Wood featured a colonial favorite known as Cherry Bounce.[129] Using a mixture of grain whisky, cherry juice, cinnamon, and other spices, it provided his customers an alternative to the hard ciders and aggressive whiskies of the day.

Another way to tame the heat was to double distill whisky. This refines the spirit by taking out aggressive headache-causing oils, cleaning up the spirit through multiple distillations. Today we take double distillation for granted, but for farmer distillers with a single still, time wasn't always a luxury they could afford. Some sold the "singlings", as they were called, and some became quite adept at taming the spirit through other methods.

This is where the term "rectification" enters the distilling lexicon. It is a term that seemed to evolve in the 18th- and 19th-centuries, covering everything from redistillation to doctoring to filtering to blending. At its essence, the term refers to fixing a spirit.

While a second distillation was the simplest form of rectifying a spirit, a more effective method for early distillers was to add milk, salts, and acids to singlings before redistillation. While the flavors of these additives could be harsh and the chemicals poisonous, the skilled distiller knew just the right quantities to avoid adding off flavors.[130] Of course, adding dangerous chemicals to spirits is a risk, even if they are being redistilled. Distillers needed a safer way to purify their spirits.

The solution was found, not in any distilling technique, but instead through filtration-- known as leaching or charcoal filtering. This purification process involves running spirits through maple wood that is fired and broken down into small pieces of charcoal. The spirit drips through the charcoal and flannel or other types of cloth are used beneath it to keep the charcoal out of the filtered spirit.[131] The result is a less aggressive spirit with reduced influence from fusel oils and harsh flavors. Add a little black tea and early distillers could even pass it off as an aged spirit.[132] To Tennesseans, with their plentiful supply of sugar maple trees, the leaching process and their spirits were a match made in heaven.

Of course, with a duo so perfectly matched, it's no surprise that Tennessee has origin stories surrounding the technique. Lincoln County distiller Alfred Eaton has long been associated with leaching. It is suggested he was the first to use the technique in the 1820s while distilling at the Cave Spring Hollow, the source of today's Jack Daniel's Tennessee Whiskey. This is one of the reasons given for it being referred to as the Lincoln County Process. The truth is, no one knows when leaching began or who the first distiller was to leach their whisky. It definitely wasn't Alfred Eaton or a Tennessean.

The earliest known record of the whisky leaching process was recorded years before the legendary distiller's birth. In 1802, a patent was filed with the U.S. Patent Office for the process by New Jersey inventor and preacher, Burgess Allison.[133] While this stands as evidence that the practice was in use at the turn of the 19th century, another event suggests its use with liquor may go back even farther. Massachusetts Senator John Quincy Adams raised concerns over the patent two years later, saying it was an example of how the patent office rules could be abused by inventors filing for long-established practices.[134]

While leaching wasn't invented by a Tennessean, nor was there exclusivity for the state in the early years, they would become the longest proponents of it. As states like Pennsylvania and Kentucky industrialized distilling, the most vocal Tennessee distillers did their best to hang onto natural processes over efficiency and output. Multiple distillations used too much fuel, multiple stills were not always financially feasible, and chemical additives unthinkable. Of all regions, Lincoln County distillers were the most vocal against the use of unnatural processes. Even when other states moved to using charred barrels for taming a spirit, many Tennessee distillers stuck with leaching and only later combined the two practices when tax laws allowed deferred taxes through aging.

Eventually leaching was marketed as the Lincoln County Process. But is this fair? What about Old Robertson or whiskies from other parts of the state? Did they also embrace it? And if Alfred Eaton, Middleton Fanning, Jr., or one of the

Tolley brothers was alive today, would they agree that leaching alone captured the spirit of Old Lincoln?

The first thing to know is that none of these legendary distillers ever publicly touted something called the Lincoln County Process. There is no record of any distiller, producer, retailer, or wholesaler referencing it in the 19th century. The first time these words appeared together was in 1896, when the *Louisville (KY) Courier-Journal* wrote a focus piece on Robertson County, Tennessee. The article mentions a Lincoln County process, but doesn't define what it entails. It only suggests that, whatever the process is, it is a more popular style than the more "pure" Robertson county style of whisky.[135]

The next use of the term is in 1905, when it was claimed on a bottle of Old White Oak Tennessee Whiskey that it was made using the Lincoln County process. But again, the details of the process it's referring to is a mystery.[136] Even Henry Kraver's Kentucky Peerless in Henderson, Kentucky sold a Lincoln County, Tennessee whisky throughout the 1910s. Obviously, there was a known style for Old Lincoln in those days, but what was it?

It is possible that, like the term rectifier, Old Lincoln whisky had a floating definition. But in reality, a deep review of articles and advertisements from the 19th century reveals the secret. There were several selling points Lincoln County used to distinguish themselves from their competition.

One of the biggest was its use of the sour mash process. Lincoln County distillers were so passionate about it; they talked down old Robertson and Bourbon distillers for not using it.

But the whiskey history buff would say, "Wait, hold on there! Didn't James C. Crow use the sour mash process in Kentucky?"

According to Lincoln County distillers, no he didn't. It was their belief that Bourbon and Robertson were using the sweet mash process, not the sour mash process. And the confusion comes down to a 19th-century Tennessee definition versus a 21st-century definition.

The process of making sour mash whisky requires the addition of mash that has been set back from the previous batch, just like how sourdough bread is made with a starter. Today, that process includes the addition of yeast to help speed fermentation. But to the distillers of Old Lincoln, they considered the addition of extra yeast, or any chemical stimulation of the yeast, to be the sweet mash process. This is not to be confused with the modern term sweet mash, which skips the addition of starter sour mash all together. In the world of Old Lincoln, if you physically added something, it wasn't natural and so it wasn't a true sour mash whisky. To avoid the use of added yeast, the distiller would set aside the cooling mash in open tubs for a couple of days, allowing it to attract wild yeast to build up energy. Getting the ideal weather was critical so as not to strain the yeast. As the industry industrialized, this long process of allowing five days or more for fermentation was dropped in favor of additives that cut two days out of the process. Lincoln County distillers sold thier process as traditional and stayed true to it through the 19th century.[137]

However, Lincoln County's claim that they were the only ones doing this is false. A late 19th-century article shows Nelson's Green Brier in Robertson County was also working with 100% natural fermentation.[138] There were likely plenty of Bourbon distillers doing so as well. But Lincoln County distillers did a better job of selling their sour mash process as a differentiating factor in their whisky.

Another commonality between Lincoln County distillers was the use of a log still. These were simple affairs that encased the still within wood, rather than using large amounts of expensive copper. Not only was a log still cost effective, it was traditional. That made it perfect for enhancing the narrative that Lincoln County distillers were staying true to their ancestors' processes.

Somewhere along the line, however, this tradition was lost. Most likely, it faded away in the late 19th century. White Oak and Kentucky Peerless both sold Lincoln County whisky in the early 20th century, neither distillery used a log still.

The third technique was leaching. While the technique was promoted in the 19th century by distillers of Old Lincoln, it wasn't a differentiating factor against their Tennessee competition. Tennessee distillers charcoal mellowed whisky from Robertson, to Nashville, to Chattanooga, to Bristol, to Memphis. In fact, if you could ask a 19th-century Tennessean what made their whisky better than Kentucky Bourbon, it would be the leaching process.

So the 2013 Tennessee General Assembly was on the right track historically when they codified whisky "filtered through maple charcoal prior to aging" as a Tennessee style. The only argument earlier distillers might make to this law is the need for aging. However, those that refer to leaching as the Lincoln County Process have inadvertently created historical confusion. It's the challenge historians face in an industry that embraces marketing and lore over documented history. But, as the Tennessee legislature proved, sometimes the truth is so strong it shines through the lore.

Chapter 10

DEMON ALCOHOL

The following story, entitled "Inquire at Deacon Giles' Distillery," originally appeared in a New England newspaper called the *Salem Landmark*. The *Landmark* started in 1834, and it ceased operations two years later. But the legacy of the newspaper would live on, thanks to this one story. It circulated in newspapers throughout the United States for over twenty years.

Its preamble sets the tone.

> *"Deacon Giles was a man who loved money, and was never troubled with the tenderness of conscience. His father and grandfather before him had been distillers, and the occupation has come to him as an heir-loom, in the family."*

The subject of this story is a religious man, Deacon Amos Giles, who is living a double life as both a distiller and a man of God. The author assumes the reader understands these are two concepts that are diametrically opposed. If they don't, the story is about to convince them. The following is a paraphrasing of the epic full-page story that both entertained and energized its readers in the 19th century:

It was a late Saturday afternoon when Amos Giles began taking stock of his freshly delivered molasses and hogshead barrels. He had a busy night of distilling ahead and wanted to make sure he had enough supplies to match the orders he had to fill on Monday. As he got the first calculations rolling about his brain, his concentration was broken by the raising of a ruckus behind him. The blather was coming from his distillery workers, who had grown disgruntled over something trivial. Before he knew it, the workers had tossed off their aprons and walked out the stillhouse door. Now angry himself, Amos went to the door and yelled out after them, but it was to no avail. They showed no signs of turning around.

Perplexed by how he could complete his orders, Amos stood there in stunned silence. But again, his determined meditation was disturbed as he heard voices coming from the other side of the building. When he walked around the corner, he saw what looked like a motley band of marauders. Most people would have cast an eye on them and turned them away. But, as fearful as they looked, the deacon wanted to show them some good Christian hospitality and asked cheerfully, "what can I do for you fellows?"

One of them looked back and said, "we're looking for work. Do you have anything we can help you with?"

The deacon asked if they knew how to distill and they each vigorously nodded their heads in the affirmative. "What luck," thought Amos. But he said, "I'm sorry but I don't have any money to pay you with, but I can pay you in all the rum you can drink."

One of the roughest looking characters, who seemed to be the leader of the motley crew, said, "no worries, we'll do it for free. Anyway, there was plenty of hot liquid where we come from 'without drinking damnation in the distillery.'"

After watching to make sure they knew how to run his stills, the deacon said he had to be at church in the morning. He wondered if they wouldn't mind if he went home and got some shut eye? They gave no protest. So Amos locked the strangers up inside the distillery so they wouldn't sneak away in the night with all of his equipment and spirits.

The next morning, the deacon was shocked to see that the men had escaped and were nowhere to be seen. But to his amazement, they had finished all of their work and left each barrel filled to the brim with rum. Satisfied, he gleefully went off to the church, where Communion Sunday was sure to bring in a good crowd.

After spending time with family and friends, Amos headed back to the distillery to prepare for the new week's spirit runs. He hoped his regular workers had caught the Sunday spirit of forgiveness and would be there waiting for him. Instead, he found the same rough and tumble men from the night before, ready to get back to work. The deacon was thankful for the help and again let them distill his rum. Having gained confidence in their sincerity and honesty, he decided not to lock them in when he left for home that evening.

When he returned on Monday morning, again the workers were gone, but they had completed their task. They had even loaded up his wagon so he could easily deliver his rum. With that, he went into town to deliver his rum personally to every tavern owner.

After his third delivery, he was preparing for another stop when he saw the first tavern owner coming at him waving a fist. What could it be, he thought?

"What kind of nonsense are you trying to pull?" the tavern owner asked.

"What do you mean?" said the stunned and concerned deacon.

"Come and look at my barrel," the owner demanded.

When the deacon saw the barrel, he was stunned. Burned into the barrelhead in red letters were the words "Weeping and wailing and gnashing of teeth. - Inquire at Deacon Giles' distillery." Confused and frustrated, Amos apologized and took the barrel back, saying he'd bring a fresh one in the morning.

Then the second man he'd delivered spirits to came at him ready to deliver a tirade. "What is it?" the deacon asked, fearing a similar situation to the first.

The tavern owner scolded the deacon. "I took a sip from your barrel to test it and realized it had a horrible message burned into the barrelhead." Amos went to look. Same red letters, but this time it said "Delirium tremens. - Inquire at Amos Giles's Distillery."

He started feeling queasy. He tested one of his undelivered barrels and watched in horror as burnt red letters appeared on the lid, saying, "Consumption sold here. - Inquire at Deacon Giles' Distillery."

Scared out of his wits, the deacon immediately returned to his distillery with his cargo and relieved every single barrel of its contents. Then he swore he would never let those demonic distillers back into his distillery ever again.

But, according to the article's author, the distilling deacon didn't learn his lesson. The story ends with the lamenting that Amos' distillery smelled like brimstone, "but he would not give up the trade."[139]

This fictionalized story seems innocent enough. Written by Pastor George Cheever of the Howard Street Congregationalist Church in Salem, his national readers saw it as a parable. It highlighted the evils of alcohol by preaching about a hypocritical man of God who doubles as a purveyor of liquid spirits. It mentioned other shortcomings as well, like his habit of working on the Sabbath, and his selling of Bibles out of his distillery office.

For the citizens of Salem, however, the story seemed a little too familiar. Friends of a third-generation Salem distiller and deacon named John Stone alerted him to the article. Incensed by the perceived slander, he and a mob of friends confronted the pastor. Unsatisfied with his response, Deacon Stone sued Cheever for slander. The judge was sympathetic to Stone's frustrations and sentenced Cheever to a month in prison and made him pay a $1,000 fine.[140]

But Cheever's goal of getting his message heard came to fruition. Readers across the country requested reprints of the article years down the road. The readers of the *Tennessee Baptist* newspaper were reading reprints as late as 1855.

The article's popularity was due to a heightened sense that Americans were being consumed by a thirst for alcohol. And the statistics back them up: While modern drinkers consume an average of 2.3 gallons of alcohol per year, in the 1830s this number was 7.1 gallons per year. And that was up from 5.8 gallons during the previous century.[141]

Those 18th- and 19th-century numbers are large by any standard. Yet it wasn't until the 19th century that the issue was seen as an epidemic.

So, why wasn't a temperance movement called for in the 18th century?

It has a lot to do with the shift from an agrarian lifestyle to an industrialized society. While taverns were popular in the 18th century, they were more often frequented by the upper classes. Farmers stayed home, taking a ladle of hard cider now and again as they came in from a hard day's work in the field. And, being at home with their families, fathers were less prone to excessive drinking in front of their wives and children. But once men took jobs away from the home, a trip to the tavern or tippling house after work allowed them to over imbibe. Add in tippling houses with a gambling element and this increased the likelihood of trouble. It hurt the family both monetarily and in terms of domestic tranquility.

There was also a sharp increase in the production of hard spirits by the 1820s. What was once a byproduct of the farm was becoming a business. With distilleries popping up left and right, more whisky was available to the saloon or tippling house. More whisky meant prices went down. As commoners drank more of it, distilleries ramped up production, creating a vicious cycle.

These factors created the perfect atmosphere for painting alcohol as a demon that needed to be tamed. The dens of sin serving hard spirits became the source of all evil in society.

In 1831, Frenchman Alexis de Tocqueville saw this attitude when he traveled to the United States. In his book *Democracy in America*, he noted "someone observed to me one day, in Philadelphia, that almost all crimes in America are caused by the abuse of intoxicating liquors, which the lower classes can procure in great abundance, from their excessive cheapness."[142] But de Tocqueville also saw the solution in another curious American trait. To him, America was a nation of joiners: for them, no problem was too big as long as there was support in numbers. Get enough people on board, and minds could be changed.

But with alcohol, finding joiners was a bit more difficult. So many people loved their beer, wine, and spirits. How could a group motivate these people to change their evil ways?

The emerging leaders of the temperance movement knew they had to be delicate initially. Once they had their hooks in, nothing would be off limits when it came to saving souls from the evils of alcohol.

Birth of the Temperance Movement

The earliest known mention of temperance in America is in 1630. The Governor of the Massachusetts Bay Colony, John Winthrop, mentioned its importance in his "city on the hill" speech. It's doubtful he was using the word in relation to drink. After all, his ship was well stocked with beer and aqua vitae when it arrived. He was also fascinated with the concept of brewing beer from maize bread.[143]

When the country was under British rule, the Crown seemed uninterested in the colonists' drinking habits. But with the birth of the United States, two temperance advocates emerged. One was Benjamin Franklin's close friend, Dr. Benjamin Rush of Philadelphia. He talked of the dangerous health effects of consuming harder spirits. The other was Methodist leader Bishop Francis Asbury. The church leader traveled across the country and to Tennessee several times, speaking out against the evils of alcohol. Yet neither thought it was necessary to meddle in people's affairs. Moderation was fine and abstinence better. But there was no need for legislative prohibitions. Even James Robertson's alcohol laws only tried to limit the availability of alcohol, not ban it.[144]

The tide turned in 1813 with the formation of the Massachusetts Society for the Suppression of Intemperance. Seeing the damage alcohol was doing to local families, men of high standing were called upon to promote the benefits of abstinence. Proving de Tocqueville's "joiner" theory, men joined the group in droves. Within five years, the organization sprouted forty chapters of one hundred men each, and they published a newspaper devoted to the subject of temperance. In it, they used their elevated status to convince the public of the virtues of curtailing alcohol consumption--especially the more powerful spirits like rum and whisky.

By the end of the 1820s, there was a growing frustration among temperance societies that their work wasn't having the desired effect. And soon organizations like the Massachusetts Society began changing their mission and tactics. The word went out that total abstinence was the only solution and that all members must swear off harder spirits. At first, beer and wine were okay, but eventually they too faced scrutiny.

In Tennessee, the first temperance society met in Nashville in August 1829.[145] Because Tennessee was one of the top three distilling states in the nation, the situation was more acute, and it was felt there was a need for more church involvement. Baptist and Methodist preachers answered the call, railing against the evils of hard liquor and using moral suasion to deter overindulgence in beer and wine.

Newspapers, which were traditionally politically biased, soon divided on the issue of alcohol. It didn't take long to realize which papers leaned "wet" and which leaned "dry."

The selling of a position started subtly. Initially papers included cautionary tales to softly sell the dangers of alcohol. In 1810, Nashville's Tennessee Gazette noted an incident where a Mr. William Cobett had fallen off of his horse and broken his neck while intoxicated. The article warned, "this awful and striking end of a fellow being should be a warning to those thoughtless persons who accustom themselves to the habits of intemperance."[146] In 1825, the *Knoxville Register* clumsily attempted a bit of intemperate humor.[147] "A man wanted to know what he should put on the sign of his tippling house - a man replied 'Beggars made here.'" This piety hit all the right notes for the drys, while wets rolled their eyes and looked for another source of news.

But taverns weren't unregulated dens of vice. Tennessee law (and North Carolina law before that) restricted the sale of liquor in taverns to under a quart with a license fee of five dollars. Tavern owners were not allowed to be "addicted to any gross immorality." They also had to post bond to the county court in case they failed to maintain respectable lodgings for travelers. If they failed to meet the agreement or didn't secure a license, they would be fined one to five dollars.[148]

The tippling house was a different matter. But Tennessee didn't wait forever to tighten the rules on those either. Between 1811 and 1823, the General Assembly added several rules, including the banning of gambling in both taverns and tippling houses. Eventually, there was an inclusion of a $3 license fee and restrictions against selling hard liquor.

Knoxville's Mayor James Park went a step further, aiming to get rid of all but the highest-class drinking establishments in the town. He raised the license fee to $100 (or $2,500 in today's money). To stop the growth of illegal tippling houses, known as blind tigers, he levied $20 fines for any establishment without a license.[149]

But the more the regulations tightened, the more tippling houses seemed to grow like weeds. By the late 1820s, tippling houses had become Tennessee's public enemy number one. The General Assembly began debating bills that looked at using Knoxville's method of higher license fees to restrain these houses. Dry newspapers attempted to help the cause by ratcheting up their coverage. Newspapers became more blatant in their biases and printing presses started rolling off special editions and weeklies to provide ammunition against the intemperate. The Enquirer of Nashville told the story of a man in Raleigh who died "from the effects of intemperance." Apparently, Major Griffin stepped into a tippling house, one of "those pests of society." It accused a patron of challenging the major to drink a full quart of liquor all at once. "He succeeded in getting it down," the journalist remarked, "and soon after fell into a profound sleep, from which he never woke."[150]

With these types of articles appearing daily throughout the state, Governor William Carroll pressured the legislature to find a solution. The issue was, tippling houses were so profitable that when they were fined they simply paid the nuisance tax and went on serving. As a result, the General Assembly put into a bill a $15 license fee and required the houses to post bond. The wets found the bill acceptable and Governor Carroll signed the Tippling Act of 1831 into law.

The Quart Law

From the beginning, the temperance movement found its greatest supporters in God-fearing Christians, especially Baptists and Methodists. In the growing Bible Belt of the south, articles from preachers found their way from strictly religious newspapers into the mainstream press. The message focused on how intemperance brought destruction to the home and the individual.

While the religious angle was powerful, there were other groups whose messages increasingly found favor. When Colonel Andrew Erwin, the former owner of Nashville's Bell Tavern, arrived at the General Assembly, he gave a rousing speech on the evils of alcohol.[151] Suppression of alcohol, especially among the enslaved and free Blacks, was another popular angle. The voice of women would grow in importance whenever it helped the cause of temperance. But with no right to vote, the best women's groups could do was to petition the General Assembly. A group of women from Bledsoe County used the opportunity of the passing of the Tippling Act of 1831 to petition for its repeal, suggesting the government was promoting alcohol sales. Their goal was the suppression of ardent spirits.[152]

Another tactic was to defeat the arguments of the "wets" by the use of doctors. The *National Banner and Daily Advertiser* ran an entire speech given by Dr. Daniel Drake MD in Cincinnati. Titled "A Discourse on Intemperance," the doctor moved beyond the tippling house to outline some of the drinking habits present in the home. He spoke about family drinking and discouraged the habit of giving children, including infants, juleps, toddies, and slings mixed with sugar and aromatics to create a tolerance to alcohol so they would have less desire for it later. He found the custom of offering drinks to guests as something that was "fraught with... mischief," and something that should be abolished. He recommended doctors should wait until they were 40 years old before drinking, suggesting habits were less likely to be carried to excess after that age. But his biggest complaint was how people were becoming reliant on the morning dram. He suggested that the body was not in a proper state to handle stimulants at that time of day, and adding bitters only led to greater intemperance.[153]

But none of these legions of abstinence advocates were making a dent in the drinking culture of Tennessee. The Tippling Act of 1831 increased the number of legal and illegal saloons five fold.[154] And in a strange twist, it would be the drys that would rally against their own bill, outraged that the state had legitimized the tippling house. So in January 1838, the General Assembly repealed the Tippling Act. With one action, all legal tippling houses had become blind tigers.

The repeal act would become known as the Quart Law of 1838. It allowed the sale of a quart or more of spirituous liquor by an establishment, but it could not be consumed on site. The legislature deemed all smaller containers illegal.[155] The law was effective in some areas of the state, but mostly it just caused a boom in defiant blind tigers. After seven years an exasperated legislature repealed the Quart Law and wrote an updated 1846 Tippling Law with some additional rules.[156] Apologists suggested that the two laws had failed because of a lack of enforcement. This would become a common theme in the future.

The Maine Law

While the Tennessee tippling law seemed to only exacerbate the problem, in New England, another solution was being bandied about—the Local Option law. This legislation allows towns and communities autonomy in writing their own prohibitions on alcohol. Rather than trying to force an entire state into the dry category, each community could decide for themselves. When several jurisdictions went "dry" other areas of the country took notice.

Then in 1838, the Boston Temperance Society lit a political firestorm when they pressured the Massachusetts legislature to pass a controversial temperance bill. Signed into law by Governor Edward Everett, the Fifteen Gallon Law put a fifteen gallon minimum on the amount of alcohol you could purchase at any one time. While not an all-out prohibition, its basic target would be the spirits drinkers that frequented saloons. But citizens of low means saw it as an act of class warfare, punishing the working classes and immigrants who couldn't afford to buy such large quantities of liquor all at once. It also targeted the small saloon owner, who didn't have the means to buy alcohol in large quantities.

But crafty saloon owners found several ways to skirt the law. The easiest method was to let a pub full of people pool their money to purchase the 15 gallons and then they'd split it between them. Another was to buy 16 gallons of spirits and then sell 15 gallons back. But the most comical way was the striped pig method. The spirits dealer would set a tent up with visitors encouraged to lay down their money to see the wonders of the striped pig. Once the money reached the hand of the vendor, the tent flap opened and into view came a pig painted with stripes. As a gift for viewing, they provided guests with a free glass of rum. No alcohol was sold, so no law was broken. Near riots would ensue when law enforcement tried to break up these events; it didn't matter, there was always a new scheme up someone's sleeve.[157]

The Fifteen Gallon Law was so unpopular that during the next gubernatorial election, many of Everett's supporters jumped ship and supported his opponent. With his defeat on election day, the Fifteen Gallon Law had claimed its biggest victim.[158] Soon after, the legislature set the law aside. In its place, Massachusetts passed a local option, with over a hundred towns opting into dry laws. New York State soon followed suit.

Maine decided to go a step further. In 1846, the legislature passed a form of statewide prohibition.[159] Like the Quart and Tippling Laws in Tennessee, enforcement would be its downfall. But, five years later, the law's champion Portland Mayor Neal Dow looked to patch up its holes.

A Quaker by birth, Dow grew up believing most of society's problems could be traced to the consumption of alcohol. Through his passionate advocacy, a bill called "An Act for the Suppression of Drinking Houses and Tippling-Shops" (known throughout the county as The Maine Law) passed through the legislature and was signed into law by Governor Hubbard in 1851.[160] Dow was determined not to let his prohibition law sink. He doubled efforts on enforcement and confiscated any liquor found in his city. Unlike the Fifteen Gallon Law in neighboring Massachusetts, Dow was determined to go after the high-end social clubs as well as the small dives. He became known as the "Father of Temperance" and took his act on the road--by 1855 thirteen states had some form of statewide prohibition.[161]

In Tennessee, the Maine Law was a hot topic during the state's 1855 gubernatorial contest. The Whig Candidate Meredith P. Gentry favored the local option, while Democratic Governor Andrew Johnson said the law was out of step with the state constitution and suggested the Maine Law was "incompatible with the rights and privileges of free men."[162]

Debate on the subject reached a fever pitch in the Tennessee General Assembly during the following year's January session. The Quart and Tippling laws had been knocked back and forth so many times, almost everyone was on board with finding a new solution.

When a prohibition law with similarities to the Maine Law reached the floor of the house, arguments rained down from both the wets and drys. Seeing the folly in the bill, Representative N. Y. Cavitt of Weakley County, a supporter in principle of the dry cause, rose and gave one of the more even-handed assessments of the problems of enacting a law similar to the Maine Law:

> *"Gentlemen have talked about these bills as though the passage of some one of them would stop the drinking of liquor, suppress the commission of crime and cause the millennium to dawn. That argument will not do. Such an imagination is fanatical. From history and tradition I have learned that in all ages of the world, men have to some extent drank as a beverage intoxicating liquors. Then reasoning by the past for the future, I conclude that man will continue to pursue the same course until his nature is changed. We have instances of prohibitory laws and their reign has been short. In England, Scotland, Ireland, Massachusetts, and New York, they have all died away, could not be enforced, and were finally repealed. More recently the mania was renewed in Maine and spread over many other States, but a re-action is already taking place there, and that re-action will follow in other States. I understand that the present Legislature in Maine are in favor of the repeal of the prohibitory law. There is one thing certain: as long as men want to drink and can produce money to pay for it, there will be some person to furnish it, whether the law permits it or not. We cannot direct the morals of the world. We have*

repealed the tippling law and now are to have in existence all the odium of the quart law without any of the restrictions of the law of 1846. That is a better law than we will get. But if that law could not be enforced I would like to know what we would do towards enforcing the Maine law? The liquor traffic has for years been a hobby on which men have rode into office. Temperance has not advanced by it. I'm sorry to see such time spent in this House when I believe our action on the subject thus far has magnified the evil. I agree with gentlemen in all they say about the evils of intemperance. I agree with them about the amount of crime that is caused by it. They may then ask me why I do not vote with them? Because I am clearly of the opinion that if we were to pass any or all of the forty three liquor bills now before us, that it would not remedy the evil."[163]

The Weakley County congressman was dead on it when he stated the Maine Law was in serious trouble. After a riot broke out in Portland and a man was killed by the state militia, Dow's popularity faded in the state, and the Maine legislature repealed the act in 1856. Other states followed suit. But the Honorable Mr. Cavitt's speech fell on deaf ears. There was no middle ground in 1850 Tennessee politics. You were either a wet or you were a dry. The battle for the hearts and minds of the people had just begun.

In the midst of all of the squabbling between the Quart and Tippling laws, little Bethel College in Carroll County came up with an alternate plan to control alcohol in the state. Wanting to "guard the morals of the youth" they proposed ridding the campus of the scourge of alcohol. To stop temptation, they proposed setting up a two-mile restrictive zone around the school where sales of alcohol would be illegal. In 1853, they sent a petition to the state legislature.[164] On the morning of December 15, Senator Benton brought the petition to the floor. It was referred to the Judiciary committee and then dropped. It was an idea that was way ahead of its time—and it would not be forgotten.[165]

Chapter 11

TROUBLE BREWING

"What hath God wrought?"

With the sending of that sinister sounding question, Samuel Morse brought America into the age of the telegraph.

It was a remarkable achievement for humankind. Before the device's invention, news and communications moved slowly and only through the mail or localized human interaction. In 1844, the idea of transmitting thirty characters a minute to a location dozens of miles away in mere seconds seemed unfathomable to most. In just a handful of years, telegraph transmission lines stretched throughout the eastern United States. The world was getting smaller.

It was also speeding up. The 1830s was the birth of America's rail age, with private firms contracting lines in the northeast and as far south as the Port of Charleston in South Carolina.

But firms in the northeast experienced growing pains immediately as haphazard development led to several failed ventures. In the sparsely populated south, the focus was on longer distance lines, which turned out to be more profitable.

When completed, the Charleston-Hamburg Railroad connected Charleston to Columbia and Augusta, Georgia. The state of Georgia followed suit, connecting Augusta, Macon, Athens, and Savannah. Chattanoogans celebrated the development of the Western and Atlantic Railroad (W&A). When completed in 1851, it gave Chattanooga direct access to Georgia, South Carolina, and their Atlantic ports. In anticipation, Nashville financiers went to work funding the

Nashville and Chattanooga Railroad. Completed in 1853, it expanded the access of Nashville, Murfreesboro, Smyrna, Wartrace, and Tullahoma to these extensive markets.[166]

North of Nashville in Robertson County, Wiley Woodard watched the progression of the railroad with great interest.

Born in 1810, Wiley was the youngest son of Thomas Woodard. Ready to grab life by the horns, at 17 he joined the state militia and quickly rose to the rank of colonel. At 18, he married Elizabeth Henry, and the two went to work growing the Woodard name.[167]

Wiley had long wanted to take his father's distillery business from a small still to a larger operation. So when the elder Woodard died, he left the Beaver Dam Creek property to the budding 26-year-old entrepreneur. Partnering with his brother-in-law John Henry, the duo began looking for creative ways to build money so they could expand the business. Wiley's cousin Wilson Pitt pitched in by helping transport their whisky to Nashville.[168]

As Wiley's own distilling operations grew, he became more curious about how the rail system could work as an advantage to his enterprise. As the Nashville and Chattanooga Railroad closed in on completion, there were talks of a Nashville to Louisville line. Adding a stop off in the Robertson county seat of Springfield would be a boon for Wiley's business. He decided the best way to secure that depot was by winning a seat in the Tennessee General Assembly. In 1849, he won his district and would eventually vote to grant a charter for the Louisville and Nashville Railroad (L&N).[169]

When it opened in November 1859, the L&N, with its Springfield depot, increased Robertson County's reach in the Deep South. In fact, Wiley could barely meet the demand, so he hired a 35 year old Irishman, Patrick O'Conner, to be his head distiller.[170] In that year, Wiley Woodard & Company sold $14,850 worth of whisky and brandy (or the equivalent of over a half million dollars today).[171] The era of the small farm distiller was over. The rail system had helped take the Woodards into the modern age.

The Rise of Brands

In those early years, the thing Colonel Wiley didn't have the benefit of was a brand. Today, branding is one of the biggest considerations for a whisky. Before the 1820s, individual brands in American whisky were unheard of.

If you were drinking at old Stump's tavern, it was a good bet you were drinking old Stump's whisky. If the tavern didn't have a still, the whisky likely came from a local farmer. If the whisky was of exceptional quality, a patron might find the name of the distiller on the barrel or they could ask the owner. The answer would likely be, "oh that's that good corn likker from old man Johnson's farm."

As transportation opened up, better quality whiskies from different regions arrived by roads or by boat. By 1808, retailers like John Wright in Franklin saw the benefit in promoting stocks of high quality old Monongahela. Four years later, Joseph Wood's store in Nashville's Deposit Alley received a supply of whisky from Kentucky.[172] He gave his customers a choice: stay loyal with Tennessee whisky or try some new spirits from up north. No one knew where any Kentucky distillers were, so he saw no point in promoting a particular distiller.

Suddenly, what did matter was whether the whisky had spent any time in a barrel. If so, it was called "old." To the whisky drinker of this era, old meant the whisky had color, didn't cause as many headaches, and was easier to drink. It was a term that went back to Scotland in the 1770s, when wholesalers peddled "very old fine Fairintosh whisky," due to newer competition not having extensive storehouses of aged whiskies.[173] The term old wouldn't enter the advertising lexicon of American whisky until regional names began appearing in the 1810s and 1820s. Old would lose its luster in the 1870s as tax benefits led to most whisky being aged. From then on, it clung to brand names and lost its original meaning.

If there was a single adjective that foreshadowed the growing need for brand names, it was the word "celebrated." Used liberally in the 19th century, it was a way for a tavern or grocer to signify the popularity of a spirit. For example, an 1846 Vicksburg, Mississippi newspaper advertisement touted Crow's "celebrated" whiskey from Kentucky.[174]

As one of the most famous brands in American whisky history, this ad for what would become today's Old Crow Bourbon provides the perfect example of how branding developed. The name Crow is written as possessive, showing that this is talking about the distiller James C. Crow, not a brand. It also doesn't use the word "old" which only attached permanently once the name officially became the brand Old Crow. And since Crow didn't come from Bourbon County, they referred to it as whiskey rather than Bourbon. So the location of manufacture mattered in 1846.

But in the early 1850s, everything changed. Distinguishing between barrels of whisky became more important. In May 1851, Nashville merchants began offering old Lincoln County whisky.[175] By December 1852, old Robertson joined the growing list.[176] Adjectives like "celebrated" and "old" joined process names like rectified whisky, copper-distilled, and sour mash.

Once the names of distillers became more prevalent, it wasn't long before branding started. In 1861, wholesaler Thompson, Sperry & Co. found the advantages to this when they provided some whisky to the *Nashville Republican Banner*. The newspaper thanked them for sending "a mammoth demijohn of Henry Kelsoe's celebrated Log distilled Lincoln County Whiskey." They even gave it a review saying the whisky "certainly transcends in purity, efficacy, and flavor, anything of the kind in the market and possesses that fine aroma which is found only in the purist liquors. We shall 'put her by' for Sunday, as we belong to the Sons of Temperance six days in the week."[177]

It is easy to conclude that branding came along because distillers saw the benefits of promotion. But there was also a safety aspect. Tennessee distillers and journalists were growing concerned with all the dangerous spirits flooding into the market. People were getting sick. The primary culprit was a specific type of rectified whisky. And the name of the town that supplied it would soon become infamous in the state of Tennessee.

Counterfeit Whisky

In 1857, an article appeared in the August 16 edition of the *Republican Banner* as a warning to wine and brandy drinkers, but whisky distillers took note as well. Dr. Hiram Cox, a chemical inspector in Cincinnati, revealed that over the course of two years, he had inspected 249 liquors of various types and found nine-tenths of them to be imitations, with a great number being poisonous. Using corn whisky as a base, additives included guinea pepper, horseradish, and enough sulphuric acid "to eat a hole through a man's stomach." [178]

Known to Tennesseans as Cincinnati busthead, ashhopper, or strychnine, these liquors were a product of unscrupulous large-scale producers and blending houses. The purpose was profit, not quality or safety. St. Louis, to a lesser degree, would join Cincinnati in this loathsome practice. Brands were a reaction, becoming a way for legitimate distillers to separate themselves from the rabble. Cincinnati's Marcus Smith's Old Reserve Whisky and Pike's Magnolia arrived in Nashville in 1851, hoping to restore the city's reputation.[179] In 1856, Houseman & Smith of St. Louis followed suit with their Julius H. Smith whisky brand.[180]

The industry adopted the practice when competitors saw the benefits of this type of branding. In the 1850s, advertisements for old "Crow" whisky in Memphis made the subtle change of removing the apostrophe, demonstrating the Crow brand rather than the man.[181] With more whisky coming from out of state, it helped whiskies earn trust with consumers hundreds of miles away.

But branding didn't stop the influx of bad whisky from Cincinnati and St. Louis. Grocers soon saw the benefit of cutting their good Tennessee whiskies with Cincinnati busthead to increase profits.

When people started getting sick from Tennessee whiskies, distillers took action. They asked the General Assembly to write a law that curtailed this practice. The result was "An Act to Prevent the Adulteration of Spirituous Liquors in this State."

The bill pulled no punches. Section one declared "the adulteration of spiritus or venous liquors by the use of strychnine or other poisonous liquids or ingredients, shall be, and the same is hereby, declared a felony." It also put jeopardy into the hands of the retailer in section three by stating "anyone who shall be guilty of selling to any person in this state, by retail or wholesale, any spiritus or venous liquors adulterated as stated in the two preceding sections of this act, shall incur all the penalties annexed to the second section of this act," which included a one to five-year incarceration in the state penitentiary. Anyone selling whisky had to post a $500 bond.[182]

It was a strong attempt to preserve the reputation of Tennessee whisky. But learning the effectiveness of the legislation would have to wait. Tennessee distillers had a bigger problem on their hands. The nation was heading for war, with the potential end of enslaved labor a major cause.

Union Men

When it came to the words he penned, Thomas Jefferson was a man of precision. Every word he wrote had meaning and a purpose. When America's forefathers decided it was time to throw off the shackles of British oppression, they turned to Jefferson to craft the Declaration of Independence. Jefferson knew just what he wanted to say. But when the delegates to the convention scrutinized and dropped some of his words, Thomas took offense.

One of the passages questioned by the members of the Second Continental Congress was a condemnation of King George III for inflicting the evils of the slave trade on the shores of America. It was a statement that was opening the door to a much freer America. But when they struck it from the document, Jefferson became incensed. He specifically blamed two states for its removal but also suggested the subject was so deeply ingrained in the culture there wasn't enough time for adequate debate. Unity was more important than dealing with an issue that could create division.

The citizens of the United States will never know of the greatness lost because of that passage being struck from the document. The names and histories lost to the distilling industry alone are significant. At the very least, it would have led to a less hypocritical stance on freedom and might have saved a lot of bloodshed in the mid-19th century.

Few states had more varying opinions on slavery than Tennessee. The east seemed to lean towards abolition, but wouldn't fully commit. Lincoln County sided more with the slaveholding states of the Deep South. But neighboring Bedford County held more Unionist sympathies.

Robertson County and its distillers don't fit any of the modern stereotypes of blue vs gray. Most of the distillers used an enslaved labor force. But they were also fiercely loyal to the United States, as were most Tennesseans before the war. What is curious are the similarities between the political beliefs of Robertson County distillers and presidential candidate Abraham Lincoln. Both agreed the North didn't have any business dictating the slavery question to the South. But they also agreed that no new slave states should be added to the Union. Both agreed "a house divided against itself will not stand." So both were passionate about the preservation of the Union. Yet no Robertson County distiller had any intention of supporting Abraham Lincoln for president. Their politics wouldn't allow it.

The political landscape of Tennessee before the war is a masterclass in the complexity of human beings. It's time to challenge the traditional stereotypes and see where the minds of Robertson County distillers were at, just before the War Between the States.

The Opposition

Weeks before the outbreak of the Civil War, a former U.S. Congressman, Felix Zollicoffer of Paris, Tennessee, was called to Washington D.C. to attend a peace conference at Willard's Hotel. The goal of the meeting was to avert a potentially disastrous conflict and the splitting of the United States into two separate countries.

Of all the people sent to talk peace, Felix was one of the oddest choices. There was a time when the onetime editor of Nashville's *Republican Banner* got into a war of words over the presidential campaign of 1852 with the editor of the rival

Nashville Union, John Marling. After Marling condemned him in an editorial, Felix challenged John to a duel[183] and, when shots were fired, both men sustained wounds but would survive.[184]

The main reason the leadership singled Felix out for the conference was his love for the United States. His wife Louisa was said to be a descendant of Pocahontas. He was the proud grandson of a Revolutionary War soldier. And he too fought for his country under General Winfield Scott during the Mexican-American War. Felix was American through and through and wanted nothing to break it in two. But he was also an enslaver and had a vested interest in preserving the status quo in the South.

When push came to shove, Felix and his allies laid their cards on the table. Not only did they want the North to promise not to eradicate slavery, they wanted the line between north and south--the old Missouri Compromise line of 1850--extended all the way to the Pacific Ocean. This would include parts of California that were free from slavery. They also wanted a Constitutional Amendment written to make this line permanent.[185] It was less a negotiation and more of a demand. With neither side willing to bend, the peace conference ended in disappointment. Knowing war was likely inevitable, Felix went home and joined the Tennessee State Militia.

Six years earlier, Representative Zollicoffer was in Robertson County at a Whig Convention attended by several Robertson County distillers, including John Yates, William Adams, Jo. C. Stark, Sheriff Green Benton, and Colonel Wiley Woodard. Tennessee had voted for every Whig candidate for president since the party's own Davy Crockett died at the Alamo. Robertson County was one of the party's strongholds. Most of the distillers at the convention disagreed with Felix's interest in extending slavery. But they at least wanted to make sure that it stayed in states like Tennessee, where it already existed.[186] With this convention, the distillers cast votes for candidates that would support this point of view.

But during the presidential election of 1856, the Whig Party fractured. Most northern members joined the upstart Republican Party, while the remaining faction joined one of the oddest named parties in American history, the Know-Nothings.

The Know-Nothings were mostly silent on the slavery issue. Their passion was behind stopping Catholic Europeans from immigrating to America. The distillers of Robertson County had no problem with Catholics, so the party didn't appeal to them.

The problem was, the Republican candidate wasn't on the ballot because Tennessee saw them as a radical anti-slavery party. So the only other choice was Democrat James Buchanan. Robertson County didn't want to be stuck without a candidate again.

To prepare for the next major election, Robertson County distillers joined the Southern Opposition Party. This was a catch-all for anti-Democrat Southerners seeking to retain slavery wherever it already existed, along with the preservation of the Union.[187]

When the delegates met in Nashville at the Southern Opposition Party's convention, they voted to join Kentuckian Henry Clay's national Union party. Their platform said they were "a party which shall stand by the Constitution and the Laws - a party which shall make opposition to the agitation of the slavery question a pre-eminent and leading feature of its policy." The convention nominated a Tennessean, John Bell, as the Constitutional Unionist presidential candidate. Bell was a moderate on the question of the expansion of slavery. This put him at odds with former Rep. Zollicoffer and his Peace Conference contingent.[188] Still, Bell won the state in the general election. But he was a distant fourth nationally behind Republican Abraham Lincoln.

The South was suddenly thrust into turmoil. Two days after the election of the Republican Abraham Lincoln, the *Republican Banner* tried to make sense of what his presidency would mean for the slavery issue. They highlighted quotes from his past speeches, including one given in Chicago in 1858, where he said "I have said a hundred times, and I have now no inclination to take it back, that I believe there is no right, and ought to be no inclination, in the people of the Free States to enter into the Slave States and interfere with the question of slavery at all."[189] It may have temporarily calmed nerves in Tennessee, but the stakes climbed higher when South Carolina seceded from the Union in December 1860.

In January 1861, a Tennessee secession referendum was called for but the measure failed by almost 12,000 votes.[190] It seemed Tennessee was staying in the Union. But within days Mississippi, Florida, and Alabama voted to secede. By February, a Confederate Constitution was written in Alabama. With that, Georgia, Louisiana, and Texas joined the Confederacy.

Not everyone in the Deep South was happy with the new Confederate government. One of the first things the government did was impose a 33 percent tax on the production of whisky. In March, the Nashville Patriot answered the woes of the Columbus (GA) Enquirer who were saddened at the loss of cheap whisky. The Patriot writer joked, "if you had imposed that tax of 33 per cent upon whisky six months ago, making it a prohibition, you might have been in the Union now." The crafty editor knew all too well how Georgians loved their Tennessee liquor. "We don't suppose Tennessee has drunk a barrel of whisky since the opening of the Nashville and Chattanooga Railroad... her whisky she ships to Georgia and other sections of the Southern Confederacy, where they have the genius to drink it, but not make it."[191]

The leaders of Robertson County tried to go on with business as usual. Days before the first shots of the war were fired at Charleston's Fort Sumter, the party met to elect delegates to the state gubernatorial convention. The primary orders of business were to establish support for distiller Jo C. Stark's congressional candidacy and to once again vow allegiance to the United States. Their statement read:

> *"We stand boldly for Union and the Constitution and will support and maintain the same as long as there is a hope for their preservation. We are opposed to the doctrine of succession, believing as we do, that it is no remedy for any of the existing political troubles that now afflict our country. We are opposed to civil war or blood shed under*

any and all circumstances, but we cannot give up free navigation to the Mississippi River."[192]

The statement started firm, but it was showing cracks. When news of the hostilities at Fort Sumter, South Carolina reached Tennessee, Governor Isham G. Harris called for an extra session of the General Assembly to recommend another referendum on secession. With Virginia and Arkansas dissolving their association with the United States, popular opinion in the state had shifted dramatically. In the referendum, 104,913 voted for secession, 47,238 against.[193] On June 8, 1861, Tennessee became the eleventh and final state to join the Confederacy.

Robertson County Unionists like the Woodards wouldn't give up hope of rejoining the Union under Lincoln's promise. It was that promise of not expanding or contracting slavery that kept Kentucky and Missouri from joining the South.

Some 30,000 troops would leave the state to go fight as Billy Yanks, most from East Tennessee.

Felix Zollicoffer, the man who so valued being an American, now fought for the Confederate States of America after they absorbed the Tennessee militia into the Southern army. They sent him to put down pro-Union uprisings in the eastern mountains of Kentucky. On a misty morning during a battle at Mill Springs, Felix came out of the fog and was staring right at Colonel Speed Fry's Union troops. Either out of mistaken identity or devious plot, he rode out and ordered the Union colonel not to fire upon his own men. Fry was not amused and Zollicoffer fell in a hail of bullets.[194]

Eventually, former Democratic Governor Andrew Johnson was tapped by President Lincoln to lead the state during its military occupation and he eventually became Lincoln's running mate, switching to the Republican party in the 1864 election.

No, there was nothing simple about Tennessee's politics or position in the War Between the States.

Chapter 12

WHISKY REBELLION

Whisky and the War

During the War Between the States, some people had little tolerance for disloyalty to the Southern cause. This is a fact Robertson County Sheriff Benton Green learned the hard way.

It was a typical Thursday when the sheriff rode out on horseback to check on his distillery. On this particular morning, his son Albert tagged along, delivering a wagon full of supplies. As he neared the home of William Morris, he noticed Will standing on the porch, staring right at him. Suddenly, he saw the body of a shotgun appear out of nowhere and aimed straight at him. Before he could react, a puff of fire and smoke came out of the barrels, followed instantly by a loud bang and a sudden sting in the sheriff's leg. His horse jumped, throwing the him to the ground.

As he tried to gather his senses, Sheriff Green heard two more shots ring out, this time from the other direction. It was his son Albert, pistol in hand, aiming to kill or wound his father's assailant. When William tried to return fire, his caps exploded. He dropped the gun and ran off into the woods. Albert came to check on his father, who had taken buckshot in his hip, thigh, and knee.[195] It was a hard lesson about the dangers lurking in his very own community, but Sheriff Green took his wounds in stride. Still, the man who stood up as a Unionist before the war would have to be more cautious with his distillery visits in the future.

Terror had come home to roost throughout Tennessee. The battle wasn't just Johnny Reb against Billy Yank; it was neighbor on neighbor. No longer could distillers limit their concerns to droughts and market swings. Markets had dried up or were inaccessible and you were never sure who you could trust.

For distillers, the Civil War bore little resemblance to the Revolution or War of 1812. In those days, distillers made profits from military contracts. General George Washington felt daily rations of rum and whisky were as important to the men's good spirits as food was to their bodies. And distillers like Andrew Jackson made a good steady income off supplying the troops.

But the attitudes toward whisky changed quickly during the early part of the war. And underneath the blue and the gray there was a subtle war between wets and drys.

On the Union side, when undisciplined Federal troops experienced a surprise defeat at the Battle of Bull Run, some blamed it on soldiers, eager to get to the whisky shop.

In the Confederacy, the *Richmond Examiner* reported "contraband grog-shops have sprung up everywhere in the city, and dens for the retail of whisky have been established not only in the backrooms of family grocers and confectionary shops, but even in more reputable establishments of trade." The *Examiner* estimated that, during the early days of the war, a single distiller in Richmond could make $4,000 in a single day (or $146,000 in today's money)! And that whisky was leading to drunken riots and a loss of grain for the poor.[196]

The Confederates believed the Yanks had a secret weapon when they seized Fort Henry and gained control of the Tennessee River. "We see that the Yankee Generals are adopting stringent measures to prevent the introduction of whisky into their camps," the Athens (GA) Post noted. "It is a wise policy. Whisky is the most dangerous of all the enemies. Drunken soldiers are not to be depended on, and still less drunken officers."[197]

In early 1862, Federal troops took Fort Donelson and occupied Nashville. A fan of old Robertson, Tennessee's military governor Brigadier General Andrew Johnson made no proclamations about distilling. This allowed distillers like Stark & Hilliard and Colonel Wiley Woodard to continue making whisky until the market dried up.

Lincoln County was a different story. Citizens were strong in the Confederate cause. Some distillers, like Dan Call and Wiley Daniel, went off to fight for the rebels. When Union troops occupied Fayetteville and Lynchburg, whisky markets were closed. Once Union troops began raiding homes and farms, the area devolved into guerilla warfare. Transporting whisky or selling it to soldiers was dangerous.

As for Union officers, the proclamation by the Confederates that they were enforcing prohibitions on troops didn't extend to the leadership.

Barrels of whisky were present at Shiloh, where General Ulysses S. Grant was accused of being drunk while Union soldiers took on heavy casualties. In truth, the drunken claims were probably more political rumor than reality. Grant only drank to excess when he was bored and lonely. But it does point to the tolerance for alcohol among the leadership.

As for the locals, tolerance of their alcohol consumption by Union leaders seemed to be a mixed bag. On September 11, the *Nashville Daily Union* reported that a Federal officer, Colonel Gillem, "caused a large number of whisky barrels to evacuate their contents into Cumberland River within the last few days. At the latest dates from Clarksville, the people of that town were all lying flat on their bellies on the river bank, with straws in their mouths, anxiously awaiting the descending nectar."[198]

Meanwhile, in Memphis, Union General William Tecumseh Sherman had the opposite strategy. He reopened the whisky shops that had been closed by the Confederates to help raise revenue to pay the local police. According to a Confederate paper, the *Missouri Democrat*, the result was chaos. "The good order of the city is gone, and the former good name which our soldiers had gained for discipline, politeness, and soldierly bearing, is fast departing. The whisky shops were opened and taxed twenty-five dollars per month each. But now they need even more police to solve the whisky shop's opening."[199]

Whether he knew it or not, General Sherman had tapped into a long-held Tennessee tradition. License fees were a way of life for the state's merchants, tavern owners, and tippling houses.

But what Tennessee hadn't seen in over forty years was a tax placed on the distiller of the whisky. A bill going through the halls of government in Washington, D.C. was about to change all of that.

The world of Tennessee whisky would never be the same.

The Excise

In response to mounting Federal war debts, the U.S. Congress presented President Abraham Lincoln with a bill that would help the government cover war expenses. Known as the Revenue Act of 1862, this temporary war measure had two primary ways of collecting revenue. It placed a progressive three to five percent income tax on the wealthiest Americans and it created a tax on luxury and vice based goods like pianos, jewelry, tobacco, playing cards and liquor. It was the first excise tax on distilled spirits since a temporary three-year measure signed by President James Madison during the War of 1812. The initial rate was set at 20 cents per gallon starting July 1, 1862, but the bill gave congress the ability to adjust the rate so they could control the flow of alcohol through higher taxes. An Internal Revenue department was created within the Treasury, headed by a commissioner.[200]

As the war dragged on in the South, the Congress of the Confederate States followed Washington's lead, placing an excise tax on wines and spirituous liquors, as well as naval stores, salt, tobacco, cotton, wool, flour, sugar, molasses, syrup, rice, and other agricultural products. Leaders brought the tax in just prior to the Battle of Gettysburg and the fall of Vicksburg. To stay ahead of the devaluing Confederate currency, which was worth only about a third of its original value by 1863, they set the Confederate excise at 8% rather than at a dollar figure.[201]

But, for the rebels, the tax was too little too late. Union General Grant had been reassigned to the Army of the Potomac in Virginia and General Sherman was about to make his final march through the South, putting an end to the Confederacy.

But even before Confederate General Lee's ultimate surrender at Appomattox Court House, Tennessee was back in the Union. It became the first state to repeal its succession amendment, thanks to Andrew Johnson's disenfranchising of Confederates during his term as military governor. With only Union sympathizers left to vote, a Radical Republican, William "Parson" Brownlow, was ushered into office in a landslide along with a constitutional amendment enfranchising emancipated Black males.

Washington saw Brownlow's presence in the Governor's mansion as favorable. But Tennessee distillers were anything but pleased. Brownlow was a teetotaller and ready to wage war against the whisky interests. Not willing to wait for the revenuers to arrive with their excise tax enforcement, Brownlow asked the General Assembly to pass such an aggressive tax on the spirit that no one could afford it.[202] At the same time a movement began with a focus on banning the sale of ardent spirits around academic institutions, showing the Bethel College pre-war two-mile law had not been forgotten.[203]

Meanwhile, the U.S. Congress was trying to figure out why the excise on whisky wasn't bringing in the revenue they expected. Just a year and a half into collection efforts, newspapers like the *New York Tribune* pointed to the increased costs associated with finding revenuers and paying bounties. In their opinion, the 20-cent tax needed to be raised. They speculated that the lost revenue was likely because of a decrease in the consumption of liquor or because distillers were cheating the government. Either way, they felt a higher tax burden would make up the difference.[204]

Bowing to those views, Congress tripled the excise tax in March 1864 from 20 to 60 cents per gallon. When revenues didn't grow, it was raised to $1.50 a gallon in July and then $2 a gallon in January 1865 (or $37 per gallon today).[205] Yet government collections still only jumped from $28,431,798 in 1864 to $29,193,878 in 1865.[206]

The Nashville Banner questioned the results, noting "the US census for 1860 reported ninety million gallons of whisky as the product that year. The last report of the revenue commissioner exhibits only ten million gallons as the yield of the fiscal year last past. What has become of the ninety million gallons? Did we drink less in 1865–6 than we did in 60?" The conclusion of the Banner was that it was all going underground, and for good reason. "Our lawmakers don't realize no product will bear a tax exceeding its cost of manufacture. The tax on whisky is by five or ten times this standard. If the tax had been .30 to .50 the revenue would have been greater than at $2."[207]

The *Memphis Daily Appeal* agreed the high costs were stifling, creating an illicit trade. But they also pointed a finger at the revenuers themselves. "The people that force dishonesty on others, soon become dishonest themselves, especially when they have resorted to a general system of "Statutory pillage." It will be remembered that of twenty-nine revenue officers on the lake frontier, twenty-eight have been officially reported as thieves."[208]

While Tennessee newspapers were concerned with the hammer of taxes that were making their way to Tennessee, most distillers in the state hadn't felt the sting yet. In 1865, Federal tax assessors stayed clear of Middle Tennessee and its rebel leanings and focused only on the First and Second Districts in the Union-friendly east. This limited Tennessee collections for the fiscal year 1865 to around $74,937 for the entire state versus $784,916 for Kentucky.[209]

In early 1865, Robertson County distillers didn't seem to take the approaching tax seriously. Maybe they thought the government would dissolve the tax, like it had in the past.

Instead, they focused on the return of Cincinnati busthead. Whisky from Queen City's stockpile was flooding into Nashville. Apparently, some of them were coming in stamped as old Robertson.

Frustrated at this new tactic, a group of Robertson County distillers took action to protect their good names. They set up agreements with two wholesalers,

Burr, Bibb & Company of Springfield and Brien & Thaxton at the corner of College and Church streets in Nashville, as exclusive dealers of their spirits. They put out a circular letting customers know that if they sought the pure unadulterated article of old Robertson, it would be available from these two sources only. The distillers' list included some of the area's biggest and most revered names, including Colonel Wiley Woodard, Stark & Hilliard, Wilson Pitt, A.B. Couts, William H. Couts, W. J. Darden, G. H. Garrett, John R. Bridges, Thomas Savage, Moses D. Woodard, and Dr. George E. Draughon.[210]

But apparently, not everyone was happy about this arrangement. A group of local wholesalers and distillers who weren't included in the deal got together at the Robertson County Chamber of Commerce and condemned the circular. In response, they:

> *"Resolved, That in consideration of that fact that there is not more than one-fifth of the distillers of Robertson County who have signed said Circular, that we respectfully invite those who have not signed the same to send their whisky to our market, freely, and that we will use our best endeavors to promote their interest; and Resolved, That until said Circular is publicly withdrawn, we hereby pledge ourselves to refrain from buying from, or selling liquors for any of the parties who have signed said circular."*[211]

The dustup would be short-lived. A danger much greater than barrels of misleading Cincinnati busthead was making its way down from Washington.

The revenue department was about to crack down on fraud and illicit distilling. To do this, the government decided on a three-pronged approach. First, they would place a revenuer at every distillery, except those only making brandy. They would force revenuers to divest themselves of any ownership in a distillery by August 1866. And they would work to source an instrument that could use the latest technologies to scientifically track a distillers' honesty. This last item would threaten the very existence of Tennessee whisky.

Measuring Failure

The turmoil the United States government and distillers were going through with excise issues was nothing new. Great Britain had been dealing with the same problem since the reign of King Charles II in the 17th century. When the tax was first introduced, the Crown made registration of stills voluntary, assuming that most distillers would comply. Instead, smaller distillers ignored the process and went on with business as usual. The government reacted by mandating registration, so distillers took to the hills. When excise men went into the hills to inspect distilleries, distillers took advantage of a loophole that said revenuers could only talk to distillers or owners and no one else. So, distillers and owners conveniently evacuated the premises when they knew a revenuer was coming. This caused another change in the law that allowed revenuers to meet with anyone at the distillery. It seems the distillers of Great Britain and Ireland had turned tax avoidance into an art form.

Another issue those distillers dealt with was the lack of a good system of measures. Determining proof was a highly inaccurate and inefficient process; while the standards of weights and measures fluctuated with each monarch and each country. But when England, Ireland, Scotland, and Wales became one with the Acts of Union in 1800, there emerged a desire to solve these problems. They standardized a single measure for the gallon across the empire, and the search began for a single hydrometer that was cheap and easy enough that distillers across the Empire could use it.

When inventors were offered a chance to submit their hydrometers for consideration, Bartholomew Sikes won over the judging committee with his efficient, accurate, and cost-effective proof-measuring device. The Sikes Hydrometer would standardize the empire's proof measurements for almost 180 years.

The Commissioner of the Internal Revenue in the United States decided on a similar tactic. He needed an invention that could optimize the measurement of spirits while preventing any tampering. Inventors were to submit their solutions to the National Academy of Sciences,[212] recommendations would be made, and then the Secretary of the Treasury would select the best tool.

The winning machine was the brainchild of a New York inventor Isaac P. Tice.[213] He designed it as a closed piping system. The goal was to take accurate measurements while keeping any mischief at bay as the spirit went through a continuous distillation between two stills.[214] With the patent in hand already and the potential for fast deployment, the treasury gave his Tice Meter the nod. It would be required by everyone taking part in the distillation process.

Mandated in April 1867, the effect on Tennessee distillers was immediate. The *Fayetteville Observer* reported in late May that "there is not now, we are told, a distillery in operation in Lincoln county. The meter was the finishing stroke. Liquor making, owing to the high price of grain and the onerous burdens of government, has not been remunerative for some time. A sickly existence was maintained, hoping for an improvement, until the new order came, fixing an immediate additional expense of $600 to $1500. Then the last of the manufacturers 'handed in his check.'"[215] The entire Fourth District, including Lincoln County, would only bring in a paltry $12,337 in taxes on whisky for the entire year—a tenth of what Middle Tennessee's Fifth District was producing.[216]

That didn't mean distillers of old Robertson in the Fifth weren't facing the same challenges. The *Knoxville Daily Free Press* lamented, "The fame of Old Robertson County must not be suffered to go down forever - there was too much in a name for that; too many a good hard dollar could be made if the thing were properly managed."[217]

Some distillers decided the only way they could survive was to buy raw spirits from Cincinnati, redistill them, and then sell them as Old Robertson. It avoided the cost of the machinery, but was ruining the name of Old Robertson, while real distillers sat idle.

But a ray of hope appeared in the form of an enterprising young Robertson County distiller. Rather than complaining, Henry H. Kirk went about creating a closed-system distillery that would achieve the goals of the Tice Meter but at a fraction of the cost. The December 21 edition of *Republican Banner* offered distillers an early Christmas present and hope for a better new year when they gave Kirk's new rival system an enthusiastic thumbs up. "Mr. Kirk has erected a model distillery (on a small scale) on the premises of George H. Garrett, one mile north of Springfield. Mr. Garrett, an old and experienced distiller, has thoroughly tested its merits and pronounced it a success, beyond his most sanguine expectations. It is pronounced by all, indeed, who have seen it, a triumphant success and Mr. Kirk has filed an application for letters [of] patent." It appeared to have all the advantage necessary and covered the entire distilling process:

> *"The boiler surpasses any we have ever seen, serving to boil the beer the second time and throwing any quantity desired of the ponytail into the mash tubs, enabling the distiller to mash one tub of beer per minute. It's very quiet. It is harmless as it is in no danger of an overcharge of steam. It goes from the boiler it passes through the whole process of distillation without being handled or seen except as it goes through a glass tube where the distiller can weigh and test it without being able to obtain a drop - it being delivered into the cistern room under the lock of the assessor. It optimizes the whiskey produced and is of high quality. It takes up a small space, and can produce from one to twenty barrels per day."*[218]

All Kirk needed to do now was wait for the patent and the approval of the Commissioner of the Internal Revenue. His first customer was George Garrett, his partner in a distilling business. Dr. George E. Draughon was also ready to buy access to the patent when approved. While it didn't bring Robertson County distilling back online, it allowed them to dream of a quick resolution to their distilling shutdown.

By spring of 1868, the Tice Meter was killing off smaller distillers. Hundreds went underground and began producing illicit spirits. This combination was punishing the nation's coffers. But rather than ditching the Tice Meter and lowering the tax, the U.S. Congress and Internal Revenue went all stick and no carrot. They announced revisions to the law in April and some of them were quite chilling. The act required the forfeiture of a distillery and all of its equipment if a distiller attempted to defraud the government. It also punished revenue agents who, if convicted of fraud, would face fines over $1,000 and serve at least six months in prison. In addition, the Internal Revenue was removed from the Treasury Department and created as a separate independent entity that could hire and fire without consulting the president or Senate. Supervisors would be appointed for each judicial district in each state and they would report directly to the commissioner. And the tax would remain at $2 per gallon, while distillers paid tax on at least 80% of the registered capacity of the distillery, whether or not they distilled that amount.[219]

The outcry was immediate, forcing the government to retreat. To appease distillers, Congress introduced a bonding period, allowing deferment of tax payments for a period of up to one year. Suddenly there were benefits to letting a whisky age. Brandy distillers caught a break and were excluded from any of the strenuous rules faced by distillers of other spirits, including the Tice Meter. And finally, the dreaded tax dropped to a more manageable 50 cents per gallon from $2.

While some of these changes were positive, it didn't soothe the frustration distillers were feeling over the complexity of the law. The bill, called the "Act Imposing Taxes on Distilled Spirits and Tobacco, and for Other Purposes," required an accountant, scientist, and attorney to understand it all. And the Tice Meter requirement was still in force.[220] The Congress and the Internal Revenue's tunnel vision on their own needs and ignorance of those they were trying to control was about to lead to some serious trouble.

The Distiller's Revolt

In the modern world, the words "Tennessee" and "moonshine" go together like a hand in glove. But before 1865, any references to moonshine in the Volunteer

State related to the rays from the white and gray orb in the sky—not to distilled spirits.

It's not that the term "moonshine" didn't exist. It did. But just not on this side of the Atlantic Ocean. When the British parliament instituted the excise tax in 17th-century Scotland and distillers took to the hills to avoid the tax, the stories of illicit distilling by the light of the moon took on a defiant and romantic character. And so, the moonshiner was born.

It's a term that any distiller of Scottish or Irish heritage might have been aware of. But with only two short periods of whisky taxation in American history, the concept of American moonshine didn't have time to exist.

This all changed when Lincoln's excise tax went from temporary to permanent. Farmers who distilled as a way of life were suddenly being asked by Uncle Sam to fork over details of their distilleries, follow their rules, and pay them for the privilege. It wasn't the way of the world they were familiar with, and it was about to make a once-peaceful countryside a lot more dangerous.

A rebellion was happening in the hills around Tazewell in Claiborne County, led by a man named Blackston Williams.

It seemed like the least likely of places for such misadventures. Claiborne County was a sleepy backwater if ever there was one. Located ten miles south of the line where Kentucky and Virginia meet Tennessee, it seemed perfectly isolated from trouble. In fact, before the war, you could count the news events that occurred in the county on one hand.

The old timers remembered when Bishop Asbury came to preach temperance on the courthouse steps in 1802. The only other incident of note happened in 1823 when old Judge Scott took a break from hearing the grand larceny case of James Martin. Back in his chambers, the judge got a little too enthusiastic with the hard cider and almost forgot the time. When he got back out to the bench and began reading his decision, the prosecution pointed to the defense's lack of a client. Martin had apparently grown tired of waiting and bolted for the door.[221]

But the war changed things in the area. Fiercely loyal Americans, most Claiborne residents had no intention of joining the Confederates, even after the state voted to succeed. And this loyalty to the North drew the attention of the Confederates who turned Tazewell into a battleground. They repelled the few Federal troops that were protecting the town, resulting in an occupation by Confederate soldiers. When a suspicious fire broke out, burning most of the town, it inflamed anti-Confederate sentiments.[222]

After General Sherman's Union troops took control of Knoxville after a late 1863 siege, there was a feeling life might get back to normal. The Unionist newspaper run by William "Parson" Brownlow was back up and nearby Greene County resident Andrew Johnson was Vice President of the United States. It felt like the old world was returning.

But Claiborne's proximity to Virginia after the war brought trouble to the area as rebel sympathizers continued to stir up violence. At one point, thirty citizens sent a petition to Governor Brownlow asking for him to send troops to the area to protect "radical Republicans" and Black citizens from attacks.

It was a county caught in a no-win situation. Then the excise law came in and complicated matters even more. Locals couldn't understand how their loyalty was being forsaken by revenuers, who were asking them to pay taxes and fees for making a little alcohol for themselves and their friends. Patriots quickly turned into outlaws.

It didn't take long for little Tazewell to be featured in the *New York Herald*. The headline read, "There is a whisky rebellion in East Tennessee."[223]

It seems Blackston Williams didn't take too kindly to the way he and his neighbors were being treated by revenue officers. He let his displeasure be known by forming a gang of distillers and outlaws known as "The League of Claiborne County." When rumors suggested revenuers were coming, the men would send word out through the hills and neighbors with shotguns and rifles would come out of the woods to help another neighbor scare off an assessor.

Terrified revenue men refused to go about their task without an armed force at the ready. The United States Army supplied Fifth United States Cavalry Company B under the command of Lieutenant J. S. Payne. But if the revenue men thought the cavalry was going to bother the men of The League, they were in for a rude dose of reality.

While on the road to Tazewell from Knoxville, The League ambushed forty cavalrymen and horses.[224] During the melee, Blackston Williams leveled a gun at Deputy Marshal Lusk, yet did not fire. But in the fire fight two of Payne's soldiers were killed. Frustrated and defeated, the troops went back to Knoxville to lick their wounds and plan a new strategy.

On their second ride up to Tazewell, Lieutenant Payne decided they needed to cut off the head of the snake. He befriended two men who promised to guide the soldiers to Williams' camp. After several wasted hours, Payne realized these men were leading them on a wild goose chase. But then someone caught the smell of cooking mash in the air. They found a stillhouse and Blackston Williams was caught in the act of making corn whisky. They arrested him, and his stills and equipment were destroyed. Soldiers delighted in dumping three barrels of low wines. The men stood guard over Williams while scouts conducted a search for other members of his rebellion.

As would be the case with many captured distillers, sympathetic neighbors offered to post bond for Blackston Williams, but Deputy Marshall Lusk kept him under armed guard until the court could hear his case in the morning.[225]

The League would continue to cause trouble for months, even while Blackston was awaiting trial. But leadership was lacking and, most times, deputies met little to no resistance. It would be a while before Tazewell would return to normal––all thanks to Mr. Lincoln's excise.

Chapter 13

THE HEARTBEAT OF OLD LINCOLN

Those Damn Yankees

For the residents of Lincoln County, losing the War for Southern Independence was a bitter pill to swallow. Not only had sons and fathers gone off to fight for a lost cause, they returned home to hear of the Federal troops' occupation and the pillaging of their farms. Worse yet, some of those Union troops remained. As an additional frustration, they were having to pay workers they once considered their property.

But none of these frustrations could stop the return of log still sour mash distilling. Veterans of the craft went right back to work, including East Mulberry Creek's G.W. Alexander, Lynchburg's Alfred Eaton, and Fayetteville's Henry Kelso. And some young upstarts were ready to get in on the tradition as well. These included William Tolley's sons Benjamin, John Dean, and William Polk, along with Alfred Eaton's son Jack. Two of the more ambitious new distillers in Lincoln County were John T. Motlow and former Confederate colonel John Mason Hughes.

But just as John T. Motlow got his distillery up and running, circumstances changed. Having at first avoided the 4th and 5th districts, Federal revenuers began making the rounds there in 1867. Suddenly, things became real for Lincoln County's distillers. The $2 per gallon tax was tough enough, but the government also wanted a complete overhaul of equipment. While Robertson's larger distilleries could absorb some of the extra cost of new equipment and taxes, the small log still distillers of Lincoln County were being eaten alive. Distillers blamed a lobby of Yankee distillers they thought were trying to kill off Tennessee whisky so they could open markets to their Cincinnati busthead.[226]

One of the biggest items bearing down on Tennessee and Kentucky distillers was the Tice Meter requirement. An inexpensive item to produce, distillers were being asked to pay from $600 to $1500 to purchase it. They saw it as an advantage for busthead producers and a scam perpetrated on sour mash distillers. The only thing that kept the meter from being the root cause of a shutdown in 1867 was that it wasn't yet ready for distribution. Tennessee distillers hoped to use this delay to lobby for its removal from the regulations before they had to purchase it. In December, a subcommittee of the House Ways and Means Committee admitted after several interviews that the Tice Meter would "avail nothing in the matter of preventing fraud in the manufacture of whisky."[227] Yet the findings of the committee and the complaints of distillers did nothing to kill the requirement.

New distillers gained an advantage in this regulated world. John T. Motlow built his distillery with many of the new requirements already in mind. By 1868, he was pumping out around five hundred gallons of whisky a month. He was a large part of why Lincoln County's tax revenues increased from $12,337 in 1867 to $44,890 in 1868.[228] But this was still far short of Lincoln County's total distilling capacity.

In reality, the government was favoring the large distillery over the small distillery. The proof was in the bloated set of regulations they introduced in the Congressional act of July 20, 1868.[229]

The regulation that hurt Lincoln distillers the most was the closed-piping system that prohibited the use of open tubs. Most of Lincoln's distillers were log still distillers. The reason they used the log still wasn't just because of tradition, they were saving on the cost of the still. So most, if not all, log still distillers had only one still. An open tub was to allow them to double distill.

The first run results in singlings, also known as low wines, that are lower in alcohol and less pure. A distiller stores the liquid in open tubs before they distill it a second time in the same still. Congress and the commissioner saw this as counter to the closed system because it allowed distillers to access the singlings during the process. So in October 1868, Commissioner Harland decided to punish this action. He ruled that not only would the final whisky, known as high wines, be taxed, singlings would be taxed separately. In other words, sour mash distillers were being double taxed, simply because they were using a single still and open tubs.[230]

Again, the Cincinnati distillers and their one-time distilled "rifle" whisky were pointed to as the villains. *Republican Banner* noted:

> *"The decisions seem to be specifically leveled at the distillers of Tennessee and Kentucky, who are the only ones who honestly pay the tax, and from whom the bulk of the revenue derived from the excise is collected. All ready the distilleries of this State have been practically suspended, under the influence of pending legislations and decisions, for three or four months. Should this decision be declared to control permanently the operations of distilleries, every manufacturer of whisky in Tennessee would be ruined. The decision is arbitrary and stupid upon its face, being wholly unwarranted by the law, and absurd in its very terms."*[231]

In December, Commissioner Rollins attempted to clarify, saying the Harland ruling did not mean the act of double distilling was being punished. Instead, distillers need only retool their distillery to free themselves of open tubs of low wines by setting up the piping system.[232] The commissioner was obviously missing the point. Not only was retooling expensive, for many this required the purchase of a second still, along with all the closed piping equipment and the Tice Meter. And it wasn't just the extra cost. Many of these distillers had been shut down for a year. Where were they going to get the funds to retool?

Knoxville Press and Messenger made it clear why people's favorite whiskies were not being produced.

> "The distiller is first required to give heavy bonds that he will fulfill all the requirements of the law, and the law makes his distillery and property a forfeit to the government in case he should violate any one of the conditions; then it taxes him on the supposed capacity, and makes him pay a tax whether he makes the amount of whisky or not; then it taxes him $2 a day for something else; then $4 per barrel for another something; then 50 cents per gallon for the main tax; then it provides him a guager, whom he must pay, whose duty it is to stamp the barrels; then a storekeeper, whom he must pay, to take charge of the whisky, then he must pay a Tice meter to measure it, and at least - stamped, branded, marked and guaged - it is shipped into market under charge of the government. Hedged around with all these taxes and restrictions, it is not to be wondered at that there are many violations of the revenue laws, both voluntary and involuntary."[233]

To show the absurdity of the law, three of the area's large distilleries, Julius T. Wolff in Shelbyville, G. W. Alexander in East Mulberry, and John T. Motlow in Lynchburg, all had to pay $600 a month in accumulated per diem tax (the equivalent of $1,300 today) whether or not they distilled a drop of spirits. Rather than hemorrhage money, the smaller distilleries simply gave up their licenses and shut down.

Even though the new law dropped the per gallon fee from $2.00 to $0.50, running a distillery was a fiscal nightmare that left distillers wondering whether it could get any worse?

Then, as if on cue, in March 1870, the Internal Revenue set technical restrictions on fermentation for distillers. This was an additional knife to the chest for Lincoln County distillers and many of the smaller sour mash distillers who were still fermenting using the natural process. The rule limited fermentation to three days, making the production of traditional sour mash, which needed five days, illegal.[234] Lincoln County distillers protested, saying the federal government was destroying the quality of whisky and purposefully trying to put all Lincoln County distillers out of business.

The results in lost revenue were seen almost immediately. In 1870, the government collected $36,189 in taxes from the 4th District.[235] Just one year later, revenues dropped to a meager $7,258.[236] By contrast, in 1874, the 4th District brought in $106,407 in revenue under more sensible laws.[237] The federal government really was pushing Lincoln County whisky to the brink of extinction. And it was hurting Lincoln County's economy as well. The *Fayetteville Observer* noted, "we have not observed any drunken men on the street for some time."[238] It was speculated that tight money thanks to the down whisky industry might be making the purchase of whisky tough.

During these years of uncertainty many of Lincoln County's old timers either passed away or gave up. Meanwhile, a crop of new distillers made plans to get going when all was settled. In 1868, Ben Tolley and Colonel Hughes partnered in a distilling operation built on leased land, owned by Dan and William Call.[239] But Tolley & Hughes would close within a year. Undaunted, Colonel Hughes started a second distillery in 1869 with Alfred Eaton's son, Jack. But Hughes & Eaton would share a similar fate as Colonel Hughes went solo. The distilling team of Holt, Hiles, & Berry opened a distilling operation that same year on land purchased from Alfred Eaton.[240] It is believed this is the site of the Cave Spring Hollow where legend incorrectly suggests Alfred Eaton invented the charcoal mellowing process.

The distillers of Lincoln County continued to struggle along until June 1872, when Congress finally got the message and simplified the excise laws and reduced costs. They abolished the per diem, barrel tax, gauger's fees, and storekeeper's salaries. The gaugers and storekeepers would now be paid by the government. To cover salaries and the lost revenue from the myriad of extra fees, they raised the per gallon charge from 50 cents to 70 cents.[241] But distillers didn't mind. Especially since the Tice Meter was removed from the regulations. It was referred to as a swindle that made its inventor rich at the expense of distillers.[242] Unfortunately, distillers who were forced to buy it couldn't get their money back.[243]

It's hard to believe, but a large proportion of Tennessee's legal distilleries had shut down for long lengths of time between 1868 and 1872; a December 1871 report showed only 22 of 48 whisky distilleries in the state in operation.[244] Names had come and gone as a result of the restrictions, and thousands and thousands of dollars of revenue for the distillers and the community had been lost.

But while most industries would have stepped quietly into their graves, the 4th District was about to rise like Lazarus and come back stronger than ever.

Assembling the Dream Team

While the tax revenues don't show it, 1873 was a banner year for whisky in the 4th District. Though the government only collected $30,309, this was the era when whisky could sit in a bonded warehouse for a year with no taxes paid.[245] The real fruits of the previous year were shown in 1874, when revenues topped $100,000.

But Lincoln County was no longer the star of the 4th District. In 1871, the state merged the eastern part of the county into the newly created Moore County. This included much of East Fork of Mulberry Creek and the town of Lynchburg. With new distilleries like Holt, Hiles & Berry, Hughes & Co., Tolley & Call, and Tolley & Eaton in Lynchburg, the new county was producing almost fifty barrels of whisky a day and still was unable to keep up with demand.[246]

But it seems not everybody was happy about all of this growth. In May of '73, an arsonist started a blaze that ripped through the Tolley & Call distillery, destroying 48 barrels of whisky, the warehouse, and the entire works. It was estimated to be a $10,000 loss (or a quarter of a million dollars in today's money), and it looked like the end for Ben Tolley and Dan Call, as there was no insurance on the distilling operation.[247] To survive, they welcomed an injection of money from Jack Eaton, who came on as a partner. These funds, along with the drive and determination of Dan Call, helped save the firm.

Daniel Houston Call was born on the family farm at Louse Creek in May 1836, shortly after the family moved from North Carolina. Dan's father, Joseph, died when Dan was just seven years of age. This meant Dan had to grow up in a hurry. He and his older brother William took care of the farm while their mother Rebecca raised her newborn baby Joseph and three-year-old daughter Sarah. It didn't take long for Rebecca to remarry and Dan had to adapt to a revolving door of step-fathers.[248] At twenty, he married Mary Jane Nelson, and the two made a home for themselves on Louse Creek.

For Dan, the spirit of the Lord reached him at an early age, inspiring him to become a lay preacher, centered in the Lutheran faith. When the war came, he picked up a gun and joined the Confederate cause. Post war, he came back home to Mary Jane, and tradition has it, they opened a little country store where Mary worked, while Dan preached and took care of the farm.

His entry into the world of distilling came by chance. In March 1869, he and his brother William leased land to Hughes & Tolley for their new distillery. But when Colonel Hughes left Ben Tolley holding the bag, Dan stepped into the partnership.

No official details exist about the Tolley & Call distillery, but it is a good bet the man manning the stills was a formerly enslaved man named Nathan Green. Known as "Nearest" or "Uncle Nearest," Dan Call touted him as the "best whiskey maker I know of."[249] Married to Harriet Flack while enslaved, the couple had four children by the time Nearest was working for Tolley & Call. He lived a simple life as a father, farmer, and a distiller-for-hire.[250] As a respected Lincoln County distiller, it's a good bet Nearest was a master at working the log stills, running five-day sour mash fermentations, and leaching whisky.

It's also a good bet that the distilleries of Hughes & Tolley and Tolley & Call had another secret weapon in their arsenal. A 5'2" firecracker of a salesman named Jasper Newton Daniel. At least, that's what his parents Calaway and Lucinda Daniel named him––everyone else knew him as Jack.

The Salesman

When it comes to Tennessee whisky legends, no name is better known than that of Jack Daniel. Yet most of his life is so wrapped up in adventure, style, marketing, and lore, that it's hard to know how to separate fact from fiction. But maybe this was the way he wanted it.

Jack was a natural-born salesman with a real knack for getting people excited about whatever it was he was selling. If a few tall tales fell in place, all the better. In fact, that was really becoming the marketing style of the era. The bigger the story, the more people remembered your whisky.

Born to Calaway and Lucinda Daniel in August 1849,[251] Jack came into a world filled with great promise. He had loving parents, nine brothers and sisters, his grandmother Bettie to get him out of trouble, and a huge plantation to roam around on. Even chores would be light, since his father had almost two dozen enslaved workers to handle the farm.

But things would not be that easy for little Jack. He never got to know his mother, Lucinda, who died of typhoid fever five months after he was born.[252] His father would quickly remarry. His new bride was Matilda Vanzant, another widower, who had children of her own. Strong willed, her presence around the home caused Jack's grandmother Bettie to move back to Franklin County with his Auntie Anne.

Being the youngest of ten and now dealing with new stepsisters to boot, little Jackie Boy felt lost in the shuffle. More than anything, he wanted to be noticed among the pack, so he started looking beyond the plantation for people who would appreciate him.

The first family he connected to were his next-door neighbors, the Waggoners. Muhulda had been a great friend to the Daniel family when her friend Lucinda died and she became an important part of little Jack's life. And her husband Felix was like a godfather to Jack, keeping his eye out for the boy throughout his youth.

It was at Felix's house that Jack met Dan Call, just after the lay preacher and his wife Mary Jane had their first child. Jack and Dan, who were around six years apart in age, became like brothers. The two could sympathize over being raised with stepparents in the house. The other important person Jack met was his best friend William Riley "Button" Waggoner. Like Dan, Button was a few years older than Jack, but then, Jack always enjoyed punching above his weight.

Over the next few years, life fell into a steady and comfortable pattern for Jack. After finishing his chores at home, he'd be off to scheme with Button or he'd offer an extra set of hands to the Calls and Waggoners.

But Jack's world quickly unraveled when the state of Tennessee voted to secede. Because of its heavy use of enslaved labor, Lincoln County stood firmly with the Confederacy. Jack's brothers Lemuel and Wiley signed to fight for the cause almost immediately, as did Button Waggoner.

The one surprise southern enlistment was Dan Call. As a Lutheran, his faith ran counter to those around him. Lutherans openly baptized the enslaved and, in the North, they were supporters of the abolitionist movement. But in the upper regions of the South, Lutherans tried to fit in with their community. So while few actively took part in the practice, they weren't always publically vocal against it.

The war years were not kind to Jack and his family. While preparing for the Battle of Chattanooga, his brother Lemuel, living in poor conditions, took ill and passed away. Back in Lincoln County, Federal troops raided their plantation, causing widespread damage. Before the war, Jack spent a good amount of time over at the Calls, but during the war the presence of soldiers in the area made it harder to travel. So Jack spent more time at home helping his favorite sister, Finetta, take care of their stepsisters Sena and Belle Thada. All the trouble and strife on the farm wore away at Calaway Daniel and on January 21, 1864 he died from pneumonia. Meanwhile Jack's older brothers James and Robert were off in Texas and Wiley Daniel was fighting off Sherman's troops in East Tennessee. Jack had suddenly become the man of the house.

The next few years were filled with legal issues for the remaining Daniel family. After Calaway's death, Matilda sold his possessions at auction, fearing she might lose the property to theft while the Lincoln County courthouse remained under the control of Union soldiers.[253] The one thing she couldn't get possession of was Calaway's land. It wasn't until six months after the war ended that she finally was granted enough money for a year's supply of food to feed the family. She finally won ownership of the property in November 1865;[254] two months later, she married Wilson Hinkle.[255]

To say life was awkward living with two stepparents was an understatement. And for Jack and his siblings, it was worse, because the children of Calaway went into a legal battle with their stepmother.

While oral tradition suggests that this was the moment Jack Daniel partnered with Dan Call in a distilling operation, there are no records to prove it. Instead, the 1866 date is more likely when Jack entered the distilling world as a salesman. His energy, gift of gab, and friendly nature could have charmed anyone in their right mind. Finding distillers willing to let him peddle their spirits wasn't hard to do in Lincoln County. Not only was his family friendly with the Eatons, his friend Button Waggoner was an up and comer in the Lynchburg business community. It's possible the stories of Jack and Button heading down to Huntsville, Alabama, to peddle whisky, date to this time. It wouldn't have been as deadly a time to travel and there were plenty of Federal troops in Huntsville to sell whisky to, thanks to Reconstruction.

Eventually, Jack would get free of his stepparents. With the help of his brother Wiley, William Tolley, and Felix Waggoner, they posted $3,000 as a guarantee and Felix became Jack's legal guardian on March 2, 1868.[256]

The doorway was now fully open for Jack to move wherever he liked and to make the whisky business his life. Jack moved in with his sister Finetta, or Nettie as he called her, and her husband Felix "Stump" Motlow. Jack was a great help around the house as the couple was celebrating the arrival of their first son, Lemuel.[257] Named after the brother Nettie and Jack lost during the war, little Lem was a firecracker himself. With the uncertainty around the family estate, it gave Jack a chance to bond with his little nephew. It also opened the door to him working for the newly established Hughes & Tolley distillery on property owned by Dan and William Call.

To improve his salescraft, and because he had an interest in running his own distillery some day, Jack learned all he could from Nearest Green. He knew that to make a great whisky he had to capture the magic of what made Lincoln County whisky special. If he had any money, he might have tried to step into the Tolley & Call business after a fire took it down in March 1873. But his inheritance would remain tied up for a few more months. When the case was finally settled, he bided his time, waiting for his next opportunity.

Then in March 1875, Lynchburg was hit with a powerful storm that caused both flooding and damaging, widespread hail. The East Fork of Mulberry Creek had become a river with hogs, sheep, and cattle washing downstream. Egg-sized hail pelted chickens, ducks, and geese to death. Colonel Hughes' new distillery also fell victim, washed some 300 ft away from its original foundation. Not only did Hughes lose his own whisky, some of the 115 barrels that were lost belonged to Tolley & Eaton. The Carriger Distillery on West Mulberry Creek was another victim, being totally washed away.[258] The local paper tried to bring levity to the situation, asking, "are the elements going into the temperance business too?"[259]

The year had been a stressful one for the Tolleys and Eatons and it was decided they should consolidate their holdings. This left Dan Call alone, looking for a new business partner. And who better to get an exclusive on than the area's best salesman, who finally had some money and freedom to invest? On November 27, 1875, a legacy was born on Dan Call's farm along the banks of Louse Creek.[260]

But before Uncle Nearest could distill the first drop of whisky, a certain government regulation, established in 1868, had to be followed. Outside the stillhouse door, the new owners were required to paint two bits of information: the name of the distillery and its Federal registration number. There in black were the words Daniel & Call and below the names, Registered Distillery #7.[261]

Death of the Old 4th

As the nation celebrated its centennial anniversary in 1876, distillers in Tennessee's 4th District were also in a festive mood. After war, ever-evolving excise tax rules, a crippling shutdown, arguments over production techniques, fire, hail, and floods, things seemed to be calming down. The district's four biggest distilleries—Hughes & Co., Tolley & Eaton, Hiles & Berry, and Daniel & Call—were experiencing a great demand for what they still referred to as Old Lincoln, even though it was mostly produced in Moore County.

But in October of that year, bad news came out of Washington once again. Green Raum, the Commissioner of the Internal Revenue, dissolved the 4th District and folded it into the 5th. It wasn't an action leveled just at this one district—Raum was under a mandate to reduce costs and having too many unnecessary districts created an expensive bureaucracy.

What Raum didn't understand was the rivalry and war of words boiling up between the makers of Old Lincoln in the 4th District and the makers of Old Robertson in the 5th. For Lincoln County distillers, the government might as well have put them in the same district as Bourbon County, Kentucky. These Robertson County distillers, in the minds of Lincoln County sour mash distillers, were sweet mash distillers who took shortcuts by adding foreign materials to their mash. To them, Lincoln County was still the genuine natural article. The fear was that Lincoln County would be swallowed alive in the 5th District while their reputation was sullied.

After ruminating over what to do next, an emergency meeting of old 4th District sour mash distillers was called. The meeting took place at Tolley & Eaton Hall on March 23, 1877, and included many of the area's top distillers.

The meeting was called to order by the chair Captain C. H. Bean of distillery #227 on a motion by John T. Motlow of distillery #4. The distillers put together a committee to draft a letter to Commissioner Raum, setting forth grievances, dangers to their businesses, and suggestions for relief.

The committee included John T. Motlow, John Eaton of Tolley & Eaton #203, J. S. McClure of distillery #22, Joel Pitts of Pitts, Parks, & Brady #209, and J. M. Stone. The letter began:

> *"Hon. Green B. Raum - Distillers of the late old 4th Collection District of this State but now consolidated into the 5th effective Oct 1, 1876. We are proprietors of small distilleries operated entirely*

by hand and known as *Sour Mash Log Distilleries whose capacity for producing spirits is estimated upon a grain basis from eight to fifty-one bushels per day, the average capacity of about 30 gallons per day, - want to provide some facts. The consolidation is not good for the government's interests and fatal to ours."*

Then they gave their list of complaints:

"Tax stamps that used to come in 12 to 48 hours without exception are now coming in over 72 hours later, often in not less than 2 to 6 weeks - the district is too big. Our customers are frustrated and going elsewhere. Surveys are coming back late, causing us to miss valuable time during the season and sometimes the yields are changed without notice from the original survey of 2 ½ gallons per bushel to 3 gallons, rendering resumption impossible, as no Sour Mash Distillery in the old Fourth District of Tennessee has ever yet been able to produce that amount of 80 percent of it for any considerable period, even under the most favorable conditions. It is our assumption the intention is to crush out entirely the Sour Mash business, and we now earnestly protest against this and appeal to you, not permit this discrimination in favor of capital and against us, who have not the capital to build costly Distilleries. This only enriches the Sweet Mash Distilleries of the Fifth District of Tennessee, who are thus enriched at our expense. We want a split so Sweet and Sour Mash distilleries are not in direct competition. We desire to pay Tax on all spirits we produce and also to produce as much as possible of pure spirits from the grain used: but as we, by the Sour Mash process, use no foreign substance or ingredient, but ferment by natural process alone, we cannot compete with the Sweet Mash Distilleries surveyed at only ½ gallon more per bushel. Our process of fermentation depends entirely on the temperature of the atmosphere and as there are no two days in the year the same tem-

*perature, we earnestly protest that to fix absolutely and arbitrarily the fermenting period, no more, no x than a given number of hours is unjust to us and detrimental to the best interests of the Government. Our interest being identical with that of the Government, we with confidence ask you to please fix the maximum period 72 hours or let us do so at present, but let us distill our beer at any time within said period, the fermenters to remain empty the remainder of it, say 24 hours or more at our option. Thus we would be enable to use our best beer when ripe, producing the most and best spirits from the grain possible by our process. Since the change, we've seen a high demand for our Sour Mash, but not over one third the quantity was produced as the same five months last year, by which the Government has lost from $50k to $150k in five months, and we too have lost in proportion during that time which has blighted our present and future prospect. We would further respectfully represent that three days from commencing business to first producing spirits in wholly inadequate to the sour mash plan, and when you remember that in the rulings we are allowed 72 hours for fermentation you well readily see it. Therefore we respectfully ask that you so rule as to allow five days, which you are hereby assured is no more than is actually necessary to produce the best results."*262

It was signed by the officers of the Sour Mash Distillers' Association of the Old Fourth District. They appointed two members of the organization to carry the letter to Washington, D.C. A follow-up meeting was scheduled for March 31 to hear the results of the meeting. The delegates apparently met with Raum, but no changes were made. From this point on, the 4th District was no more.

Conspicuously absent from the proceedings were Daniel & Call of the old #7 distillery, which had its number changed to #16 with the district change.

Perhaps Dan was becoming too interested in building his new church. Or maybe he was at home with Mary Jane, who wasn't too pleased with him being in the whisky business. Whatever the reason, he agreed to turn over the distillery to Jack. On October 1, 1877, the 28-year-old salesman signed a lease to continue using Dan Call's stillhouse and, with Uncle Nearest manning the stills, the Jack Daniel Distillery was born.[263]

Meanwhile, times were changing with Lynchburg distillers as well. Possibly worried about the new competition brought on by the folding of the 4th District into the 5th, Tolley & Eaton invested money in building a large steam distillery at County Line. But not everything went smoothly. Apparently, mistakes were made in the equipment's setup and several runs of whisky were ruined. When the assessor presented them with a bill for the bad batches, they successfully lobbied Congress to release them from the taxes due.[264]

In 1879, Kentucky congressman John G. Carlisle did the whisky industry a great favor when he introduced a bill increasing the bonding period from one to three years. The Carlisle Allowance, as it would come to be known, gave distillers the ability to mellow their whiskies longer in barrels, giving their whiskies a chance to compete with the quality of Tennessee's short-aged charcoal-mellowed whisky. It meant the larger distilleries would no longer have a barn with a single-level warehouse. Carlisle had introduced the era of multi-level warehouses.

By 1883, it appeared all the fears of the loss of the 4th District were for naught. The combined 5th District was a powerhouse and members of the old 4th were holding their own. It's true they would never compete directly with Old Robertson's three biggest players, who held a combined 700,570 gallons of whisky in their warehouses, but the Lincoln and Moore County distillers were doing quite well for themselves. Tolley & Eaton's steam distillery was fourth largest at 67,275 gallons. Joel G. Pitts, who used a Nashville distributor, was the sixth largest with 52,762 gallons. And Jack Daniel was the eighth largest at 34,579 gallons.[265]

Now the most eligible bachelor in Lynchburg, Jack upped his image. He bought himself a high-rolled planter's hat, frock coat, fawn vest, fancy linen shirt, and broad bow tie, establishing his trademark look. He was also following in his father Calaway's shoes by acquiring land. On one plot, he topped it with a marvelous estate. In just ten years, he went from living with his sister Finetta to having his sister Bette and her husband living with him.

But, seeing the growth of Tolley & Eaton, Jack knew he had to up his game. With his lease term up with Dan Call, he decided it was time to find a distilling property of his own. He needed a place to spread his wings, build warehouses, and increase his output.

The best property in town for making whisky was just east of Lynchburg. It was the site of the old Hiles & Berry distillery. After the duo split up, the old distilling operation lay dormant, waiting for a new suiter. On June 14, 1884, Jack paid $2,180.40 for the 142 acre tract that included the legendary Cave Spring Hollow. He erected a new brick distillery and simple wooden office, with the sign outside reading Jack Daniel Distillery #514. Jack had finally found a permanent home.[266]

Chapter 14

AGAINST ALL ODDS

Johann Phillip's Dream

The *Helena Sloman* was a modern marvel. In only the 12th year of transatlantic steamship voyages, *Sloman* had ditched the old paddle wheel for a highly efficient screw propeller––soon to become the standard of the industry. Finally, travelers were no longer at the mercy of the wind and waves. Seafaring was evolving, and this ship was a shining example of that progress.

During her first two journeys, *Helena Sloman* hauled over three hundred European immigrants to America. On her maiden voyage, she brought fifty-three-year-old Heinrich Engelhard Steinweg and his wife and seven children to New York from Germany. Fourteen years after his arrival, he would anglicize his last name and pin it to his thriving piano business: Steinway.

On *Sloman*'s third journey, Johann Phillip Nelson, a 49-year-old candle- and soap maker, booked passage in the steerage compartment for his family. His dream was to have his five children find similar success to Steinway on American shores.

The ship was under the command of Captain Paul Nickels Paulson, a seasoned officer from the vessel's home port of Hamburg, Germany. On board were 36 crew members, 144 passengers, 100 tons of iron, and 150 tons of French and German merchandise destined for New York Harbor. After leaving the German port, the ship stopped at Southampton, England, before heading into the North Atlantic.

Three weeks into the trip, the passengers had a reason to be thankful for Captain Paulson's steady hand at the wheel. The seas had become a boisterous affair, with wind, rain, and heavy storms setting the passengers on edge.

But the rough seas shouldn't have been a surprise. Britain and the North Atlantic had already been dealing with unseasonably cold weather for a couple of months. A violent gale in early October had wreaked havoc, driving boats ashore and causing wind damage as far away as the Scottish Highlands.

The first break in the weather came on a Tuesday in late November, when the seas calmed. But as nighttime drew up under a blanket of clouds, the ship rocked aggressively, teasing danger. The next four hours were intense as a fearful gale grew up out of the North Northwest. Then at 11 p.m. a fierce rogue wave crashed with intense violence against the stern and starboard quarter of the ship, sweeping waves of ocean water across the deck. The cabins flooded with water, and the ship quivered from stem to stern. Sleep for the passengers and crew was impossible as the ship creaked and moaned all night. Relentless waves pushed and tossed the vessel from side to side.

As the morning light revealed gray, overcast skies, and a calmer wind, passengers breathed a sigh of relief. But as the day wore on, Captain Paulson noticed the crewman at the helm seemed uneasy. He asked if something was wrong, but the seaman said all seemed fine. Unsatisfied with the response, he took the wheel and turned it 360 degrees. To his dismay, the ship wasn't responding.

Looking over the stern, he saw the rudder had parted from the ship and was tangled and dangling in chains. The massive wave that had struck the ship the night before had apparently done more damage than he expected. This would require all hands on deck... including the passengers. The rudder weighed at least four tons and would take every ounce of energy to rescue. They set the chains on a pulley and endeavored to lift the rudder, but its weight was too great. Both chains snapped, and the rudder sank quickly beneath the waves to the bottom of the icy North Atlantic. Then the First Engineer reported the engine was jerking so violently, he feared the wave had compromised the propeller as well. Nighttime was falling, so the captain ordered it shut off until they could inspect it the next morning.

The next day, the crew lowered lifeboats into the water to inspect the damage. The news was grave. Not only had they lost the rudder, but apparently it had ripped about 12 ft off the stern and part of the keel from the boat. Keeping the boat stabilized in another storm would be difficult and, to make matters worse, she was taking on water.

They immediately began pumping water out of the boat and attempted to seal the cracks. And, as if the crew and passengers weren't already on edge, another hurricane-like storm battered and tossed the ship for the next thirty-six hours. The mizen sail and stabilizing trysail were ripped and torn away from the ship. With no rudder or propeller, and the sails in tatters, things were looking pretty desperate.

As the storm subsided on Saturday morning, they saw a smaller sail-powered ship about ten miles away. They sent distress signals, but to no avail. But they weren't far off from the coast of Nova Scotia. Surely another ship would spot them.

They put up with more storms, including rain, sleet, and snow, for the next couple of days. Some nine days after the disastrous rogue wave had dismantled their ship, they spotted another vessel off the mast-head. Once again, the *Helena Sloman* sent distress signals, this time in both German and English, just to make sure. Times were getting desperate. The ship was taking on an inch of water per hour.

To everyone's great relief, the other ship responded. It was an American packet ship, the *Devonshire*, under the command of Captain Henry R. Hovey. Captain Paulson had his men prepare a lifeboat so emissaries could give the captain of the *Devonshire* the desperate news.

Learning of the ship's condition, Captain Hovey called on his best men to help transfer all the passengers and crew from the wounded ship to the *Devonshire*. But the aggressive waves weren't playing fair and wreaked havoc on the little lifeboats. There was great relief as each lifeboat unloaded her passengers.

It was a joyful moment when Johann Phillip Nelson saw his entire family standing safely aboard the *Devonshire*. His lifeboat was just about to touch the water when everything went wrong. The force of the waves grabbed the little boat and, before the passengers realized what was happening, it slid under and struck the steamer's bow. The force of the blow made it pitch and roll over, tossing all eleven of its inhabitants helplessly into the water. Two passengers quickly grabbed onto the lifeboat. Crewmen from the *Sloman* reacted quickly and threw a rope over the side, but only one person grabbed hold.

For Johann Phillip, he had unknowingly sealed his fate before the ship ever left Germany. After receiving proceeds for the sale of his home and business, he had converted it all into gold coins. Then he had a coat tailored with hidden pockets inside to carry his gold coins. The weight of the extra-heavy coat and coins was too much. With his horrified family watching from the deck of the *Devonshire*, Johann and eight other souls slipped beneath the waves. In an instant, the Nelson family patriarch and the family's fortune sank to the bottom of the cruel North Atlantic.[267]

Carrying On

For 15-year-old Carl Diedrich Wilhelm Nelson, there was little time to recover from his father's sudden and tragic death. As the oldest boy, he had to stand up and take his father's place. And without a penny to their names, times were desperate for the Nelsons when they reached New York City.

As luck would have it, Carl, who Americanized his name to Charles, found work in his father's trade as a candle- and soap maker Hayes & Schultz.[268] His mother took care of the family while he brought home meager wages. The day to day became a struggle for survival. In the 1850s, New York had grown to over half a million people, most of whom were immigrants. There wasn't anywhere to breathe. It was time to look beyond the city's borders.

Several of Charles' German friends on the Lower East Side talked of moving west to Cincinnati. Located on the Ohio River, it was the sixth-largest city in the United States, but only one-fifth the population of New York. With a larger proportion of German immigrants living there, it seemed like the perfect place to settle. So, the Nelsons moved west.

The first five years in the city were hard for Charles. He worked in the sweaty Cincinnati stockyards as a butcher, saving every penny he could.[269] He was his father's son, after all. But Charles wanted to own his own business. When another immigrant, Ernst Blersch, offered to pool his money into a produce and grocery business, Charles jumped at the chance.[270]

Unlike the filth and disorganization of the stockyards, this little store gave Charles an opportunity to put his gift of organization to work. For Charles, everything had to have its place, and every business decision needed to be measured against potential outcomes. The little grocery became the cleanest, fairest, and best-run shop in the area. The hospitality offered by Charles and Ernst was second to none and they always stocked top-quality goods.

In 1859, Charles met a Cincinnati girl, Louise Brengleman and the two made a bond.[271] It was a short-lived relationship. She died in March 1862, while giving birth to their only child, Charles Jr.[272] Life seemed destined to challenge him.

Charles and Ernst had been talking about expanding and Charles had great interest in the opening markets in Nashville. With the Federal occupation of the city, things would hopefully be calm enough for him to move down and get things established. Charles liked what he saw when he arrived and began looking for a place to set up shop.

But when he returned to Cincinnati, he had one more thing to take care of. After the death of Louise, he began courting Louisa Rohlfing. A Cincinnatian since her family arrived from Germany when she was six, Louisa was an inspired choice for Charles. She agreed to move with him to Nashville and the two were married on March 4, 1863.[273] Before they left town, Charles took care of one other family matter. He promised his brother Adolph there would be a place for him in Nashville as well.

It was time for the Nelsons to make their mark.

The Athens of the South

The decade between 1850 and 1860 saw Nashville go through a great metamorphosis. The dusty old frontier town, turned state capital in 1843, had absorbed some of the cosmopolitan feel of cities back east, the population had nearly tripled to 16,988[274] and many of the archaic structures from the early settlement were gone. In their place, the streets were filled with the finest in modern architecture.

The railroad and telegraph had changed everything. What was once a city unto herself was wide open. With products shipped in and out through Georgia, Alabama, South Carolina, and up to Kentucky with ease, Nashville became a boomtown. Even the financial downturn of 1857 that depressed the rest of the country had little effect on the city.[275] Lower city rents meant businesses could sustain profits, and so not a single business closed.

One of the strongest draws of this revitalized southern city was the University of Nashville. Born as Davidson Academy in 1785, the struggling school became the pride of the South in the 1820s thanks to Dr. Phillip Lindsley of the College of New Jersey. Under his guidance, the standards of the curriculum rose to levels that impressed his contemporaries back east. With a highly respected female academy as well, Nashville earned a reputation as the Athens of the South.

The growth of the town's economy, its educational structure, and its pleasant, healthful weather made it an ideal place for the Nelsons. Charles found a homesite on South Church Street and the perfect building for his business at 24 Market Street,[276] just a block from the river. It had formerly been inhabited by a clothing store and was a suitable space to get started. But Charles needed a little more capital to get started and so he added another partner to the venture, opening as Nelson & Pfeiffers.[277] Once they were on their feet, Ernst agreed to have Charles' brother Adolph join the firm and the name was changed in 1865 to Charles Nelson & Co. and the business moved to 22 North Market Street.[278]

While the grocery and produce sold well at Nelson's store, the whisky he stocked--by chance rather than design--was selling like hotcakes.

It was surprising to Charles, who saw little distilling activity when he moved to town. In the 1840s, a large state-of-the-art facility called the Nashville Steam Distillery had been built after the owners saw the success of Old Robertson and Old Lincoln, but it failed within a handful of years.[279] And the building sat barren. The distillers that followed, like A. A. Hall and Howard Sims, had only moderate success.

Where whisky thrived in Nashville was in the wholesale business. Grocers like Lanier & Morris, Hugh McCrea & Co, and Mizell, Hooper & Co. sold barrel after barrel of whisky to the growing number of taverns and smaller retail grocers. Along with Robertson and Lincoln, they sold Tennessee's own Jo. Newson's celebrated Whisky, Old Bourbon, Old Monongahela, and Tennessee White Whisky. With easier access to transportation, Nashville salesmen, or "jobbers" as they were called, worked territories throughout Tennessee and into Alabama and Georgia before the war.

As there were only a handful of established wholesalers in the city, Charles put his research and organizational skills to work and began stocking barrel after barrel of the finest whiskies he could find, along with sherry wines, rums, gins, and brandies. He also stocked Brazilian coffees, Cincinnati lager, and a variety of different food items. In a nod to his father, and to attract other German immigrants, he continued stocking candles and soap. It didn't take long for his reputation to grow and soon he outgrew the facility. So he moved up the street to 7 South Market Street.[280]

Initially, the move into whisky seemed like an inspired choice. But in 1867, with the postwar demand for Old Robertson and Old Lincoln rising and the excise man choking off supplies, barrels were getting tougher to find. The enterprising Charles seized the opportunity. He learned what regulations he needed to follow, and began seeking a building suitable for a new distillery, bonded warehouse, and rectifying house. He found the perfect spot just a couple hundred yards away at 18 and 20 South Market Street (now 2nd Avenue). These attached buildings were perfect as they opened onto both Market and Front streets (now 1st Avenue).[281] Charles and Ernst ran the store while Adolph took over the management of the warehouses and they prepared the space for the distilling equipment. Meanwhile, Charles placed an advertisement in the Republican Banner seeking one hundred chords of clear green sugartree wood.[282] He'd learned what made Tennessee whisky special, and he was ready to provide his customers with the best he could. But he would have to do it without his brother. In September, Adolph left the grocery and whisky business to take over management of the Sherman House on 139 North Market.[283]

It didn't matter. Charles was so meticulous in what he was doing, his charcoal-mellowed whisky got money rolling in, while other distillers were still in a lockdown over the Tice Meter regulations. The state-of-the-art downtown distillery was churning out eight barrels of copper-distilled whisky per day. His warehouse had room for two hundred barrels, but he never reached capacity.[284] He was churning through barrels at breakneck speed. He decided he needed a second distillery, so he secured a location further south on Mallory Street and quickly got the operation up and running. But in August 1869 a fire ripped through the building, doing $1,600 in damage--and Charles had not insured the facility. No worries though, Charles was an energetic go-getter, and he wouldn't let the fire get him down. He had workmen remove the debris and put carpenters and coppersmiths to work on the rebuilding project. It took less than a week to get the distillery back up and functioning.[285]

But with the continued growth of the city and the number of wholesalers crowding Market Street, the danger of another fire was palpable. If only to protect his business holdings, Charles wanted to diversify and find somewhere outside the city where he could establish a distillery away from other fire traps. Charles needed something close and accessible. He loved the reputation the Woodards, Pitts, and Draughons had established for Robertson County whisky. So he started looking north for his next opportunity.

Greenbrier and Belle Meade

Just east of the town of Greenbrier, Tennessee, along the Rocky Fork of Long Branch Creek, sat a vacant distillery looking for an owner. It was once the home of a distiller and rectifier named Charles Palmer. He built his modest gristmill and log still operation just in time to catch the tail end of the initial postwar whisky boom. But thanks to the Federal government's expensive requirements for sour mash distillers, Palmer was going broke trying to meet and exceed the requirements, buying two copper stills, two steam engines, and a large steam boiler.[286]

The fifty acres of land his distillery sat on were owned by Henry and James A. White. Seeing their renter struggle, they offered it to a local real-estate man named Travis Winham in August 1869.[287] When Palmer's operation failed, he abandoned the property and Winham was stuck on what to do. Distillers were cash poor thanks to the long-term shutdowns, so interest in the property was extremely limited.

When the highly successful Nashville wholesaler and distiller Charles Nelson inquired about the property, Winham jumped at the chance to sell it to him. The Robertson County address and land for expansion brought Charles' pen to the dotted line. His $3,600 purchase price included the land, the gristmill, springhouse, and all the equipment and fixtures. October 20, 1870 stands as the date the Charles Nelson's Greenbrier Distillery was born, but in name only.[288] There would be plenty of work to do to get this distillery up to Charles' standards.

Just as he was getting ready to start on the redesign, Charles learned that a local inventor and distiller Henry H. Kirk had just received a positive ruling on his patented "Kirk's Improved Distillery" design. This would allow Charles to distill as close to the old Robertson County way as he could while following the rules of the Federal government. For $500, Charles purchased the rights and went to work retooling his new distillery.[289]

Feeling a bit overwhelmed with three distilleries and a wholesale grocery to run, he decided it was time to take on a new partner. Enter John N. Sperry, a fellow wholesale grocer with big plans to get into the distilling business. Sperry was a longtime neighbor of Charles, having established Sperry & Co at 21 South Market Street a couple of years before.[290] He was a commission merchant dealing in cotton and whisky. But in November of '68, his store had gone up in flames thanks to a fire at his neighbor's J. R. Paul & Co.[291] John was able to save his stock of cotton, bale rope, bagging, and whisky, but much of it was damaged. Insurance covered the losses. Nevertheless, he needed a partner and formed Sperry & McCrory. The new firm decided to go big by buying the Spring Brook Building at 36 South Market and 15 South Front streets.[292] But John and his new partners didn't see eye to eye. So, when Charles Nelson approached John about a potential partnership, Sperry jumped at the opportunity.

The plan was to ditch the distillery at 18 and 20 Market Street and build the most modern distillery in the area inside the Spring Brook Building. As part of the combined partnership, Charles included the Greenbrier and Mallory Street distilleries and the grocery as well. It was a little empire.

Once completed, the new Spring Brook Distillery was a large three-story operation. It featured a large copper pot still that was able to produce sixty-five to seventy barrels of proof spirits each day. On the third floor sat one of Tennessee's first copper column stills, some twenty-five-feet tall. The distillery produced Old Robertson and rye whiskies along with gin, brandy, and cologne spirits. They even produced a spirit they called Bourbon. A local reporter was in awe of the operation upon first reviewing it. "It is one of the most complete in the South and is destined to do a heavy business. 2,000 gallons every twelve hours capacity. We predict that the product of Spring Brook Distillery will soon become famous throughout Tennessee and the South." To entice direct purchases, a salesroom was added to the 36 South Market Street entrance.[293]

Meanwhile, the Mallory Street distillery continued to operate, taking on some special projects, including an attempt to see if they could make whisky from cottonseed.[294]

The Greenbrier Distillery turned out to be a workhorse and model of efficiency, while keeping to tradition. The water for the facility arrived by gravity from the springhouse up on the hill. Brick, stone, and iron warehouses with red roofs were positioned close by the distilling operation. Grain bins were filled with rye, corn, and barley. They used a fancy new roller mill in place of the old gristmill. In terms of process, contrary to the accusations of Lincoln County distillers, Nelson's used natural fermentation in their sour mash process--making use of the full ninety-six hours allowed by law. It was a process they would use until the day Prohibition shut them down. Whisky was double distilled on full-size copper pot stills, and they ran the spirit through sugar maple charcoal before barreling. They also made bourbon and rye; and, according to an industry trade magazine, Bonfort's Wine and Spirits Circular, these had "the same general characteristics of similar goods distilled in Kentucky and Pennsylvania, but are more refined and delicate in body and flavor."[295]

The attention to detail and the absence of much of their competition thanks to the excise issues made Nelson & Sperry an instant success. In January 1872, the Nashville Union American reported "416 barrels of whisky taken out of bond at Charles Nelson's Green Brier distillery. We understand this is the largest lot of whiskey ever taken out of bond at any one time in the fifth district of Tennessee." That was saying a lot, as the 5th District was king.[296]

This was only the beginning for Charles Nelson and John Sperry, although they wouldn't achieve their success as a team. Whether it was a conflict of visions or too many tigers in a cage, the partnership came to a close in November 1872. Charles gave up interest in the Spring Brook business and store; he kept Greenbrier Distillery along with his store on South Market Street with his offices down the street.

Sperry & Company continued their success at Spring Brook Distillery through 1875 and sold Old Robertson whisky that was made in Nashville. Later in the decade, John would find new partners and establish Sperry, Wade & Co. Tired of the lurking danger of fire in a downtown area, the firm moved two miles outside of town and reestablished the distillery. In May 1878, they built Belle Meade Distillery at Bosley's Springs just off Harding Pike, out near the historic Belle Meade racetrack and breeding ground.[297] The home of famous racehorses like Bonnie Scotland and Enquirer, the property soon became famous for Belle

Meade whisky's dominance over the market. Their stunning success must have surprised even Charles Nelson, their main rival. The *Memphis Daily Appeal* gave a glowing report of Sperry's new enterprise:

> "It is an established fact that the whiskies from Belle Meade for the past two and a half years have far exceeded in the number of sales of any distillery ever run in the State. Out of about 10,000 barrels produced since January 1878, up to the present date, only 450 barrels now remain in the hands of the proprietors unsold. They are now running day and night to enable them to meet demand. They have three large brick bonded warehouses, fire-proof, with a storage capacity of 15,000 barrels, and are in every way prepared to take care of whisky sold in bond."[298]

With the money he made, John did what many successful distillery owners did--he got into banking. He was a founding member and director of the First National Bank of Nashville. He also expanded the operations on Market Street and invested in a new distillery run by John L. Price. Unfortunately, Price had a bit of a temper and was arrested for wounding a revenue officer after striking him on the head with a hickory club.[299] It appeared John wasn't always the best judge of character. Three years earlier, his partner W. J. Wade was fined $50 for assaulting Charles Nelson on South Market Street.[300]

Regardless of the actions of those around him, John N. Sperry had one of the most storied runs as a distillery owner in Tennessee history. Unfortunately, all of his fireproofing and moving out to the country was for naught. A fire ripped through the new distillery in the early morning of August 30, 1885. It was a total loss and his insurance fell short of what was lost.[301] Not only did it end the Belle Meade Distillery, it caused John to retire from the business. He would go on to become a very successful banker.

Meanwhile, at Greenbrier, the H. H. Kirk distilling equipment was a stellar success. Of course, Charles had expected this as the whisky it produced for George

Garrett & Co. had won "best new whisky" at the 1871 Robertson County Fair.[302] It wasn't long before Greenbrier's whiskies were outselling all of his Robertson County competitors.

Beyond his whisky endeavors, Charles stepped up his efforts in the community. He founded the Nashville Musical Union and Nashville Trust Company, serving as the first president for both. He was also a family man. As a father to three boys and three girls, he always made plenty of time for them. And he was a charitable man. His obituary stated, "Mr. Nelson was in the fullest sense a public-spirited citizen. Every enterprise intended for the good of Nashville received his hearty support and generous help."[303] Charles hosted one big event every year, the "Nelson's Annual Jolity" barbecue, which the Nashville American said, "was simply not to be surpassed."[304] And while he returned multiple times to his hometown in Germany and was accepted as a hero, there was no doubt he was an American through and through and was fiercely loyal to his adopted home country.

Charles' wholesale business eventually moved to 66 South Market Street and his oldest boy, Charles Jr., joined the business as a bookkeeper. Charles was determined to make a successful business for his family, just as his father had attempted to do for him.

The day the Belle Meade Distillery burned was the last time Charles Nelson had to worry about competition in the state of Tennessee. Until the day he died and years after, Nelson's Greenbrier far outsold any distillery in the state.

If only his father could have seen him running a hugely successful family business, with his loved ones gathered around him. He truly had achieved Johann Phillip's dream.

Chapter 15

THE GOLDEN AGE OF OLD ROBERTSON

Message in a Bottle

Sir Kenelm Digby was a true Renaissance man. He was an entrepreneur, inventor, alchemist, philosopher, privateer, politician, and, most of all, he loved food and drink. In fact, a book released after his death, *The Closet of the Eminently Learned Sir Kenelme Digbie Kt. Opened* (or simply *The Closet Opened*), revealed recipes he collected for everything from black pudding to mead. A man of boundless energy, inventiveness, and curiosity, it makes one wonder when he had time to sleep.

From birth, Kenelm lived outside the norm. He was born into a Catholic family while his homeland England was still struggling over Henry VIII's decision to break from Rome. When he was two, his father Sir Everard Digby was involved in a failed scheme to blow up the House of Lords, as a protest to anti-Catholic King James I. The Gunpowder Plot of 1605 most famously claimed the life of Guy Fawkes, but it also led to the torturous death of Kenelm's father. This relationship to Catholicism and his rebellious father would leave a cloud of suspicion around Digby. But it didn't stop him. Instead, he seemed desperate to show his worthiness while walking away from his religious upbringing. He spent his early adulthood traveling extensively throughout Europe, meeting royalty, statesmen, and the brightest minds, all while wooing the ladies.

At age 24, he befriended Prince Charles, the future King of England, and was knighted by James I. When the prince ascended to the throne as King Charles I, the country was involved in several conflicts. The king gave Sir Digby a commission to plunder any Flemish or Spanish ships he could find. On one adventure, he traveled to Algeria and used his charm to free fifty of his enslaved countrymen. After several more adventures, he returned to England and tried to settle down with his wife Venetia and start a family. But she died suddenly, and a distraught Digby drove himself deep into scientific studies and the glasswork he had established.

A connoisseur of wines, Digby put his inventive mind into improving the drink he loved. In the 17th century, wine was stored in barrels for the entirety of its life, soaking up tannins and over-oxidizing. Bottles were available, but they were rare and expensive.

Making glass was a highly skilled, laborious, and dangerous endeavor. It took someone stoking fires all night just to get to the required temperature of 1500 degrees Fahrenheit. Once molten glass was extracted from the kiln, a laborer had to work quickly while also avoiding being badly burned. The glass was then blown and shaped. It took hours of sweaty and dangerous work to create a few thin and fragile bottles, which were not suitable for transport.

Sir Digby was determined to solve this problem, so he devised a wind-tunnel blower that could make the fires hotter, faster. Then he increased the ratio of sand to potash and lime to give the bottle more heft. His experiments led to higher-quality bottles that could be produced in less time, earning him the moniker "the father of the modern bottle."

The bottles of Digby's era were squatty globes with short, fat necks. The volume of liquid they could hold depended on the amount of air the blower could produce before the molten glass solidified. Future advances allowed for taller and taller bottles and, by 1770, Digby's short, stout bottle morphed into the modern whisky bottle shape. Yet glass bottles remained a luxury item. Taverns would reuse them like drinking glasses. Storekeepers might keep a few empty bottles on hand, but it was more likely they would use cheaper ceramic pots and jugs.

The first real breakthrough for glass whisky bottles came in the first decade of the 1800s, when British glassmaker Rickets of Bristol built a machine that could mold small bottles and reproduce them with consistency of shape. When the patent was opened to other manufacturers, the cost of bottles and the speed with which they were made improved. For wine drinkers, the fermented juice of the grape found its way into larger bottles. Whisky drinkers used small glass liquor flasks, which fit nicely inside a coat pocket for a convenient nip. As time passed, these flasks went from simple bottles to decorative decanters. In the 1840s, embossed flasks featured the faces of presidents, emblems, quotes, or scenes of significance, and were cleaned and refilled by a local grocer or tavern.

The earliest use of the full-sized whisky bottle by merchants appears to have occurred in Scotland in the 1830s. It took another decade before the practice reached America and even longer to get to the frontier. Even then, this was a rarity since ceramic jugs were less expensive. Because grocers filled the bottles, the name of the distiller would not appear on the bottles unless hand written. Still, during the early 18th century, beyond occasional convenience, there was no compelling reason to attempt mass bottling of whisky, especially since the whisky seemed to get better the more time it spent in the barrel.

That all changed in the mid-19th century when consumers lost trust in the businesses that were producing their food. Several food scares and stories of tainted whisky caused the public to question the quality of the products they were putting into their bodies. Whiskies were being adulterated with extenders, coloring agents, and poisons. Finding a "pure" barrel of whisky was getting harder and harder. Even pharmacists got into the act of extending their supplies (and profit) of medicinal whisky by adding water.

Soon consumers were willing to pay more for the genuine article. In response, wholesalers began marketing words like "pure" and "genuine" to convince the public their product was unadulterated. In 1860, a distiller named S. T. Suit went one step further. He sold his "pure Bourbon Whisky" in bottles, hand-filled at his

Kentucky Salt River Bourbon Whisky Distillery, and shipped directly to grocers and pharmacists. This allowed him to guarantee the quality of his product. It gave him a firm leg up on the competition and his became one of the most trusted brands among druggists.[305]

The mid-1880s saw significant advances in bottle making with the development of semi-automatic machines. But they were slow to be adopted thanks to the old-fashioned glassblowers who lobbied against them.

Then, everything changed. In 1895, the Commissioner of the Internal Revenue grew frustrated with brands like Hiram Walker's Canadian Club, which was bottled-in-bond, crossing the border in droves, while American distillers were restricted to exporting spirits in casks rather than bottles.

In his end-of-year report, Commissioner Joseph Miller noted "the attention of this office has repeatedly been called to this discrimination against the products of American distillers, and it has been urged that if spirits were allowed to be bottled-in-bond, each bottle to have affixed thereto an engraved stamp bearing the signature of the collector, a large export trade would be secured." He asked Congress for "an act authorizing the bottling of spirits in bond."[306]

Kentucky's 5th District Congressman Walter Evans, one-time Commissioner of the Internal Revenue under President Chester A. Arthur, took the lead and crafted what was then known as the Evans Bill or Bottling Bill.[307] Today we know it as the Bottled-in-Bond Act of 1897. Not only did it level the playing field with Hiram Walker, it created confidence in boasts of purity, and it created a high demand for glass bottles. The use of the bottle was further boosted when Michael Owens of the Libbey Glass Works in Toledo developed a fully automated glassblowing machine.[308] His 1903 patent was the death knell for the ceramic whisky jug and would see the glassblowing industry slowly lose its dominance.

As for Tennessee whisky, an early proponent of bottling was Judge John Woodard. Partner in the wholesale whisky house Moore, Woodard & Co., in 1868 he saw a great opportunity to reinvigorate the area's distilling reputation by bottling "Pure Robertson County" whisky. The plan was a great success. Between November 1868 and May 1869, the Springfield wholesale location sold almost $25,000 worth of his bottled whisky (over half a million dollars today).[309] It would be this kind of forward thinking, from whisky men like Judge John Woodard, that would help Old Robertson move quickly ahead of its Lincoln County competition in the hearts and minds of Tennessee whisky drinkers.

The Judge

At the close of the Civil War, there was a comfort in knowing the great distilling legends of Old Robertson were back on task, making their high-quality spirits. Thomas Woodard Jr., Colonel Wiley Woodward, Jo. C. Spark, and Wilson Pitt were all present and accounted for in the late 1860s. But there was also a new generation of distillers on the rise.

One of the most celebrated of the new generation of distillers was John Woodard. Known to the community as Judge Woodard, John was the oldest son of Thomas Jr. and Winifred Woodard's eleven children. He was born in 1825 in a log cabin on the family farm six miles north-northwest of Springfield.

As a youth, John watched his father distill on the farm, and used to play down in Booger Bottom Cave, the source of the distillery's limestone-filtered water. With its water some 700 ft within the cave, his father damned it up and built a copper-piping system to bring its water into the distillery. The family had made enough money off the whisky that, by the time John was a teenager, his father built a sturdy Federal-style brick home for the family.[310]

But whisky wasn't John's first love. He wanted to study and learn about the law. He took a job in Adairville, Kentucky, near the spot where Andrew Jackson killed Charles Dickinson in a duel, and made enough money as a clerk in a dry goods store to put himself through school and buy a small farm. Soon after graduating from school and joining the bar in 1851, the clean-cut and sharply dressed lawyer won a judgeship in Robertson County.[311]

John's leadership skills and firm convictions made him a standout in the Southern Opposition Party before the war. This conviction earned him a seat in the General Assembly. During his first term in Nashville, he found many admirers after he gave each of the whisky-drinking congressmen a black bottle of whisky at Christmas.[312] But that same legislature would break his heart during the next session when they openly lobbied for succession. Judge Woodard was a fierce Unionist and never apologized for his loyalty to the United States, even after Tennessee voted to join the Confederacy.[313] After the war, he threw his support behind Republican President Andrew Johnson, who just so happened to be an unabashed fan of Robertson County whisky.[314] John returned to the legislature after the war, but his father passed away in the middle of his first term.

For John, the death of his father came as a hard blow, but he knew what he needed to do. Already speculating on numerous properties, he purchased his father's distilling equipment.[315] John rode out his term in the State House, then came home to go full throttle into the whisky business.

His first step was to get into the whisky retailing business. In the past, establishing a wholesale business on Market Street in Nashville would have been the first choice. But the one-time sleepy town of Springfield was emerging with a wholesale industry of its own, thanks to its new rail stop on the Louisville & Nashville line. He partnered with William Moore and Thomas Green, opening their Moore, Woodard & Co. wholesale shop with rectifying capabilities and whisky provided by G.H. Garrett and Henry H. Kirk.

During the first few years, the company focused on bringing in high quality spirits from other firms. This won them accolades from the likes of the judges at the Robertson County Fair, where one of their preferred distillers, M.O. Mason, won first prize in the old whisky category for his twelve year aged st ock.[316] Eventually, after Thomas Green left the firm and the laws for distilling were simplified, the newly christened Woodard & Moore stretched itself into distilling.[317] In May 1873, they sold their first branded whisky, distilling at John Woodard's Silver Spring Distillery and using grain sourced from the county.[318] They would enhance the name in 1876, calling it "Celebrated" XXXX Silver Spring Distillery Whisky. With the popularity of Robertson County whisky, they decided to try their hand at the Nashville trade and opened a wholesale business at 13 North Market Street in 1877. There, they stocked Silver Spring along with

Lincoln County, Bourbon, and rye. Within two years, the demand was so great between Springfield and Nashville that another distillery was set up and the Belle of Tennessee brand launched. With the use of bonded warehouses, they provided whiskies with extra age up to seven years, even before the Carlisle Allowance opened up the three-year tax-free bonding period.[319]

John wasn't the only Woodard selling his whisky in Springfield. His uncle Colonel Wiley sold his whisky exclusively through the Springfield house of Thomas Pepper & Co., who opened their doors in 1868. Wiley's whisky still held onto its great reputation, even after the excise forced changes in his distillery layout. His son Pete helped keep his father's business online through the turmoil, creating his own patented process for making whisky that complied with the law.[320] This open competitor to the patent created by H.H. Kirk was just as successful at making a quality product. Colonel Wiley's whisky won a gold medal at the Robertson County Fair for the best new whisky (meaning white dog coming right off the still). He distilled corn and wheat whiskies and used triple distillation to make a clean and neutral spirit.[321] It didn't hurt that he was still employing the charcoal mellowing process to keep the spirit clean and drinkable. He soon expanded his markets into Midwestern states like Michigan, Wisconsin, and Kansas.[322]

In 1872, the wholesale house of Hopkins & Lawrence would attempt to duplicate the success of Woodard & Moore and set up their large shop. Then they bought the John R. Bridges distillery, about 2½ miles east of Springfield near Wartrace Creek.[323] Hopkins & Lawrence expanded their stock to include Joel Pitts Lincoln County whisky, Davidson County's "Richland" whisky, and John R. Bridges "Mountain Dew." The duo later added C.S. Pearce as a distiller and opened an additional shop in Nashville.

In short order, Springfield had become a whisky town. With just around two thousand people in the area, it had a staggering twelve wholesale whisky houses and nine rectifying establishments. Within a few years, its houses brought in almost a million dollars combined annually (that's nearly $23 million today).[324]

With his keen sense of awareness, Judge Woodard realized the town desperately needed a bank. Not only was the whisky business raking in cash, so were important ancillary businesses like farms, gristmills, metal workers, and--especially so--the cooperages in nearby Coopertown. In August 1872, the Springfield National Bank was established with $60,000 capital,[325] and Judge John Woodard as its president. The deposits were so strong on its first day that it kept the community solvent through America's Financial Panic of 1873.[326]

The Woodard Family Tree

With Robertson County, first distiller arguments can be made between Thomas Johnson, Benjamin Menees, or even the old Scotsman Thomas Kilgore. The most dominant distiller in its history is easy--it was Charles Nelson by a country mile. And the family with the greatest impact on the reputation of old Robertson is clear--the Woodards.

Their family tree has many distilling branches and, by extension, they connected to several other successful distilling families. A dissection of their tree shows how tight the distilling community was in old Robertson.

The patriarch, Thomas Woodard, who brought the family name to Robertson, had four sons. Two of them, Colonel Wiley and Thomas Jr. were distillers. And three sons would have distilling offspring of their own.

Since a lot of first names were reused, nicknames became commonplace. Thomas Jr's nickname was Dinktum and Wiley became Colonel Wiley. The oldest of the brothers, "Old Bill" had a son, James. It's not clear if Old Bill or James ever distilled, but James' son Moses ran the Silver Spring Distillery owned by his uncle, Judge John Woodard.

Colonel Wiley was so prolific with his distilling genes he had three sons and a daughter that would own and run their own distilleries. Daniel Woodard, who was known as "Pete," worked for his father Wiley for over thirty years before entering a distilling partnership with J.W. Bowling in 1866, though the partnership didn't last long. Instead, he went into the wholesaling and rectifying business.[327]

His brothers G.H. and G.R. Woodard opened their own distillery in 1871 using their brother Pete's distillery patent.[328] This gave them a leg up during the Tice Meter fiasco. It's possible James Woodard was also a partner in this distillery. If it is the same one, it burned down in 1873. The distillery's lack of established reputation led the local newspaper to claim it was Colonel Wiley's distillery that burned down, instead of his sons'.[329]

James married into another successful distilling family, when he took the hand of Nannie L. Draughon, daughter of Dr. George E. and Tabitha (Couts) Draughon.[330] This also tied the Woodards to the Couts distilling family through James' mother-in-law Tabitha.

Even one of Colonel Wiley's daughter's got in on the distilling legacy. Josephine Woodard married distiller Jordan Stokes Brown. A Confederate veteran from the battles of Perrysville and Murfreesboro, Jordan returned to Robertson County and went into the dry-goods business in Springfield. When the couple married in 1867, the pressure mounted for him to enter the whisky business. He saw how Springfield was being transformed by the wholesale industry and started his own house. A couple years after Wiley's death, Jordan purchased land along Wartrace Creek in Robertson County and established the Wartrace Distillery,[331] where he and Josephine made J.S. Brown & Co. Hand Made Sour Mash "Old DDDD" Whiskey.

While all of Colonel Wiley's children were finding great success, Wiley Woodard & Company itself continued to excel. 1875 was a banner year, with the distillery taking in $75,000 (around $2m today).[332] Wiley wasn't shy about letting the youngsters know how it should be done. But the spark was soon taken from his eye. A crippling paralysis took over his body, and he spent the last two years of his life confined to bed. He passed away at 68.[333]

One of Colonel Wiley's great friends throughout his life was his cousin Wilson Pitt. The son of Arthur Pitt, he was in many ways Colonel Wiley's opposite. Wilson loved the life of the farmer distiller and didn't need to go far beyond his roots. He spent his life raising cattle and hogs, growing crops, distilling, and feeding spent grains to his livestock. It was a simpler and quieter life than the

Colonel's, but Wilson let his spirits do the talking. If you had a barrel of Pitt's Best or even the lesser-aged Honest Wils, you knew you were tasting something special. Wilson almost gave up distilling when the Federal excise tax restricted how he could make his whisky, but customer demand brought him back. He continued his impressive distilling career for another decade.

On the sad day in 1880 when the news of Wilson's death echoed throughout the community, the writers at the Clarksville Tobacco and Leaf unfurled a touching tribute to his character:

> *"He was never sued nor did he ever sue anyone. Such was his devotion to his business, and he was never absent from his home two weeks at one time during his life. His home was always open to his friends and many who shared his bounty will regret to hear of his death. Mr. Pitt belonged to no religious denomination, but was liberal in his donations to all. He was a man of noble impulses - his heart ever open to the appeals of charity and his hands ever ready to administer to the necessities of the destitute never turning away empty those who come to him hungry. Of Mr. Pitt, it may be truly said that he was the "noblest work of God" an honest man."*[334]

Wilson's sons would become successful distillers in their own right as the Pitt Brothers.

The Long Slow Fade

While no one in Robertson was going to touch the output of Charles Nelson, Judge Woodard always came in a respectable second. Much of his success came down to his striving for quality. When most distillers were sticking to the one-year bonding period, Woodard & Moore were selling John and Moses' XXXX Silver Spring Whisky and Belle of Tennessee at two to seven years old.

The Judge would retire as a rich man, amassing a fortune of nearly $1 million during his time in the whisky industry ($34 million in today's money).[335] Not bad for someone who didn't jump in until he was almost forty. In the early 1880s, before his official retirement, he built a home near Columbia, Tennessee, so he could enjoy the fruits of his labor.

For Judge Woodard, the timing couldn't be better. He left at the very peak of Robertson County's success. The golden years had some ill effects on the region. Wanting to feed as much grain as possible to the industry, Robertson County farmers exhausted the land by not rotating crops. Their yields dropped during the first few years of the boom. More and more farms moved into tobacco. The boom for sawmills and charcoal resulted in the removal of a large number of oak and sugar maple trees. Passengers on the L&N would get a firsthand look at the blight. By the 1890s resources were being shipped in from other markets.

While Charles Nelson's operation never seemed to slow, John Woodard's operations eventually wound down. And only a handful of Robertson County distillers remained by 1890, including the Pitt Brothers, Pete Woodard, J. S. Brown, and the short-lived Duncan & Bros. John R. Bridges and Sons continued to produce their Mountain Dew whisky, but they diversified into tobacco. When George H. Garrett hit hard times, he filed for bankruptcy, leaving Henry H. Kirk without a distillery and John Woodard with the property.[336] Jo. C. Stark's operation with B.G. Hillard survived into the 1880s, but the two longtime partners would close the business early in the decade, ending in a land dispute at Robertson County's Chancery Court.[337]

As for Dr. Draughon, he had stayed true to the tradition of making copper distilled sour mash whisky in the old Robertson way. In the late 1870s, he doubled his distillery's capacity due to demand. But a freak accident almost took his business and his life away. While rolling a barrel, the head popped off, spilling whisky that quickly found an open flame. Within minutes, the distillery was in ruins and George was badly burned.[338] What might have sent other men to another occupation only strengthened George's resolve. He rebuilt the distillery and was soon back to earning high marks for his whisky. Dr. George E. Draughon would go out strong, closing the business while it was still profitable.

It was quite a run for Old Robertson. The postwar years were highly successful. But an enemy was on the horizon. No, it wasn't Old Lincoln. It was the teetotaller and the threat of Prohibition.

Chapter 16

TIGHTENING THE GRIP

The Hunt

For the better part of six decades, a growing tide of voices rolled, crested, and sank as legislatures across the U.S. acquiesced and then backpedaled on the issues of temperance and prohibition. The problem appeared to be a lack of leadership. Neal Dow's voice rang the loudest until the Portland Rum Riots sullied his name. Susan B. Anthony attempted to stand for temperance, but her connection to the suffragette movement kept her from winning over male voters.

All of that changed in 1879, when a non-political organization, the Woman's Christian Temperance Union (WCTU), shifted focus under its new president Frances E. Willard. Frances helped channel the group's energy, clarified the organization's mission of removing alcohol from society, and united temperance forces behind that singular mission.

But for all the ladies she drew to her side, there was still a major problem. They didn't have the vote. Frances could stir up the crowds and build her organization, but she had to depend on getting male voters to elect temperance-friendly representatives on behalf of their wives. It was a daunting task.

A solution came to Frances in the form of a Connecticut-born science teacher named Mary Hannah Hanchett Hunt.

A graduate of the Patapsco Female Institute near Baltimore, Maryland, Mary loved science. She had a particular fascination with the subject of alcohol and its effects on the human body. She gathered research and put together educational materials for her local school district in Boston. Then she traveled across Massachusetts and used her scientific arguments to convince school boards to put her books into the hands of children. In this way, she could teach the next generation about the dangers of intemperance.

Mary's education plan intrigued Frances, who invited her to the WCTU's National Convention in 1879. It didn't take long for Frances to see the wisdom in Mary's long-term approach of reaching future voters through early education. She named Mary the superintendent of the WCTU's Department of Scientific Temperance Instruction in Schools and Colleges.

With the power of the WCTU behind her, Mary cast a wider net, trying to get her materials into schools across the northeast. She also trained an army of WCTU members on how to approach and pressure school boards.

When these attempts failed, she realized the only way to get her books into schools was through the state legislatures. But it was still a time when most politicians avoided taking too firm a stand on temperance, fearing the creation of any unnecessary wedge issues. She used the politicians' fear of losing their seat against them. Starting in Vermont and Michigan, she entrenched herself in state politics, found allies, organized citizens, and watched those opposed to her books get booted from office.

Not only did Mary Hunt's books get into the schools, teachers were required to pass tests confirming their understanding of the dangerous and harmful effects of alcohol and narcotics. To maintain the laws, Mary and her team would return to states that were wavering, or where issues were found, and she would again pressure the legislatures to play along or face a reckoning at the ballot box. When school boards ignored her materials, Mary used the local WCTU chapter to put pressure on them to act.

It took almost a decade before a committee of scientific scholars debunked a good number of Mary Hunt's theories. But by then, every state and territory under U.S. control, mandated the use of her anti-alcohol materials. This emboldened her to simply brushed their conclusions aside.

When the history of U.S. Prohibition is told, names like Frances Willard and her WCTU, Wayne Wheeler and his Anti-Saloon League, and William Jennings Bryan with his impassioned speeches and political wrangling take the spotlight--and for good reason. But without Mary Hunt's indoctrination of future voters on the evils of intemperance, their "noble experiment" of Prohibition might never have come to fruition.

The Four-Mile Fight for Rural Tennessee

Back in Tennessee, the disorganization of temperance forces was still being felt in the state's General Assembly throughout the 1870s.

The decade opened with arguments over the redesigning of the state's constitution. Hot topics up for debate were Black male suffrage, the abuse of power by Governor Brownlow, and temperance. The first two issues were solved by a poll tax and letting a simple majority override the governor's veto.

The third issue was the constitutionality of giving the citizens the right to vote their municipalities wet or dry. Known as the local option, it was seen by temperance supporters as the best way to show a state how temperate communities were healthier and more productive. But there was a hitch. Tennessee's Constitution gave the exclusive rights of enacting laws to the General Assembly. "Wet" lawmakers knew any attempt to pass a local opinion in Tennessee might be deemed unconstitutional. To overcome this, they attempted to add a clause to the Constitution that would specifically allow the local option, but the measure failed.

The forces for temperance in the legislature weren't ready to give up that easily. In 1871 and 1873, the General Assembly put through bills to enact the local option. The first attempt failed, but the second attempt made it all the way to Governor John C. Brown's desk. As expected, Brown vetoed it due to constitutionality concerns. All that was required was a simple majority to override his veto. But the legislators knew Brown was right––the bill would never make it past the State Supreme Court. His veto held.[339]

With the local option off the table, temperance advocates went back to the drawing board. Desperate to find a solution, memories of Bethel College's attempts to build a two-mile alcohol free zone around their school returned to the minds of legislators. They realized the power to grant and shape school charters was under the purview of the General Assembly. If they couldn't have local communities vote against alcohol sales, they could circumvent the system by adding alcohol-free zoning restrictions to future school charters.

While the selling of liquor by grocers and other retails was a concern for the drys, the real target of this legislation was the old tippling house, now known by the fancy French-sounding name saloon.

Evolving from the French word "salon", this stylish rebranding was no accident. In the United States, salon was used for bachelor clubs and elegant drawing rooms, tavern and tippling house owners saw the word saloon as a way to give their establishments an air of respectability and class.

Thanks to financial incentives and ownership by brewers like Pabst, Miller, Busch, and Nashville's own William Gerst, saloons became quite popular with the lower classes, who were offered free, salty lunches with plenty of beer to quench their thirst. The financial input of brewers and their competitive nature put saloons on what seemed like every corner. The heir of respectability was short-lived. And this massive growth made the saloons an easy target for the drys.

The saloons also became a primary target of religious groups throughout the state, though their efforts fell flat, especially in the cities. The saloon was too big a draw and religious arguments weren't as effective. So the temperance crusaders would have to take to the countryside. And help for this crusade would arrive in 1877, as the Tennessee General Assembly constructed a law that would push the battle for the control of alcohol directly into the hands of the temperance movement.

Known as the Four Mile Law, it prohibited alcohol sales within four miles of chartered institutions of learning in unincorporated areas.[340] What gave it teeth was when incorporated areas began to repeal their charters of incorporation. Now any community that didn't want retail grogshops or saloons in their town only needed to unincorporate, then have their schools rechartered.

Distillers and wholesalers saw no danger in the new legislation and ignored it. But many of the communities frustrated by the lack of a local option, embraced it. In fact, it shocked people to see how many towns were willing to forgo their incorporated status just to get rid of the saloons in their community.[341]

It wasn't long before the rural saloon started disappearing. Saloon owners tried to fight back. They decided to test the constitutionality of the law. They pushed the case of Elizabeth Rouscher of Knox County all the way to the State Supreme Court. Elizabeth was charged with selling alcohol within four miles of East Tennessee University. The high court upheld the ruling in the case and declared the Four Mile Law constitutional. By 1880, large swaths of rural Tennessee were dry.[342]

For the purveyors of temperance, it might have been time for a victory lap. But there was a sense among the faithful that they had the liquor interests on the ropes, and this was no time to give up the fight. In their minds, the people of Tennessee had spoken. It was time to rid the state of the scourge of alcohol all together. And their blueprint for doing this would come from a distant state out west.

The Kansas Amendment

When it comes to temperance, there were few states that embraced the concept more from a legislative standpoint than Kansas. When it became a state in 1861, it inherited the local option from its territorial government. This drew organizations like the WCTU and New York's Independent Order of Good Templars to the state.

Unlike politicians in the rest of the country, Kansas legislatures had no problem picking a side. The state's Republican party was a strong promoter of temperance policies by the mid-1870s. When Republican Governor John St. John came into office, he believed the people had given him a mandate to rid the state of alcohol. He immediately pressed the Republican-held legislature to get a bill on his desk. What they gave him was a constitutional amendment banning "the manufacture and sale of intoxicating liquors." Put before the people in a referendum, the voters passed it by a slim margin—as of November 1880, the entire state of Kansas was dry.[343]

Like the Maine Law in the 1850s, Kansas Prohibition became a rallying cry in Tennessee. But just like Maine, if the drys of Tennessee had waited to see the results of the amendment, they might have thought twice.

The number of saloons in Kansas actually increased after the passing of the amendment.[344] The frustration over the lack of law enforcement led a Kentucky-born Kansas housewife, Caroline Amelia Nation, to take matters into her own hands. Looking to exact revenge on the saloons for the death of her alcoholic husband Charles, she ditched the routine of singing songs of protest outside the saloons, and started wielding an axe. With it, she smashed up any saloon she entered. Carrie Nation would become famous for her antics, and soon saloons were posting signs that said "*All Nations* Welcome But *Carrie*." This was a warning sign of the ineffectiveness of legislation without enforcement.

But even if the Tennessee prohibitionists were paying attention to the failure of the amendment, they didn't care. They were on a mission from God, just like Carrie.

So where were the distilling interests during all of this? Fighting for changes in bonding laws. After all, this is why they formed their trade organization, the National Distillers and Spirits Dealers' Association, a couple years earlier.[345] But during the fall of 1882 another organization formed, looking to counter the WCTU. Their original name was the National Liquor Dealers and Manufacturer's Protective Association of the United States. Their first order of business at their Milwaukee convention was to rebrand themselves. They needed a name that was friendly and approachable—something that sounded like a cause. After all, they were peddling alcohol, while their opponents were passionate clergy members and women with children to protect. They decided to make it a battle between freedom of choice and freedom of body and soul. The name they chose? The Personal Liberty League.[346]

But in Tennessee, distillers and wholesalers seemed oblivious to it all. They were too busy looking at their fat profits. Spirituous liquors had become the state's top industry--why would the citizens of Tennessee kill their cash cow? To the distillers, the saloon was the real issue.

Adding to the distiller's confidence was the high hurdle temperance crusaders would have to jump to get a constitutional amendment passed in Tennessee. It was no simple task. First, it would have to pass the General Assembly by a majority vote in both houses, then it would have to wait a year to be voted on again. Plus, it took a two-thirds majority to get the amendment put into a state referendum. It seemed the distillers were right to believe this was too tough to accomplish, when measures failed to get out of the House in both 1881 and 1883. And since the legislature only met biannually, that meant a referendum met in 1885 couldn't meet a public vote until 1887. If the temperance forces were going to get this done on the third attempt, they would have to channel their inner Mary Hunt, and needed the same temperance organizations that sealed the deal for the Kansas amendment, marching in lockstep for Tennessee.

The WCTU, who had only a small organization in the state, boosted their numbers when they heard there was a growing chance for victory. Churches organized, social clubs formed, and organizations like The Order of the Good Templars attacked the issue with zeal. Since Tennessee's Republican and Democratic parties weren't quite ready to endorse Prohibition, efforts would have to go district by district and candidate by candidate. To get everyone marching in lockstep, a state temperance convention was held in Nashville on May 22, 1884. With the two major parties not willing to add temperance to their platform, delegates debated joining the Prohibition Party, which had recently formed in the state, but went the Mary Hunt route by attacking candidates who opposed the amendment.

One measure the convention considered adding to its platform was the elimination of the manufacture of spirits in the state.[347] This had to take a few distillers and wholesalers by surprise. The adopted language for the amendment was "no person shall manufacture for sale, or sell, or keep for sale as a beverage any intoxicating liquors whatsoever."[348] Distillers were on notice.

When the 1885 General Assembly met, they approved the right of the public to vote on a Prohibition referendum in 1887. Senator McDowell would form the Tennessee Temperance Alliance with a goal of further organizing the troops for this critical fight.

The Referendum Fight

"Untrue Report" read a headline in the *Nashville Daily American*. The story was a distiller's response to an article in the *Nashville Union* titled "Scoundrels at Work," with the more incendiary subheadlines, "Dastardly Outrage of Springfield Whiskyites" and "Using Dynamite to Intimidate the Foes of the Rum Power."[349]

There was little doubt that tensions were at an all-time high. The people's vote on the Prohibition amendment was on the way that fall and there was a lot at stake. Partisan newspapers did their best to stoke the fires any way they could.

The Daily American article surrounded a devious and dangerous act committed in Springfield. It seems that a Mr. Duncan was giving a speech on the evils of alcohol when he was started by the explosion of fireworks near his feet. The *Nashville Union* assumed it was an attack by distillers against a prohibitionist. Instead, it was a group of boys, angry about an ordinance against the sale of fireworks in the town. The *Daily American* noted, "Everyone knew it was a prank of some mischievous boys except Mr. Duncan and the nameless correspondent who seized the opportunity to make Duncan a martyr and raise a sympathy for the prohibition cause."

The article then extolled the virtues of Robertson County distillers and the lack of violence in the community. "Until the last court there had not been a murder case on the docket for years, and for months last fall the doors of the jail stood wide open. The whisky dealers here are as much respected and contribute as much to the cause of Christianity as any man in the country." It was signed by nine distillers including John W. Stark & Co, Jordan S. Brown, Daniel Woodard, and James Woodard.[350]

Meanwhile, the *Daily American* and *Chattanooga Commercial* printed an old letter by the late-Andrew Jackson criticizing prohibitory laws. They reminded people that Tennessee's hero, Old Hickory, had once been a distiller.

Prohibition advocates, feeling they had the church vote in their back pocket, expanded their reach to tip the scales. Of the electorate in Tennessee, the Black vote constituted about one-fourth of the total. Most were against the amendment. It brought back memories of slavery and Tennessee's laws that forbade the purchase of liquor for the enslaved. What made it a tougher sell is the fact the Ku Klux Klan were clear advocates for the amendment.

Women became a double-edged sword for prohibitory forces. They were the perfect martyrs, having suffered at the hands of drunken and sometimes violent husbands. And many had lived through poverty, watching their life savings being poured into the saloons. It made them sympathetic characters. But they had no say at the ballot box, so they let their voices be heard by organizing rallies and gathering at polling places with their children at their side. But this turned off some of the very voters they needed to encourage. Nashville attorney John Vertrees turned against the amendment in the papers, seeing it as a ploy for gaining women's suffrage.

Vertrees also suggested that the law would be ineffective as the legislature would be too shy to pass enforcement laws.[351] Meanwhile, the *Chattanooga Times* argued it was impossible to enforce prohibition in a single state.

As polls opened on September 29, every town across the state bustled with activity. Street demonstrators held signs; clubs and organizations flew flags. In Morristown, the WCTU placed a huge banner at the courthouse polling places that said "Thou God Seest Me." Children were taken out and paraded. Free lunches were served. Music filled the streets and crowds gathered around the polling places.[352]

Some polls provided different color ballots so onlookers could see if the voter was for or against the amendment. Boos would rise when a red anti-vote was cast and cheers when a blue ticket went in the box. In Chattanooga's Third Ward, every time a vote went her way, a woman would yell out, "God bless you, you're a man."[353] The police were thankful for the women's presence as they felt the violence and language were kept at bay during the proceedings so that "delicate ears might not be offended."[354] More than a few men stopped off at a saloon to drink a pint of courage before heading through the mobs to cast their vote—except in Knoxville, where saloons remained closed for the day.

In the end, the measure failed by 27,633 votes.[355] East Tennessee had given the greatest support for the amendment, while Nashville and Memphis had the ultimate power in striking it down.[356] It was said to be the largest poll cast up to that time.[357]

Those in the temperance movement were beyond confused by the result. They just couldn't believe the state had turned against them. This put them into a search for scapegoats.

Some questioned the wisdom of having women and children at the polls, thinking it was too heavy-handed. Others questioned the use of clergy and the Bible. The capper was the Black vote, which went overwhelmingly against the amendment.

The prohibitionists licked their wounds and carried on. The anti-prohibitionists celebrated with a dram of their favorite spirit. But the prohibitionists would have their day. They just needed a little more time for Mary Hunt to work her magic on the next generation of voters.

Chapter 17

MEN OF MYSTERY

To those who never bought a bottle of spirits on Market Street, the face on the front page of the June 11, 1894 *Nashville Banner* could have been anyone from a Civil War general to a beer baron. His square jaw, strong brow, and deep-set eyes brought a serious look to his face. His dark suit and white shirt gave off an air of distinction. Yet within this stern and professional demeanor there was a kindness in his eyes, and his white beard gave off a grandfatherly vibe.

For the longest time, that sketch in the *Banner* was the only known image of George A. Dickel. A highly successful spirits wholesaler, George's reputation in the Nashville whisky community was unimpeachable. He was also an active member of several civic organizations. He served in the Nashville Commandery and held the Order of the Golden Cross. He was a Mason with the Cumberland Lodge. And the Knights Templar dubbed him Sir George Dickel.[358]

That his death was front-page news spoke volumes about his character. Living in a time of temperance, most whisky men had their occupation buried or excluded from their obituaries. And their death notices usually appeared deep within the paper. But not George. There was no escaping the fact he was a whisky man, and a highly celebrated one.

During the 20th century, the name George A. Dickel became associated with a whisky that always played second fiddle to its Lynchburg neighbor. In the 19th century, however, there were few men in the industry who stood taller than George Dickel.

The Forgotten Past

It's no surprise that George Dickel's life ended up a mystery considering the confusion surrounding his birth. His obituary in the *Nashville Banner* claims he was born on February 2, 1818, in Grünberg, Germany. However, in the 1870 U.S. Census records from Davidson County, he was listed as being from Darmstadt, Germany, some sixty miles to the south.[359]

The *Banner* obituary tells of George's arrival in Nashville in 1847. His first job was as a firefighter, serving with the then famous Deluge Fire Company No. 3.[360] Known for their speed and efficiency at putting out blazes, these firemen earned extra compensation from insurance companies if they were first to the scene. George used these bonuses to build his bank account.[361] He also gained exposure to Nashville's business community. The fire company stayed heavily invested in community affairs and put on shows for the people of Nashville.[362] This exposure led George into the Masons, becoming a Master Mason in 1852.[363]

One of the people George became acquainted with during the city's parades was George C. Banzer, a frequent assistant marshal for the parades[364] and the owner of a confectionary store on Union Street.[365] It was at 40 Union Street where George Dickel opened his first store He manufactured and repaired boots and shoes.[366] Not long after they met, George Banzer passed away, leaving behind his wife Louisa and several children. Over the next few years, George grew close to the Banzers, especially the eldest daughter Augusta. A young woman with refined tastes and a social sense that matched George's, They were a perfect pair. As she grew into adulthood, a relationship blossomed and the two were married on January 30, 1860. But George knew life as a cobbler would not bring Augusta the lifestyle she deserved. His opportunity to find a more lucrative business arrived when he met another German immigrant, Meier Salzkotter, a recent transplant from the eastern part of the state.

Like George, Meier's early years are a mystery. Born in Harstein, Prussia on June 22, 1826, little is known about his upbringing.[367] At 23, he left his homeland, boarded the ship Francis in Bremen, Germany, and arrived in New York City on August 24, 1848. Meier's plan was to settle in Philadelphia and find work as a shopkeeper.[368] He arrived in Knoxville in the 1850s and tried his hand at running a wholesale liquor and cigar shop on Main Street.[369] Seeing a bit of success, he opened a wholesale and retail gentleman's clothing shop down the street.[370] At the same he fell in love with Cecelia Schwab, the fifteen-year-old daughter of a Nashville merchant. The two were married by a justice of the peace in 1857.[371] Life was moving at a fast pace and Meier was faced with both businesses failing. He and Cecelia were forced to move in with her family. It's possible Cecelia's father Abe took pity on Salzkotter and purchased his liquor inventory, because soon after, A. Schwab began advertising its Knoxville wholesale liquor business in 1859. Meier then went to work for his father-in-law as a bookkeeper.[372] He also renewed his vows with Cecelia in 1860. By then, Meier was in Abe's good graces and he gave the young man an opportunity to work as a bookkeeper in his Nashville store. Meier was ready for the challenge. So, in December, he and Cecelia headed west.

Things started well enough in Nashville. The store was doing a good business and Cecelia was pregnant. But when shots were fired at Fort Sumter in South Carolina and Tennessee joined the Confederacy, war was all around. Soon the liquor wholesaling business dried up. Back in Knoxville, Abe hedged his bets and slowly entered the dangerous but lucrative smuggling trade. It was a risky business, but Schwab was soon scoring some big sales selling across Union lines. By the end of 1861, the Nashville store was still doing an honest business, but Meier had another mouth to feed. Felix Salzkotter was born on December 20. Whether it was pressure from his father-in-law or the need to feed his family, Meier took Schwab's Nashville operation slowly into the smuggling trade.

He wasn't alone. Nashville became a hotbed of smuggling activity. Most were still using the tried and true wagon for transportation. To keep from being discovered, they hid their illicit payload under sacks of grain or salted meats; if the load was oversized, they might go as far as to cover the items in manure. Salzkotter wasn't impressed. If everyone was doing the same thing, the chances of getting caught would increase exponentially. Then he heard of a carpenter named John L. Smith who had built some false-bottom wagons for two local smuggling rings—the Friedenbergs and Besthoffs. Basically he used wood planks to add a secret compartment of two and a half to three inches to the wagon bed. It was just enough space to ship bottles of quinine and other medicines to the Confederates. Meier paid five dollars for the first wagon, but then decided selling these wagons to other smugglers could make him a pretty penny. Unfortunately for him, word got around and on January 3, 1863 local law enforcement came beating on his door. Meier was arrested and taken before federal authorities. He tried to deny the charges, saying he had never bought a false bottom wagon. He also claimed the liquor found at his home was partially stock that was to be sold legally and some was payment for his work with Schwab. But Mike Friedenberg, the carpenter Smith, and others testified against him. He was accused of running quinine and other medicines between Louisville and Nashville. He was also said to have personally delivered goods to Knoxville in false-bottom wagons throughout the summer and fall of 1862. There was nowhere for Meier to turn.[373] He was charged as a spy for the Confederates, and his liquor was seized and distributed to hospitals. From there, they sent him to Alton, Illinois, to serve out his time in a former penitentiary that was being used as a makeshift army prison camp. He was paroled on March 2 and made his oath of allegiance to the Union.[374] When he returned home, he found his wife Cecelia had taken a lover. Meier tried to reconcile with her for the sake of their child Felix, but within days, she was back to her adulterous ways. Then, on October 28, 1863, she left Nashville for good. She made her way to Louisville, Kentucky, where she found a "house of ill fame" on Madison Street and became a lady of the evening. By May 1864, Meier was in court seeking a divorce. When Cecelia didn't appear for the divorce proceeding in Nashville, Meier was granted the divorce and custody of two and a half year old son Felix.[375]

It was time to start life over again; he decided to leverage his relationships within the German community. One man he had befriended was George Dickel. The shoe business was doing okay, but with the war coming to a close, Meier's talk of his experience in the wholesale liquor business intrigued George. Meier, who had used the railroads in his days as a smuggler, persuaded George of their ability to expand a wholesale business beyond Nashville. George needed to start small, so instead of jumping right into wholesale, he sold his shoe business and established a smaller liquor store at 23 South College Street and hired Meier to manage it.[376] The business did well enough that the next year he moved the store to a larger space at 12 South Market Street.[377]

The new business was just a few steps from Charles Nelson's establishment. Whether the two whisky legends were friends is unknown, but Meier definitely knew Charles' brother Adolph. Not only were the two part of a local German citizens' group,[378] Adolph was also a witness at Meier's divorce proceedings against Cecelia.

It appears from the record that Meier stepped away from the business in 1867 to once again try out his entrepreneurial skills, but by May 1868, he and his new partners were declaring bankruptcy.[379] With hat in hand, he came back to George, who by that time had expanded into a full-fledged liquor wholesaler. He even added rectifying to his arsenal. But George might have jumped the gun on that last activity, as he soon faced a U.S. government charge of rectifying without a license.[380] That seemed to bring an end to the idea of producing in-house whiskies.

Dickel proved to be adept at building relationships in the community, but he was slow to grow the business. What he needed was a dynamic outside salesman. He didn't realize he had just what he needed working in his backroom as a bookkeeper. The charisma and salesmanship of the young man he called Manny was about to supercharge the future of George A. Dickel, & Co.

The Secret Ingredient

Victor Emmanuel "Manny" Shwab was a born salesman. He had drive, instinct, a great sense of humor, and a chameleon-like personality that helped him open a variety of new doors for the Dickel organization.

Born in Youngstown, Ohio, in 1847, Manny attended Crocker's School at White Springs Creek, just a dozen miles north of Nashville. Upon graduation, he moved to the city and quickly found employment with Dickel. It may have helped that Manny was the son of Abe Schwab and Meier's brother-in-law. The family connections would grow even stronger when, in July 1871, Manny married Augusta Dickel's sister Emma Banzer. That meant Manny was George Dickel's brother-in-law too.[381]

Once Manny's sales talents were realized, the company's sales and customer base grew. Having Manny selling set Meier free to travel and expand the company's inventory. With what was described as a painful death for his ten-year-old son Felix, Meier threw himself into his travels. His new products made Dickel's the place in Nashville to find fine French brandies, and Irish and Scotch whiskies. They also stocked the best of Old Robertson and Old Lincoln.

This change in the company's fortunes didn't go unnoticed and in 1872, Meier was made a partner of the firm. But not all of Meier's transactions went smoothly. One of his trips to the old country in 1874 turning into quite a mess. After purchasing fifty thirteen-gallon casks of Cognac, he sent them to the port in Le Havre, France, where he could get approval for shipping to the US. When Meier got back to Nashville, he expected the barrels to be just a couple of days behind. Instead, they were still sitting at the Customs House in New York. When he inquired about their status, he was told that Dickel would have to forfeit the casks to the U.S. Government. It seems the measurements at the docks showed the barrels only contained 12 ½ gallons each. By law, each cask was to have no less than 13 gallons. It was a simple case of evaporation. But what they were implying was that George A. Dickel, & Co. was trying to avoid paying full customs duties. Luckily, George had friends in high places who vouched for his honesty. Eventually, the government processed the brandy and sent it on to Nashville. This led a local paper to suggest the appointment of a local appraiser "to avoid New York customs' stupidity."[382]

Another challenge that reared its ugly head for the firm was fire. Although Nashville had ditched many of the old wooden structures from the frontier days, it remained a tinderbox waiting for a spark. Of all the places in the city where the fear was greatest was along Market Street, with its excessive number of warehouses filled to the rim with barrels. And on August 14, 1874, George got the dreaded 1 AM call saying there was a fire at his store. Apparently, the blaze started at his neighbor's, the Rock City Paper Mill Company. George feared the worst. The firm had just received 150 barrels of fresh Lincoln County whisky, which added to the existing 750 barrels. Luckily, the fire walls built between the two businesses held. But unfortunately, the fire hoses flooded Dickel's business, causing some unintended damage.[383]

The fire was nothing more than a speed bump. By 1875, the firm had established such a fine reputation throughout the region that they were shipping copper distilled sour mash whisky, imported wines, and champagne to locations as far away as New York, the Carolinas, out west to Missouri and down south to Alabama and Georgia.[384] All of this growth expanded their goals. No longer were they willing to settle for being the biggest wholesaler in Nashville. They wanted to become a principal supplier to the emerging western United States.

This gave George A. Dickel & Co. the opportunity to spread Tennessee whisky to more regions of the United States. Manny was so confident in the quality of Tennessee whisky, he even sold it in Kentucky, which was starting to challenge Illinois and Ohio as a center of industrialized whisky production.[385] Manny had such a great impact on the business that in 1881, George and Meier invited him in as a partner.

Shortly after, once again, fire wreaked havoc with the business. The great Nashville fire of May 1881 was one of the worst on record. It started in the late morning when an alarm bell sounded at the corner of Market and Church streets—the opposite corner from Dickel's business. It started in the cellar of the Warren Brothers paint store and was well underway before employees noticed flames kicking up through the elevator shaft. Oil paint and thinner only intensified the blaze. When firefighters arrived, they couldn't get water to come out of the hoses. Suddenly, a fear gripped the crowd and business owners grabbed what they could from their buildings. Once the water finally flowed, the fire was already inside Dickel's establishment. It didn't take long for the entire building to be engulfed in flames. Meanwhile, the sizable crowd that had gathered jumped out of their skins when a deafening explosion echoed down the streets. The fire was inside the Pearse, Hopkins, and Lawrence wholesale liquor warehouse. It sounded like a war zone, with barrels exploding like artillery. Six hundred barrels of whisky, plus brandy and other spirits, went up in flames along with the building, which was owned by John Sperry's brother Henry.

The damage to the wholesale house of Pearse, Hopkins, and Lawrence totaled $20,000. Dickel's losses were at $75,000, with only $40,000 covered by insurance. The firm temporarily relocated to 36 South Market Street.[386]

One of the more curious items in the record is a lawsuit filed by George A. Dickel, & Co. against Jack Daniel. Allegedly, the Lincoln County distiller owed Dickel's company $2,000, and payment wasn't forthcoming.[387] Shortly after the filing in Circuit Court, Dickel dropped the case. Historically, this is significant. It shows that George Dickel likely sold Jack Daniel's whisky in his store at some point. Eventually, the two businesses would become rivals.

Over the years, neither fire, war, nor temperance workers could keep George A. Dickel from the daily affairs of his business. But by 1886, the 68-year-old was slowing down. He still helped in business negotiations and helped keep up the management of the store, but more and more, he was turning the day-to-day operations over to Manny and Meier. With George stepping back, Manny had more opportunity to expand the business beyond wholesaling. His first step was to set up an exclusive partnership with a local saloon. This was following the trend started by German brewers like Adolphus Busch, Frederick Miller, and Joseph Schlitz, who put up capital for saloons and then supplied them with signage and spirits. Manny had his eye on the popular but highly questionable Climax Saloon. It wouldn't have been George's first choice, but Manny made the highest bid at $27,000, and the building was theirs.[388]

Of all the saloons in Nashville, the Climax had one of the rowdiest and more violent reputations. It was a real old-time saloon. Not only could you get your drinks on the first floor, you could gamble on the second, and visit a lady of the evening in the brothel on the third. They made an exclusive deal to sell their liquor in the bar. But when reporters questioned Dickel's reputation, the chief of police, J.H. Clack, stood by the company's president saying that while Manny was a whisky man and his company owned the building, he said "so far as I am informed he has no interest in the business."[389]

While the Climax was a questionable move for Manny, his other purchase cemented George Dickel's legacy in the world of Tennessee whisky.

Seeing the example set by Charles Nelson and John Woodard, Manny knew he needed to establish his own brand of whisky. The question was how? He could start his own distillery, but he was at a disadvantage. The Woodards brought with them a century of distilling heritage. Charles Nelson had built three successful distilleries before rebuilding the Greenbrier facility. Manny didn't have time for that. He needed to find an established distillery with home-grown talent, a great reputation, and easy railroad access. He found it all close to the Tullahoma train stop on the way to Chattanooga.

Cascade Hollow

Since the days of David Crockett's travels into the interior of Tennessee, the springs and creeks that flow through Bedford and Coffee counties have seen their share of water powered gristmills both large and small. Some of those mills bred stillhouses. Before the days of the excise, Flat Creek was a popular area for stills with Philip Burrow, John Holt, Simpson Neice, and Leslie Bobo being some of its early producers.[390] After the war, distillers like E.A. Call, J.S. Newton, Finis E. Cunningham, and Julius Wolff developed successful operations despite the Tice Meter controversy.

The area known today as Cascade Hollow would see its rise in the distilling world thanks to a Lincoln County distiller named Mathew Benton Sims. A onetime partner with Tolley & Eaton and owner of his own M.B. Sims & Co. distillery in Flintville, he thought the location held promise, moved his wife Lucy and three daughters to Coffee County and bought in on the distillery. By 1883, Mathew had 22,813 gallons of whisky aging in bond.[391]

Much of that output was because of his new partnership with Bedford County's McLin Hezikiah Davis.

From the outside, it might have appeared McLin "Ki" Davis was a long shot. He didn't have a background in distilling. His work experience included being a merchant and telegraph operator at the Normandy general store. But distilling is where McLin really shined. When Mathew tested him out on the stills, he could see McLin had a gift. The two worked so well together, McLin bought a third of the business, buying out R.J. King in October 1883.[392] The reputation of the M.B. Sims Distillery at Cascade Hollow now rested with McLin. It wasn't long before Mathew's Masonic brotherhood in Lynchburg had to admit McLin was something special. It was McLin's goal to make the best sour mash whisky money could buy.

Over his first five years, McLin developed such a strong reputation, they drew the attention of the Nashville wholesale house of George A. Dickel, & Co. Manny Shwab became such a fan of the whisky coming out of Cascade Hollow, he offered to buy out Mathew Sims. On March 14, 1888, Victor "Manny" Shwab became a two-thirds owner of the Cascade Hollow distillery.[393] From that day forward, McLin Davis' top quality whisky would be sold exclusively to George A. Dickel, & Co.[394]

None of that Sweet Mash

With a distillery in hand featuring a high-quality product, Manny wasted no time in touting it as some of the best whisky around. He also took a jab at "sweet mash" whiskies masquerading as sour mash and Cincinnati spirits being sold as "pure sour mash."[395]

It's true that the word "pure" was being abused by a wide range of distillers and this wasn't just in Cincinnati or St. Louis. The Whisky Trust in Peoria, Illinois, was the biggest offender. In fact, when the State of Illinois took them to court to shut down their trust, it appalled them to see how the company sold grain spirits with added flavors and colorant as pure bourbon or pure rye whisky. It was truly an age when integrity was in short supply among the whisky barons.

Manny also took a shot at Robertson County, suggesting some deception in their sour mash claim. He pointed to a rule change that came down after sour mash distillers asked the government to allow them five days for fermentation and to tax them on a lower yield. In response, the government allowed it, but a distillery had to declare if they were "sweet mash" or "sour mash," they couldn't be both. To validate their choice, a form had to be filled out. What Manny was alleging is that sweet mash distillers were filling out both forms. Then, after giving the sweet mash survey to the government, they showed the sour mash survey to customers.[396]

Whether true or not, Manny would do whatever he could to take a bite out of his competition.

To further convince the whisky buying public, he invited the *Nashville Banner* into the Cascade Hollow distillery to have a look around. It sounds like Manny was along for the tour to keep the reporter on message:

> "Mr. V. E. Shwab, the active manager of the firm of Geo. A. Dickel, approves of Davis' attention to detail. He wants his as the model brand of the Lincoln county type. They have a mill on site and use white hominy corn. A little rye is added. Into the mash tub is ejected a certain quantity of hot potale from the still and into this is allowed to flow the meal while a wooden rake revolves to thoroughly mix the mean and water. When cooked it is cooled by the cold spring water flowing through copper pipes coiled in the tub. It is turned over into one of the 4 fermentation vats. A little yeast from one of the fully fermented mashes is added to assist in the process. Sweet mash would have used a chemically prepared yeast. When the beer is ready to drink, it is pumped into a wooden still by siphon pump. Steam through copper pipes boils the beer. The vapors are condensed as low

> wines and are passed into a doubler (a copper still) for redistillation. Another condenser is used and the resulting liquid is pumped into the leaching house. Ten feet high, six foot wide leaching tubs are packed and pounded firmly with a quantity of the finest wood charcoal. Maple wood. It takes days for it to drip through the charcoal. Sweet mash distillers put color in, but sour mash doesn't."[397]

It is interesting to note the hallmarks of good Lincoln County whisky were still intact at Cascade Hollow in the 1890s: Log stills; leaching; and slow natural sour mash fermentation.

To further convince the market of the legitimacy of his sour mash process, Manny started an advertising campaign in 1890 stating: "George Dickel's whisky is SOUR MASH as verified by the honorable Collector of the Internal Revenue for the Fifth District."[398] They used a government collector's name at the end to validate it. Manny's attention to detail meant this statement had to be updated every couple of years. With George in ill-health, Manny sought a brand name to carry the whisky well into the future. He wanted one that would honor his mentor, but also wanted a name that could live on its own. Since the whisky came from the Cascade Hollow distillery, he rebranded the whisky as George A. Dickel's Cascade Whisky.

As with the Dickel wholesale business, Manny had bigger plans outside of Tennessee for the Cascade brand. In 1892, he shipped a barrel of Cascade whisky, painted red, white, and blue, to the Democratic National Convention in Chicago. On the side he had painted, "if the nominee is as free from faults as Cascade whisky he will be sure to win."[399]

While Manny was looking forward, the past started slipping away. Meier Salzkotter was taken away suddenly, killed by a heart clot on August 3, 1891—he was 65 years of age.[400] With George Dickel still in poor health, Meier's share of the company went to Manny.

Then came the sad but inevitable end for a bedridden George Dickel. The *Banner* reported, "his wife, son-in-law and other relatives were with him at his last moments. He was perfectly rational to the last and spoke with calmness and precision of his temporal affairs. He died in perfect peace."[401]

Sir George Dickel had passed away, but his name would live on, thanks to Manny's aggressive work promoting the quality of George A. Dickel's Cascade Sour Mash whisky. Two years after his death, wholesalers couldn't keep it in stock, even though it cost 50% more than its Lincoln County competitors.

History remembers George Dickel's name mostly because of the brand that still bears his name. Yet people know little about the man himself. And fewer yet know the names of the talented team that built and carried on his legacy. But maybe they wanted it that way. After all, why shine the spotlight elsewhere, when your whisky is doing a grand job of speaking for itself?

Chapter 18

WATERFORD WANDERER

Looking for a Home

What a wondrous scene. Glancing out the window of the Nashville to Chattanooga bound train, young Jim Kelly couldn't help but think of his homeland as he watched the scenery passing by. Rolling green hills and placid, brilliant blue waterways, this place made it easy to get lost in a daydream.

His mind suddenly wandered to his life's path. He wondered if coming to America was really the right decision. As a young lad, fresh from school, he'd left County Waterford to get into the wine trade in Dublin. He enjoyed living in the city, but he couldn't help but feel like he was stuck fighting for scraps. His friends were all talking about the great opportunities overseas, so he took a chance, sold everything, and took a job as a sailor to pay for his voyage to New York in 1863.[402]

While most of his friends took jobs on the docks, in factories, or at one of the city's many slaughterhouses, Jim wanted to make his mark further west. With a war going on, there weren't a lot of safe places to go, but he took a chance on Nashville, Tennessee. He thought the slower pace of the frontier town might help him find a suitable business opportunity.

The place looked like it held promise, but there was a tentativeness about the people. He arrived just as the Battle of Nashville was raging at the edge of town. He initially took a job with R.H. Singleton and helped produce their Nashville

Business Directory.[403] Soon after, he took a job as a bookkeeper at the *Nashville Daily Bulletin*.[404] The money was nice, but he was stuck behind a desk most of the time. He waited for other opportunities, but nothing seemed quite right.

After a year at the *Daily Bulletin*, Jim became restless. He decided to head back to New York to see if he could get into the international wine trade. But first, he needed to collect a debt from a friend that had recently moved to Chattanooga. From there, Jim could catch the rail line north to Virginia and beyond.

As the train steamed ahead over the Tennessee River, he started having second thoughts about heading back east. But he wasn't sure what else he could do.

Jim and Johnny

When Jim reached Union Depot at Chattanooga, the 22-year-old Irishman looked around to see if his friend had arrived. As he stood there waiting, he couldn't help but notice the sound of hammers in the distance. Wandering out of the limestone and brick structure onto 9th Street, he noticed a street filled with activity. Construction was going on all around him. It was 1866 and the last physical scars of the Battle of Chattanooga were fading away. Jim liked it there. There was an energy of renewal. When he spotted his friend walking up from Market Street, he wasn't disappointed that his buddy said he didn't have the cash to pay him just yet.[405] Something about this place was drawing him. He decided to stick around to see what the town could offer him.

With the light sandwich he had on the train wearing off, he went on a hunt for something to snack on. He walked to the corner of 9th and Market streets, past the Kaylor House and into a dry goods store. He bought some fruit and then struck up a conversation with the owner, Daniel Kaylor. Jim knew a grocery was always a great place to get tips on the local job scene. But, to his surprise, Mr. Kaylor offered him a job in his store.

It was while working at Kaylor's that Jim made the acquaintance of another ambitious young man, John G. Webb. As a sprightly twelve-year-old, the young Pennsylvanian had run away from home, hoping to help the boys in blue win the war. Johnny caught on with the 78th Pennsylvania as a drummer boy and quickly won over his regiment with his enthusiasm. They would remark that he was never late for reveille and his shining face made the early morning wake-up calls much easier to bear. [406]

After the war, a teenage Johnny found himself stranded in Chattanooga. Kaylor, who was a sucker for ambitious young talent, gave the young man a job sweeping out the storeroom and stocking shelves.

Jim took to the little ball of energy right away and asked Johnny if they might go into business together. It was a grand offer to Johnny, but neither of them was exactly flush with cash. Overhearing the plight of the two boys, Mr. Kaylor said, "boys, if you want to set up your own fruit cart business, I'm happy to rent you out space in my storeroom for your supplies." The boys jumped at the offer.

Knowing the boys' financial situation, he didn't ask for his payment up front, thinking a week would be sufficient for them to make a few sales so they could pay him. On the day he went to collect the $30 due, Johnny was nowhere to be seen and Jim was in the back room leaning against an apple barrel. Even in his scruffy, torn up jeans and unkempt shirt, Jim gave off the appearance of all business.

When Mr. Kaylor asked where Johnny was, Jim said he was on the slow train to Georgia, selling fruit to his captive audience.

"Do you boys have the rent money together yet?"

Jim took the last bite of the apple he was eating, walked to the back door and tossed the core at a stray dog sniffing around their stock.

"Well, I tell you, Mr. Kaylor," Jim said, "we haven't but $28 between us and if we pay you $30 we will be $2 below zero. It's mighty hard to make money on no capital. If I had $300 you would see me swim like one of my apples in a tub of salt water."

Mr. Kaylor smiled and said, "Come, now, if that's all you want."

He wrote out the check to James W. Kelly. Jim took it down to the First National Bank and cashed it in. After three months Jim and Johnny made enough money to pay Mr. Kaylor back and they soon left his stockroom and set up a storefront of their own on Daniel Kaylor's block.[407]

Kelly & Webb was a success right out of the gate. The two young entrepreneurs put every dollar they made into growing the store's inventory. But six months into their ownership, four straight days of heavy rains put the business in danger. Flooding consumed the town and the force of the Tennessee River brought down the Military Bridge downtown. The new business owners were determined to weather the storm. But when they heard stories of people drowning in their homes, they sought higher ground.

When the storm was over, the store was in a miserable state. Desperate locals had broken the windows of their storefront and pilfered through their supplies. Kelly & Webb survived, but faced another threat to the business the following September when a waiter at the nearby Crutchfield House tripped while carrying a tray of lighted oil lamps. The glass burst, the oil ignited, and within moments, the entire first-class hotel went up like a torch. The fire quickly jumped across the street as a March gale blew in from the north. Now the Kaylor House was in danger and Kelly & Webb's light-wood-framed business was right next door. Since Chattanooga didn't have a fire truck, stopping the blaze wasn't easy. Every able-bodied person grabbed a bucket and tried to douse the fire the best they could.

The intense efforts of the community saved the Kaylor block and the Kaylor House.[408] It looked like Kelly & Webb dodged a bullet. But, once inside, they saw the damage inflicted by vandals, who had seized on the moment to pilfer the store of many of its goods.

Daniel Kaylor had seen enough and sold out the business to his partner R.L. Bowdre. R.L. turned part of the house into the Bon Ton Billiard Saloon, first known as "The Bar" at the National, and stocked it with wine, liquors, and cigars.[409]

A visit to the Bon Ton rekindled Jim's interest in the wine trade, so he furnished Kelly & Webb's shelves with French wines, English porters and ales, and a variety of tobacco products. While Johnny wasn't interested in the liquor trade, he did like the idea of diversifying. So he added a bakery and catering services for weddings. The pair made an agreement. Whatever business they got into, they would always offer the best. Their advertisements boasted, "the choicest of everything in their line to be found in the city."[410]

Three years into the business, Kelly & Webb were getting rave reviews for "their character as reliable business men."[411] They were also getting interested in female companionship. As an entrepreneur and the star drummer of the Silver Cornet band, Johnny was one of the town's most eligible bachelors. But when he met Hattie Johnson, the daughter of a former Union officer, he was quick to supply her finger with a ring.[412] Marriage suited Johnny so well, it got Jim thinking about his childhood sweetheart Lizzie, back in Waterford. With John in Chattanooga to handle things, Jim went off on an extended vacation to Ireland to court the love of his life.[413]

Upon his return to Chattanooga, James W. Kelly spread the joyous news. Lizzie had agreed to marry him, with a grand wedding planned in Ireland the following year.

Wanting to impress her with his business empire, he opened a European-style gentleman's billiard room. He rented out a space, purchased the finest "Brunswick" tables, and invited the sophisticated gentlemen of Chattanooga to visit.[414]

Jim married Elizabeth Jane Short in Waterford on September 3, 1870, and the happy couple came to their new home in Chattanooga.[415] At first, Elizabeth was like a fish out of water. She was the exact opposite of her husband. While he had a showy personality, she was quiet and reserved, with a touch of melancholy. She was a warm host, delighted in smaller gatherings, and loved to play euchre, whist, and other card games. The couple became a steady presence in a town that doubled in size every decade for the rest of the century.

Jim and Johnny continued to grow the business. And in 1871, they added whisky to their inventory for the first time. Their initial inventories included Monongahela ryes and Bourbons from larger distillers out of state. As Tennessee whisky flowed again after the excise debacle, Jim put his focus on Robertson County whisky.

By 1872, John felt like he was holding Jim back from his dream of running a wholesale spirits shop. They dissolved the partnership and Jim established J.W. Kelly & Co. John opened his own John G. Webb grocery next to the old Crutchfield House, now rebuilt as the Read House.[416] He also bought into the Commercial Hotel, where his wife Hattie took care of guests. It was an amazing run for the dynamic duo, who had built impressive fortunes as a team. And all thanks to a $300 boost from a gracious Daniel Kaylor.

But while Jim had found a home, John was ready to head off to greener pastures. After befriending a man named Dan Duffy, he went off to St. Louis with his wife and child, and became a ticket broker. He eventually used his fortune to get into the development of medicines.

John and Hattie lived lavishly, but never outspent what they were bringing in. When he eventually split with Dan, John went to New York and worked full time in the ticket broker business. His offices were in the Astor House Hotel and on Canal Street. He used the money he made to build a beautiful estate on the Hudson River for Hattie and their little one, and he frequently invited his friends from Chattanooga to come and stay with him. When they did, he treated them with lavish luxuries.

He seemed to have it all. But on August 12, 1892, the *Chattanooga Daily Times* dealt a shattering blow:

> *"John Webb lies in death in a cemetery near New York City, leaving behind him a large fortune and hundreds of friends all over the country who will ever remember him as a man of splendid business talents, with a heart as big as the world."*

Unbeknownst to many of his friends, John suffered from heart disease. It was hard for his friends to believe that such a firecracker had been taken so cruelly. He was just 42 years old.[417]

The Chattanooga Liquor Trade

Free to explore the world of wholesale liquor in Chattanooga, J.W. Kelly initially had little competition. In fact, prior to the Civil War, the town was nearly dry. And not because of any law passed in the Tennessee General Assembly. The town's teetotalling founders served as an inspiration.

Chattanoogans only built a couple of distilleries and they were simply extensions of their gristmills. James S. Schneider opened the Chattanooga Mill & Distillery just before the Civil War. He had big plans for expansion and hired John J. Faulkner, a well respected southern rectifier, in January 1862. But selling whisky in a war zone wasn't easy, and the business quickly shut down.[418]

The Bell Mill & Distillery, near the banks of the Tennessee River, became the first post-war distillery in Chattanooga. But it too never took off. In 1869, the city sold the property at a chancery sale.[419]

North of Chattanooga, there were plenty of distillers but they all made brandy. Only Roufus Friddle, a small-time distiller, occasionally made up a batch of corn-based spirits.

The boys in gray returned from the war with a thirst for liquor, so wholesale liquor houses seemed like the business to get into. J.M. Doherty & Co. was the strongest player in a thin field. But as the town's saloon culture developed, Doherty expanded the business into rectifying and distilling. It wouldn't be until his partner D. Kirkpatrick bought him out[420] in July 1869 that he would sell in-house distilled white corn and copper-distilled whiskies. But D. Kirkpatrick & Co's bestsellers remained Old Robertson, rye, Bourbon, along with locally distilled apple and ginger brandy. When Kirkpatrick retired in 1873, the firm changed its name to E.B. Edwards & Co. and increased its focus on rectifying, at the expense of corn whisky.[421]

The other company J.W. Kelly considered competition was Betterton, Ford & Co. It was founded by two Virginia Confederate veterans, Elijah R. Betterton and Nathan C. Ford, who saw Chattanooga as the gateway to the deep south. While Elijah came directly to Chattanooga from Virginia,[422] Nathan spent time in Knoxville where Elijah's brothers William and J.N. Betterton ran their own wholesale whisky firm. William also ran his own distillery in Kingston, Tennessee. Betterton, Ford & Co. opened their Chattanooga wholesale in February 1870 at 717 Market Street. A couple of years later, William's distillery in Kingston burned to the ground twice.[423] Frustrated, he left to join Betterton, Ford & Co. to complete the team.

J.W. Kelly always focused on quality, whatever business he was in. When he opened his wholesale liquor operation at 253 Market Street, he stocked the best spirits he could find. He also was an early proponent of building trust in names. Seeing his competitors selling generic Old Robertson and Old Lincoln, he went a step further. He cut exclusive deals with longtime distiller John T. Motlow in Lincoln County and Dr. George E. Draughon in Robertson County.[424]

In February 1876, Kelly's low-cost competition, Betterton, Ford & Co., split up.[425] William went to Texas and Nathan Ford went into the wholesale tobacco business. Elijah wasn't ready to give up selling liquor just yet, so he moved the firm six blocks away to 141 Market Street. This put him right across the street from E.B. Edwards at 174 Market Street and just a block south of J.W. Kelly's firm.[426] While they were in similar businesses, the competitors all had a unique mix of products. For high-end spirits, Kelly's was the place, while Edwards had the best rectified spirits, and Betterton brought the value. But the low-cost approach put Betterton on the shaky ground and eventually he sold out to E.B. Edwards.

As soon as he merged his stock with E.B. Edwards, Elijah headed south along the rails and began selling for his new firm.[427] But the old Confederate was in for a shock. Edwards sold the business to a former Cincinnati liquor wholesaler, Moses Frank. Working for a Yankee wasn't quite what Elijah had in mind. When M. Frank & Co. re-established the firm at the corner at Ninth and Market, Betterton broke away and established a new business under the name Betterton & Co. He decided his best move was to add rectifying to the business, so he could make more profits, while still emphasizing value. One of his specialties was a process called compounding, where he would infuse fruits and spices into his whiskies. Some thought he was just covering bad distillate and lowering himself to Cincinnati busthead standards. But he eventually won over many of his critics.

While E.R. Betterton tried to get a foothold in the market and Frank's business went through several owners, J.W. Kelly established himself as a man of the community. His philanthropy started back in 1869 when the civic-minded firm of Kelly & Webb furnished 25 gas lamps and fixtures to light the streets of Chattanooga. J.W. then became an active board member of the Irish National League. He also liked to chime in on political affairs, especially regarding whisky legislation. He invested heavily in land and quickly doubled and tripled his money as the city grew. He also continued to run his high-class billiard hall. With all of this activity, he decided to lighten his burden. In 1876, he partnered with Alabaman and ex-Confederate soldier George Davenport.

Davenport was a top-notch networker. In no time, he had developed strong relationships with grocers across Alabama, Georgia, and down to New Orleans. In terms of stock, he got Kelly & Davenport into the medicinal spirits field. His chief brands were Lawrence and Martin's Tolu Rock & Rye and Duffy's Pure Malt Whisky. He also looked to leverage the growing popularity of Kentucky Bourbon, so he made deals to stock popular brands like McBrayer, Ripy, and Bond & Lillard. Locally, he made a deal with William Copeland's Lincoln County brand for his spirits. He also sourced regional corn whisky from North Carolina and Stone Mountain Georgia. Throughout the 1880s, it was Kelly & Davenport that led the wholesalers of the town.

But all was not peaches and cream. The state's push toward a prohibition amendment in the mid-1880s rattled some nerves. Once a date was set for a prohibition referendum, liquor dealers and distillers across the state organized to defeat the amendment.

In early July 1887, Kelly represented Kelly & Davenport in Tullahoma at a huge closed-door meeting at Montgomery and Davis Hall. There he met some of the biggest whisky names in the state including Manny Shwab of George Dickel & Co., Charles Nelson of Nelson's Green Brier, Tolley & Eaton, Jack Daniel, and a rising star revenuer Joe L. Spurrier, along with a host of smaller distillers, rectifiers, and dealers.[428]

Kelly came away from the meeting sensing the demise of retail liquor in the state. So he talked George Davenport into selling off the retail arm of their wholesale liquor business to Ed Mullery's store on Market and Ninth.

Then, in what seemed to be a monumental error in judgment, J.W. decided he wanted to rent the barroom of the Read House. Most thought the owners of the house had taken him to the cleaners. He paid an incredible $698 a month (the equivalent of $23,000 today). The previous rental rate was $211 a month, and the bar was just a room with no fixtures.[429] The move may have been the last straw for George Davenport, who withdrew from the business less than a month later and moved on to establish a wholesale dry goods business with his sons.[430]

But the Read House deal was a stroke of genius. J.W. saw a value where no one else did and ended up subleasing the room for a huge profit. He made $10,000 profit in the first three months alone.[431] The bar became one of the most popular hotel bars in the south and paid for itself with ease. As part of the sublease, J.W. Kelly was to be the exclusive provider of spirits, adding even more to his profits.

Wait. Wait. Wait. Boom!

For a town that once had a dry reputation, Chattanooga shifted into saloon central by the end of the 1870s. Yet the area was still devoid of any distilling beyond rectifying. Harry Kaylor tried to change that in 1876. He opened a log still distillery at Kaylors Mill at the base of Cameron Hill.[432] Initially he sold a handful of barrels to E.R. Betterton. In 1879, he sold out to J.B. Gilkerson, who ordered two 374-gallon stills, hired distiller T. Rachel from the old Kingston distilleries of William Betterton, and stocked grain silos with corn and rye. The distillery got up and running, making one hundred gallons of whisky a day. But within a month, financial difficulties shut the operation down and a buyer couldn't be found.[433]

The closest whisky distilling got to Chattanooga in the 1880s was when local wholesaler George W. Cureton opened the Fox Mountain and Poplar Spring Distillery thirty miles southwest of the city in Rising Fawn, Georgia. The Cureton wholesale shop at 704 Market Street sold his "pure handmade copper distilled sour mash whisky" alongside Lincoln, rye, and corn whisky.[434]

Then, in 1890, the local news reported that whisky men had selected a distillery location at Kelly's Ferry, eight miles west of downtown Chattanooga. The operation was the brainchild of E.R. Betterton and deputy sheriff and saloon owner Sam Cate.[435] But eventually the deal fell through. Then Betterton reached out to several potential investors, including J.W. Kelly, with an eye on developing a city brewery. But even with $100,000 in capital available, the American Brewing Company, as it was to be known, died with a whimper.[436]

Betterton wasn't the only one looking to establish a brand beyond wholesaling. J.W. Kelly believed rectifying was his step into the world of branded whisky. After adding stills to his establishment in 1891, he went heavily into promoting the wholesale house. In 1895, he began touting J.W. Kelly as "the Oldest House" in Chattanooga, established in 1866.[437] Of course, this wasn't when he started selling spirits, it was when he and John G. Webb started their first fruit stand. But as the 20th century approached, there seemed to be a need to establish "oldest" claims in the whisky industry. In fact, six months before the Kelly advertisements appeared, Jack Daniel made his own longevity claim. In the *Lawrence Democrat*, an ad proclaimed "Jack Daniel's old time sour mash whisky, the purist in Tennessee. The records at Washington D.C. show this Distill has been in operation longer than any in the United States."[438]

As for a stand-alone Chattanooga distillery, the 1890s looked to be another lost decade. Even Internal Revenue assessor Fred Fox complained about how boring his job was. There were only two rectifiers to visit and no distilleries. He needed a hobby for the other 29 days of the month.[439]

But all of that changed in 1897. Chattanooga finally got a distillery with staying power. It would come from Elijah R. Betterton, of course. After his failure seven years before, the crafty old wholesaler knew he needed someone with experience to help see it through. He partnered with William Mark Tolley, a third-generation distiller and the son of William Polk Tolley. Having distilled in the isolation of Kelso, he welcomed the chance to move his operations into the highly accessible and busy city of Chattanooga. The plan was to have the distillery operational before the summer of 1897. They purchased a quarter acre and leased another ten acres below Smartt Springs. The distillery began its first run of whisky on May 7, 1897. With an output of one hundred bushels a day, distilling started in a big way in Chattanooga. Seasoned distiller H.L. Maxwell ran the controls and produced both Lincoln County and corn whisky. Meanwhile, E.R. Betterton & Co. wholesale expanded its product line. New brands included Old Overholt Pennsylvania Rye, Sam Clay Bottled-in-Bond Bourbon, and Cascade Whisky from Manny Shwab's distillery.[440] By December 1898, they would have their newly branded White Oak Tennessee Pure Sour Mash whisky on the market.[441]

When William Mark Tolley's uncle John Dean Tolley saw the success his nephew was having in town, he decided it was time to get in on the action. John Dean wanted to prey upon what he saw as a fatal flaw in the Tolley & Betterton distillery––its location. Smartt Springs was a good deal north of town, making access to transportation more difficult. Partnering with James S. Cannon, John Dean Tolley filed a charter for the Lookout Distillery in November 1897.[442] By February 1898, Chattanooga had its second distillery in full operation.

The new Lookout Distillery was an instant success. When it quickly outgrew its footprint on Montgomery Street, John Shamotulski, one of its investors, opened up more land for the operation. In short order, the distillery was producing a thousand gallons of corn whisky, rye whisky, and brandy per day.

Being a bit of a showman, John Shamotulski wanted to give his distillery a little added flair. So he had two Angora goats killed and stuffed in what he referred to as a "belligerent manner." He placed them outside the distillery and attracted a lot of attention, including, according to the Chattanooga Daily News, "dogs who wanted to pounce upon the stuffed animals."[443]

With this influx of new distilleries, J.W. Kelly felt it was time to release his first batches of in-house rectified whisky. He branded it Deep Spring Tennessee Whisky and touted it as the "purest and best," and good for medicinal purposes.[444] He also began looking for property to construct more warehouses. With the government opening up longer bonding periods, he hoped to use the full eight years he was being given, tax-free.

As the Chattanooga business community took in all the advancements of the last six decades, it was time to celebrate. Not only had the town's population grown exponentially, it was once again made whole with the rebuilding of the Walnut/Market Street Bridge that had been lost in the floods so many years ago. The Chattanooga Business Expo of 1900 brought the business community together to show off the future. The distillers took full advantage. J.W. Kelly was there introducing his new brand Silver Springs while also giving out samples of his Deep Spring Whisky. Distiller J.S. Cannon represented Lookout Distilling and demonstrated wildcat distilling on a forty gallon still. Not to be outdone, E.R. Betterton showed off his White Oak Tennessee Sour Mash Whisky and did his own demonstrations on a fifty gallon still.[445]

Then, in a shocking move, the Tolley's sold the fast-growing Lookout Distillery. Whether spooked by a rash of warehouse fires in Lincoln County or the ratcheting up of rhetoric by prohibitionists, they wanted out of the business. J.D. Tolley sold out to a distiller from Sparta, F.H. Wakeman. For the price of $42,000, Wakeman brought the Old Mountain Spring and Queen of Tennessee brands out of the wilderness and into the city.[446] Seeing a great opportunity, he went right to work and doubled the capacity of the already booming distillery and added another warehouse. He concentrated his efforts on Lincoln, corn, Bourbon, and rye, with J.S. Cannon continuing to man the stills. Then he opened an office and another warehouse at 980 Market Street.

Seeing the advantage Wakeman and the Lookout had with their proximity to town, E.R. Betterton decided it was time to really build something grand downtown on the Tennessee River. In October 1902 he unveiled "the largest plant of [its] kind south of Louisville." Located on the Market Street wharf, Betterton wanted it to rival the great distilleries of Dublin. At its peak, it produced seven barrels of whisky a day and featured a large cattle barn with room for 125 heads. The mash bill comprised 12 ½ percent rye, 12 ½ percent barley, and 75% percent corn. They said they used the Lincoln County process, but no log stills were present in the facility. They also referred to leaching as rectifying, showing how that term was being used in various ways.[447]

The explosive boom in Chattanooga whisky was not to be stopped. On the south side of town, yet another distillery was being built by Abercrombie and Price along Chattanooga Creek, called the Chattanooga Distillery. The owners poached J.S. Cannon from Lookout Distillery and launched operations just over a month after the White Oak Distillery. With the pressure on to make back the $10,000 investment, the firm began selling their Old Tennessee Club Lincoln County Sour Mash Whisky.[448] They showed how some Tennessee distillers still only saw barrel aging as a supplement to their leaching process. With just a 12 month old spirit, Chattanooga Distillery felt a year was more than enough time in a barrel, saying, "this brand is mellowed by age and a trial is all we ask."[449]

Where was J.W. Kelly during this massive explosion of distilleries? Planning his own, of course. By this time, J.W. and Lizzie were living a comfortable life, so it only seemed right that Kelly should get his dream distillery. It would be the fourth distillery in Chattanooga in seven years, and it would be the largest. The $40,000 operation featured a three-story steel framed distillery, the first of its kind in the state. And there was no better distiller to have at the helm than J.S. Cannon, so Kelly lured him from his Chattanooga Distillery perch.[450] The Deep Spring Distillery launched in 1905 with an unheard capacity of 5,000 gallons of whisky per day.[451]

As hard as it may be to believe, yet another distillery was being constructed at the same time as Deep Spring. It was J.H. Abercrombie's second try at a distillery, having left Chattanooga to Scott Price.[452] But the new distillery, which was to be called Chickamauga, never got off the ground.[453] The owners sold the land to the Chattanooga Southern Railway to recoup some of the investment.[454]

It was the end of the days when poor old Mr. Fox was bored out of his mind with only two small rectifiers in town. Now Chattanooga demanded at least three United States guagers.[455]

As for J.W. Kelly, what a life he had constructed for himself. His decision to stay in Chattanooga had been an inspired one. Not only was he a well-respected man about town, he was a successful entrepreneur in two ventures. Best of all, he could share his success with his soul mate, Lizzie. They were Chattanooga's model of the ideal couple.

But while Lizzie was extremely proud of her husband's accomplishments, what she really hoped was that he would slow down. She always felt James worked too hard. And although she probably wouldn't admit it, she wanted more time to spend with him. Instead, she took what she could get, which usually turned out to be the Sunday socials with friends.

One particular rainy Sunday in March, J.W. took the unusual step of excusing himself from his wife and friends. He was tired from the week's activities and wanted to take a noon-time nap. Lost in conversation, Lizzie heard the ringing of the clock and realized it was 2:30 p.m. She went upstairs to check on him. When she said his name, he didn't move. She nudged him, then suddenly seized up in horror. Panicked, she called down to her friends to help, but it was too late. He had died of a brain aneurysm.

It was the end of an impressive life for the jovial Irishman. The *Chattanooga News* summed up his life and his relationship with Lizzie:

> "His friends, business and social were legion and few men came nearer being liked by everyone who chanced to be associated with them. Personally, Mr. Kelly coupled the Irish wit and good nature with a splendid command of the English language and a natural brilliancy of intellect. This combination made him a most delightful man socially and created a circle of friends about him that was never broken. Their wedded life has been a most beautiful one. The devoted wife is almost prostrated by the death of her husband."[456]

Lizzie never recovered from the death of her soul mate. For the next few months, she lived a sickly existence. The house was like a morgue. Fearing for her life, Lizzie's niece came from England to watch over her. As the eighth month without her husband approached, Lizzie fell into a most desperate condition; 238 days after J.W. Kelly left this world, and she likely counted every one, she too was gone. Cause of death, a broken heart.[457]

Chapter 19

THE REVENOOR

The Hero of the Revenue

When Mr. Lincoln's excise arrived in Tennessee, responses to it ranged from compliance, to indifference, to indignance, to opportunism.

In 19th-century Tennessee, those that saw great opportunity for profits in the illicit spirits trade were known as wildcatters. As their name suggests, these renegade distillers were highly unpredictable and potentially deadly. For a revenuer on a hunt, they could expect anything from a quiet and polite submission to the scattering of buckshot and gangs coming out of the hills.

To the revenuers of the Internal Revenue and local law-enforcement officers, the risk versus monetary reward was hardly worth the effort. But for those whose exploits were big enough to receive print coverage, they could become as famous locally as Wild West lawmen like Bat Masterson, Wild Bill Hickok, and Wyatt Earp. It was the age of stories and heroes. In Tennessee, several revenuers gained fame and notoriety through the local press.

One man journalists became preoccupied with during this time was U.S. Deputy Marshal Joe L. Spurrier. At a glance, it was hard to know what to make of him. He had all the appearance of a desk clerk masquerading as a gunfighter. His widely pronounced flat-brimmed hat with its Stetson-like crown gave way to sleepy eyes and a large, unkempt goatee. Though they did not hire him to hunt down wildcatters, he soon developed a flair for it.

With Tennessee and Kentucky under his jurisdiction, Spurrier became experienced in the ways of moonshiners. His instincts made him the go-to man when 'cats needed to be subdued. He was a new breed of revenuer––too young to have served in the war, but observant enough to understand the impact it had on those he was tracking down. He was brave, but he wasn't reckless. He never forgot he was a family man and took the utmost precaution when faced with overwhelming odds.

In July 1888, he was hunkered down with a team of agents in the woods of Clay County, his target was the "Humpy" Pennington distilling operation. Recently arrested for violations of the revenue laws, they had set Humpy free on bond. When Spurrier and his agents found his new setup, Pennington's fetching twenty-year-old daughter was at the controls. It was a reminder that wildcatting was usually a family business.[458]

One of the biggest of the wildcat legends was J.W. "Old Bill" Thompson. Word was that Old Bill had an operation big enough to produce a barrel of 'shine a day. Thought to be the oldest wildcatter in the upper country, his stills were also the best guarded. They stumbled upon the wildcatter working one of his secondary stills. And after arresting him, Spurrier took two of his best men up into the woods along Wolf River to look for Thompson's primary operation.

After following a series of creeks, they came upon a short and deep gorge, where they found the operation set up alongside Kettle Creek. They left their horses some distance back to keep the whinnying from giving away their presence. Spurrier was sure that word of Old Bill's arrest would have already made its way down through the moonshiner's network. The friends and family of the old wildcatter would be on high alert. The three officers sat in an elevated position awaiting the still operator. Soon, a woman appeared, looked at the still, then looked around for any sign of intruders. Then another woman showed up, followed by three men. They all sat down and began drinking distiller's beer while the men smoked pipes.

Suddenly the man closest to the still put up his hand. And in an instant, eighteen men appeared around the camp with double-barreled shotguns and Winchester rifles. Spurrier listened intently as the wildcatters talked about what they would do if they found a revenuer. The three lawmen sat frozen for five hours before they finally felt safe enough to head down the revenue and back to their horses.

After the incident, Spurrier confessed to a reporter from the Banner, "there is no use trying to do anything with those people with less than fifty brave and well-armed men."[459] Two years later, Spurrier captured two of Old Bill's men after getting the jump on the operation when it was less guarded. In addition, they destroyed a 100-gallon copper still, cap and worm, 1600 gallons of beer, and 30 gallons of single-distilled low wines that the old timers called singlings.[460]

While wildcatters could be dangerous, what made them even more dangerous were the power hungry revenuers. There were many men who joined the force just so they could legally shoot a man. The worst offender was Deputy Bud Lindsay.

Bud didn't take any guff from people he considered lowlifes. One of his targets was a wildcatter named Kitts. With his backups hiding behind nearby trees, Lindsay walked onto Kitts' farm and, without a second thought, asked if he could buy a gallon of whisky. Well, no wildcatter in his right mind would offer to sell whisky to a stranger. When he refused, Lindsay pulled his pistol and pointed it at Kitts' face. Fearing for his father's life, Kitts' 14-year-old son came out of the barn and threw a rock at the revenuer. Sensing trouble, Lindsay's shadows came out from hiding and relieved him of his pistol. With no still to be found and no sale made, the revenuers left the scene.

As they made their way down the road, Lindsay asked for his pistol back. With gun in hand, he wheeled his horse around and rode back at a full gallop to Kitts' farm. Lindsay smashed into the front door of the cabin and put two 44-caliber bullets in Kitts, killing him instantly. Hearing Kitts' son behind him, he spun around and shot at the boy, but missed. Instead, he hit his little sister, who was standing near. Then Lindsay's men came in and threw him to the floor. It wasn't the first time Lindsay had killed a man while on duty. In fact, he had spent time in jail for a previous killing. He tried to claim it was a killing in self defense, but it was revealed at trial that Lindsay had an outstanding grudge against Kitts.[461] Although the little girl did not suffer serious wounds, she lost her father.

Joe Spurrier detested men like that. They gave revenuers a bad name and riled up wildcatters who saw the government as oppressive and out of control. It was because of these badge-wearing outlaws that most wildcatters kept shotguns by the door. And the sign of a revenuer made some 'shiners down right trigger happy.

Of all the wildcatter hotspots in Tennessee, Lincoln County was one of the busiest, boldest, and most dangerous. In fact, Lincoln was like a second home for Spurrier. It was there that he had taken down some of the largest distilling setups in the state. One of his first captures was an operation near the Alabama state line with output as big as Old Bill Thompson's in Clay County. The wildcatters hid the stills within a thick, deep, and almost impenetrable thicket. But it was more than just well hidden. Deputy Marshal Spurrier said it was "one of the best equipped wildcat stills he'd ever seen and the only one he ever found fitted with a steam boiler." It had two wooden stills with a barrel a day capacity. The stuff produced there was so good, a local rectifier admitted it was some of the best juice he'd ever tasted. Upon discovery, Spurrier's men destroyed all the equipment and dumped all the mash, singlings, and finished spirits. Yet they never found the distiller.[462]

It was a frustration of the job. Rarely were arrests made. The communication networks of wildcatters were sophisticated. They usually knew when a revenuer was on the prowl. Wanting to avoid confrontation, they would head off into the woods, sacrificing their equipment and spirits.

If a revenuer caught a wildcatter, the next issue they had to deal with was the sympathetic community. Most of the area's citizens were customers of moonshiners. This led to courts going easy on offenders. And even if they convicted a wildcatter, after serving time they would be right back to distilling within a year. Some were so bold, they would go back to working after being released on bond.

And then there were those wildcatters who didn't want to be trifled with or disturbed. Some had a mean streak a mile long. And wildcatters, like the mafia of the future, knew how to send a message. A tipster found this out the hard way when he woke up to find a bunch of hickory switches, some seven feet long, sitting on his doorstep. The accompanying note told him to leave the country, or else.[463] To the wildcatter, the crime wasn't the illicit distilling, it was ratting on the distiller.

Spurrier respected those citizens willing to take the risk to turn in an offender. But tips weren't always from well-meaning people. Sometimes they came in from wildcatters looking to get rid of the competition. Worse, some of these tips were traps for unsuspecting revenue officers. Spurrier had seen it before and always trusted his gut when it came to potential deceit.

One of those suspicious tips landed on Spurrier's desk in his Nashville office in early autumn 1892. The writer, who only gave his initials H.S., said he'd discovered contraband brandy hidden in the woods in Lincoln County. He offered to lead officers to it. The next day, another letter appeared, giving a day and location for a meeting. With his customary precaution, Spurrier asked Deputy J.E. Pulver to join him as backup. When the two arrived at the location, six miles outside of Flintville, they found five barrels of unregistered brandy. They found the score on the property of A.J. Patrick. When the tipster didn't show, the two lawmen arrested brothers A.J. and T.E. Patrick for having the illicit spirits on their property. The Patricks had once run a licensed distillery, but they had shut it down before their arrest. It was all for naught, as the court acquitted the brothers when their case came before a judge at the Fayetteville Courthouse.

It disappointed Spurrier, but he didn't let it bother him. Then another letter arrived from "H.S." In the letter, the tipster apologized for not being there to meet the officers; he had been called away. Then he let the revenuers know he had discovered an even bigger score. It was highly unusual to get two tips from the same informant, but Spurrier decided he had to check on it, and if the score was as big as was being claimed, he would need plenty of reinforcements.

Nervous about getting cornered in the backwoods, Spurrier contacted a friend in Lincoln County, David L. Harris. Harris knew the territory well and his home was a perfect staging point for the expedition. It was just three miles to Flintville from his residence. For added protection, Spurrier brought four revenuers with him, including Deputy Pulver, Deputy Cardwell, Deputy S.D. Mather, and Deputy E.S. Robertson. As they talked over strategy the night before, none of the men felt good about the situation. Spurrier said, "Boys, it's a desperate undertaking. We will either find the brandy or else half of us will never come back alive." Joe knew, such was the life of a lawman.[464]

Twenty Barrels of Brandy

At 7 a.m., with the team prepared, Spurrier led the men from the house. The tipster had given them instructions to walk along Stewart's Creek from Fayetteville. Suspicious of an ambush, the team decided it was best to approach from the opposite direction.

About a mile from the meeting point, the team stopped off at Noah Cooper's house to alert him to their presence. Then the six men started out along the trail on mule and horseback with Spurrier and Mather in the lead. Their backups, Cardwell and Pulver, rode some 25 ft behind and Robertson and Harris another 25 ft behind them. About halfway to the meeting point, Robertson was in a daydream with his eyes looking at Mather and Spurrier. Just then, he noticed a puff of smoke rising from a log beside the two men, before a vicious crack broke his train of thought. Mather slumped and fell from his horse. In an instant, another crack came from behind the log and Spurrier fell helplessly from his horse. Deputy Pulver barely had time to coax his mule in the opposite direction when another shot hit Deputy Cardwell. The mule under Cardwell bucked and jumped, throwing the helpless lawman to the ground, a move that likely saved his life. Robertson and Harris slid off of their mules and tried to find the best protection they could. Robertson thought he saw an assailant duck behind the log. He aimed and waited for the man's head to pop up and, when it did, he sent a slug right through the back of the moonshiner's head. The body jerked as he hit the ground, dead. As for the other assassins, they all escaped into the woods.

The lawmen that were able went into triage mode. It was quickly ascertained that Captain Mather was gone the second the wildcatter fired the first shot. He had six buckshot in his right side, one in the rear of his head, two in the right shoulder, and one in the left. Deputies Spurrier and Cardwell were alive but in critical condition. Sickened by the sight of his friends lying helpless on the ground, Deputy Pulver ran to Noah Cooper's house to round up a posse. With their horses and mules gone, Robertson and Harris scurried off on foot to find help. As luck would have it, a local farmer, Bud McClellan, was riding into town with a wagonload of apples. The deputies offered him money if he could help them transport the two wounded officers back to the Flintville train station. He agreed.

They arrived in Flintville at 1 p.m.. The train for Nashville wasn't scheduled to arrive until 3:30 p.m.. They summoned a local doctor to keep the officers stable. Cardwell's right arm was broken, and he had twelve buckshot under that arm. The wildcatter had shot Joe Spurrier with a Winchester rifle; the ball penetrated his shoulder and severed his spine, paralyzing him.

As Spurrier lay in the depot waiting for the train, he spoke to Pulver and Robertson, "Boys, I have not long to live. I have nothing to leave my family. Promise me that you will see that they are cared for. Tell my superior to give my son and daughter employment at the custom house that they may not come to want. Another thing, boys, go home and resign your commissions. It is only a matter of time until you meet with my fate if you remain in the business." Shortly after, his friend Deputy Cardwell passed away.[465]

Telegrams coming into the Nashville Customs House were confusing at best. The noon-time message said, "S.D. Mather killed. S.C. Cardwell and J.L Spurrier not expected to live. Notify Mrs. Cardwell and children to come immediately."

Shock and disbelief ran around the office in Nashville. Most had seen the second letter and its claim of twenty barrels of unattended brandy. They knew Lincoln County's reputation, but none of the officers thought the worst could happen to either Spurrier or Cardwell. Both were the most cautious of men. Spurrier had a wife and several children. He was only forty and well respected.

Deputy C.S. Cardwell was only thirty-seven and had recently come from Kentucky to help in the uprisings in Tennessee. Deputy Mather had spent ten years in the Internal Revenue and had a wife and grown daughter in Franklin County. He was forty-eight.[466]

Joe Spurrier was the only one of the three to make it back to Nashville alive. The local news conveyed the feeling of the community, while giving an update on the agent's condition. "The feeling in the State is strong against the brutal assassins and if they are captured they never be tried, but lynched forthwith. Col. Spurrier's death is hourly expected."[467]

It turns out, the one casualty for the wildcatters was T.E. "Elbus" Patrick, the man who Spurrier and Pulver had arrested on their first trip to Lincoln County. To cover his tracks, T.E. had told his family he was off to Indian territory.[468] The sheriff immediately arrested four men: T.E.'s brother A.J., brothers Cooper and Morgan Petty, and James Epps.

As for Spurrier, there was little hope for his recovery. He was in terrible pain and spent most nights in a restless state. He told the papers he'd rather die than be crippled. Yet somehow he kept on fighting. There was talk of bringing his assailants to his bedside for identification, but officials feared the stress might kill him. Instead, they took his official statement of the events.[469] Soon after, the brave and well-regarded lawman passed away.[470]

The trial was set for May 1893 for A.J. Patrick, James Epps, and Morgan Petty. They dropped charges against Cooper Morgan due to lack of evidence. Newspapers kept a riveted community abreast of trial details.

The trial was held in the United States Circuit Court at the Customs House in Nashville. When the accused took their seats, they placed Patrick next to the defense attorney while old man Epps and Morgan Petty sat in the prisoner's dock. Moments after the gavel fell and order was called, the defense threw a bombshell. They claimed that Joe Spurrier's bedside statements should be deemed inadmissible because he was not of sound mind when he gave them. Apparently, these were additional statements made by Spurrier just before he died. The judge ruled in the defense's favor.[471] It wasn't a good start, but the rest of the trial went off as expected, at least until the verdict.

They found the defendants "not guilty."

To casual followers, the past editions of the papers gave no hint of this turn of events. Reading that headline had to be quite a shock for Nashville citizens. But in the courtroom, the verdict was met with applause and relief.

There was one flaw that was made clear in the courtroom, but not in the papers. It was the fallibility of Joe Spurrier's early recollection of events. They couldn't reconcile how a man paralyzed by a gunshot could make out his assailants while falling helplessly from his horse—especially if they were all masked. They also noted that he was beyond the log and his assailant before the gunshot.

The other problem was proving a conspiracy. The judge reminded the jury of the lack of prosecutorial evidence in proving the collusion of the men. He said that if T.E. Patrick had lived, it was doubtless they could convict him on the evidence at hand. Thanks to the judge and defense casting doubt, the jury set the men free.[472]

The trial did nothing to slow illicit distilling in Lincoln County. Two years later, Deputy Collector Walter G. Rutledge found a thirty-gallon still about a mile from where Deputy Marshall Spurrier was shot.[473]

The following year, the same agent captured and destroyed an illicit distilling operation only two miles from the spot. This distiller was so brazen, he or she didn't even attempt to conceal the sound of the steam engine, which was easily heard from the road. However, there were no spirits on-site and the one man they saw near the stills ran away. The owner of the land claimed he was very sick and that he didn't know there was a still on his property.[474] Spurrier's war would go on without him.

The 19th-Century Wildcatter

To the Internal Revenue, the rampant activities of the wildcatters came as a shock. Every time it seemed like they were getting a handle on the problem, another statistic would blow away their illusion. The 3rd District was the most obvious offender. In the 1870s, there were twenty-five legitimate brandy distilleries but no legal whisky distilleries. Meanwhile, there were over 300 illicit distilling sites in that same area.

What surprised revenuers the most was how easy it was for these distillers to acquire equipment. Although stills were available in Nashville, wildcatters knew that buying one of those was the fastest way to get caught. Instead, wildcatters sourced copper and made their own stills or found someone who could. But black-market stills weren't cheap. The smallest of stills might run you $200 from an illicit still-maker versus $25 in Nashville for a legitimate one. For some families, it took every penny they owned to acquire a still. Once purchased or bartered for, that first still was precious to the small distillers. Once they made enough money, they became less concerned with the loss of a still to a revenuer. But the smaller operations clung to their stills, and poorer families passed them down to the next generation.

There were hundreds of ways to keep a revenuer from discovering a still. Some built small sheds they could easily dismantle at the first sign of a revenuer. Many took to ravines with extremely steep bluffs where revenuers might never look. Some even built their stills into the chimney of their home to make their activity look like a normal bit of home life. The harder things to conceal were the beer, singlings, and final spirits.

A wildcatter named Joe Hooper had an ingenious way of hiding his whisky. He hollowed out a tree, stored his liquor inside, and slept in the tree branches when revenuers came by. Another moonshiner named Wilkerson built a massive still, but hid it on a bank under trees and earth. He bragged a revenuer could be ten feet away from it and never see it. To add to the ruse, Wilkerson set up small stills around the area as decoys for the revenuers to find. However, they finally caught him when he hid his decoy a little too well. Eventually, an aggressive agent sniffed out the large still.[475]

Saturday was the best day for wildcatters to distill. Revenuers were less active, opening up a more free-spirited atmosphere. Distilling became an event, with the moonshiner's family and friends coming together to watch the run. They spent the rest of the evening and the next day downing the spirits in copious amounts. If there was any left on Monday, they would take it to the local grocery and sell or barter it for supplies. The grocer continued the deception by putting the new spirit in their old stamped barrels of revenue-approved whisky, topping off the supply. Some of these barrels took years to empty, although dates on the stamps meant they couldn't keep the ruse up forever.

Wildcatters also benefited from makeshift communication networks. In Wilson County, local miners allied with their illicit distilling neighbors. When miners spotted revenuers in the woods, they sent runners to warn the distillers. As payment, the miners received a fresh supply of spirits. This teamwork was necessary for survival.[476]

Middle Tennessee had the larger wildcat operations. East Tennessee had the smallest stills but sometimes several distilling operations per wildcatter. And, as with legitimate distilling, West Tennessee was light in wildcat activity.

While they may seem like birds of the same flock, legitimate distillers did not like wildcatters. Like the police versus a criminal, only one had to live by rules. Legal distilling meant paying license fees, buying required equipment, paying for barrel stamps, etc. Moonshiners could distill whatever they had and made 100% profits. It is part of the reason distillers got over the Tice Meter controversy and became friendly with storekeepers and gaugers.[477]

Eventually, society would romanticize the moonshiner as the frontier pioneer, standing up for freedom. But as the *Memphis Commercial Appeal* reminded its readers, there was another side:

> *"As a rule, the people who engage in this work are an indolent, imprudent, lazy class, who poorly tend little patches of corn on a hill. Their wives and children are illiterate and their surroundings foster ignorance and idleness. They do not pursue any line of business. Just enough to stave off starvation is enough. Frequently their cabins*

have no floors, and their furniture is what they have made of woods surrounding with their axes and saws."[478]

Unlike some of their 20th-century counterparts, the 19th-century moonshiner rarely got rich off their efforts. It was a hard life. But for many, wildcatting meant survival.

The Never-Ending Job

As the wildcat infestation continued to grow, revenuers found it easier to take down several operations on a single trip. In January 1871, a large mounted raid by revenuers in the eastern mountains saw the destruction of seven distilleries, fifteen thousand gallons of mash, and eleven stills over eight days.[479] A year later, a summer raid led to the discovery of seven illicit distilleries in Lincoln County, nine in newly formed Moore County, plus two more in Franklin County. In all, twenty thousand gallons of beer, three hundred gallons of singlings, and one hundred bushels of grain were disposed of.[480]

To counteract the large number of revenuers and troops coming into the area, the more violent wildcatters looked to lure revenuers into an ambush. The goal was to get the agents into an area where the wildcatters had the upper hand. Then they would fight guerilla warfare style, just like they had in the Civil War.

To make peace, the government occasionally offered amnesty if wildcatters turned in their stills. In 1877, U.S. Senator Isham G. Harris and Internal Revenue Collector R.F. Patterson held a barbecue north of Paris, Tennessee. They invited wildcatters down from the hills to meet their neighbors. It was a great success, as over one thousand people attended. Senator Harris gave a speech outlining how embarrassing wildcatting activity had become for the state. He tried to appeal to their competitive nature by showing how Tennessee tax revenue's deficiencies were making Illinois and other states look bigger than Tennessee in terms of distilling prowess. After appealing to their better nature, he asked the crowd if they would stand by the law. It was said, not a single "no" was uttered. Those that signed the pledge willingly agreed to post bond in Paris. They also allowed the destruction of their stills and product, in return for leniency in sentencing during their court hearings.[481]

Some of the tougher cats to catch were the legal distillers who were making extra on the side. Charles Brantley had applied for a license to distill in 1868, but the Tice Meter controversy kept him from renewing. When revenuers found his equipment in working condition and high wines, milled corn, and beer around, Brantley blamed it on a man named Nichol, who had come in and tried to distill on his equipment without his permission. He said he only had the milled corn for his farm animals. Others corroborated his story. They held him on $700 bond.[482]

A legal distiller in Cocke County, Charles Pasour hid some of his extra non-taxed whisky in his shuck pen. When revenuers discovered it, they destroyed two illicit stills and over four hundred gallons of illicitly made whisky.[483]

It might seem that men were the only ones leading their families in wildcatting activities, but Mollie Miller of Polk County broke that mold. Her rise came thanks to a rival wildcatter ratting on her father, Sam. Sam Miller wasn't one to go down without a fight. A battle took place in Sevier County and it led to the death of three revenuers. It's possible Mollie may have taken out one or more by her own hand earning her a reputation as a ruthless leader of her own family. During the 1860s and '70s, her gang was notorious for taking out their aggressions on revenue officers. But she never met a judge and jury, and died in her home in 1873.[484]

The Putnam County War

One of the most famous wildcat battles took place in the late Summer of 1878. Under the orders of Colonel W.M. Woodcock, the Collector of the Revenue, a group led by collectors James Davis and S.D. Mather was on a mission to take down several operations in Putnam County. They had just spent an exhausting morning chasing down a single illicit brandy distillery. After chasing shadows for most of the day, they eventually found the distillery, broke up the stills, and dumped the brandy. Tired from the day's toil, the officers retreated to Spring

Creek hoping to stay at the home of a kindly old gentleman, James Peak. But when Mr. Peak's son came to the door, he told them they didn't have enough room for the officers and that they should head down to Mr. Barnes' house. Exhausted, but willing to do as the man said, they made their way from Waterloo Falls to near where the Barnes house was located. But just before arriving, a stranger stopped them and said Barnes didn't have accommodations. So the agents turned around and headed back to Peak's home.[485]

When they arrived, collectors Davis and Mather went inside to chat with Mr. Peak. Deputy Mather enjoyed hearing the stories Mr. Peak had to tell. And at 102 years old, he had plenty of them. He was born weeks after the signing of the Declaration of Independence. A less interested Commissioner Davis stepped outside to chat with the two men guarding the door, Lee Ayers and J.M. Phillips. He asked Phillips to accompany him down to the garden so they could find some feed for the horses. When they got down the hill, a partridge caught Captain Phillips' eye. He pointed it out to Davis, who saw more than just a bird. Six men were running through the trees behind it on a nearby hill. Davis whispered something in his partner's ear. Then the two men made a break for it. Trying to find the shortest route he could, Captain Phillips jumped over a fence, with Davis right behind. While Phillips was airborne, a bullet stung him in the side. He yelped, "Oh Lordy!" Soon a swarm of men came out of the bushes. Davis made his way to the house, with Phillips close behind. Soon, every man with a weapon was engaged in a firefight. After Mather confirmed Phillip's wounds were not fatal, he ran outside to join in the battle.

For forty minutes, shots rang out from all over the woods. One revenuer, Press Smith, took three bullets in the arm but still held his ground. Frustrated, he yelled at the guerrilla fighters, saying, "Come out and fight like men!"

At one point, the man thought to be the leader of this angry band, William Campbell Morgan, appeared from behind a tree. He took aim and fired, then disappeared into the woods.

The hostilities ceased for about an hour. Collector Davis sent two men out to alert Commissioner Woodcock of their plight. Not only did they need about a hundred men, they needed ammunition. As soon as the two men were off, guns started blazing again. With bullets running low, the revenuers decided the safest place to be was inside Peak's home. In response, Campbell Morgan's men laid siege to the hilltop residence.

All night and throughout the next day, tensions ran high. Morgan's men would occasionally take shots at the house and the revenuers would return fire out of the windows of the little two-story log house. A brave Dr. Martin of Cookeville came up to tend to the wounded. He only stayed about a half hour. There wasn't any water and only a little food. As day turned to night Mather remarked that you would have thought there were "a thousand men around us, from the sound of the bugles, shouting and firing, many of the balls penetrating the house." It was a second sleepless night, and no one knew how long they could hold out.[486]

The next morning, as rain fell, the men in the woods started firing their guns in frustration, and to keep them dry. A peace committee approached the cabin. Two of Campbell Morgan's men said they brought terms of peace. Davis let them in and asked if he could meet Morgan face to face. The emissaries went back to their camp for an hour or two, then when they returned, they asked for a presidential pardon for all the men. Collector Davis said that was a promise they didn't have the right to make. The men returned to Morgan to give him the news. They said Morgan had heard Collector Davis had orders to kill him on sight and all he was doing was defending himself. He told them, if the government wanted to serve him, it had to be by someone other than Davis. If that happened, he would gladly go to Cookeville to post bond. There was no objection, and the men surrounding the cabin dispersed. The Putnam County War appeared to be over.[487]

Morgan's biggest regret in the melee was the wounding of Captain Phillips. He had great respect for him as a revenuer. And when Colonel Woodcock and Collector Davis learned that bit of information, they sent Captain Phillips up to see if Morgan was willing to come in. When they arrived, Captain Phillips and Major Wagner found Morgan sitting near the Roaring River. The three men sat for hours while Morgan unloaded all of his concerns. He claimed to have a letter in his possession that said Davis was out to kill him. He said he held off on posting bond because of Davis' presence, but he had no intention to do any more shooting.[488]

It would be six more months before Campbell Morgan made his first appearance in the U.S. Circuit Court in Nashville. The court had offered amnesty for the wildcatter and Campbell's lawyer, General George H. Morgan, confirmed its legitimacy. Hoping to avoid a scene or violence, they kept Campbell's court appearance a secret. When they announced his name in the courtroom, an audible gasp of surprise came from the gallery. Campbell went through the motions of asking the judge for amnesty. At that moment, Collector James Davis came over and offered his hand in friendship to his onetime enemy. The two had a good long chat and then walked over to the Capitol Building. Along the way, they agreed to let bygones be bygones.

A reporter later asked Campbell why he became a wildcatter. He said "illicit distilling had been carried on in the mountains more through ignorance of the law than say any wish to violate it." There was a belief in his community that only monied men could run legitimate distilleries. Because of this, the locals felt they had every right to make small quantities outside the law. When the reporter asked him why he made alcohol, Campbell said it wasn't because he drank whisky. He didn't. He only made it to pay for his farm.[489]

That day in court was an incredible turning point in the life of Campbell Morgan. No longer a man ignorant of the law, he joined its cause. He was so helpful to agents in putting down wildcatting, they appointed him as a Deputy U.S. Marshal. He became a pillar of the community. Eventually, he was asked to run for sheriff, which he did. During his maximum of three terms as sheriff, they say crime all but disappeared in his community.[490]

His old adversary turned friend, James M. Davis, wouldn't be so lucky. After taking down over 3,000 violators of the Internal Revenue laws and 700 illicit distilleries during his career, the thirty-four-year-old collector met an ambush in the mountains near McMinnville in March 1882 and was shot dead.[491]

There were no guarantees in the life of the revenuer.

Chapter 20

WOMEN OF MYSTERY

Standing in the Shadows

"Woman with an unusual history dies; aged 100."

This provocative headline was the lead into what was a truly unusual obituary for the time. Featured on the front page of the July 18, 1920 edition of the *Nashville Banner*, it told of the death of a formerly enslaved woman named Nancy Patterson.

Short on details, it encourages more questions than it delivers answers. It describes Nancy as a "comely mulatto" woman, who nursed an Irish distiller named Barney Patterson back to health. At first she sounds like a servant, serving Barney meals and never sitting at the same table with him. But then it says they had several children together that all died young. And in the end, she inherited all of his property.[492]

So, who was Nancy Patterson? In the history of Tennessee whisky, she's a very important person. But you would never know it from her lack of coverage by historians nor by her obituary.

Such is the difficulty in researching the women of distilling. Too often they are a footnote to their husband's legacy. Yet women have played an integral role in the craft's history.

In fact, women's role in distilling goes all the way back to ancient Mesopotamia in the 2nd century AD. It was then that a female alchemist named Mary the Jewess developed one of the earliest known copper stills. But after the development of this critical invention, the coverage of women in distilling fades.

As did their coverage in general society. For most of the Dark and Middle Ages, leaders painted powerful women as sinful and subservient women virtuous. There was little in-between. The few that broke through had to be strong willed while wielding immense power, like Joan of Arc or Queen Elizabeth I.

When the Black Death made its way across Europe in the 14th century, women initially took on the role of caretakers and healers. Distilling was a natural occupation for the females in the household, who provided tonics to help ease sickness. But as the plague ravaged the Continent, superstitions emerged. Soon widows and landowning women became the targets of witch hunts. A potential charge of witchcraft pushed women to get out of the spotlight for any talents that could be deemed supernatural.

But with the Industrial Revolution and the Victorian age, the role of the women in distilling reemerged. But only as a hearth skill. Women of note were more often than not celebrated for their position as homemakers or child bearers.

In whisky history, Helen Cumming's story is a great example of this. A farmer's wife and homemaker, Helen and her husband John lived in the Scottish Highlands in the days of rampant moonshining. She was a skillful distiller who brewed up batches of whisky in her kitchen. To keep out of trouble, she became friendly with the excise men who patrolled the area, and often invited them in for a meal before they made their rounds. When they arrived, she hid her distilling operation from sight. While the agents ate, she went out back and raised a red flag on a pole to alert the area's moonshiners that a revenuer was in the area. She kept up this subterfuge until the Excise Act of 1823 was passed, making taxes much lower on whisky production. As illicit distillers came out of the shadows, Helen's husband John established the Cardhu Distillery. Whether Helen took part in the business was clearly less important to the 19th century storyteller.

When husbands passed away, some left their distilleries to their wives. Several of these women quickly displayed a savvy business acumen. When Ellen Jane Corrigan inherited the Bushmills Distillery from her husband Patrick in 1865, she took a strictly Irish brand and expanded it into global markets. Mary Anne Locke inherited the Locke Distillery (now known as Kilbeggan) and doubled the distillery's output during her ownership. Even Helen Cumming encouraged her daughter-in-law Elizabeth to grab the reins after her son Lewis passed away. Elizabeth took one of the smallest distilleries in Scotland and made it attractive to larger firms. Soon, John Walker and Sons acquired Cardhu and made its whisky a core part of their Johnnie Walker blend.

In the 1890s, Tennessee boasted not just one, but three successful women distillery owners and one with strength in the wholesale business. Yet, few details exist about their exploits.

The first of these women is Josephine "Josie" Brown. Upon the passing of her husband on October 14, 1890, she became the sole owner of the Wartrace Distillery near Springfield.

To get a sense of Josie's story and the other female distillery owners, it requires turning to the biographies of their husbands and filling in the gaps with our imaginations.

Josie's Husband Jordan

Jordan Stokes Brown was born to Samuel and Lucy Brown in October 1845. Growing up in a family of meager means, he took a job as a clerk in a general store at fifteen. At seventeen, he broke away from the farm and joined the Fourth Tennessee Cavalry on the side of the Confederates and fought at the battles of Perrysville and Murfreesboro. After the war, he moved to Springfield and started a dry goods business. Not long after arriving, he fell in love with Colonel Wiley Woodard's daughter Josephine and the two were married on February 7, 1867.[493]

It would have been easy for Jordan to leverage the relationship with his famous father-in-law to propel himself into the whisky business. But Jordan desired to make a name for himself through his own efforts. To build his wealth, he took the profits from his dry goods business and began investing in property around town. Eventually, he made his way into the whisky business when he partnered in the wholesale house of Brown & Ragsdale.

The firm survived among stiff competition until March 1882. It was then that a fire that started at the Springfield Register newspaper office spread to his establishment, burning the store to the ground. Having recently purchased property for a distillery and with insurance money in hand, Jordan made the fateful decision to go full force into the distilling business.[494]

It was a historic property, situated on Wartrace Creek; the grounds included a cabin built in 1796 by Joseph and Nancy Ann Hart.[495] He used the cabin for his office and built the Wartrace Distillery next door. There he produced J.S. Brown's Sour Mash Robertson County Whisky, which was sold as "the purest and best make for medicinal and family purposes."[496] Going up against heavy hitters like John Woodard and Charles Nelson didn't bother him in the least. Even though he was late to the game, Jordan not only held his own--by 1888, he was doubling his capacity to keep up with demand. How involved Josie was in this success is unknown, but her Woodard distilling genes couldn't have hurt.

However, Jordan and Josie saw their lives turned upside down in 1890. It started when a terrible drought caused corn prices to skyrocket across the state. The entire district suffered. By September, Charles Pierce of the Internal Revenue noted that 38 of the 5th District's 58 distilleries were shut down.[497] Most distilleries used the downtime for repairs, including Wartrace, Greenbrier, J.R. Bridges, Duncan & Company, and the new Kinney + Co. who had bought out John Woodard's operation.[498] Jordan diverted his attention by spending his time on construction projects and in his job as Vice-President of the Springfield National Bank. But then, his rebuilt wholesale liquor business was lost to another devastating fire, thanks to an arsonist.[499]

The stress quickly caught up with Jordan and only a few weeks later, he started complaining about severe pains in his stomach. His diagnosis was inflammation of the bowels. His doctors tried to treat him, but he only got worse. Less than two weeks after his 45th birthday, Jordan Stokes Brown died.[500] It was noted that he left Josephine with a fortune of half a million dollars, as well as the distillery and ten children to provide for.

In all reality, Josie could have easily sold the business and property, then spent the rest of her life doting on her children and grandchildren. Instead, she took the bull by the horns and embraced her position as owner of the Wartrace Distillery. While her day-to-day functions in the business are unknown, the distillery continued to thrive under her ownership.

When she died on February 10, 1940, the Tennessean called her the richest woman in Robertson County, noting her wealth came from her late husband, who was a "local merchant and banker." While it mentions her famous father, Colonel Wiley Woodard, they list him as the founder of the Springfield National Bank, not as a distiller.[501] If their distilling prowess was passed over, it's no surprise her twenty-year stint as a Tennessee distillery owner was too. With no recognition of these facts, her legacy in the industry faded into obscurity along with Old Robertson whisky.

Only fourteen months after Josephine Brown inherited the Wartrace Distillery, her neighbor Louisa Nelson found herself in the same boat. And again, we must look to her loving husband to piece together her story.

Louisa's Husband Charles

For those who knew Charles Nelson, his death on December 13, 1891 came as a complete shock. At just 57 years old, it hardly seemed fair that such an outstanding businessman, citizen, and father should die so young.

Charles had lived an incredible life and overcame great odds. His friendly nature, drive, and determination brought him through every hardship. He wasn't a man given to bragging or boasting; he felt action was the best way to communicate.

Charles was a man with diverse tastes. He was a big fan of music and, in a town that would become known as Music City, U.S.A., he was one of the early promoters of the town's music scene. That passion flowed down to his children: His son, Charles Jr., became a professor of music in Ohio and his daughters would all graduate from Vassar College with backgrounds in music.

But if you asked Charles what his greatest accomplishments were, he would put family above all else. A passage from his obituary in the *Nashville American* said it all:

> *"When he hung up his hat he laid down his cares, burrying himself in the bosom of his family. He was not only a father upon whom his children could lean, but he was to them a companion in whom they could confide and with whom they could make free. He was to them at one and the same time father, brother, sweetheart, and friend. Stern when sternness was necessary, yet gentleness was the prevailing ingredient in his royal nature. He ruled by the divine attribute of love, and if his children feared him, it was not the fear that he would visit punishment upon them, but the fear that they might displease him. In all family matters he would with knightly grace defer to his beloved wife, whose word to him was law. Seldom do we find a happier, more perfect home than this one."*[502]

In other words, Louisa was his rock. The true embodiment of the statement "behind every great man is a great woman."

When Charles died, Louisa, like Josephine, embraced the role of distillery owner. It was a huge undertaking and she thrived in the role. For the next nineteen years, Nelson's Greenbrier remained the busiest distillery in the state. In fact, the only thing that would stop Louisa was Prohibition.

Robertson County whisky made its way into the 20th century under the leadership of Louisa Nelson and Josie Brown. In fact, they would go down as the last two distillery owners in the fabled history of Old Robertson.

When Louisa died in February 1918, she had been out of the business for only eight years. Yet her obituary in the Tennessean, titled "Noble Woman Passes

Away," mentioned nothing about whisky or of her incredible ownership of the brand. In fact, reading it, you would think her husband Charles was a merchant, not a distiller. To readers that didn't know her, her legacy was motherhood and, while described as "a woman of strong character and many amiable traits," it was her children's devotion to her that mattered most.[503] It appears 19th-century Victorian principals were still at play and whisky was not to be promoted in the era of prohibition. Sadly, the part she played in the whisky industry wouldn't be publicized for another nine decades.

Augusta's Husband George

Of all the Tennessee wives who were said to have inherited distilleries in the 1890s, the one who seemed to enjoy the fruits of her husband's labor the most was Augusta Dickel. And this is exactly what George wanted.

When George Dickel passed away in June 1894, his shares of George A. Dickel, & Co. passed to Augusta with the instruction that she should sell her part of the business.[504] Instead, she remained an owner of the company until the day she died in September 1916.

While historians occasionally mention Augusta, she is usually characterized as being disinterested in the distillery and business affairs. Instead, a vision is painted of a woman living out her days on an endless holiday, traveling back and forth between Europe and the United States.

It's true that Augusta was a frequent traveler overseas, but she also actively took part in real estate transactions in the years following George's death.[505] As for the distillery, it was never owned by George A. Dickel & Co. Why would Augusta suddenly inject herself into a business she only sourced whisky from? When it came to the whiskey, at most, she owned a piece of the George A. Dickel Cascade brand with Manny and any wholesale inventory.

When obituaries appeared in *Nashville American* and *Nashville Banner*, she was mentioned as the wife of George A. Dickel, but her relationship to owning or running the company was ignored. More focus was placed on her surviving relatives and her decline while living at her summer home in Charlevoix, Michigan. The Michigan papers at least disclosed her worth, which was said to be over $2,000,000 at the time of her death.[506] She was buried alongside her husband in Mount Olivet Cemetery in Nashville.

Nancy's Partner Barney

Out of these four Tennessee women, the one who is best documented is the one from the smallest distillery. In fact, there is as much known about her as there is about her partner, Barney Patterson, whose name is associated with the distillery. Yet her life story still contains plenty of mystery.

Nancy was born on her father's farm near Tullahoma in 1830.[507] James Puryear was a wealthy landowner who had moved his family from Virginia to Tennessee in the 1810s. When his wife died, it left him with a household of children and several enslaved people. Nancy was born as the result of a sexual encounter between James and one of the enslaved women on the farm.

By all accounts, Nancy was a beautiful and caring girl. As the story goes, when she was in her late teens, an Irishman named Barney Patterson came to live on the farm. He had been in a terrible accident while working on the nearby railroad. Apparently, he slipped and his foot got in the path of a moving railcar where it was forcefully amputated. James took the wounded man into his home, and Nancy tended to him as he convalesced.

In 1852, Nancy's father James was growing old and feeble, and he feared that if he died, his daughter might be traded or sold off as property to another plantation. Noticing how devoted Nancy was to Barney, he sold his daughter to the Irishman for $1000, along with 75 acres of land along Norman Creek. The $1000 was never paid, which seemed to be the agreement. The purpose for James was to protect Nancy, not to make a financial gain.[508]

But from there, the story gets fuzzy. Some say the couple left the state to elope. Others say they had a child, but that it didn't survive. Barney would claim she became his servant after emancipation. There is no documentation showing that

Nancy and Barney were ever married. But even if they were, they had to be careful about disclosing it. Tennessee state law forbade interracial marriages. The punishment was one to five years in the state penitentiary. Nancy eventually became a Patterson. But did she simply take the name of her enslaver, as was common in those days, or did she actually marry Barney or consider him a common law spouse?

Whatever the situation, they weren't being overly cautious. When a census worker came by the house in 1870, they listed Nancy Patterson as a wife. But they also listed her as white. However, Barney was listed as residing in a different house.[509]

If Barney disowned the property when it came to the census, he didn't disown the farm or on-site distillery that was built around 1872.[510] The operation was a success. A lot of that was because of Nancy, who ran the place and kept the workers and Barney in line. Early on, the distillery focused on brandy, but eventually distilled whisky.[511] Knowing distilling was beyond his abilities, Barney hired John W. Maddox as his head distiller.

But in 1879, Barney became suspicious that Maddox was siphoning some of his liquor. He and a storekeeper named Elkins kept watch and caught the distiller breaking into the cistern room. Maddox was arrested and taken to the courthouse at Tullahoma and then processed for transfer to the Davidson County jail. During the transfer, Maddox escaped, never to be heard from again.[512] Suddenly losing a distiller would have panicked many distillery owners. But Barney had been watching Nancy and knew she had been keeping tabs on the process and learning how to distill. So she stepped right in and took over as Barney's head distiller.

Like with everything else, Nancy took right to the craft. It wasn't long before she was churning out a hundred gallons of spirits per month. As to the quality of the spirits? By all contemporary accounts, Nancy had a great reputation as a distiller. J.A. Lloyd, a former gauger, called her "an excellent distiller" and superintendent. She was both hardworking and industrious.[513] Four long-time friends, Jasper Tyler, Mike Olehan, Thomas Sharrock, and Peter Anthony, all said she was a woman of boundless energy. She ran the distillery, looked after the farm, worked the fields, milked the cows, and did the housework. They each called her the "boss" distiller, and a fine one at that. Mike Olehan went as far as to say she was "the best one in the country." She distilled both brandy and whisky, which is known because in November 1885, revenue men found several barrels of unstamped brandy in the house. This led them to seize 67 barrels of whisky and 30 barrels of brandy. Barney ended up in court because of it.[514] This would be one of two incidents that would hurt the distillery in the 1880s. The other is when an arsonist burned down Wilholt's Mill, where Barney had a large load of grain waiting to be ground.[515]

In 1881, Barney was growing nervous that Nancy might not get all she deserved if he died without putting his wishes for her down on paper. He contacted his attorney Thomas Myers and had a Deed of Gift drawn up. In it, he gave her rights to all his real estate holdings.[516] Then, in November 1890, he felt like a will would be more appropriate. He had his friend William Kiely draft it. The will made Nancy executrix, and turned over any and all property to her, after debts were covered, for the rest of her natural life.[517] But after it was drawn up, he decided to hold off on getting it witnessed—fearing it might cancel out the Deed of Gift and create confusion.

A couple of days before he died on October 9, 1894, Barney decided it was time to get the will witnessed and asked two long time friends, William Kiely and John Bennett, to sign it.[518]

Upon his death, Barney's niece and sister hired an attorney and took Nancy to court. They claimed Barney was not of sound mind when the document was executed. A trial was set and then postponed until August 1896. One of Nancy's chief witnesses, William Kiely, was moving to Kentucky, so his story had to be taken in a deposition. The prosecution attacked the validity of the will, but Kiely and Bennett relayed the story of being called in by Barney to sign the documents. They claimed he was of sound mind. They also gave his reasoning for leaving his property to Nancy. Not only was she his partner through life, she had saved his life during the war several times and he felt that she was the reason they survived financially through the years.[519]

The prosecution, on the other hand, was more interested in tearing Nancy down. Witnesses were called who claimed Barney was under the devil's spell. Others claimed he would confide in them that she was controlling him. Other witnesses claimed Barney feared Nancy and that he would do anything she said. But, when pressed, none of the witnesses could recall seeing any of this anger and her "boss" reputation came from Barney's insistence that she handle the money during any transactions. Perhaps the only time she appeared aggressive to anyone was when she shut the saloon down Barney was running on site because he was drinking heavily and the saloon was causing trouble.[520]

Meanwhile, the witnesses that vouched for her character were locals and storekeepers who said she was a wonderful person. Barney's lawyers and the signers verified the signatures and handwriting. Everyone for the defense agreed that Barney was of sound mind.

Yet none would claim that Nancy and Barney were married. In fact, almost all vouched for the virtue of the pair. One storekeeper that had lived in the house said he had never seen Nancy eat her meals with the men. Another said when he stayed in the house, he had a room and Barney had a room, but he didn't know where Nancy slept.[521]

This was the era when the "Plessy v. Ferguson" Supreme Court ruling of "separate but equal," and a host of Jim Crow laws were being introduced. Perhaps Nancy, who did list herself as a wife during Reconstruction, was a little more worried about a backlash in these troubled times. Whatever the reason, the subject of her being Barney's wife was ignored through the trial.

It took almost four years for Nancy to win the lawsuit, but she eventually did. And the whole time she continued to distill at the Norman Creek distillery as the boss and owner. In fact, she continued to sell whisky and may have distilled right up to Tennessee prohibition. If so, she would join Josie Brown and Louisa Nelson as three of the distillery owners who stayed at their post until prohibition brought everything to an end. And while there is more documentation surrounding the life of Nancy Patterson, her story and those of her female compatriots are still incomplete.

But before wrapping up the story of Nancy Patterson, there is one last intriguing detail left to cover. It is an interesting ending that only adds more questions to the life of Nancy. In 1900, when a U.S. Census worker came by to gather household details, Nancy was more than happy to oblige. The entry stated Nancy Patterson was the owner of the property and the farm. They listed her as a landlord and head of household. As for her marriage status, she was listed as a widow. And for her race, for the first time, she was listed as Black.[522]

"Woman with an unusual history dies, aged 100." Unusual indeed.

Chapter 21

THE SHOT THAT KILLED WHISKY

Since the days of Evan Shelby, Tennessee whisky had grown from a few small farmer distillers to become one of the largest distilling states in the U.S. Even with Kentucky far surpassing it in volume, Nelson and Daniel kept Tennessee whisky on the lips of national and international drinkers.

But troubled times were ahead. After surviving war, a rebellion, the Yankee taxman, and a prohibition amendment, the Four Mile Law shut off the backcountry from liquor sales. The goal of temperance leaders was to rid the state completely of its spirits. They would try just about anything to stop the scourge of alcohol, legal or not. For whisky interests to survive, they needed to conjure up a miracle.

Stoking the Flames

The early years of the 1890s were a hot time for Old Lincoln. One of the prominent leaders of the boom was Jack Daniel.

After purchasing the land at Cave Spring Hollow, Jack worked diligently to build a solid foundation for his business. In the early 1890s, Jack Daniel's Old Time Distillery wasn't the biggest distillery in Lincoln, but the whisky's reputation was quickly surpassing that of its local competition. One advantages of the location was the perfectly temperate limestone-filtered water source the cave provided. It was so prized, even his neighbor, Tolley & Eaton, asked if they could pipe water out to their own distillery.[523] An amiable Jack was happy to oblige.

There was another change that occurred after the move to the hollow. Longtime distiller, Nearest Green stepped away from the stills when the operation moved to Cave Spring Hollow. His son, George, was around 20 years old at the time and likely took on more responsibilities at the distillery. Meanwhile, it is said that William Hughes, the son of Colonel Hughes, worked his way into the job of distiller for Jack after Nearest left.[524] Unfortunately, all 19th century distillery records were lost in a 20th century fire, so the positions attained by George and William are left to oral tradition.

There was another fresh addition to the team: Jack's nephew, Lem Motlow. Since he was a little boy, Lem had looked up to his uncle and wanted to get into the business. But Jack was determined to make Lem earn his way into the business. There would be no handouts. To work for Jack, Lem had to start out doing hard labor on the farm, slopping hogs, and feeding cattle. Once Jack felt his nephew was ready, he invited him to his new distillery to learn the trade. Lem learned how to distill, but he also learned the business side of things and kept the books. He was being groomed to be Jack's right-hand man.

As for Jack, he wanted his distillery to be self-sufficient. So he purchased as much farmland as he could to keep up with the distillery's grain requirements. But eventually, the demand for his whisky forced him to contract for grain. One of his suppliers was Button Waggoner's father, Mathais. Once all of this grain was processed in the distillery, the spent grains helped fuel another successful venture for Jack––the cattle trade. This was another area where Jack excelled. He was almost as famous for the quality of his herds as he was for his whisky. In his eyes, he had created the perfect ecosystem.

As Jack amassed wealth, everything he spent the money on was to develop his reputation, grow his business, or to help friends and family. In his mansion, he hosted parties and entertained. He became the talk of the town.

By the mid-1890s, Jack's distillery was running at about half the output of Tolley & Eaton's nearby County Line Distillery. But Jack was playing the long game. He had long strived to make the number seven and Jack Daniel's name on the side of a barrel mean something to wholesalers and saloon owners.

After the Internal Revenue commissioner called for a bottling act, Lem and Jack moved from ceramic jugs to quart bottles with their Belle of Lincoln brand.[525] The Belle of Lincoln name played on Jack's standing as the area's most eligible bachelor. Whether or not that was the intention, it was an effective way to build mystery around a brand. Soon, people were talking about who the mysterious "belle" could be. Anything that kept his whisky in the conversation was a plus for Jack. While Belle of Lincoln was quick to be put in bottles, Jack Daniel's No. 7, didn't get its fancy square bottle design out to the market until later—eventually being advertised in bottles in Georgia, and Alabama in 1903, followed by Tennessee in 1904. The square design set Old No. 7 apart with an iconic design with white labels and then eventually black and green.[526]

Jack wasn't the only one of Calaway Daniel's boys that made himself a success in the whisky business. Jack's older brother, Wiley, opened W.B. Daniel & Co. But while he built a nice sized business, he would never compete with his brother. Built in the late 1880s, it would survive for a decade.

Wiley long held out hope that the L&N line would open a depot in Lynchburg. To see the success a depot could have, Wiley only needed to point to Springfield and Flintville. Robertson County's distilling thrived once a depot was established. Little Flintville in Lincoln County was also seeing distillers drawn in. William Copeland opened two distilleries nearby, one in Flintville and the other in Stonesborough. Ben Tolley owned the Tolley Brothers distillery near Lois, and John Dean ran Tolley & Eaton in Kelso. Lincoln County was benefitting from the transportation outlets, but Wiley and the other Moore County distillers never saw their extension.

Maybe it was just as well. While the Gay Nineties were a hot time for liquor sales across the nation, Tennessee was getting hot for another reason.

A frightening trend was growing across the state. Distilleries, warehouses, and liquor businesses were going up in flames. Many of the fires were suspicious in nature, taking place when the distillery wasn't in operation, pointing to arson.

F.E. Cunningham of the Tullahoma Distillery, saw one of his newly built bonded warehouses go up in flames in July 1887. He lost 119 barrels of spirits.[527] Then there was the fire in Springfield in 1890 that took out J.S. Brown and J.W. Starks' liquor wholesaling businesses. This was followed in 1891 by fires at J.M. Million and Duff & Co, which saw both of their saloons torched, along with several additional buildings near Cleveland, Tennessee.[528] A week later, Easterwood & Grant's distillery in Winchester burned thanks to someone placing an incendiary device inside the facility.[529] J.A. Pasour heard the news his distillery went up in flames as he was going into Knoxville to get it reinstated after revenuers shut it down.[530] Even a government warehouse in Tazewell, the site of the onetime whisky rebellion, went up in fiery flames with nearly 800 barrels of whisky lost.[531]

The Tolley's were the worst hit. In 1898, the Tolley & Cannon distillery near Fayetteville lost 55,000 gallons of whisky to flames. Luckily, insurance covered some of it.[532] Then Ben Tolley's distillery on Louse Creek was destroyed by fire soon after.[533] And Jack Eaton paid the price for having 94 barrels of whisky stored in Ben's warehouses. The fires spooked Jack Eaton so badly he hired armed guards to protect his facility in Tullahoma.[534] Then Tolley & Cannon went up in flames and the pair had to lobby the government to rescind the $70,000 in taxes owed on the burnt-up barrels.[535] All the fires made J.S. Cannon's move to Chattanooga seem like a no-brainer.[536]

In an era where smashing up saloons was commonplace for prohibitionists, questions were raised as to whether this uptick in fires might be the work of temperance crusaders. An editorialist at the *Nashville Banner* saw firsthand how the prohibitionists were reacting to all the carnage. As he looked at the bulletin board in the office, he saw the news of the fire at William Copeland's Lincoln County distillery that claimed 650 barrels. He thought to himself, at least it was only 650. Then a man came up behind him and said, "Thank God! Six hundred and fifty barrels of hell–fire where it can't do any more damage to anybody." The reporter said, the man "expressed the hope for the day when every saloon in Nashville burned down and each man inside would at least get a good scorching."[537]

If they hoped to rid Tennessee of its prized Lincoln County whisky, they were doing a good job. John Dean Tolley saw the writing on the wall and left his distilling business altogether in 1902, deciding instead to seek public office.[538] Jack Eaton was so desperate to get away from the fires, he left Tullahoma all together and opened distilling operations in Memphis. Copeland attempted to reopen after their fire, but financially they couldn't do it.[539] It was a shocking turn of events. By 1901, legendary Lincoln County was down to only one whisky distillery.

But it wasn't just flames that wreaked havoc on the southern end of the 5th District. In the late 1880s, the government intensified its campaign against violations of the revenue laws by legitimate distillers. In 1887, William Copeland was fined $100 and spent three months in prison for violations of the law.[540] Tolley and Cannon closed for violations in 1897, with the two owners also thrown in jail, all thanks to five illegally stamped barrels.[541] And it wasn't just in the 5th District: The entire state saw arrest after arrest of legal distillery owners. The smallest infraction could easily send a distiller to jail.

The one distiller that seemed immune to Internal Revenue issues was Jack Daniel. The *Nashville American* made note of that fact when they came to Lynchburg to do a profile on the town in 1896.

> *"One remarkable fact in connection with this distillery is that it has never suspended operations. It has run continuously except at night and on Sundays, and the records of the Internal Revenue Commissioner's office in Washington today show that Jack Daniel's distillery has been in continuous operations longer than any distillery in the United States. This is something very remarkable and a fact which adds largely to the fame of this mammoth distilling plant."*[542]

The article dated that continuous operation back to 1881. This suggests that Jack might have been distilling at Cave Spring Hollow a couple of years before he purchased the property in 1884.[543]

But Jack's good fortune was about to end. Revenuers soon began looking for any abnormalities with the distillery. An investigation went on for a year before the Jack Daniel's plant was seized in 1898, with Jack Daniel charged with illegally removing whisky from bond and reusing tax stamps. In total, 161,000 gallons of whisky were seized. But Jack wasn't arrested. A newspaper article surmised it was because Jack had friends in the revenue department. He posted bond, and the distillery was back up and running in short order.[544]

End of an Era

Ever since intemperance became an issue in Tennessee, the two major political parties steered clear of the issue. By the late 1880s, however, a weak Republican party saw an opportunity to gain traction by painting Democrats as supporters of the saloon and whisky interests. Initially, the strategy didn't bear fruit. Between 1889 and 1895, Republicans in the General Assembly blamed Democrats for their failure to pass a bill allowing the Four Mile Law in incorporated towns.

But in the middle of the 90s, Tennessee Democrats had a change of heart. The national scene was changing, and the local electorate took notice. There was a new organization leading the charge for temperance. It was Wayne B. Wheeler's Anti-Saloon League. A lawyer by trade, Wheeler was relentless in his attacks against the saloon and alcohol interests. His powers of persuasion brought many fence sitters into the fight. It also helped that his organization wasn't tied to the divisive issue of women's suffrage. This helped him pull in support the WCTU never could. One of the ASL's most valuable weapons was former Democratic presidential candidate William Jennings Bryan. Not only was Bryan one of the best stump speakers in America, he was also a staunch prohibitionist. At one point, he attempted to raise income taxes to cover the potential loss of revenue if the government enacted prohibition. But the plan backfired when the Supreme Court declared the income tax unconstitutional in 1896. Bryan saw Wheeler's Anti-Saloon League as an ally in getting a constitutional amendment, allowing the income tax to be reinstated.

In Tennessee, it would be the state-run chapter of the Anti-Saloon League that finally swayed the votes to get the Four Mile Law amendment passed in 1899.

Again, the law restricted the sales of intoxicants within four miles of schools in unincorporated areas. But this version also added incorporated municipalities under two thousand people.[545] The only caveat was that the municipalities had to reincorporate after the passage of the amendment. A large number of small towns quickly scheduled referendums on reincorporating.

It was already tough enough for rural whisky drinkers to find a good bottle of hooch. As far back as 1874, this east Tennessean had felt the effects of the Four Mile Law and Kentucky's Local Option Law:

> *"Allensville KY voted Local Option three to one. Russellville ditto. Olmstead had a four mile liquor law already. Elkton voted whiskey back to where it was in the days of "Auld Lang Sine." Its an outrage that our people should have to send away to Elkton to get legally a first class article of family disturbance. Maj Cox says our liberties are going. One by one we cross the river."*[546]

A quarter of a century later, Major Cox's prophecy was coming true. The move into small incorporated towns wasn't enough. The prohibitionists were out to squeeze the state dry town by town if necessary.

With a win under their belt, the prohibitionists pushed the new legislature for an extension into towns under four thousand people. But the Senate rejected it, which sent the Tennessee Anti-Saloon League into a rage. The House revised the bill, increasing the number to five thousand people. Known as the Peeler Bill, it made it through the House, but when the Senate discussed the bill, a clever anti-prohibitionist had it amended to cover towns under 104,000 people, not five thousand. The goal was obvious: Kill the Peeler Bill by making an exaggerated mockery of it. It was a dangerous game to play though. If it passed, it had the potential to ban the sale of alcohol throughout the entire state. With the new amendment, it was rejected by a three-vote margin.[547]

Prohibitionists cried foul. They accused the liquor interests of paying off senators. After an investigation, it was discovered that distillers and brewers around the state had raised $2,400 to defeat the bill. J.H. Brengleman of the Charles Nelson wholesale house in Nashville confessed to the scheme and detailed who was involved. Brengleman said not a single penny had been used corruptly. At most they spent $400 to get an opinion as to whether the law was constitutional.[548] Soon Manny Shwab was sucked into the fray. Away on a trip to Florida, his brother George had to stand in for him. He told legislators, "whiskey had been sent to the hotels and to the Capitol, he could not tell how much or whether or not it was paid for. He also knew of a case where whiskey had been sent out by express for a member of the Legislature."[549] With no money trail, they couldn't prove corruption. But if the scheme did anything, it showed how far the liquor industry would go to stop prohibition.

The next big bill came in 1903 when again there was an attempt to get the Four Mile Law extended to towns of five thousand or less. Known as the Adams Law, the bill that created it sailed through the General Assembly. Its passage sent shockwaves through the state's liquor interests.[550]

To the surprise of Old Robertson fans, Springfield held a referendum on rechartering their town. When the town's vote was in, the *Chattanooga Daily News* wrote, "truly the day of miracles has not passed. Think of Springfield, so long the headquarters for the pure and unadulterated stuff––old-fashioned Robertson County Sour Mash Corn, which made babies grow and men good natured and lively, but never 'drunk.' While Robertson County for half a century has been the home of good liquor it is now really a temperance county."

With Springfield going dry, the days of Old Robertson were numbered. Distillers could still distill and wholesalers could still sell to wet areas, but that was it. By May 1, 1903, Springfield's six saloons closed their doors for good.[551] The Pitt Brothers kept their wholesale house open until 1907, but eventually moved to Kentucky. The Pitt Brothers Distillery continued to operate, as did Nelson's Greenbrier and Wartrace, but there was little hope for the glory days of old.

The mood of the state had turned so anti-alcohol that the saloons of Fayetteville saw the writing on the wall and shut themselves down. W.C. McLeod, John Hughes, Tom Eagin, J.W. Milam, W.T. Yates, Style Buchanan, and E. A.

Evans all quit the business.[552] Weeks later, the town easily passed its referendum and Lincoln County's largest town went dry. In fact, by mid-April the only three holdout towns under 5,000 were Winchester, Raleigh, and Lynchburg. Winchester narrowly missed passage by 27 votes, while Raleigh went with the rest of Shelby County into the wet category, and Lynchburg drys protested the election.[553]

With former distilling centers dropping like flies, sad news hit Springfield. Just twenty-two days after giving up the hooch, the town learned that John Woodard, one of the wealthiest men in the state, and the second to last symbol of the great Woodard distilling family, had passed away. It must have felt like the death of Old Robertson was at hand.

The Political Machine

After a century-long list of legendary distilling names, Tennessee whisky was about to meet its greatest antagonist. He was Sumner County lawyer turned politician and newspaperman, Edward Ward Carmack.

As an up and comer, he spent two years in the General Assembly in the 1880s as an anti-prohibitionist. A fact that his opponents would use against him in the future. When he lost reelection, he went to work for the *Columbia Herald* for a time. Quickly proving himself, he stepped up to Colonel Duncan Cooper's *Nashville Herald*. When Cooper sold his interest in the *Herald*, Carmack moved to the *Nashville American* and became the paper's editor. It seemed nothing could stop Carmack's ascent in the newspaper industry. In February 1892, Carmack heard that the post of editor at the *Memphis Commercial* had opened up. Proud of his young star, Duncan Cooper gave Carmack a glowing endorsement that helped him seal the post. It was there that Carmack learned how to use a newspaper to promote his own political beliefs. One of his pet themes was the superiority of traditional southern living.

But the political arena was where Carmack wanted to be. In 1897, he ran for the U.S. House of Representatives and won the seat, defeating three-term Rep. Josiah

Patterson after a bitter campaign. Carmack quickly gained favor with Democrats in the General Assembly. And when U.S. Senator Turley declined to return to Washington, the General Assembly chose Carmack to take his place.

The man who replaced Senator Carmack in the House seat was fellow Democrat Malcolm Patterson. A Vanderbilt graduate and Memphis lawyer, Patterson was the son of Josiah Patterson, the man Carmack had bounced from office in 1897. Patterson had served as his father's manager through the campaign. The angry words passed during that campaign created an animosity between the two men that simmered into the new century.[554]

In the 1906 primaries, Senator Carmack began his reelection campaign while Rep. Patterson looked to unseat the sitting governor, John Cox. By this point, the question of temperance was no longer if a candidate was wet or dry, it was how dry they were. This kept the Tennessee Anti-Saloon League on the sidelines during the primaries. But Carmack's opponent, former Governor Robert Taylor, used the senator's past anti-prohibition stance against him. Carmack had reimagined himself as a defender of temperance and a supporter of the Four Mile Law, but Taylor had an easy time painting him as untrustworthy.[555] Rep. Patterson, on the other hand, mostly focused on election reform and getting the party out of the hands of "machine politics." He also confirmed his support for the Adams Law and its further extension into the cities, as long as the people voted for it. Carmack lost the primary to Robert Taylor, while Rep. Patterson sailed through the primary and on to the general election. Patterson was almost upended when his Republican opponent accused him of public drunkenness. But in the end he won the governorship easily. Both Patterson and Carmack headed to Nashville, but while Patterson went to the governor's mansion, Carmack began plotting to take his place.

For Patterson, his time as governor got off to a rocky start. He pushed a bill that would finance improved roads by taxing saloon keepers $300 a year for beer sales and $1,500 a year for whisky sales. But temperance leaders weren't about to justify sales of liquor to build the state's infrastructure, so they lobbied to have saloons taxes removed from the bill.[556] The revised bill was passed and signed by the governor, but an angry Patterson began vetoing what he saw as pet anti-liquor bills to spite them. One of those bills tried to force the mining town of LaFollette dry, weeks before it held a referendum on recharter. Patterson was opposed to this kind of forcing of laws against the people's will. The bill became a battle of wits between the wets and drys. The wets argued that the town had ballooned to over 5,000 people in the last year, so it was exempt. Drys argued that the Adams' Law took the population from the last census into account, not the current population.[557] For Patterson, all he had to do was hold onto his veto and wait for the election. When the town finally voted, they went 698 to 23 against recharter. As for the legislature's attempt to ram it through anyway, Patterson vetoed the bill and told voters he did it because the bill didn't follow Democratic ideals.[558]

Rev. E.E. Folk, the leader of the Tennessee Anti-Saloon League, immediately went to war against the governor. Their biggest ally was about to become Edward Ward Carmack. In the fight with Patterson, things were about to get nasty.

The Fate of Knoxville

By March 1907, just about every town in Tennessee had been rechartered so as to invoke the Four Mile Law. Nashville, Chattanooga, Memphis, LaFollette, and Knoxville stood as the last footholds for purchasing whisky, beer, and wine in the state.

Wanting to protect the liquor trade of the city's, anti-prohibitionists railed on the job losses the Four Mile Law would bring. But Senator Carmack was having none of it, saying towns like Knoxville would survive without their beloved saloons and wholesalers. He chided the opposition, saying, "the tattered vagabond wallowing in the gutter adds nothing to the prosperity of a community."[559]

Of the five remaining cities, Knoxville seemed the closest to giving up their spirits. Carry Nation visited the town in late November 1906, declaring it wicked. The citizens welcomed her with open arms.[560] Those that cheered for her knew all too well about the violence and murder that happened in places like the Bowery down along Crozier Street. The Bowery was Knoxville's den of prostitution, gambling, drugs, fights, and gunplay. It had been that way since the Gay Nineties and no self-respecting citizen would be caught near it.

But there were a couple of saloons that anti-prohibitionists could have pointed to as having some measure of class and respectability.

One was Sullivan's Saloon in Irish Town. Its owner, Pat Sullivan, did what he could to make it hospitable for visiting dignitaries and the respectable ladies about town. Patrons went to calling it "Pat's Barn" because the watered down beer was served in a massive sized mug. There was elderly woman that always seemed to be there. It was said she stored her whisky in her cane.

The other respectable establishment was Johnson's Saloon, down on Gay Street. Johnson's was where everyone felt welcome and no one dared get out of line because there was too much respect for its owner.[561] But there had been a time when you wouldn't have been caught dead in the old Johnson Saloon.

In the 1870s, if you were looking for crime, drunkards, and debauchery, Gay Street was the place to find it. And the old Johnson Saloon felt like the instigator of all the mayhem. When John Johnson was manning the bar, there were plenty of fights and sometimes he was in the middle of them. It was also a notorious den for pickpockets. And its drunk patrons didn't seem to mind churning up trouble outside the saloon. In fact, George Carter's barber shop next door saw what cheap rotgut could do to a man, when a normally peaceful Mart Teasley pulled a pistol and shot at Carter after a heavy drinking session at the Johnson Saloon.[562]

But those were the early 1870s when John Johnson ran the place into the ground. Two years after it was boarded up, another Johnson came in and re-established the bar. The new owner––no relation to the old––was determined to build a respectable saloon where all peaceful men could come in and enjoy a responsible drink of the finest liquors available in the area. And while there was pricey liquor there, Johnson's was open to all social classes. The only thing was, you had to follow the rules. The budding entrepreneur with the hopeful attitude was Cal Johnson.

To say Cal started with nothing but his wits and personality is an understatement. A native of Knoxville, he worked odd jobs after the Civil War, saving every penny he could to establish his own business. When a contractor named John Long held an administrator's sale on a building at the corner of Gay and Vine streets, Cal bought in.[563]

What Cal saw was a building surrounded by a rough and tumble community that felt like it needed a shining light to bring it all together. His building was nothing but a slapped-together shack, just like the other structures on Gay Street. But what sold Cal on the building was the beautiful dark-stained bar John Johnson had left behind. He gave the building a fresh coat of paint and hung a sign by the old elm tree that stood out front. There was something Cal liked about that old tree just as much as he loved the bar. Maybe it was because it was the only one on the entire street.[564]

Once he opened his doors, he turned away gamblers and ruffians. Only customers who were respectful could stay. He instructed his employees never to open the bar on Sundays. This was a rule Cal was quite adamant about. The only thing that wasn't squeaky clean about his establishment was the brothel on the second floor––a staple of the era. But after reading a news story about a sick woman who had to send her daughter to a brothel on Gay Street to find her father, Cal transformed the second floor into storage space.[565]

The profits from Cal's saloon went straight into land investments. He knew owning property was the way to success. He also involved himself in charities, including joining a committee with J.N. Betterton and Henry Allen to raise money for a destitute widow.[566] His prosperity soon drew the attention of local reporters. "By industry and fair dealing [Cal] has acquired considerable property in this city." It wasn't long before locals started lobbying for him to run for alderman in the Fifth Ward. Cal was a soft-spoken, independent man, and he wasn't sure he would be the best candidate for the job. But eventually he won the spot. And again, the local news raved that the voters of the fifth "can't do better than to elect Cal Johnson."[567] In an era of temperance, it was a rare thing to see a saloon owner receiving so much praise.

In 1883, Cal decided it was time to build a more handsome and sturdy framed structure for his patrons. It was the first framed structure on the street. Then he worked to have the old dusty walkway out front replaced by a wooden sidewalk. The only caveat was that the elm tree had to be protected. So the town built the sidewalk around it.

The new building and Cal's way of taking care of his patrons made the Johnson Saloon one of the best in the city. The friendly atmosphere was second to none. And if Cal wasn't busy with some other endeavor, he might tip his hat to you when you walked in the door. He especially went out of his way to tip his hat to the businessmen he respected.

Cal had other passions, too. One of his biggest was horses. Oh, he loved horses. And his growing fortune allowed him to purchase a top-quality stable of racing horses. He raced them all over the south, winning cash prizes and investing in more winning horses. Eventually, he got up the nerve to build his own race track in East Knoxville.

As for drawing talented horses to his track, that wasn't a problem. The *Knoxville Sentinel* wrote:

> *"All he has to do is write to some of his horse owning friends and the stables will be filled with their and his horses all challenging for a purse. The area is ready for some fast horse flesh. Johnson, who owns the track agrees to make it available for free, for the event, and will share with others the receipts and expenses. He is energetic. Johnson has been in the race horse business for many years and has extended acquaintance among horsemen of the country. They all know him."*[568]

His favorite race horse was Dan McClung. According to Cal, he ran one hundred races and only lost one, and that was just because he cut his foot. Cal had little money when he started racing Dan back in 1883, but the horse eventually made him a rich man.

Horses, property, saloons––it seems Cal excelled at everything he did. It was because he wouldn't settle for second best.

When whisky was finally available in bottles instead of barrels, he sought the best brands he could. According to Cal, his whisky was "100 proof, and the people who drank it knew they were getting the best."[569] He looked for the same in his horses and his properties. Whether he realized it or not, this infectious spirit made it into his community. Gay Street had moved from the dregs to a well-respected neighborhood, just as Cal had hoped.

But in March 1907, the fate of Cal's saloon and the other saloons of the city fell in the hands of the voters. Cal knew many of the saloons in the city were a menace. How could the voters know that the wicked ways of some saloons weren't the ways of ol' Cal Johnson? Unfortunately, he couldn't get a separate trial in the court of public opinion and the Four Mile Law didn't consider responsible actors who ran a tight ship.

On the day of the election, a parade of ten thousand women and children marched through the streets of Knoxville. The writing was on the wall. For every vote to keep the saloon, there were two votes against it. When the tally was announced, there was singing in the street. Singing everywhere, but inside Cal Johnson's saloon.[570]

Cal would not let it get him down. He turned the saloon into a soda shop and removed all the alcohol from the premises. At least he still had his property, and he still had his racehorses. He diversified his business holdings by buying and refurbishing the old Lincoln Theater.[571]

Cal's 38 years of running one of the most respected saloons in town was at an end. The law and the people had spoken. And Cal always stayed within the law.[572] It didn't matter, though. Cal was one of the wealthiest people in Knoxville and one of the richest in all of Tennessee--not just in money, but in respect and friendship.

Three months later, Cal was at his racetrack, checking on his horses. A reporter from the *Knoxville Sentinel* was there to gauge his reaction to a new law that was taking away his ability to race his horses. The two made their way over to Cal's pride and joy, Dan McClung. The horse was now over 30 years old. Cal said, "he has some gray in his coat, but he is gay as a colt, and when he goes out to run, he appears that he could give some young horses some trouble." If it were anyone else, you might have thought he was speaking metaphorically about himself. His wife had passed, his saloon was gone, and his racing days looked to be at an end. But there was always a glimmer of optimism in everything he said.

"Dan," he said with some melancholy, as he brushed a fly away from the old horse's face, "you have lived to see your last race. But Dan, the grass is just as green as ever. My memory of your fine racing is just as green as the grass, and the legislature can legislate you out of a job, but they cannot legislate against me loving you just like I did when racing horses was an honorable business in the eyes of the law. Old Dan, if it was not for that law, we would show them something yet."[573]

The Showdown

The year 1908 promised to be a year of extreme politicking between the Democratic rivals for governor. And for the first time, prohibition was at the top of the agenda. Malcolm Patterson was up for reelection and his challenger in the primary was none other than former Senator Edward Ward Carmack. It was sure to be a campaign filled with vigorous attacks, as the two longtime rivals not only had their own venom to spit but also had the Tennessee Anti-Saloon League to appeal to. Who would win on the alcohol question?

The south was already falling like dominoes to the prohibitionists. Alabama and Georgia were already dry. North Carolina was on the precipice. When Knoxville went dry, that left only four wet municipalities in Tennessee; and Chattanooga saloons were losing their battle with local religious factions.

Neither Carmack nor Patterson would commit to promoting statewide prohibition. But Republicans were ready to force them to commit to something. The problem was, both Democrats had holes in their swing. Patterson had vetoed Democrat's pet liquor bills, angering lawmakers; but Carmack was a little too cozy with Memphis city officials who were anti-prohibitionists.[574]

Meanwhile, the liquor interests spent most of the time out to lunch. Just like in 1887, it took until March to organize the statewide Model License League with a focus on saloon reform. Part of their strategy was to get the remaining saloons to be good citizens through firmer licensing standards. They were also seeking compensation for saloon owners who were being forced out of business. With a legislature unwilling to pave roads with saloon "blood money", this was a big ask. It showed how out of touch the liquor men were with public and legislative sentiment. That didn't stop them from attacking Carmack. They said, if he was against the use of alcohol, he should punish the drinkers. In that, he would learn how against this idea of prohibition people really were.[575]

In reaction to the League's formation, Carmack decided it was time to take a firm stand, saying the saloon had "sinned away its day of grace in Tennessee. It will not be reformed and therefore must be destroyed."[576] The saloons responded with posters accusing stump speakers of being freeloaders looking to crush the state's farmers. Others used fearful rhetoric, including one that told every farmer to "assert his rights and use every effort to suppress this growing evil of prohibition, which is jeopardizing the livelihood of upwards of six million people and threatens to precipitate the greatest financial crisis this country has ever known."[577]

Distillers who were feeling the pain from the loss of most of Tennessee, Alabama, and Georgia's revenue now faced a bigger problem. Edward Carmack was coming for them. On April 11, he released his platform and at the top of the list was "the entire abolition of the liquor traffic" in the state.[578] For E.E. Folk and the Tennessee Anti-Saloon League, this was all they needed to hear. Carmack was their man. Even the WCTU, which had lost power but was still active, threw their support behind the former senator.

Then a bombshell hit. *Collier's National Weekly*, a newspaper with around half a million readers, produced an article called "Who Killed Margaret Lear?"

It was a rehashed story about the assault and killing of a 14-year-old white girl in Shreveport, Louisiana some three years earlier by a Black man, who was drunk on gin. The article's purpose was clear. It was to demonize the gin makers and the Model License League. It did so by preying on the deepest and darkest racial prejudices of the day in a most deplorable way.

The main attacks in the article were levied on a St. Louis spirit branded as Black Cock Vigor Gin. The gin bottle featured a white woman wearing what was interpreted as revealing clothing while holding a black rooster.[579]

Newspapers, especially those sympathetic to temperance, reprinted the article multiple times throughout the campaign. Then Knoxville editorialists condemned Chattanooga saloons for selling it. Patterson was then associated with the product. But, Patterson denied ever knowing anything about the gin, let alone endorsing it or promoting its production.[580]

It wasn't long before E.R. Betterton found himself in the crosshairs. Chattanooga's dry paper railed against his Tom Boy Gin that featured a picture of a "beautiful and fascinating white woman," suggesting it was sold specifically in saloons frequented by Black men.[581]

The Hamilton County Board of Excise Commissioners met to decide Betterton's fate, the fate of other bottles of gin, and issues surrounding the saloons. The St. Louis gin was found to be indecent with its photo, but Betterton's was not considered lewd. In their judgment, they decided:

> *"The proof failed to justify a conviction for the use of 'The Tom Boy' label. It also finds that the exposing of a picture of any woman's face or figure on a bottle or otherwise is improper and destructive of the respect which all men owe to their mothers, wives, and sisters. Hence the Commission orders that such practice is discontinued."*

They further stated that nude or suggestive pictures in saloons where only men gathered showed bad intent.[582]

When primary day mercifully arrived, the vote count was so close that it took a couple of days to confirm the result. But, in the end, the Margaret Lear tactic failed. Carmack didn't dispute the result, but the Tennessee Anti-Saloon League and WCTU both claimed bribery, corruption, and ballot-box stuffing. And, once again, women were blamed for the loss because of their mere presence at the ballot box.

Even though Carmack didn't dispute the results, he was bitter and sought revenge against the governor. The best weapon he could wield was the one he started out with. He made a deal with Luke Lea, the owner of the upstart *Tennessean* newspaper and on August 23 announced he was now to be the new paper's editor. Along with the position, he was made the "exclusive dictator" of policy.[583] He knew he wasn't going to stop Governor Patterson's second term: The Republicans were too weak and disorganized. But he could damage his reputation for the rematch.

The problem was, Patterson wasn't Carmack's only target. As the general election approached, Carmack started spreading his vitriol to those he felt were confidants of the governor. But the wet *Chattanooga Times* saw through his tactics. "*The Tennessean*, in the hands of a very accomplished politician and brilliant word juggler, never lacks for something to say. It erects a straw target today, and shoots it full of holes tomorrow."[584] One of Carmack's favorite targets was his old boss, Colonel Duncan B. Cooper. In Carmack's mind, Cooper had betrayed him by working for Patterson during the election.

Immediately after Patterson defeated his Republican challenger G.N. Tillman with 53.7% of the vote, Carmack increased his attacks. Cooper tried to let the personal attacks roll off his back, but by the end of the week, the colonel had heard enough. He penned a letter to Carmack asking him to stop the attacks on his character. After all, he was a private citizen and no longer a public figure. But he didn't want to hand deliver the letter, so he sought a proxy.

The following Monday morning, the colonel was sitting at the Tulane Hotel in Downtown Nashville chatting with E.B. Craig, a friend of Carmack's from Chattanooga. Craig hadn't expected the discussion to focus on Carmack, but Cooper asked him to do him a favor and to go ask Carmack to stop his attacks and take him the letter. Craig obliged and went to the offices of the *Tennessean*. When Craig returned, he appeared somewhat dazed and reported that Carmack had refused to see the letter and berated him for bringing up the subject. Yet Craig said he agreed not to use Cooper's name in the future.

Then Cooper met with Governor Patterson at the Maxwell House Hotel. They were joined by the colonel's brother-in-law, James Bradford, who also happened to be his son Robin's law partner. Patterson and Bradford tried to calm Cooper down, but he was getting more and more agitated. Robin and James agreed that nothing good could come from confronting Carmack directly. But Bradford said he had a good connection with an ally of Carmack's and he'd give him the letter to deliver. Bradford went off to see his old friend, but when he didn't return with news, Cooper went up to his son's law office to get an update.

Unfortunately, Bradford's contact was out of town. Again, Bradford implored the colonel to pocket the letter and let the situation go. His son Robin conquered. Moments later, the phone rang. It was the governor, asking to speak with the colonel. After the call, Duncan asked his son to join him at the governor's mansion.

As the two made their way to the door, James Bradford stopped them and suggested that maybe they should take a back way out of the office. A chance meeting with Carmack on the streets wouldn't be advisable. Better to take streets he wouldn't normally be on. They did just that, walking through the Arcade and up through Union Street to Vine.[585]

At that same time, Edward Carmack was leaving the *Tennessean*, heading home to his apartment on Seventh Avenue. As he walked, he recognized Mrs. Charles H. Eastman and her husband further down the street. He called out a hello to her and waved. She waved back. When she lowered her hand, Carmack saw two figures walk around the corner behind her. Suddenly, one man started rushing in his direction. It was Colonel Cooper.

Carmack had feared this confrontation might come. Especially since Cooper seemed to be making him out to be the bad guy with people like his friend Craig. He sensed things were heading to a boiling point. As a precaution, he had purchased a pistol to defend himself. He fumbled in his pocket and felt for the trigger. Cooper yelled something out at him and in a gut reaction Carmack pulled the pistol out and tried to aim it towards the colonel, but the Eastmans were in the way. He jumped to the side to get them out of the line of fire when he spotted the Colonel's son aiming a Colt automatic revolver right at him.

At that moment, the sound of gunfire echoed and ricocheted off of the sides of nearby buildings. One man grabbed at his shoulder. The other man spun around, reached out for a lamppost, but missed, and fell into a gutter, grabbing his face. His weapon fell helplessly to the ground.[586]

Chapter 22

OL' DAN IS DEAD

Martyr to the Cause

If Carmack knew what hit him, he didn't know it for very long. Any of the three bullets that entered his body could have killed him. Robin Cooper was an excellent shot.

When the Coopers and Eastmans gave their accounts of the event, they didn't match up. Mrs. Eastman, a supporter of Carmack, saw the newspaper man as defending himself. The Coopers claimed Robin, who had taken two bullets himself, shot in self-defense after Carmack hit him. There were no other reasonable eyewitnesses. The best that could be offered was that the sound of a pistol was followed by rapid fire shots, most likely coming from the Colt.

Amid the scene of a lifeless body and his bleeding son, Colonel Duncan Cooper stood dumbfounded. How did it come to this? He wandered over to Robin and put his arm around him, attempting to hold him up. Robin's wound came from a shot that had entered near his collarbone. The colonel helped his son over to the office of Dr. R.E. Fort, who examined Robin, got him stable and made arrangements for him to be sent to St. Thomas Hospital.[587]

Outside, several hundred people had gathered. The police were doing their best to investigate and hold the crowd back at the same time. It was a half hour before the coroner removed Carmack's body. And the crowd stayed deep into the evening, checking out the blood on the sidewalk and talking about what had happened earlier in the day.

Robin was charged with murder and his father, Colonel Duncan Cooper, charged as an accessory to murder. It was hard to know where things went so wrong. Carmack and Duncan were friends at one time. Carmack had even praised Duncan when his endorsement earned him the job at the *Memphis Commercial* in what seemed like a lifetime before. Although the colonel hadn't fired a single bullet, he would soon be on trial for the killing.

The following Sunday, the largest gathering in the history of the Ryman Auditorium took part in a memorial for Carmack. When speeches concluded, resolutions were read. "In his death, the city has lost a fearless editor, the State one of its foremost citizens, the country one of its ablest statesmen. Of him a Senatorial colleague said: 'He was the most brilliant man who has appeared in the Senate on either side of the chamber during my term of service.' In him civic virtue had a knightly champion, prohibition a mighty advocate, and hearth and home a dauntless defender." The resolutions that followed showed exactly what cause he would be a martyr for. The first resolution stated the deplorable way he died, the second resolution stated "that we renew our allegiance to the principles of prohibition and pure politics." The third was "that in devoting to his memory we redeclare our determination to drive the liquor power from the State of Tennessee." And the fourth to "condemn the spirit of lawlessness rampant in our State." What's interesting is that Duncan Cooper wasn't a liquor man. But it didn't matter. The prohibitionists were out to make his son's gun a symbol of the liquor industry.[588]

Newspapers filled the holidays with articles pushing both for and against prohibition. The recently elected General Assembly, being more dry than it had ever been, meant the table was set. The hopes of the prohibitionists were all centered on January 1909 and the next session of the legislature.

To remember, a time when two political parties were more in sync requires going back to the Era of Good Feeling during James Monroe's terms as president. It was the time just after the old Federalist Party of Washington and Adams had given up the ghost; this left the Jeffersonian Democratic-Republicans standing unopposed, save some internal opposition. The only faction on the outs on January 4, 1909 were the supporters of Governor Malcolm Patterson. The rest of the Democrats split off and joined the Republicans. It seemed like the *Memphis Commercial Appeal* was ready to proclaim the death of the Democrats in Tennessee.[589]

The first days of the new term in the Senate were heated. Senator O.K. Holladay, a Democrat from the rural country east of Nashville, took center stage as soon as the last new senator was sworn in. The new alliance was eager to get a speaker named so they could get down to business. And Senator Holladay didn't even seem to care if that meant having the minority party win the speaker's post.[590]

The bill he wanted on the floor was the "Statewide Bill," or what was later referred to as the Holladay Bill, after its author. The goal of the bill was to outlaw any sale of liquor within four miles of any school, regardless of the town's incorporation status.[591] Angered, Memphis and Chattanooga sent council members to Nashville to protest the extension. When the vote was delayed, Governor Patterson declared the bill tyrannical, and promised a veto.[592]

But before the bill hit his desk, the governor found himself fighting another unexpected bill. The new one was co-authored by Holladay. It was known as the Manufacturer's Bill. If passed, it would outlaw all distillation of spirits within the state. It would be a stake through the heart of Tennessee distillers.[593]

But first, a special evening session was called to allow all voices to be heard on the subject of the Holladay Bill. Crowds of people filled up every inch of space in the Capitol. Amazingly, there were no incidents to report of, even though both sides of the argument were passionate about their cause. The statewiders far outnumbered the anti-prohibitionists, but leaders from both factions had an opportunity to share their views.[594] After the House passed the bill, it went to the Senate. It met little resistance. The split Democrats voted fifteen for and twelve against, while all five Republicans voted for the measure. As of July 1, it looked like the Tennessee saloon would be dead, all but for the coming veto of Governor Patterson, but all they needed was a simple majority to override it.[595]

Next up was the Manufacturer's Bill, which the few remaining wet papers called the Confiscation Bill. This was because it confiscated the livelihood of distillers and rectifiers.[596] Statewiders didn't want to let the liquor interests gain any momentum, so they pushed the bill through the Senate within a breakneck ten minutes.[597] With the House following suit, it headed to the Governor's desk within a week of the Holladay Bill passing. As expected, Patterson vetoed both, but the unified General Assembly easily overrode him. Distilling in Tennessee would have to be shut down by January 1, 1910.

From that day forward, the only liquor sales allowed would be wholesale transactions to points outside the state. The state couldn't regulate this, because interstate commerce falls under federal law. It was figured, to get that solution, Tennesseans would have to wait for national prohibition.

In less than two weeks, the General Assembly tore down 125 years of legal distilling history in Tennessee. And all thanks to a firefight in the streets of Nashville.

Trial of the Century

After putting the liquor interests in their place, the state shifted its focus to the fate of Colonel Duncan and Robin Cooper. Four days after Carmack's killing, a grand jury arraigned the two, and the court held them without bond. For good measure, a co-conspirator was added to the trial. The authorities also accused ex-Davidson County Sheriff John D. Sharp of being an accessory to murder.

The trial was to begin in Nashville on January 20 and media outlets like the *Chattanooga News* and *Knoxville Sentinel* set up a special leased telegraphic wire so they could get reports in instantaneously.[598] Within days, a media circus commenced with reporters from Chicago, New York, and Cincinnati arriving on the L&N railway or by motor car.

But things quickly ground to a halt. First, an elongated jury selection delayed the trial. It was hard to find a juror in Nashville that wasn't familiar with the news surrounding the case. Then Judge Hart had a bellyache which delayed the trial longer. And then the judge dismissed a juror due to his bias towards the governor.

Once the trial got underway, Judge Hart had to admonish the lead attorneys, who were getting hot under the collar, rehashing past elections. "Gentleman, this is no matter of politics, and please keep it out."[599]

It was almost two weeks before testimony was heard. The first to appear on the stand was Mrs. Eastman, the only eyewitness to the crime. She was a charming woman, exuding a strong intellect and refinement. Her silvery gray hair gave her a regal appearance, and she cut a sympathetic figure. Revealing the story from the beginning, she put special emphasis on one specific memory on that day. "I told Col. Cooper that he had not given Mr. Carmack a chance and that I would rather be the dead Senator lying there in the gutter than to be him alive." To that came a light applause from some members of the audience, which caught the defense attorneys by surprise.[600] If the Coopers thought self-defense was going to make this case a shoo-in, that reaction said there was some momentum against them.

Day in and day out, the witnesses appearing for the state and defense tried to make their cases. Governor Patterson and James Bradford both appeared for the defense. Robin Cooper's testimony was the first chance the jury had to hear the full story from the defendant's side. Additional detail emerged, showing the cynical tone of Carmack's *Tennessean* toward Duncan Cooper. They also revealed that Carmack had in fact opened Cooper's letter when Craig brought it to him. Apparently Craig wasn't honest with Carmack's response. Instead of saying he'd back off, he actually dug in. Carmack pleaded, "if the *Tennessean* never again used Cooper's name, the public would believe that the paper had been bluffed, and it would lose caste."[601] When it came time for final arguments, the lead attorneys went into great filibusters, with the state talking for fifteen hours and five minutes and the defense going on for eighteen hours and ten minutes. The judge read his charge to the jury on March 17.

When the first ballot came in, things weren't looking good for the Coopers. Five felt murder in the first degree was justified, six saw it as second degree, and only one man called for acquittal. But each time they polled the jury, they came back deadlocked.

On Friday 19, as each juror was polled, the words acquittal rang out. But it wasn't for the Coopers. The jury couldn't understand why ex-Sheriff John D. Sharp was added to the trial, so they let him go.[602] As for the Coopers, their verdict remained unsettled.

On Saturday morning at 9:30 a.m., most of the observers were sure another deadlock was coming, so the courtroom wasn't as boisterous as it had been. Then the verdicts were read. As each individual juror gave their verdict, the tension in the room grew more and more. Could it be an actual verdict? When the one holdout on acquittal changed his vote to murder in the second degree, the courtroom knew the jury was unanimous. The Coopers were to be sentenced to twenty years in the state penitentiary at Brushy Mountain. The judge set bail at $25,000 each. Their attorney immediately called for a mistrial, which the judge denied.[603]

But not so fast. Shortly after, the criminal court cited forty-six errors during the trial. They overturned the guilty verdicts, which brought about a retrial. The major errors were in Judge W.M. Hart's charges to the jury and his choices of what evidence and testimony should be stricken from the record. Those that were excluded included the conversations of Bradford and the Coopers on the day of the shooting.[604]

It would take a year, but in April 1910 the State Supreme Court overturned the case against Robin Cooper, allowing for a retrial. But they sustained the conviction of his father, Duncan Cooper. Within a couple hours of the decision, Governor Patterson pardoned his old friend the colonel, saying neither man received a fair trial.[605] This sent the state and press into an uproar. But in November, Robin's second trial led to his acquittal.[606] The long drama was over. The only victims would be Edward Carmack and Governor Patterson, whose pardon of the colonel lost him any support he still held among the voters.

Governor Patterson would never hold high public office again. He would, however, become a member of the Anti-Saloon League and toured the nation in favor of national prohibition. Duncan Cooper died twelve years later at the ripe old age of 78. But Robin wasn't so lucky. After riding off from his home with a stranger in September 1919, he disappeared. Not long after, they found his body in a creek. Newspapers speculated his death resulted from unpaid gambling debts.[607]

No Distiller's Holladay

It was the largest seizure of liquor and distilling equipment in the south, up to that time. Apparently, Sterling S. Price had cooked up a scheme where he stole spirits from his own distillery, the Chattanooga Distillery Company. He did it by using a rubber pipe to siphon-off spirits after the gauger left for the day. As punishment, the feds confiscated $185,000 worth of property and the state revoked the distillery's company charter. It was the last raid before the passage of the Manufacturer's Bill.[608]

After the Holladay Bill passed, distillers held out hopes they could get it declared unconstitutional. But when asked if either of his bills would survive under the microscope of the courts, Senator Holladay confidently said yes. The Statewide Law was basically the Four Mile Law. There were challenges to it in the past and it always passed the constitutional sniff test. But the Manufacturer's Bill was a new concept. How would it hold up?

With all the investment and progress made by Tennessee distillers over the last decade, they weren't about to see it all tossed away so easily. A fight was soon to come.

The Dying Days of Tennessee Distilling

The first decade of the 20th century and last decade of Tennessee distilling before Prohibition was a time of triumphs and heartaches.

The unexpected death of the great McLin Davis foreshadowed the loss of an entire industry in 1898. For Manny Shwab, it was a great blow. At just 46 years of age, McLin passed away while convalescing at a treatment center in Battle Creek,

Michigan.[609] Still, he left Manny in great shape. He had just overseen the transition from log still distilling at Cascade Hollow to the use of a modern column (beer) still and doubler. And according to oral tradition, he also left behind a phrase that would become Cascade's eventual slogan—"mellow as moonlight." It was McLin's belief that mash mellowed when cooled by the light of the moon was superior.[610]

But, like the Chattanooga Distillery, Shwab too would see his distillery seized by the government under two counts of fraud in April 1909. Over 500,000 gallons of Cascade whisky were put under government control.[611] It was insinuated that the seizure was politically motivated. Not long after, the feds turned the distillery back over to him, but he still had to pay a $10,000 fine on a distillery that was shut down by the Manufacturer's Bill.

The only cheerful news for Manny that year was the marriage of his daughter Augusta Dickel Shwab to McLin Davis' son Paul.[612]

Even with the shadow of Prohibition looming, Jack Daniel's brands had a great last decade. Some of it was attributed to Lem Motlow taking more of a lead role in the company. Where his uncle was a traditionalist, Lem saw the future and demanded growth strategies. This led to several confrontations between the two men. Lem was adamant about three things: increasing production; adding brandy to the distillery's offerings; and entering the company's brands into spirits competitions. Jack would fight him tooth and nail on each of those subjects.

The first victory for Lem was when his uncle, at the last minute, told him he'd entered Old No. 7 in the great Louisiana Purchase Exposition, also known as the St. Louis World's Fair. The festival was a celebration of Jefferson's famous acquisition of Louisiana Territory, and people came from all over the world to see the splendor of the event. Organizers filled it with great new inventions and innovations, and there was plenty of entertainment too. It saw the introduction of the x-ray machine, the personal automobile, the electric streetcar, and cotton candy. Brands like Dr. Pepper made their national debuts there and in the spirits competition Dewar's Scotch took home the grand prize for best exhibit while Jack Daniel's won a gold medal for world's finest whisky.

Another victory for Lem came in July 1906 with the completion of a brandy distillery, which at two hundreds bushels of fruit per day was the largest of its kind in the state.[613]

Then in winter 1907 an event occurred that would see Jack Daniel give up ownership of his distillery. It all started after Jack made an early morning visit to the office. Needing to get into the safe, he realized he didn't remember the combination. In frustration, he swung his leg back and gave the safe a powerful kick. The safe didn't open, and Jack fell back in his chair, grabbing his throbbing foot. For weeks, Jack hobbled around but refused to have his foot looked at. By April, he just couldn't get around like he used to, and he turned the company over to two of his nephews: Wiley's son Dick Daniel and Finetta's son Lem Motlow. However, Lem apparently wasn't interested in having a partner and so ended up buying his cousin out. Lem had gotten his wish, but not the way he wanted. Still, it allowed him to ramp up production of Jack Daniel's. And it was just in time, as the company would lean on that supply for years to come.

With the changing of the guard, Jack Daniel's wholesale outlet, run by Spoon Motlow, put out a full-page ad in the *Chattanooga Daily News*. The ad featured Jack Daniel's diplomas from the World's Fair in 1904 and a spirits competition in Liege, Belgium in 1905. It also included "The Story of Lincoln County's Whiskies." Filled with glory, it told how the name Old No. 7 was born out of Jack Daniel making the first seven-year-old whisky. It told of log stills and why the distillery shifted to copper stills. It described the old-time process of stirring the mash and conveyed why they had shifted to machines. It also gave the 1860s as the decade when Jack registered the distillery. And while it told the story of "slaves" making Lincoln County's whisky in the old days, gone were the names Tolley, Eaton, Alexander, Motlow, Kelso, Hughes, or indeed any other historic names. Of course, this made sense: it was an advertisement by a Jack Daniel's wholesaler, not a historical document. But it foreshadowed the soon-to-be-lost history of Tennessee whisky.[614]

Stretching tales and crafting stories became an art of distillers in the last decades of Tennessee distilling. When it came to E.R. Betterton, he didn't ignore history--he rewrote it. After saving his company by moving the White Oak brand to Ohio, he decided to create some amazing boasts. Not only did he proclaim White Oak "the South's most famous distillery," he went on to say it had been running since 1870. But even worse, he suggested Betterton had "more pure whisky sold than from all others in Tennessee combined." Ouch.[615]

Before Betterton left Chattanooga, sales of whisky had never been better and saloons were at peak capacity in June 1909. Everyone knew July 1 signaled the end and those that could afford to stocked up. It wouldn't be illegal to own whisky, just to sell it within the state.

You could also sell whisky into the state, so Manny Shwab and Lem Motlow moved their businesses to Hopkinsville, Kentucky. From there, they placed price lists in Tennessee newspapers and shipped whisky to loyal customers. Other locations that attracted Tennessee distillers and wholesalers included Evansville, Indiana and Paducah, Kentucky.

Sadly, E.R. Betterton's beautiful waterfront distillery sat vacant while he took his White Oak brand to Cincinnati. Meanwhile, saloons that remained open after the 1st rebranded themselves as "soft drink stands."

A few distilleries held firm, hoping for a change in the law. These included the once highly lucrative Wakeman Distillery, formerly known as the Lookout, and J.W. Kelly's Deep Spring Distillery. Carl White, the president of Kelly's former company, was ready to be a test case for the new Manufacturer's Bill. John H. Conner of J.W. Kelly, along with Wakeman Distilling Company and Chattanooga Brewing, filed a bill in Chancery Court in Chattanooga testing whether the Holladay Bill could prohibit wholesale dealers from selling within the state.[616]

When doomsday arrived on January 1, 1910, forty distilleries made it to the final day of distilling, including White Oak, Deep Spring, Wakeman, Greenbrier, R.H. Cate in Knoxville, Chattanooga Distilling, two of Ezekiel E. Gouge's distilleries including Bristol Distilling, the Pitt Brothers, Cascade, Jack Daniel's, Jack Eaton in Memphis, and Lem Motlow's brandy distillery.[617] Jack Daniel's would begin construction of a St. Louis distillery, with plans to also build in Alabama.

With all the whisky being shipped across borders through mail order, new federal laws inspired by temperance looked to slow the practice. No longer could spirits be shipped Cash on Delivery (COD), packages could no longer be labeled with fictitious business names to hide spirituous contents, and all packages shipping whisky had to plainly state that fact on the package.[618] It was an effort to bring shame on those who would dare buy whisky, brandy or rum.

Playing with the Border

Long-time distiller Ezekiel E. Gouge of Carter County, Tennessee was entering what is thought to be his thirtieth year of distilling when Tennessee's legislature pushed to end his reign. He'd already fought the law once in 1907, when Bristol, Tennessee, went dry but lost. Now, with the Manufacturer's Bill, he was out to test this law's constitutionality. He started his distilling back up in August at the Bristol Distillery while lawyers in Memphis, including former secretary of the treasury John G. Carlisle, of the Carlisle Allowance, attempted to get the law overturned. A group of distillery owners, possibly including Gouge, promised the attorneys $2,250 for expenses and $5,250 if they could delay enforcement of the bill until their spring distilling season was complete.[619]

To get the public behind him, Gouge promised the city of Bristol, Tennessee, that he would double his capacity if the Manufacturer's Bill was killed. But if the Supreme Court denied it, he would move his distillery across the street into Bristol, Virginia.[620] The Virginia side had been dry, but voted itself wet after Tennessee showed its hand.

There must have been some glimmer of hope for killing the Manufacturer's Bill. Chattanooga's distilleries went wide open with distilling in October and others committed to the process as well, including Gouge in Bristol. As for wholesalers, J.W. Kelly got confirmation from the Supreme Court that liquor dealers in Tennessee could still legally ship out of state. It was a small consolation.

The high court dragged its feet on its decision on the Manufacturer's Bill and delayed the announcement past November, yet all appeared lost.[621] So on

December 1, E.E. Gouge announced he was finishing up rectifying his last eight thousand gallons of corn whisky in Bristol, Tennessee. In the new year, he would have a larger distillery built on the other side of the border.[622] The gauger at Cascade Distillery in Tullahoma announced they would close down with some 400,000 gallons of whisky in bond.[623] Their Hopkinsville mail-order ads let it be known "If you can't get it in your town, we will supply you direct. Sent by express prepared to the nearest railroad station - nothing sold COD. We carry great supply at our Hopkinsville KY branch house."[624]

On January 1, 1910, with the Manufacturer's Bill in force, every legal distillery made their decision. Many closed-up shop for good, while others headed for greener distilling pastures.

Making Lemonade

There were a few saloon owners who wouldn't give up without a fight. The Conger Saloon in Sequatchie County was run by a former Nashville saloon-keeper, W.P. Conger. He'd found one of the rare spots in the state that wasn't touched by the Four Mile Law. The saloon became known as "The Oasis." W.R. Hamilton, superintendent of the Tennessee Anti-Saloon League was not pleased and promised to go after the building's owner Colonel A. M. Shook. If that didn't work, Hamilton said he had "other remedies to apply."[625] It wasn't long before a suspicious fire claimed what was likely the last legal saloon in Tennessee.[626]

In Knoxville, Cal Johnson had followed his morals and dropped his lucrative and well-respected saloon as soon as it was outlawed. It just wasn't worth the trouble, nor the ding to his reputation. He could find other ways to pass his time. His establishment of one of Knoxville's first moving picture theaters was a testament to his instincts as an entrepreneur.

Then in 1908, Cal hit the national news after one of his projects caught the attention of the President of the United States, Theodore Roosevelt. Apparently, before Cal's wife Alice died in 1906, she had purchased a life insurance plan without Cal's knowledge. Cal felt he had plenty of money and wanted to put this new sum to good use. But he also wanted to choose something he knew his wife would appreciate. Wanting to see his community improved, he became interested in a Christian organization that was having a significant impact on some of the less fortunate young men in his area. He contacted the organization about establishing a branch in his neighborhood. Cal would buy the building at 514 East Vine and pledged to help the organization financially.[627]

On a chilly November afternoon in Washington, D. C., President Roosevelt gave an address during the laying of the cornerstone of the Colored Y.M.C.A. building in the nation's capital. During the address, he spoke of Cal F. Johnson and his benevolence toward the people of Knoxville. "A colored man, born a slave in Knoxville, Tennessee, was so much impressed with the value of the Y.M.C.A. work among white young men that he gave a piece of property costing $2,000 to the Young Men's Christian Association." It was the largest gift given to the organization in Tennessee's history, up to that time. It was one of Cal's proudest moments.[628]

In September, Cal remarried, taking the hand of Maggie Irwin of Jonesborough. He was ready to start the last chapter of his life. Ever faithful to one of their favorite sons, the *Knoxville Sentinel* introduced Cal more fully to its readers. A reporter followed Cal out to his stables and collected the details. It introduced the late-Colonel Hu L. McClung of Knoxville, the man who held Cal's rights prior to emancipation. It talked of his saloon at Gay and Vine, and of his renovation of the Lincoln Theater. The February 1910 article concluded by informing readers of the sad news that his favorite horse had passed on.

"'Old Dan is dead,' said Cal Johnson."

> *"Cal was patting him on the head as he passed. Cal attributes his horse racing success to Dan. Dan was put to stud 15 years ago. The day before he died, Cal was with him. Dan tried to get up but couldn't and pitifully drooped his head. Cal caressed him, fed him soft feed from a bucket and the old horse laid his head against Cal and seemed happy. 34 years ago, Cal bought Dan at Sevierville. He was looking*

for a saddle horse and paid Snapp & Toomey $75 for him. He broke him, but he was not a saddler. He wanted to trot. His pedigree was looked up and it was found that he was sired by Denmark and the dam was a famous mare owned by Col. Chas. M. McGhee. Dan leaves a record that can be boasted by the owners of few horses. He started in fifty races and was first in forty-eight of them and ran second in the other two. The horse ran at every track in East Tennessee, Atlanta, Macon, and Chattanooga. The best time ever made by this horse was 2:31. This was in a muddy race in Chattanooga. Cal never permitted anyone else to drive him. When he took the horse to his first race at Maryville, his friends laughed at him. The horse won. Then he'd go on the win race after race while Cal cleaned up taking in thousands upon thousands of dollars. 'He was the best horse I ever saw,' said Cal. 'I named him Dan McClung, McClung being added to his name because I was owned as a slave by Pleasant McClung. I never struck the horse a lick in my life. He loved children but hated every woman but my wife. Dan, my wife and I were together for 30 years. Dan had not been in a race for fifteen years, but I would not have taken $10 or $20k for him. He made me money and it was my duty to take care of him in his old days.'"[629]

Three years later, Cal got out of the soft-drink business and rented his old saloon out. He could have sold the property easily. He had offers of up to $25,000 for the house and the lot.[630] But the place had too many memories. And he knew he couldn't let that old elm tree go. He did all he could to protect it. In fact, the news would follow its progress until the day it was finally choked off by the pavement and chopped down.

Cal had seen Gay Street go from a rough neighborhood to a series of dilapidated structures, and finally to a desired thoroughfare. He probably wouldn't have admitted it, but it was largely due to him. He wouldn't even take full credit for his brilliant success. "I was raised by the best people in East Tennessee. The best people in the world, I might say, raised old Cal Johnson, and I've tried to live up to their teachings. I have never been in trouble and I have always run an orderly place."[631]

Meanwhile, the rest of the city was filling up with bootleggers, blind tigers, and locker clubs. It may have been the way of some people, but it wasn't Cal Johnson's way.

Chapter 23

THE BOSS AND MEMPHIS

Edward Hull Crump. In the world of Memphis politics, he was a kingmaker. When he died in 1954, the man known as "The Boss," left behind quite a void.

At first, he might not have looked that powerful to those on the outside. But behind his circular black glasses and piercing glare was the mind of a master manipulator. His genius not only allowed him to control politics from the mayor's office in Memphis; for a time, his Shelby County contingent held sway over the General Assembly of Tennessee as well.

Statewide Prohibition was his greatest tool. He watched the Democratic party split over the subject, and then he pounced on that weakness to build his power base. He grew so strong that lawmakers had to write a law to stop him. When they finally did, he was already so entrenched in the political system that he became a sort of Wizard of Oz, magically pulling the strings and guiding players in whatever direction he deemed necessary. He was so powerful that when he passed away at eighty years old, no one could figure out how to replace him. It seems there could be no heir apparent, as there was only one Boss Crump.

When it came to liquor and the saloons, the Boss seemed disinterested. This disinterest makes his early career a perfect metaphor for the city's whisky history. For some reason, the largest city in the state ignored distilling. But they didn't ignore the saloon. Apparently Memphians were more happy consuming alcohol, rather than making it. That saloon culture would earn the town a reputation as that "small hell on the Mississippi."[632] The Boss was apparently a product of his city.

Before learning about the political rise and fall of Boss Crump, it is worth taking a few moments to dive into the limited history of Memphis whisky.

Oh Distilleries, Where Art Thou?

Finding a distiller in the 19th-century history of Memphis is about as tough as finding a prohibitionist politician without a private stash of liquor. And maybe for good reason. According to a newspaper called The Ledger, the stuff coming out of Memphis was pretty rough. In one issue, they quipped, "it has been gravely asserted that when snakes were banished from Ireland they took refuge in Memphis whisky."[633] In another issue, they pointed out the stuff had to be diluted so much that "Memphis whisky drinkers consume more water than do the temperance people."[634]

The first record of a distillery in the city doesn't show until distiller John A. Hughes offered a reward of $500 for the arrest and conviction of the person who burned down his distillery in 1858.[635] He didn't rebuild. Instead, he sold the land. That is the entire known history of Memphis distilleries prior to the Civil War.

After the war, T.J. and J.W. Megibben opened a wholesale liquor business called Megibben & Brother, at 281 Main Street. J.W. lived in Memphis and T.J. owned a distillery in Cynthiana, Kentucky. The brothers saw a great opportunity to use Memphis as a wholesale distribution center. They came out swinging, stating "the impression that there is no good whisky in Memphis is erroneous."[636] They soon began advertising their good old Megibben whisky in their wholesale advertisements. But there is no evidence they ever distilled a drop in Memphis and by 1871, a family squabble ended the Tennessee end of the business. T.J. went on to embed himself in the Kentucky distilling industry.

The first known attempt at building a distillery in Memphis post-Civil War wasn't until 1882 when Kentucky-born Colonel S.H. Haynes made a splash by putting up stills on Monroe Street, naming the business the Memphis Distillery Company. But his ownership of the distillery was short-lived. A Peoria, Illinois-based organization known as the Distillers & Cattle Feeders Trust made him an offer and took over the business. Haynes went off into politics. The trust shut down the facility to rid its midwestern-based operation of any distilling competition on the Mississippi.[637] After they shuttered the doors, Memphis was without a successful distillery until the end of the century.

Why was distilling such a failure in Memphis? The answer was easy to spot. All it took was one glance at the Mississippi River and the daily arrival of flatboats to its docks. Why make whisky when barrels of old Monongahela, Bourbon, Old Robertson and some of the finest whiskies available are floating right by their doorstep?

The Genoa Connection

When it came to whisky, where Memphis shined was in the wholesale world. The few houses that opened were highly successful. Antonio Vaccaro ran the oldest whisky house in the city. Born in Saint Peter di Rovereto near Genoa Italy in 1824, Antonio thought he would find his greatest opportunity in New Orleans. But after two years, he decided to move up-river to the rough frontier town of Memphis.[638]

He initially rented a small store from Parker & Harris at the corner of Jefferson and Front streets. There he established a fruit and cigar business. It wasn't until 1848, when he merged with James Boro, & Co. that he added a full line of groceries and liquors to his inventory. Three years later, he established himself as the leader of the firm and changed the name to A. Vaccaro & Co.

The Vaccaro name would be a staple in the wholesale liquor and import business for nearly fifty years in Memphis. Other firms like H.H. Mette and H.H. Potter came and went. It wasn't until the 1870s that Carbery & Casey and B.J. Semmes, along with a host of smaller firms, turned up the heat in the liquor wholesale business. Each firm had its own personality and clientele. Vaccaro pursued customers in Memphis; Carbery quickly established a sales team throughout the south; Semmes would align himself with Charles Nelson's distilling operations. No one else in Memphis seemed to show any interest in rectifying, distilling, or creating their own brands of whisky. The closest anyone would come was Antonio's nephew, Domenico Canale.

Born in Genoa, Italy around the same time Antonio arrived in Memphis, Domenico was a teenager before his family left the old country for a new life in America. Upon arrival, the energetic young man went to work for his uncle. He spent his time running fruit carts through the streets of Memphis before and during the war.[639]

After the war, Antonio invited his brothers into the business, making Dominic feel like the odd man out.[640] Dominic and his brother Peter would establish a confectionery under the name Canale & Bro. in 1866,[641] but the venture failed. Licking their wounds, the brothers went back to clerking at Vaccaro & Co.[642] In 1868, when a fellow Genoan Lorenzo Solari asked if Dominic was interested in going into business together, they opened a grocery store at 82 Beale Street. That wasn't the only partnership Dominic would enter into with a Solari. Lorenzo's sister Catherine caught Dominic's eye, and after a brief courtship, the two were married at St. Patrick's Church on August 10, 1869.

In 1870, Dominic added a side business as a commission merchant dealing in liquors and groceries at 280 Front Street.[643] The side venture didn't last long and it might have strained the partnership. By 1873, Canale & Solari were through.[644] In the long run, it didn't matter. The two young businessmen were about to embark on successful careers on their own. Dominic went right back into the grocery business, opening a store on Madison Street. His dream was to bring the best of Europe to Memphis. His store was well stocked with a wide assortment of pricey French and Italian wines, meats, cheeses, and local produce.[645]

What supercharged his business was the inspiration Dominic gained after a trip to New Orleans in 1877. It intrigued him how stores sold high-quality goods, but somehow kept their prices low. He accumulated a list of distributors and filled his store with high-quality and exclusive goods that made his store stand out. The demand for his goods led him to seek a larger building for his business.

In 1880, D. Canale & Co. established themselves at 329 Main Street between Monroe and Union streets. This new building came with ample space in the cellar for preserving large supplies of fruits and wines.[646] This was key to keeping his inventory safe from the scorching, humid summers of Memphis. Canale's eventually earned the reputation as one of the best locations in the south for tropical fruits, specialty olive oils, and fine wines.

Through the 1880s and '90s, Dominic kept up a steady business and integrated himself into the business community of Memphis. He was a charter member of the area's Chamber of Commerce and a director at several banks. He spent those two decades traveling to Italy and South America with Kate and his family, always keeping an eye out for exotic goods.

His early flirtation with whisky happened after he returned from New Orleans in 1877, but it would become a bigger focus shortly after his uncle died in 1899. A. Vaccaro & Co had been the most trusted name in Memphis whisky, wholesaling for five decades. But upon Antonio's death, the company went into bankruptcy.[647] It may be a coincidence, but not long after D. Canale & Co was advertising Hunter's Baltimore Rye, and a variety of Scotches and English whiskies.

Then, in June 1903, a most curious entry landed in the Miscellaneous section of the want ads of the local paper:

> *"LOST - Somewhere between Court square and the railroad station, a leather bag containing a diamond ring, $46 in money and a bottle of D. Canale & Co.'s Old Dominic Whisky. Finder can keep diamond ring and money if he returns the bottle of Old Dominic Whisky to NOAH GOODTHING."*[648]

Suddenly, Memphis had a whisky brand. It wasn't the first. Alfred Eaton's son Jack had moved to Memphis in 1899 and opened a distillery and wholesale business. But Dominic was the first to advertise his whisky.

That creative classified ad ran for a few weeks, using Dominic's proper spelling of his name. But the next month, the newspaper added a "k" to the end of his name, and the Old Dominick brand was ready to roll.

The creative advertising continued. More want ads appeared, with Old Dominick's whisky as the subject. The brand sponsored a shooting competition at the Bluff City Gun Club and provided an Old Dominick medal for the winner. They even used tax records for advertising. Whenever a new shipment of whisky or Cognac came in from Europe, Dominic would have the tariff payment posted in the newspaper. It was a subtle way of telling clients what new stock he had. Eventually he bowed to traditional advertising, but again his ads stood out. Instead of just posting the picture of a bottle, he included a series of illustrations and statements like "it pleases the stomach and tones the system,"[649] and "Like Old Rip Van Winkle, our Old Dominick Whiskey has had a long sleep."[650]

Corporate filings in 1905 show no mention of a distilling operation, so it is likely D. Canale & Co. sourced their whisky in the days before Tennessee Prohibition. Labels carried the words "distillery bottlings" but didn't specify which distillery was making the spirit. While it could have been Jack Eaton, it's not likely, since Jack was a competitor in the wholesale business.

As a side note, Jack Eaton became the only known successful distiller in pre-Prohibition Memphis. His business lasted ten years until the Manufacturer's Bill shut him down. It wasn't an easy ten years. He had to survive two disasters. The first was a flood that had two thousand of his barrels bobbing up and down in the water for a week.[651] The second was a fire that almost took a life. A heavy-set firefighter named Thomas Sauerman of Company 6 had attempted to jump to higher ground, but when he climbed atop a barrel, the head gave way and he fell into burning whisky. Luckily, a buddy nearby heard the screams and immediately turned the fire hose on him. Sauerman fell out of the barrel, picked up his hose, and went right back to work. Thanks to his teammate, he was spared severe burns and helped save the building.[652] The distillery was back up and running, and made it all the way to the last legal day of distilling in the state. He would be the last of the Tolleys and Eatons to shut down their stills.

After that point, since there was no whisky being made in Tennessee, Old Dominick's whisky had to come from another state. They contracted with several Kentucky distilleries, including Susquehanna Distillery (#63) in Milton, Daviess County Distillery (#2) near Owensboro, and the Marion County Distillery (#372) in Louisville.[653] They purchased "fine old Bourbon" with ages up to fifteen years. Dominic sold his whisky using several health claims, including "used in every hospital in Memphis" and "recommended for medical purposes by every physician in Memphis."[654]

Because they couldn't sell whisky to Tennesseans from a Memphis location, they moved their wholesale business to Helena, Arkansas, seventy miles to the south on the westside of the Mississippi. From there, they sold whisky and other spirits back into Memphis through mail order.

In the waning days of advertising, as their markets slowly were squeezed off, they made an aggressive push into the State of Mississippi. As Dominic's sons took over, the number of products showed they'd really committed to the whisky side of things. But in 1912, they had a scare when Arkansas nearly passed their own statewide prohibition. Soon, D. Canale & Co. saw the writing on the wall and was pushing hard to make profits. One of the last big products they advertised was the Dominick Toddy in 1914.[655] Based on the old English drink, it offered an alternative to drinking straight whisky. But if people in Arkansas and Mississippi fell in love with it during the cool winter months, the next year they'd lose their opportunity to stock up on more. Arkansas passed the 1915 Newberry Act and followed its southern compatriots into the dry category. D. Canale's run in the whisky business was at an end.

Dominic passed away in 1919, but his family carried on. But instead of focusing on liquor and groceries, they moved deeper into manufacturing. One of their big sellers was D. Canale Italian Gravy. Showing they hadn't given up on their boldness for claims, the ad proclaimed, "every retailer sells it."

High Stakes Shenanigans

On the Friday before election day 1909, the *Memphis Commercial Appeal* ran an advertorial written by Dr. R.B. Maury called "Reasons Why Crump Should Be Elected." It was a puff piece that extolled the virtues of mayoral candidate Edward Hull Crump. It talked of his rise from nothing to becoming president of the Buggy & Harness, Co. and it proclaimed that Crump was the one man who could eradicate the political wrangling that was holding the city back. The good doctor reminded voters that Crump's opponent, J.J. Williams, was simply another machine politician in the mold of Malcolm Patterson.[656]

But the question had to be asked. Was Dr. Maury really that clueless about the man he was endorsing, or was this just another case of advertising through political expediency, rather than truth? In reality, the man who would become known as Boss Crump was about to become the poster child for Tennessee machine politics.

A term lost to the past, machine politics referred to the boss system. A relic of the Gilded Age, the most infamous example of 19th-century machine politics was Tammany Hall in New York. Through a system of patronage came a political hierarchy that allowed one man, elected or not, to control the direction of a city. These bosses pulled the strings and the people under them danced. Prohibition and machine politics eventually gave rise to men like Al Capone. In Tennessee, the two most prominent bosses were Nashville's Mayor Hilary Howse and Memphis' Mayor Edward Crump.

While Howse used the boss system to control Nashville, Crump used his Shelby County contingent to get his way in state politics. Neither man was interested in having the state General Assembly tell them what to do. So when legislators voted to remove saloons from the state, Crump and Howse did nothing. And their political underlings soon followed suit.

It didn't take long for saloonkeepers to realize they had free reign to do as they pleased. They posted signs in their bars reminding the people who were downing pints of beer that selling intoxicants was illegal. It didn't take long for a federal judge to notice there were over seven hundred active saloons in Memphis, with federal licenses, running in open defiance of the law. J.P. Striker, a hotelier from Detroit, came down for a visit and marveled at the lax enforcement in the hotels he visited in Tennessee.

> "There is one thing that prohibition in Tennessee and the rest of the south does not prohibit, and that is the sale and consumption of liquor. More of it is being disposed of in Tennessee than before the state went dry. I went to Memphis and Nashville to see the conditions. At a leading hotel at Memphis I found that they work six bartenders and make no bones about running. It happened to be a Sunday when I was there and there was a convention or meeting of some sort in town. The head bartender told me they ought to take in about $600 that day... Prohibition in Tennessee allows the hotel and saloon men to do business without paying any license. It causes men to break a law, something they would not do otherwise. It is a farce, and men who live in Georgia tell me the state of affairs there is the same."[657]

But not all acts were this blatant. Nashville hotels tricked law enforcement by pouring alcohol from teapots. Locker clubs were glorified saloons, allowing people to bring their own hooch and drink it with friends. Some saloons changed their names to soft drink establishments, yet still secured federal liquor licenses. And the businesses flourished because none of them had to pay state alcohol taxes.

All of this infuriated the Anti-Saloon League. They held meetings in several areas and pushed for laws that would punish public officials that were weak on enforcement. At the very least, they wanted tax revenues collected if the government wouldn't prosecute saloonkeepers.

There were a few public officials that weren't under the thumb of the boss system. One was Davidson County Attorney General Jeff McCarn. He conducted a series of sting operations that saw the arrest of over two hundred alleged violators of the law.[658] The problem was, the grand juries were sympathetic to the whisky interests, according to McCarn. Frustrated with his cases being thrown out, he launched an investigation in February 1910.[659]

In Memphis, authorities exasperated by the boss system went right to federal court, where they asked the judge to shut down 114 illegal saloons. But the federal judge dissolved the injunction. Then he reminded prosecutors the feds could not enforce state laws.[660]

Governor Patterson pointed to all this lawlessness as he kicked off his reelection campaign. He gave a big "I told you so" to the prohibitionists, saying "universal experience has taught that no law of this character can be enforced against the will of the people." As a solution, he advocated repealing the manufacturer's bill, saying it "does not possess any element of common sense, or of ordinary fairness." He also pointed to the deconstructing of the Statewide Law, giving Memphis, Chattanooga, and Nashville citizens the ability to "exercise the power of local government and decide the question for themselves."[661] Meanwhile, the Republicans, who only controlled the governor's mansion for a total of four years since the Civil War, saw an opportunity to run on strict enforcement. Their gubernatorial candidate, Ben Hooper, won the general election over Patterson by twelve thousand votes.

But if Governor Hooper thought he was going to have an easy time getting Nashville and Memphis under control, he was sadly mistaken. And the two city bosses were about to get the upper hand.

This shift of power started in the General Assembly, where Democrats had grown comfortable with control. But that all changed in 1911, when a faction of prohibitionist Democrats split off and voted with Republicans. This new prohibition-focused block became known as the Fusionists. The Democrats that were part of the Fusionists would paint the remaining Democrats as being in the back pocket of the liquor industry.

An astute observer, Boss Crump realized the Fusionists and Democrats had nearly the same number of votes. And even though he was ignoring the saloon activity in his city, he didn't support the liquor industry. In this mindset, he could play both sides, and so his Shelby County contingent became a swing voter in state politics. And this is how Boss Crump went from being in control of his own city to controlling the entire General Assembly. All he had to do was throw his allegiance to either the Fusionists or Democrats. And it wasn't long before everyone was lobbying for his support.

Crump's power became evident in 1912 when Governor Hooper came up for reelection. He was in desperate need of Crump's support. But Crump seemed to be ready to push the Fusionists back toward the Democrats. Then, when Hooper won the election, former Winchester mayor Jesse M. Littleton accused him of giving patronage to the "Crump whisky machine" to swing votes in his direction.[662] Hooper had to publicly deny it. Being tied to Crump made him look like a hypocrite when it came to enforcement of prohibition laws.

To counter the Crump rhetoric, Governor Hooper went on an all-out attack against the bosses. In his inaugural address, he asked the legislature to enact laws that would allow him to remove any local official for misfeasance, malfeasance, or nonfeasance.[663] This would put a target on Crump's back and Crump took it personally. He called Hooper a liar and two-faced hypocrite. He said, "I blush with shame when I realize that such a man is Governor of this State."[664] Crump decided it was time to show the governor who truly wielded power in Tennessee. When the governor's enforcement bills were up for a vote, the Crump faction defeated every one. And because of this, the Fusionists lost their edge and U.S. Senator Luke Lea blamed the governor.[665]

Then the General Assembly devolved into a circus. With the Fusionists losing power, the Democrats put forth a new election bill that would give them a political advantage. The Fusionists had no way to stop the bill, so they left the State House and made their way to Kentucky. Without a quorum, they hoped to delay the vote on the bill until the next legislative session.[666] But the plan backfired when the remaining Democrats voted anyway and avoided taking a roll call, thus allowing the vote to stand.[667] The Fusionists were incensed. Hooper urged the General Assembly to hold a special legislative session. He had five major law changes he wanted enacted. The biggest was the Nuisance Law, which allowed saloons to be shut down and their property confiscated. He also wanted to make the shipping of liquor illegal and to reduce mail-order quantities to a gallon or less. But it was the fifth law that looked to shift the balance of power in the General Assembly: His proposed law that would allow the governor to remove city and county officials.[668]

On the day they were to vote on the bills, armed prison guards stood around the Capitol building in case there were any outbreaks of violence between the politicians. The Senate passed the governor's bills, but Speaker Stanton kept them from coming to the floor for a vote in the House. Hours before he was told "unless he ruled as desired by Hooper, a revolution would follow." Stanton accused Hooper of trying to threaten his life with the presence of the gunmen. Stanton held firm and the session ended with the bills being dropped.[669]

In Chattanooga, the near passage of these bills sent law enforcement on a crusade. Within days, a slew of saloonkeepers were charged and indicted. Hamilton County Circuit Court Judge McReynolds offered to cancel saloon keepers' sentences if they stopped selling alcohol and gave up their licenses. Seventy-eight took him up on the offer.[670] In Nashville, Judge A.B. Neil warned liquor dealers they had until October 1 to turn in their federal licenses or they would face justice.[671]

Yet the citizens of Nashville didn't seem to care. When Mayor Howse ran for reelection, he won handily. His crusade to run his city the way his citizens wanted him to had the *Memphis Commercial Appeal* calling him "a 'living protest for the right of self-government."

Eventually, Governor Hooper won the day on the liquor issue, at least in the General Assembly. His four anti-liquor bills passed the legislature. But Boss Crump showed he still had the Fusionists in his back pocket when it came to the governor's attempts to get public officials removed from office. The removal bill was tabled by the senate.[672]

After the vote, Judge Neil went on a crusade, taking down a number of saloons. The *Knoxville Journal and Tribune* declared "Nashville dry as the Sahara."[673] Shelby County Attorney General Z.N. Estes threatened to shut down any saloon still open by March 2, 1914. The *Commercial Appeal* was somewhat cautiously amazed by the disappearance of liquor traffic on that day. They couldn't pronounce John Barleycorn dead in Memphis, but he seemed to be on life support.[674]

With the saloons somewhat settled, Estes decided it was time to go after the liquor traffic using boats on the Mississippi. But within weeks, Nashville and Memphis saloons were back at it, reapplying for federal licenses. Memphis saloon keepers felt the Nuisance Act was unconstitutional and several had no problem lining themselves up as potential test cases for the law. True to his word, Attorney General Estes went on the warpath and, on March 19, some of Memphis' biggest names, including Canale, Lucchesi, Vaccaro, Ragghianti, Tucker, and Eaton, were in court posting bond.[675]

Of all the convictions, it was liquor dealer J.J. Persica and J.P. Lynch of the Park Hotel saloon who would serve as the test case for the Tennessee State Supreme Court.[676] To their chagrin, the court upheld the constitutionality of the Nuisance Act. The convictions of the two men and Fred Ragghianti would stand, and they all served six months in the workhouse.[677]

With the new law solidified, many Memphis saloons turned into locker clubs and riverboats moved to the Arkansas side of the Mississippi River. Memphians could still get a drink, but it required a little more legwork. General Estes continued his work against soft drink stands and locker clubs.

Saloon activity eventually returned to both Nashville and Memphis. Mayors Crump and Howse continued to turn a blind-eye to the liquor traffic in their cities. But their underlings weren't always so willing to give in. In mid-March, Judge Neil sentenced the city's most prominent saloon owner, William Luigart and others, to a work crew working on a county road for thirty days. He was fined $50.[678] The *Memphis Commercial Appeal* took a more definitive stance declaring "the action of Judge Neil today has made a desert of Nashville, so far as intoxicants are concerned."[679] But without Howse's support and the support of law enforcement, the saloon keepers only smirked as they filled their customer's mugs and shot glasses. The Anti-Saloon League blamed Judge Neil for his ineffectiveness and threw their support behind Circuit Court Judge G.N. Tillman.

But no matter who they backed, the fight against the saloon was akin to swatting gnats at a picnic.

Once Again, it's Kansas

Frustrated that laws were not slowing the liquor trade, the prohibitionists once again looked outside the state for answers. Politicians and newspaper editorialists began scouring the country for prohibition enforcement success stories. Once again, Kansas appeared to have the blueprint, yet their journey to this success wasn't easy.

For over thirty years, the Kansas government struggled to get the saloons under control. They became a national embarrassment when Carrie Nation's axe revealed their ineptitude in controlling the liquor trade. They'd gone through the same problem Tennessee was now facing. Not only was it easy for local officials to ignore the law, it was in their best interest to do so. Local bosses like Howse and Crump won their elections by large margins. To them, those statement victories obligated them to serve the desire of the people rather than the state. Kansas officials finally realized that if the city bosses didn't support judges and law enforcement, they might as well be putting out house fires with teaspoons.

Like with Tennessee, the Kansas legislature tried several ways to curb the abuses. At first, they amended search and seizure laws, but this led to corruption. The state tried to enforce their Nuisance Act, but these were ridiculed. And, worse yet, they made the saloon keeper a sympathetic character. When they finally realized they had to cut the head off of the snake, the resulting legislation became known as the Ouster Law.

This idea of targeting public officials was nothing new in Tennessee. Time and time again, Governor Hooper tried to get the Fusionists to support the removal of public officials. The issue was the control those officials held over the legislature. But what potentially made the Kansas law more palatable was its narrowed focus on mayors, rather than judges and other public officials.

The ineptness of Governor Hooper's enforcement tactics made the Kansas "Ouster Law" something he desperately needed in 1914 to retain his office. But its introduction into the minds of Tennesseans came too late. The Fusionist control was fading and Democrats broke off and returned to their party's candidate, Thomas C. Rye of Paris, Tennessee. Rye promised to make up for the failures of the Hooper administration in terms of law enforcement. Two surprise supporters of Rye were mayors Crump and Howse. It was a case of strange bedfellows. But for the first time, Crump was in need of support.[680] The head of the Anti-Saloon League, W.R. Hamilton, decided he didn't want to endorse Hooper or Rye. Yet when his organization overruled him and threw their support behind Rye. The summer turned into a stressful war of words between Hamilton and Rye. With the added connection to Howse and Crump, it was too much for Hamilton and he resigned his post.[681] But if he had held on just a little longer, he might have changed his mind. The opinion of most was that Rye was against the measure. But soon Rye turned on Crump and Howse, stating that he wouldn't put up with officials not enforcing the laws. He was ready to consider the Kansas Ouster Law.

When the state elected Rye by a large margin, Hooper said the governor-elect's liquor friendly platform "succeeded in deceiving a considerable number of prohibitionists in the state, but it deceived no liquor man."[682] But in Governor Rye's inauguration address, he took a hardline against the saloons and lax law enforcement. His agenda included banning liquor advertisements, regulating soft-drink stands and locker clubs, increasing the power of the courts, eradicating liquor shipments, and holding city officials accountable. And he had one advantage Hooper never had—an entire General Assembly that was on the same page.[683]

The legislature went right to work on his measures, but added some radical ones as well. No more advertising, no more liquor as a gift, and no more mail order. They even looked to banning medicinal use. One house bill went as far as to say a person twice convicted of selling intoxicants would be rendered infamous and lose their right to vote. Another looked to make it a capital crime to take a fourth drink.

But the most anticipated bill of them all was the Ouster Bill. With all the fresh prohibitionist blood in the legislature, there wasn't a lot of opposition to it. Those that spoke out against it were Crump and Howse, along with Senator Luke Lea. Some formerly wet newspapers said it went too far and warned that the other party could use it when they were in power. To them, it had the potential of turning "into an instrument of injustice and deviltry."[684] But the bill sailed through both houses of the legislature and Governor Rye signed it into law.

As written, the Ouster Law not only provided for the removal of state, county, or municipal officials who neglected their duties–they could also be removed if they "in any public place be in a state of intoxication produced by strong drink voluntarily taken or who shall engage in any form of gambling, or who shall commit any act constituting a violation of any penal statute involving moral turpitude." Not only could the law be invoked by the governor but also by the state attorney general, a district attorney general, a county or city attorney, or any ten citizen freeholders. The determination of guilt would be in the hands of a judge, not a jury. And if they rendered a guilty verdict, they would immediately remove the official from office.[685]

Howse and Crump were well aware of the huge target on their backs. Even if they cleaned up their act, any small failure on their part would put their positions in jeopardy. Both men decided it was time to capitulate and show good faith in the law.

With the Ouster Law victory, Governor Rye and the General Assembly took advantage of the unified atmosphere and passed more laws. Soft-drink stands could no longer sell drinks with over one-half of one percent of alcohol in them. Pure food and drug inspectors were given "full power" to enter these establishments at any time and test the contents being sold. If alcohol was found, the business could have most of its property seized and sold. Locker clubs would face lesser penalties that included fines up to $500 and imprisonment for up to six months. Medicinal spirits could only be distributed by prescription, had to be filled within three days, and could not be refilled. And to throw a Mary Hunt tactic in the face of anti-prohibitionists, they made the fourth Friday in October

Frances E. Willard Day in public schools. On that day, children were to "be taught the evils of intemperance."[686]

With the Ouster Law in effect, it didn't take long for lawsuits to be brought against both Crump and Howse. Both used the fall of 1914 to sweat it out under appeals, hoping to get the State Supreme Court to declare the law unconstitutional. As they awaited the court's decision, they continued to campaign for reelection. On election day, Memphis and Nashville citizens returned both men to office.

By the end of 1915, the strength of the wet faction was unquestioned. Even Senator Lea, who had stood with Crump and Howse, did a 180. He used a speaking opportunity in front of the Jack Daniel's Old Time Distillery in Lynchburg to let his new position be known. Senator Lea called for a national prohibition amendment to once and for all put an end to liquor and lawlessness. He knew this would be a tough audience, but said, "I know that you have respect and confidence for the man who expresses his honest opinions." Apparently, the crowd bought into his new opinion, because his follow-up speech at the Moore County Courthouse was standing room only.[687]

As for Mayor Crump, he continued to plead his case.

> *"I freely admit that no attempt has been made to close the saloons. I felt that I could serve the people better by devoting my energies to the up building of this city along constructive lines. I have felt that public sentiment was not in favor of the abolition of the saloons. The people of Memphis have shown on three or four occasions that they were opposed to prohibition. However, the law was passed over their protest. I am not making the fight in the interest of the whisky business. I do not want the people to overlook the fact that I am subject to a recall.*"[688]

In the end, the Tennessee State Supreme Court had the final say and, in February 1916, they declared the Ouster Law constitutional. But, in a twist, they also affirmed that the current lawsuits only applied to the previous term, so neither man could be removed by the old judgements. However, that didn't mean they were not liable for past sins. State Attorney G.T. Fitzhugh declared he would wait until Crump took office before starting proceedings again.[689]

The Boss was out of options. On February 22, in a secret meeting of the city commission, Crump took the oath of office to honor the people's vote and then resigned two minutes later.[690] When they heard the news, prohibition forces celebrated. The man who had made a mockery of the statewide law for so long was gone. Mayor Howse would soon follow.

With control over the General Assembly and the death of the saloon, the prohibitionists then went on the attack against the wholesale trade. No more receiving orders for intoxicants, no storage of liquor with the intent to sell, no clubs with liquor on hand for distribution, no use for religious or medicinal purposes, and a second violation of the Four Mile Law became a felony, punishable by a prison term of one to two years. Labeled the Bone Dry Law, it passed the Senate by a thirty to two vote and House by a convincing eighty-four to five count. By March 1, 1917, the prohibitionists had finally conquered Tennessee—in terms of legislation.[691]

And Tennessee wasn't alone. All of its neighbors were also dry, save Kentucky. But it wouldn't be long before the Bluegrass State joined their ranks.

The next step was a national prohibition amendment, and William Jennings Bryan made it possible thanks to his successful lobbying for an income tax amendment. No longer was the country reliant upon revenue from liquor. Eventually the dry politicians, WCTU, and Wayne B. Wheeler would win that too. And for a blueprint in enforcing the law, the U.S. Congress would have both Kansas and Tennessee to show them the way.

Meanwhile, Memphis had a new mayor. But the old one was still making headlines. In a surprise move, Boss Crump endorsed the law that had him thrown out of office.[692] He also made it a point to turn against the liquor interests. But if anybody thought they had Crump under their thumb, nothing could be further from the truth. Crump was a master politician who didn't need the office. He had the trust of the people and an organization seated throughout the government. Everyone would continue to look to him for answers. And this made him a kingmaker in Memphis politics. Sure, the Ouster Law had the power to get rid of a mayor, but Crump knew it could never get rid of The Boss.

The Couch Affair

The day the press announced that Boss Crump was stepping down, no one in Memphis was happier than Captain John M. Couch of the Memphis Police Department. In 1916, he was the city's best weapon in the battle against vice.

Captain Couch made headlines that February, when he took down a big game of Policy being run by a local saloonkeeper. Policy is a lottery run by scammers. It was popular all over Memphis, and it preyed on the poor. It gave the player a chance to win big, but mostly it just enriched the racketeers running the game. Couch's raid scored 26 arrests, including the saloonkeeper that ran the game.[693]

But even more than bringing down racketeers, Captain Couch's passion was taking down blind tigers. Liquor became his enemy as he saw his own department facing troubles brought on by spirits. His greatest hero was Carrie Nation and, when she visited the town years before, he made sure he was there to greet her. She was so impressed by his zeal that she presented him with one of her hatchets as a keepsake.

But Boss Crump always seemed to stand in the way of the captain's mission. Several times, he was called to the carpet by the mayor for arresting men who were on his payroll.

Couch blamed this disregard for the law as the reason for the troubles he was seeing in his own department. Over and over, he saw patrolmen falling down on the job due to liquor. In one incident, patrolman James F. Flanigan failed to make his regular call-in to the station. When Couch found Flanigan out of his wits on alcohol, he took his star and his gun and suspended him. He offered to take Flanigan home in the emergency wagon since he was in no shape to drive, but Flanigan refused. Two hours later, Flanigan entered the captain's office and put his fist upside Couch's head. Officers at the station had to pull the two men apart when Couch retaliated. Flanigan was fired and Couch blamed the alcohol.

Couch's boss, Chief Perry, had to agree. He told the *Commercial Appeal*, "no man who drinks to that extent can stay in the department."[694] The Flanigan situation frustrated Captain Couch, and he vowed not to see it happen again. But unfortunately, two of Couch's own junior patrolmen were suspended after being caught over-indulging on alcohol on the job. This got Chief Perry fully invested in shaking up the police department. He gave a mandate to his captains and sergeants that the men under their charge do "police duty" and that he wouldn't be "satisfied with anything less." He finally felt emboldened to lay down the law, thanks to Boss Crump's resignation from office.[695]

The embarrassment surrounding his patrolmen's indiscretions led Captain Couch to double his efforts. But it would not be easy. The law seemed to be filled with escape routes for offenders. When Couch caught Mrs. A.E. Griswold with a dozen bottles of cold beer in a wash can, he charged her with violating the Four Mile Law. But she ended up claiming that she'd bought the suds to make ravioli with them. Acting precinct Judge Neely saw no way to convict her and let the woman go.[696]

In early May, the captain brought in H.L. Goldklang, charged with selling liquor on Sunday. But again Couch lost the chance for a conviction when the accuser admitted he'd only had his boss, Goldklang, arrested because he was mad at having his wages garnished.[697]

At the end of May, Couch thought he'd scored big when he raided a blind tiger run by grocer L. Bisio. But Bisio skated after claiming he couldn't open the safe with the ill-gotten gains inside. It would take a second raid and a safecracker to finally bring the man to justice.[698]

While Couch wasn't having the greatest success, City Hall noticed his efforts. Mayor Ashcroft, the current mayor, saw Couch's never-say-die attitude and hired him as a special agent. Captain Couch was to be answerable only to the mayor, with the specific duty of enforcing liquor laws. Couch admitted the task would be "a hard one, but he would pull off his coat and go for it."[699]

The summer of 1916 in Memphis would become known as the great blind tiger hunt. Couch arrested so many people that he soon saw a rash of repeat offenders. The saloon keepers were so used to lax enforcement that they never expected Couch to hit the same place twice. When he did, they would find themselves back in court. Throughout the summer, "More Four-Mile Arrests" became a common headline in the papers. In the second week of July alone, twenty-two offenders sat before the grand jury, many thanks to Captain Couch. But he didn't seem to put a dent in the traffic. He wondered how long he would have the confidence of the mayor. With all of this money being spent by taxpayers, it was basically catch and release, catch and release. He realized he was going to have to go to the source of the booze to stop this illegal activity. He needed to target the wholesalers, who hadn't as yet been killed off by the Statewide Law.

His plan was foolproof. Have the city set up a soft-drink stand and get the word out to wholesalers that it was a blind tiger in need of liquor. They found a spot near a ballpark to the south of town and set up shop. They had no intention of selling liquor but had to make the place look legit. Couch brought in liquor from previous raids to hide in the storeroom. Customers were served soft drinks by an out-of-towner rather than by an undercover officer so as to not tip their hand. Once the wholesalers came in and solicited the business of the blind tiger, the police had all the evidence they needed to take down the wholesalers.

It was a brilliant plan. And when they had secured liquor from eight unsuspecting wholesalers, they called it a success, shut the operation down, and served warrants on the offenders. Once the warrants were issued, the entire scheme made headlines in the *Commercial Appeal* and across the state.[700]

But the celebration was a bit premature. It seems that in the excitement of setting up the sting operation, no one thought to get a federal liquor license for the operation of the fake blind tiger. The article in the *Commercial Appeal* drew the attention of the Feds. They enjoyed all the evidentiary quotes provided by Captain Couch.

Catching the local government with their pants down was funny enough for the revenue agents, but the icing on the cake came from the wholesalers. As far back as J.W. Kelly[701] and E.R. Betterton, it was well known how almost militant the Feds were about having a posted federal liquor license in a drinks establishment. Those two men both spent time in a jail cell, not because they didn't have a license, but because they did not post it "in plain view." Somehow, these wholesalers didn't notice the lack of a license on the wall of the fake blind tiger.

To clear the department's name, Captain Couch informed the U.S. District Attorney they didn't sell any liquor during the operation. The DA suggested he wouldn't charge Couch as it fell into the revenue's jurisdiction. In the end, it would be a minor snafu amid a very successful six month long tiger hunt.[702]

By January, the police department promoted Captain John M. Couch to chief of detectives. He had done an incredible job arresting some six hundred people on charges of breaking the Four Mile Law and gaming. The newspaper did a full writeup to celebrate his accomplishments.[703] A photo appeared in the *Commercial Appeal* showing the car that was used in the raids. It had traveled some eighteen thousand miles all in an effort to bring down the liquor traffic of Memphis. A closer look at the photo showed Officer Morehead holding the hatchet the late Carrie Nation had presented to Captain Couch ten years earlier.[704]

Few were the success stories during the decade-long struggle under the Four Mile "statewide" law, but Captain Couch was one of them. He'd long suffered under Boss Crump's disregard for the law and cronyism. He finally caught a break when his own chief saw the light. His determined vigor caught the eye of a man whose job depended on the enforcement of the law. And when given the tools and some creative latitude, he made a success of the effort.

For a brief shining moment, Memphis had become a city for the prohibitionists to be proud of.

Chapter 24

LAST RITES

When it came to city politics in Tennessee, the boss system of Nashville and Memphis grabbed the headlines in the early 1910s. But down south along the Georgia line, Chattanoogan's wanted something different. The man with a plan to provide that system of government was Thomas C. Betterton. The son of whisky man Elijah R. Betterton, T.C. was a man with a mind all his own. After watching his father make headlines for several years, the move of E.R. Betterton and Co. to Cincinnati gave T.C. a chance to step out from his father's long shadow. T.C. took a key interest in government and he helped establish a commission-style government in the city. He also served as Chattanooga's fire and police commissioner.

A man like Captain Couch in Memphis would have felt right at home under T.C.'s leadership. He had a passion for honesty and integrity. And T.C. would quickly become the pride of Chattanooga.

So it was quite a surprise to the town's citizens when they picked up the October 2, 1915 evening edition of the *Chattanooga News*. Its bold headline read "T.C. Betterton Under Arrest: Gruesome Charge Filed Against Chattanooga's Police Commissioner."[705]

The word "gruesome" conjured up dark images in the minds of readers. Many of the older crowd had grown up reading the macabre stories that so engrossed newspaper readers of the Victorian era. But after pursuing a few lines of copy, greedy eyes soon gave way to eye rolls.

What crime did he commit? T.C.'s company had been shipping whisky across state lines and breaking federal law. But it wasn't the fact he was breaking the law that was so gruesome. It was the container he used to ship the whisky.

Creative Packaging

Born at the close of the Civil War, not long after his father Elijah was released from a Union prison camp, T.C. grew up around whisky. But he wasn't at all interested in following his father into the liquor trade. What did interest him was his father's side business. Elijah was a stockholder and secretary for the Chattanooga Coffin & Casket Company.[706] T.C. went off to Vanderbilt University to get his education, going on to become an ordained minister within the Methodist Episcopal church. He came back to Chattanooga in 1907 and became general manager of the coffin company.

It was still months before the Nashville shootout between Carmack and Cooper, so liquor was still being made and sold in Chattanooga. As T.C. took the reins, he learned that the company had in stock a good amount of whisky for the salesmen to take as gifts to regional undertaker conferences. Nothing greased the wheels of coffin sales better than White Oak whisky.

When E.R. Betterton & Co. moved their wholesale business to Cincinnati at the start of Tennessee prohibition, they left some whisky behind. There were no rules against storing whisky, so there seemed little concern with it remaining in the storeroom. And since gifts of whisky were still acceptable, salesmen continued to take bottles with them on the road.

But once states fell to Prohibition, T.C. put an end to the practice of giving White Oak whisky as gifts. It might still have been acceptable thanks to the interstate traffic rules, but T.C. wanted to protect the company's reputation and wasn't sure if a federal license would still be required.[707]

In the first couple years of Prohibition, T.C. would spend his time as police commissioner dealing with several alcohol-related issues. One of the biggest issues for Chattanooga was cross-border traffic. Wholesalers were taking full advantage of a loophole that allowed for interstate liquor traffic. A few from Chattanooga set up shop in nearby Rossville, Georgia, and began shipping whisky back into Tennessee.

Then, in 1913, the U.S. Congress tried to appease prohibition states by stopping the practice through the Webb-Kenyon Act. This new law made shipping of alcohol between states into dry counties illegal. But the bill was challenged as unconstitutional.

While waiting for the decision from the high court, Chattanooga's Judge McReynolds pushed whisky merchants into an agreement that they wouldn't ship whisky in or out of the state from within a twenty-mile radius of Chattanooga. If they did, it would mean either jail time or time in the workhouse. J.W. Kelly & Co, and E.R. Betterton & Co were two of the signers.[708] When the U.S. Supreme Court declared the Webb-Kenyon Act constitutional in January 1917, the law on shipping was finally clear. No alcohol was to be distributed inside or outside of Tennessee.

But it wasn't this law that put T.C. Betterton on the front page of the *Chattanooga News*. It was Section 240 of the Federal Penal Code. That law prohibited shipping intoxicating liquor from state to state, unless the shipper labeled such a package on the outside showing "the name of the contents, the nature of the contents, and the quantity contained within, with the name of the consignee." Violations came with a $5,000 fine and confiscation of the goods.[709]

Apparently, the U.S. Department of Justice heard rumors that this act was being violated in Chattanooga and they put Inspector Webster Spates on the case. The target of the investigation was T.C. Betterton's Chattanooga Coffin and Casket Co.

When the press caught wind of the investigation, T.C. Betterton had to defend his company's honor while simultaneously trying to win the office of Police Commissioner. He firmly denied the allegation, saying his shipping clerk assured him that no whisky was being sold. But Inspector Spates wasn't buying it and he came down from Washington to comb through the company's invoices.

The gruesome act he discovered was revealed in an invoice from May 11, 1914. At first, it looked like a standard shipment of coffins and boxes to Murphy's Furniture Company in Anniston, Alabama. But upon closer inspection, the invoices showed more than just coffins on order. There were also quart bottles of White Oak whisky, specifically numbered, so the receiver knew which coffins the whisky was in. Then he found similar receipts for August 12 and October 5 of that year and two more in 1915. Since they didn't ship the coffins with the word "whisky" clearly marked on them, they violated Section 240.[710]

Those five invoices were just the tip of the iceberg. There were several hundred more clearly marked in the record. It seems that after T.C. shut down the salesman's face-to-face whisky giving, the practice continued through shipments.

A raiding party arrived at the coffin factory at 11a.m. and by noon T.C. Betterton and three employees found themselves in Federal Court. Surprisingly, T.C. didn't deny the charges. Apparently, when Inspector Spates brought the invoices to his attention, T.C. could only shake his head. He posted bond the following morning.

After the Saturday headline, T.C. wrote full details in the next day's paper about what he thought had transpired. He had specifically told his employees not to ship whisky. He claimed he didn't know they were doing it. And it couldn't have been him, because he didn't have a key to the whisky room.[711] It was plausible deniability. But many in town weren't buying it. This led to questions about whether this potential "criminal" had the right to be police commissioner.

The following month, a trial looked to determine who was guilty of this crime. Was it T.C.? Was it the company? Or was it an employee? Frank Fox, the shipping clerk, looked to be the prime target of the investigation. But questions surfaced over T.C.'s lack of control of his own company. Did he not review invoices from time to time? Did he really have no clue they were shipping out quart after quart of whisky?

The prosecutor for the Feds was District Attorney Lewis Coleman. The defense attorney was Judge J.J. Lynch. Co-council for the defense was Assistant State Attorney General T. Pope Shepherd, a protégé of prosecutor Coleman. This relationship between legal teams built an underlying tension into the proceedings.

Even before the trial began, Lynch attempted to get the case kicked by the judge, saying his clients would admit to all the government's charges and would bow to their sentence. But Coleman wasn't having it. He felt there was something sinister going on and he wanted a trial.

Once proceedings began, there were plenty of theatrics in the courtroom. The prosecutors said it was "preposterous" to think T.C. Betterton didn't know about the scheme. It was his job to police the prohibition laws. How could he not see what was going on in his own organization? Then the prosecutor showed the jury an invoice that had "in plain view" a drawing of a hand at the bottom of an invoice pointing to the added White Oak whisky. [712]

The defense countered by having witnesses confirm that T.C. had in fact given the order not to provide whisky to customers. But on rebuttal, the District Attorney said "If he didn't want the liquor shipped, why did he give the shipping clerk [Mr. Fox] the key to the whisky box?" The defense replied, the clerk had to have the key in case E.R. Betterton in Cincinnati needed them to ship up some whisky.

The trial turned personal when Lynch accused Coleman of bribing witnesses to testify against T.C.. He closed his arguments by asking the jury to acquit T.C., not only because he was innocent but also because he had to deal with being called a "damned rascal."

Incensed, Coleman closed out his arguments by saying, "I didn't think there was money enough to buy Pope Shepherd and little Jimmy Lynch to get up here as they did this morning and accuse me of dishonesty." Then he turned to the jury, dropped his head and said with a sarcastic edge, "I hope you will acquit Lewis Coleman."

Tired of the barbs, Judge Sanford instructed the jury to ignore the personal attacks and politics, "which would be regretted upon reflection." Then he instructed the jury to determine if it was the company or individual that was at fault and to keep in mind reasonable doubt. It was also important to weigh whether either side had been "frank, truthful, or actuated by feeling and animus against the defendants." He also told them to ignore any prejudice and feeling of public sentiment.[713]

When the verdict came in, T.C. Betterton was acquitted, but the shipping clerk and the Chattanooga Coffin & Casket Company were both found guilty. They charged the company $150 per case for ten cases. The clerk, Frank Fox, had to pay $50 per case for ten cases. In addition, each had to split the $900 in court costs. Some felt the judge had lowballed the penalties. Coleman said the embarrassment brought to Chattanooga by such an immoral use of the coffins as a storage box warranted a bigger punishment. Judge Sanford held back on the moralistic question and explained that he set the fines low because the company was apparently unaware of the activity of its clerk.[714]

The scandal didn't hurt T.C. Betterton's reputation at all. He would continue on as Police Commissioner for the rest of the decade and at the head of the coffin business for most of the rest of his 65 years.

Just one month after the trial had put an end to the fiasco, members of the fire and police departments surprised Commissioner Betterton with a beautiful silver loving cup "in token of their regard for his courage, fidelity, honesty and impartiality in the administration of the affairs of his department." When T.C. stood up to receive the award, he was so overcome by emotion, he could hardly project his voice. It appeared the honor of the Betterton name had survived the great whisky coffin controversy.[715]

Seeking a Silver Lining

While Tennessee seemed dead set on burying its whisky industry, there was one man who refused to go down to the General Assembly's demands. It was longtime Carter County and Bristol distiller Ezekiel E. Gouge. He didn't have interest in fighting the state in court, and so instead moved his Bristol Distillery a mile north across the Virginia border.

Feeling he had outwitted authorities, he opened his new Bristol Distillery on a large plot of land near the Virginia and Southwestern shopping center. This new distillery produced up to five hundred gallons of corn whisky a day. It also had ample space for a hog farm. He kept his hogs fat and happy, filled with protein from the distillery's spent grains.[716] With his stills up and running, it seemed there was no stopping Ezekiel E. Gouge.

But after a year of strong production, everything that could go wrong did. He started 1911 with a devastating cholera outbreak within his hog population. He tried to make the best of it by selling his slop to area farmers.[717] Then, just after he applied for his wholesale license, his government storekeeper shut him down. Ezekiel was accused of pulling whisky out of his warehouse without paying taxes. The Federal authorities seized his distillery and ten thousand gallons of whisky.[718]

For a precious year, the Bristol Distillery sat silent while its owner awaited his trial. The government offered him a $20,000 settlement, but he declined, knowing he was in the right.[719] In the end, they found him not guilty. But that didn't bring back the lost distilling seasons. With southern states quickly falling to Prohibition, he knew he'd lost valuable time.

The business and its brand Happy Valley thrived until Virginia passed statewide prohibition and banned manufacturing of spirits. By this time, there was nowhere else to go. Ezekiel's career as a distiller was over. On October 31, 1916, the Bristol Distillery distilled its last drop of corn whisky.

But that wasn't the end of Ezekiel E. Gouge's whisky story. Just a month and a half after being shut down by the State of Virginia, the Feds came knocking. Again, they seized his warehouses of whisky. They accused him of cheating the revenue, saying he owed them $160,000 for back taxes accumulated over the previous three years. Ezekiel couldn't believe that he was being charged again.[720]

According to the government, the $160,000 shortfall resulted from grain calculations that suggested more whisky was being made than was being reported. Ezekiel hired two attorneys to help him fight the government's claims. Before the ruling came down, the government informed him that any business or personal property he owned in December 1915 was subject to seizure.[721] All the property he'd gained throughout his life would be put up for auction on April 23, 1917, to cover his debt to the government. It was a devastating blow. The distiller was getting on in years, and would have no way to recover from this government confiscation of his property. Even his glorious home, which the Chattanooga News called "one of the costliest in the state" was sold. Unfortunately, the event only raised $35,700 of the total $160,000.[722]

As if things couldn't get worse, a month later Ezekiel was being accused of another crime. They charged that he'd bribed an official to keep him from revealing the incorrectly measured malt. It was a charge that was eventually dismissed.

In another incident, twenty barrels of whisky mysteriously disappeared from the seized Bristol Distillery warehouse. Accusations flew left and right. Some believe the government had confiscated them and placed them in the basement of the Bristol, Tennessee Post Office. When asked about it, Postmaster John I. Cox feigned ignorance.

Then the story took a strange turn. With the case still in limbo, the great Spanish Flu pandemic spread across the land, killing hundreds of thousands of people. When it found its way into Bristol, it took a heavy toll on the population.

In response, Bristol, Virginia, put in a request for medicinal whisky. The state provided thirty gallons to relieve suffering patients. Yet Tennessee wasn't ready to help its half of the city. Bristol, Tennessee Mayor Clarence King, had heard the rumors about Ezekiel's twenty barrels of whisky possibly hiding in the basement of the post office. He quickly called the Internal Revenue office in Knoxville for permission to use some of the whisky to relieve the citizens of Bristol, Tennessee. A revenue man made his way to Bristol, went to the post office, and pulled two barrels from the basement. The barrels were next taken to the courthouse where they were siphoned into bottles by a former saloonkeeper. Next thing you know, the mayor was out on the front steps of the courthouse, filling hastily obtained prescriptions for quarts and pints of E.E. Gouge's confiscated corn whisky. All 120 gallons were sold out in four hours. Ezekiel's whisky wasn't doing himself any good, but at least it was helping someone.[723]

Eventually, they dropped the criminal charges against Ezekiel E. Gouge and the government settled for $5,000 and the whisky they confiscated from the warehouse. The settlement came on December 28, 1919, three weeks before enforcement of the Volstead Act.[724] The final cruel blow came the following June when an arsonist burned Ezekiel's distillery to the ground. Luckily, there was no whisky inside, just five hundred bushels of what became burnt popcorn.[725]

As for the whisky in the post office, the government decided another cruel joke needed to be perpetrated. They called for a public auction of 750 gallons of 110-proof corn whisky. The Feds held the event at the post office building. But the government had no intention of selling it to any third party. Their plan was to outbid the highest bidder, regardless of cost. When word got around, the bidding stopped at $10.50 per gallon.

If there was a silver lining to the story, at least they put the five-year-old corn whisky to good use. In the end, they sent 540 gallons of whisky to a government hospital in Perryville, Maryland in nine sixty gallon sealed iron barrels.[726] If that number seems short, it's because gallons were lost on evaporation. But then, there was also a subtraction of gallons that ended up in the bellies of some very needy influenza patients.

Saying Goodbye

The 1910s were a tough decade for the former distillers and distilleries of Tennessee. There was a great finality to that January 1, 1910 date. With the Manufacturer's Bill in full effect, there was little for distillers to do but move on or find another way to fight.

J.W. Kelly's president, Carl White, was one of the main holdouts. He attempted to keep making whisky for out-of-state sales until the Hamilton County sheriff shut the Deep Spring Distillery down. White continued to hope for a change in the law and held onto the distillery. In the meantime, he bought half interest in Henry Kraver's Kentucky Peerless Distillery.[727] The Deep Spring whisky they sold had a new slogan: "The whisky without an unkind thought." White also produced what may have been the only Lincoln County, Tennessee whisky ever to be made out of state.

R.H. Cate & Co. was the biggest distillery in Knoxville before Prohibition. They kept their doors open to the very end, then promoted their spirit from Middlesboro, Kentucky. Their ads featured the slogan "Every drop is honest whiskey," mentioning it was available "just over the dry line." There would be some confusion when the owner, R.H. Cate, showed up in Chattanooga with a new home. He had to explain that his son was the one running the Kentucky side of things.[728]

As for Jack Daniel, he spent the years after the safe incident in a slow and steady decline. He was putting on weight due to inactivity and his inattention to his foot only made it worse. He decided it was time to be baptized as a Primitive Baptist, the church of his father. The ceremony took place in Mulberry Creek. Suddenly rumors circulated that because of Jack's new faith, he wanted his name stricken from the whiskey he made famous and its distillery. Lem tried to quash the rumors immediately, saying, "Captain Daniel has joined the Baptist Church as reported, but he has not made any statement regarding the business with which he was so closely identified from 1865 to 1907."

In the waning days before prohibition, Lem confirmed in a newspaper article that Jack's church did not expect him "to give up on his values." He stated that the company would move its stock to St. Louis when "the lease of good will extended by Tennessee for so many years has expired." He noted the company would walk away from the Jack Daniel Old Time Distillery, valued at $100,000. But he said "if it is the law, we must obey it and take with good grace our apportionment. We are sorry for the good people of Lynchburg."[729]

On October 9, 1911, Jack Daniel passed away at his home surrounded by family and friends.

At the same time, Lem was in the midst of running a mule business and riding the train back and forth from St. Louis, where he was trying to re-establish the distillery. Then, in 1914, an October fire ignited in a warehouse near the distillery. Rumors flew that there was no more Jack Daniel whisky to be had. In reality, it was just one warehouse that had burned, although it was filled with precious private stocks of whisky. Lem quickly calmed fears by placing ads in the paper that assured customers there was a good supply "up the hollar" at Lynchburg. The ad featured Jack Old No. 7, 10 year, 14 year, 18 year, and a variety of brandies including a 10 year Tennessee apple brandy. It wasn't the only fire Lem would deal with in that decade.[730] The distillery in St. Louis also burned in 1913.

Manny Shwab would take the Jack Daniel's and J.W. Kelly lead and set up in a new state. First, George A. Dickel & Co. set up its wholesaling business at 8th and Water Street in Hopkinsville, Kentucky. They established a relationship with a Louisville distillery for new distillate. Then they opened a bottling room at 827 W. Main Street, Louisville, Kentucky.[731]

But Manny soon suffered from a case of bad timing. Just a year after setting up the bottling hall, on December 18, 1919, he posted a full equipment inventory of the plant in the *Louisville Courier-Journal* saying "Everything must go." Kentucky and soon the nation was going dry.[732] Carl White and Henry Kraver shut down Kentucky Peerless. With the introduction of National Prohibition, Lem would be one of the last to go. He shut down the Jack Daniel Distillery in St. Louis but held onto a warehouse where he stored his barrels of whisky.

In a final blow to the industry, Manny Shwab passed away in November 19 24.[733] Had he lived another week, he would have read the sad news that the old Cascade Distillery, where McLin Davis had perfected the formula for his whisky, had burned to the ground. There was a great note of finality in both events. It could truly be said, the death struggle was over. Tennessee whisky was dead.

Chapter 25

A DIFFERENT KIND OF PROHIBITION

War of the Roses

For the greater part of the 19th century, the subject of temperance was intertwined with women's suffrage. That was due in large part to the passionate women who broke through the Victorian-era stereotypes of quiet homemakers and childbearers to stand up for what they believed in. Women like Susan B. Anthony, Frances E. Willard, and Mary Hunt used their speeches, lobbying, and organizational skills to bring men to their cause. Yet, for this effort, they faced decades of ridicule. If one of their issues made it to a ballot and failed, the women who had supported it by standing outside the polling place were blamed for the loss. It was hypocritical and hard to justify.

Eventually, women helped state after state adopt various forms of prohibition measures and finally on December 18, 1917, they found enough votes in the U.S. Congress to get the 18th Amendment to the states for a ratification vote. Once the amendment passed and the alcohol question was out of the way, it only seemed fitting that a vote on women's suffrage was next.

The 18th was simply taking alcohol off the table, while the 19th Amendment meant women had to convince men to willingly dilute their votes, turning that power over to their mothers, wives, and daughters. This was no simple task. But women had already done the unthinkable. They got the 18th Amendment added to the Constitution without casting a single vote. It was no longer possible to deny their intelligence and abilities with any kind of credibility. Still, it was going to come down to a fight. After getting a bill through Congress, three-fourths of the state legislatures, filled with only men, needed to ratify the amendment before it would become the law of the land.

Congress completed the first step on June 4, 1919, and the ratification vote got off to a quick start. The Midwest was quickly on board, with Illinois, Wisconsin, Michigan, Kansas, Ohio, Iowa, and Missouri, all ratifying within a month. New York, Pennsylvania, Texas, and Massachusetts joined them. But suddenly the process bogged down. By the end of the year, only 22 of the 36 required states had ratified the amendment.

Women waged campaigns in the western states and those along the Mason-Dixon line, where they felt the amendment had the best chance of success. There was a feeling the southeast was a lost cause, so they mostly ignored it. The process churned away and, by March of the following year; the lobbying had gotten the total up to 35 states. But then the vote went into an endless stall. It felt like the remaining states were in a defiant mood, with no one willing to blink.

After banging their heads against the wall in states along the eastern seaboard, they finally realized some effort would have to be made in the southern states. Women spent the summer working the border states of North Carolina and Tennessee with all their might. But neither General Assembly was in a hurry to move. As the summer neared a close, both states begrudgingly put ratification votes on the docket. This brought on fierce lobbying, and one of the amendment's leading advocates, Carrie Catt, founder of the National American Woman Suffrage Association, parked herself in Nashville for the duration.

When the week of August 16, 1920 finally arrived, women held their collective breath as both the North Carolina and Tennessee legislatures prepared to cast their votes.

All eyes turned to Nashville, where the Volunteer State had the first shot at it. The governor was for ratification but had no vote. It was all up to the General

Assembly. As expected, the Senate passed it easily at twenty-five for and four against. But the House of Representatives wouldn't be so easy. Speaker of the House Seth Walker was a firm anti-suffragist. He could kill the measure simply by calling for a vote to have it tabled. If it was, it would be six more months before they could hold another ratification vote.

When the day of the vote in the House arrived, the positions of the representatives were not a secret. Each wore a rose on their lapel to show where they stood on the issue. A red rose meant the congressman was an anti-suffragist, and a yellow rose meant they were for suffrage. A simple look around the room showed the house was evenly split.

As expected, Walker called for a vote to table the measure. As roll was called, each representative cast his vote according to his rose. In the end, the vote was deadlocked at forty-eight to forty-eight. Walker called for a revote and again the noes and ayes followed along with the flowers on the lapels.

It was clear no one was changing sides. Seeing that he could escape blame if the vote failed, Walker decided to risk it and, rather than calling for another vote to table the measure, he called for votes on ratification. If this vote ended in a tie, the measure would fail.

Again, the representatives were called upon one by one for their votes. They stood up and gave their aye or no. With every passing vote, Speaker Walker's muscles loosened, knowing his decision was about to get him out of a fix. The roses didn't lie and everyone was staying loyal to their cause.

Then the name Burns was called out. The gentleman slowly rose from his seat, but didn't say a word. He seemed unsteady. His rose was red and so was his face. He seemed to be fighting some inner demon. But when his mouth opened, a sudden confidence came over him and he firmly said, "Aye!" Audible gasps were heard throughout the room. When the final vote was cast, the ayes had it. A few people cheered, but most of the room realized the vote wasn't over. By Tennessee state rules, forty-nine to forty-seven wasn't a constitutional majority. They needed one more aye vote for ratification. In a surprise move, Speaker

Walker changed his vote to aye. Women in the gallery jumped from their chairs and a loud cheer echoed throughout the chamber.[734]

The newspapers didn't know how to react. Neither did Representative Harry T. Burns' anti-suffragist allies in the House. Immediately, charges of bribery were levied against the young representative. But this only angered Burns, who released a statement to the press saying the members of the House should know him well enough to know his character. But to satisfy their curiosity, he gave his reasons for changing his vote.

First, he gave his moral and legal reasons for the yes vote. He truly believed the country had an obligation to give all people the right to full suffrage. It was a rare chance to "free American women from political slavery." He also wanted his party to be remembered for passing the act. But it is his third reason that is most remembered by history. He said, "I know that a mother's advice is always safest for her boy to follow, and my mother wanted me to vote for ratification."[735]

That advice came in a note he had received that morning from his mother, Febb Burns. It said:

> "Dear Son--Hurrah, and vote for suffrage and don't keep them in doubt. I notice some of the speeches against. They were very bitter. I have been watching to see how you stood, but have not noticed anything yet. Don't forget to be a good boy and help Mrs. Catt put 'rat' in ratification. Ah, ah, your MOTHER."[736]

Burns admitted he'd worn the red rose because that's the way his constituents wanted him to vote. This despite him being "for suffrage as a matter of moral right." The letter from his mother gave him the courage to follow his morals.

Beneath the noise of the women cheering after the House vote, Speaker Walker had motioned for reconsideration of the ratification, but it was shot down the next day. That same day, the North Carolina House voted against ratification by a seventy-one to forty-one vote. But the vote was meaningless. When Tennessee Governor Roberts sent the ratified amendment to Washington, the long struggle for women's suffrage was over. American women no longer had to lobby men to fight for what they believed in.

A Volunteer's Perspective

On January 17, 1920, most of the nation woke up to a great hangover and a morning headline proclaiming the death of John Barleycorn, the patron saint of booze. It was the first day of national Prohibition, the so-called noble experiment, and it was a huge event in states that were losing their access to alcohol.

Yet the newspapers in the Volunteer State were mostly free of references to Prohibition. Instead, the papers focused on the Russians, Navy morale, and a probe into crimes against women in Mexico.

There was one eye grabber, though. It was an advertisement placed in newspapers across the state by an organization promoting their Prohibition Enforcement Campaign.

> *"Booze and Bolshevism. Bolshevism flourishes in wet soil. Failure to enforce prohibition in Russia was followed by Bolshevism. Failure to enforce Prohibition HERE will encourage Bolshevism, disrespect for law and INVITE INDUSTRIAL DISASTER. Bolshevism lives on booze."*[737]

Shameless in its approach, each ad set a monetary goal for each city in a week-long campaign. In Nashville, the goal was $80,000, while they asked Chattanooga citizens to contribute $45,000 and Knoxville $60,000. The use of fear by those both for and against prohibition was nothing new to Tennesseans. Citizens of the Volunteer State had already learned the "noble experiment" wasn't so noble. That knowledge, and a ten-year preview of Prohibition is a big reason why Tennesseans and their journalists were disinterested in the blowout drinking parties held on January 16, 1920.

Yet there is an assumption that all Americans had a similar experience on both the day national Prohibition arrived and the day it left. But, as with most blanket historical statements and stereotypes, this was far from the truth.

To celebrate, Tennesseans needed access to alcohol. New Yorkers could toast the night away because their bars were still well stocked. But on that same last day, Tennesseans were surrounded by dry states. Getting alcohol was tough and flaunting it was dangerous.

Inside the state, everything from locker clubs to soft-drink establishments to saloons had long since been shut down. Of course, if you had a rich friend who had stocked up ten years earlier or a friend with a connection to a moonshiner, you might have a drink, but otherwise you would have to seek a blind tiger. Moonshiners were able to distill up their own celebratory concoctions, but open celebrations would make them a target.

But even if Tennesseans could get together with friends, what was there to celebrate? Nothing was changing in Tennessee. The alcohol laws on January 16 and January 17 were no different. The only ones who had a reason to celebrate were those in charge of state and local law enforcement. There was a promise of more federal support in the fight against moonshiners and blind tigers.

It wasn't just the first day of national Prohibition that was different for Tennessee; it was much of the experience. Some assume that Tennessee and Kentucky had similar experiences with Prohibition, but this too is a fallacy.

The difference once again comes down to Tennessee being under statewide prohibition for nearly a decade longer than Kentucky.

Kentucky still had warehouses full of whisky in January 1920. In Tennessee, however, distillers in 1910 had to ship their whisky out of state so they could take advantage of clearing their inventories through mail-order sales. By 1920, Tennessee warehouses were mostly dry. White Oak, Cascade, and Jack Daniel's stocks were in Ohio, Kentucky, and Missouri.

When the government offered Maryland, Pennsylvania, and Kentucky distillers licenses to sell medicinal whisky, they had full warehouses to pull from. Tennessee was bone dry. That meant brands like Nelson's, Cate, Gouge, and

Eaton had no way to preserve themselves. Meanwhile, brands like Four Roses and Old Overholt remained viable as their names appeared on bottles of medicinal spirits throughout the thirteen-year whisky drought. Perhaps a little Jack Daniel's whiskey made it into prescriptions, but, if so, the juice came from St. Louis. Dickel's Cascade whisky eventually became a Kentucky Bourbon and gave up all connections to Tennessee.

Another way Kentucky preserved its brands was through the Whisky Trust. In the early 1890s, the government broke up the original Distillers & Cattle Feeders Company of Peoria, Illinois as a trust. But after taking a couple years off, smaller organizations formed out of the fragments and eventually merged again at the end of the century. In 1899, one of these branches, the Kentucky Distillers & Warehouse Company, formed and purchased every Kentucky distillery, warehouse, and trademark they deemed worthy.

The Whisky Trust avoided Tennessee. The only distillery they purchased was the Memphis Distillery Company, only to shut it down. Perhaps they considered the slow fermentation and charcoal-mellowing processes counter to their speed distilling techniques. And most Tennessee distilleries were much smaller and less industrialized than the big Kentucky distilleries.

Whatever the reason, the Whisky Trust would eventually benefit the heritage of Kentucky whisky. And that all was possible thanks to company president Seton Porter, who saw the repeal of Prohibition as a real possibility. Under the former trust's revised names of National Distillers and the American Medicinal Spirits Company, he purchased warehouse after warehouse of old Bourbon along with Pennsylvania and Maryland rye stocks. He also held the names of some of the biggest historic brands in Kentucky Bourbon history. When Prohibition was repealed, he flooded the market with brands from Kentucky, Pennsylvania, and Maryland. Again, Tennessee's early entrance into Prohibition left them out in the cold.

These disadvantages are a primary reason Tennessee's 19th-century whisky history was lost to the ages.

The Bootlegger and a New Kind of Moonshiner

The place where Tennessee had the greatest advantage during national Prohibition was in something they probably weren't very proud--at least at first. The state had a wealth of well-seasoned moonshiners. And, much like their ancestors, the Tennessee moonshiners of the 1910s were producers of some of the highest quality corn likker, white lightning, or mountain dew that the state had ever known. In the early days of statewide prohibition, their product had to be good, otherwise they wouldn't be able to sell it to their main clientele: their neighbors.

While 'shiners were scattered throughout the state, most made their homes in the mountains, hills, hollers, and ravines of East Tennessee. For Carolinians and Tennesseans, a trip to the Great Smoky Mountains was an opportunity to visit friends and family and to get spirits to take back home. But the moonshiners of that day were still quite protective. Unless you knew someone, you weren't getting any hooch.

This became a problem as the Bone Dry Law hit Tennessee. People in Nashville, Chattanooga, and Bristol were getting more and more interested in securing spirits. The moonshiners were good at distilling, but they didn't travel far from their own homes. They needed a network of distributors who could take their spirits to the masses. Enter the crafty smugglers known as "bootleggers."

The job description of a bootlegger can be surmised by their name. A myth relating to the etymology of the word goes back to Neal Dow's Maine Law in the 1850s. It was said the streets of Portland were filled with boot-wearing smugglers who lifted pint-sized bottles and flasks with ease from their oversized boots. But this isn't really where the word came from. Bootlegging, like moonshining, was a term that came from the old country.

Bootleggers came in two main types: Wholesalers and hip pocket bootleggers.

The wholesaler was the trusted connection to the moonshiner. They would take the hard drive up into the mountains, purchase ten or more gallons of 'shine from the distiller for around a dollar per gallon, then they would fill up jugs and jars and take their score down the mountain. Wholesalers faced low risks when selling to certain networks like blind tigers, soft-drink establishments, business clubs, and hip pocket bootleggers. Things got more sketchy when they attempted to enlist the help of hotel porters and cab drivers, who were easily caught by undercover police.

The biggest danger for the wholesaler was a roadblock or a sheriff's deputy out on patrol. The car was the key. Over time, bootleggers became skilled mechanics and learned how to fine-tune their automobiles to outrun the law. They also learned not to overload their vehicles, since revenuers were smart to look for cars riding low under the weight of excessive liquor.

The riskier job was that of the hip pocket bootlegger. These were the bootleggers who worked the streets. To protect themselves, they carried very little moonshine in case they got caught. At most, they brought just a couple of bottles so as not to rattle. The problem was, there was always a danger of soliciting an undercover cop. With that, there would be no excuses. The profits per sale were much bigger than for the wholesaler, which compensated them for the added risk. Their supplies would come from wholesale bootleggers who charge $3 to $5 a gallon. The hip pocket bootlegger would then put the liquor in bottles and get a nice fat profit, usually tripling their money.[738]

As states like Virginia and Arkansas went dry, the demand for Tennessee moonshine and corn likker only increased. Bootleg networks became more sophisticated, moonshiners began focusing on quantity over quality, and the growing influx of money increased the level of greed in the system. By the time the Volstead Act arrived, prices for moonshine had skyrocketed. Greed wasn't the only reason for the high prices. Bad weather in the wintertime meant supplies were low. Bootleggers took advantage by squeezing profits from whatever supply they had.

When cities ran out of moonshine, locals took it upon themselves to make their own liquor. City spirits became known as bathtub gin. Chattanooga alone estimated 1,500 people in Hamilton County were adding five hundred gallons of spirits to the market every day.[739] And the distillers weren't always the people you would suspect. One of the bigger operations uncovered by law enforcement was run by Mr. and Mrs. E.C. Johnson. When authorities raided their home in

Nashville, they found two hundred gallons of rum and a large still. The tip came from bootleggers in the notorious Black Bottom part of the city. The Johnson's neighbors were quite surprised by all the sirens and law enforcement officers. To them, the old aristocratic neighborhood had always been a "law abiding" place.[740]

Beyond the bootlegger, the other critically important person in the moonshine network was the still maker. A good still maker was worth their weight in gold and usually swimming in profits--especially after a revenuer raid where they smashed moonshiner's stills to bits. A certain blacksmith in the Tennessee hills made a fortune on his stills. He pumped out one a day, making $35 on each. He had a backlog of customers and those customers needed him on the job. So he was one of the first they would warn when revenuers were in the area. Several times, law enforcement arrived at his door, but they always found him shoeing a horse.[741]

The best still makers figured out ways to make their copper creations easier for their customers to transport. Up in the Land Between the Lakes on the border of Kentucky and Tennessee, Casey Jones became famous around the area for his square stills that were easily transported on the backs of flatbed trucks.

The automobile was one of the biggest advantages modern moonshiners and bootleggers had over their ancestors. No longer did a 'shiner have to abandon their stills at the first sign of a revenuer. They just packed it up and disappeared. But not everyone could afford a vehicle at first. In that case, they went back to the old school ways of hiding stills in caves and ravines. A few set up wide networks of stills so that when one was seized, another could go into operation.

To the old-time moonshiners, it was well understood that the best time to distill was in the cooler months on the edges of winter. Those conditions always made the best hooch. It was like they were channeling McLin Davis. The cool temperatures during fermentation made an extra-special spirit, and the impeding of bootlegger traffic, thanks to bad roads, also meant spirits sat in the barrel just a little longer.

Distilling continued to be a family affair. Wives and daughters were just as active in the trade as their men. As a local law enforcement officer noted, "the ladies know moonshining brings profits and prosperity. It means an automobile, which is the highest level of luxury in the mind of a mountain woman. The dream is that someday prosperity will lead to a nicer farm in the valley."[742]

But the new breed of distillers and bootleggers that came into the area with Prohibition were less about family and more about fat profits. And because the distribution networks had moved beyond local clientele, there were fewer repercussions for bad hooch. With no government overseers, these new members of the network started cutting corners.

Initially, bootleggers and moonshiners used some disgusting but fairly harmless techniques, like adding color by emptying a spittoon of tobacco juice into a batch or throwing in prune juice. Others simply watered down the whisky, but then added pepper to give it some additional heat. Another way bootleggers added heat while cutting the spirit was by using products produced on their own makeshift stills. Created out of household goods like a tea kettles and stew pan, their drawback was that they allowed less control over dangerous heads which contained poisons and the less desirable flavors of the tails.

As Prohibition went on, whisky additives became much worse. Some of their most disgusting and dangerous additives included manure, lye, poison ivy, mercury, or chemicals that gave the whisky a kick. The lye was used to speed up fermentation. The problem is, distilled lye comes out clear and deadly.

It wasn't just additives that poisoned spirits. Some moonshiners would forgo pricey copper stills for sheet iron stills. And some new distillers had no issue with leaving poisonous heads in their spirits, which could lead to blindness.[743]

Naturally, the moonshiners who took pride in their distillate and their family heritage disliked these unscrupulous invaders in the market. "Old distillers say, while there may be honor among thieves, this new breed of bootlegger and moonshiner have none. It has become every man for himself."[744] Sadly, the government had incentivized this kind of activity by forcing distilling into the shadows and away from proper regulation. As if to add insult to injury, these purveyors of poisonous hooch paid the same $500 fine if caught as the quality 'shiner competition did.[745]

As this new breed of 'shiner permeated the mountains, the level of lawlessness increased.

Before Prohibition, people could visit the Great Smoky Mountains and head down any road they liked. But, during Prohibition, moonshiners assumed strangers were undercover revenue officers. This meant all bets were off. The visitor could state their business, but from that moment on, they should expect plenty of eyes and gun barrels pointed at them.

Another dangerous aspect of black-market bootlegging was the uncertainty surrounding the clientele. Meeting the wrong person could mean a quick and painful death. One of the more notorious cases of violence occurred in East Tennessee, close to Cleveland. A wealthy farmer, James Pierce, was found barely alive along the side of the road, a machine hammer by his side. It was said his head had been beaten into jelly by the instrument. The sixty-year-old bachelor had been missing for nearly a week. Pierce had apparently gone off with a bootlegger named Asbury Fields. It was known around the area that Pierce normally carried between $500 and $2,000 in his pockets. Fields violently beat him and stole his money.[746] Eventually, authorities apprehended him. Fields was tried, found guilty of murder, and sentenced to death. Fields proclaimed his innocence and a doctor diagnosed him as a "mental defective."[747] He tried to saw his way out of prison, using soap to cover his tracks. (It wasn't clear how he got the saw.)[748] He died in the electric chair in the state prison on February 18, 1922, less than six months after being charged with the crime.

Prohibitionists continued to believe legal liquor and saloons were the reason for lawlessness. Anti-prohibitionists argued that its absence made things worse.

Prohibition Chaos

On the national front, Prohibition wasn't getting off to a good start for the government. The number of illicit stills immediately increased in the months following January 1920. Costs to enforce the law were estimated to be around $88,000,000 annually (or $1.3 billion in today's money). Meanwhile, the country lost any remaining liquor revenue it had received. During the first year of National Prohibition, they confiscated over six thousand stills, with 386 coming from Tennessee.[749] But this was clearly just a fraction of the actual distilling capacity in the mountains and around the Highland Rim of Tennessee. These outlaws had had ten years to learn how to hide.

The national government was finding the same issues with enforcement that Tennessee faced a decade earlier. Leadership just didn't care. President Wilson, who had vetoed the Volstead Act, showed no support for the law. When President Warren G. Harding took his place, there wasn't much difference in attitude. The rum runners quickly established themselves along the Atlantic coast and speakeasies flourished. The first signs of enforcement came from Assistant Attorney General Mabel Walker Willebrandt. Put in charge of Prohibition in 1921, she eventually became the government's best weapon in the fight against the bootleggers.

The treasury department had its own leader in the fight to enforce Prohibition: Assistant Secretary to the Treasury Roy Asa Haynes. But Haynes' over-the-top use of propaganda over actual enforcement was seen as a joke. But, in reality, his options were few. The president and congress weren't making money available to do any more.

By 1923, Haynes felt his only weapon was to give daily pep talks in the nation's newspapers. In July, he attempted to turn moonshiners against bootleggers by suggesting they were paying 50 cents a gallon to moonshiners and selling the spirits for $32 a gallon. He worked to get sympathy for federal agents by pointing out the risks they encountered in their daily raids. Then he gave instructions to druggists and physicians on how to get supplies of medicinal alcohol while following the law. But some of his talks were clearly based on feelings rather than facts. One suggested men of stature were now following the dry laws. And another suggested city moonshining was on the decline.

But sometimes there was real insight when his numbers were interpreted by others. This April 1923 article from the *Chattanooga Daily News* based on Haynes report gave a genuine sense of the danger revenuers faced.

> *"The modern moonshiner is a desperate criminal, unlike the distillers of the pre-Volstead days. Thirty federal agents have been killed by moonshiners and bootleggers and two accidently in the line of duty over the last three years. Fully 100 state prohibition officers have been killed during the 3 year period. In the past, the humble moonshiner sold what he could asking for a few dollars a year, injuring no one. Rarely would a revenoorer be dropped. Arrested, he would take his punishment gracefully. The new blood is a business. Tear gas and bear traps for this new breed. Moonshiners have no rules in combat, but officers can only fire in self-defense."*[750]

In his listing of the deaths of federal revenue officers, it was interesting to note that only one killing, Irbey U. Scruggs (Knoxville TN) occurred in Tennessee during that three-year period. Ironically, the moonshining areas of Tennessee, Virginia, and Kentucky were much lighter on deaths than one would expect.[751]

The stories carried by local journalists in the early days of national Prohibition were quite dark. The one-time wet *Chattanooga Daily News* assessed Prohibition and its troubles in April 1922. "Mountaineers, forgetting long-standing feuds, unite in bootleg cause to fight revenuers and circumvent prohibition. So far, hundreds on each side slain. Moonshine has replaced romance along the train of the Lonesome Pine." The story was grim. "Ten thousand illicit stills in daily operation. Three hundred thousand gallons of raw 'moonshine' whisky being made and marketed every week—all despite the earnest and tragic efforts of the revenuers to halt the flow and dam the source." The paper raved on: "Twelve million gallons estimated, of this white whisky is estimated to have flowed into the hands of distributors in the last twelve months. Thirty thousand men women and children engaged in the family business operating these stills. Ten thousand arrests within a year and little progress made. Three hundred revenuers hiding along the trails and fifteen hundred sheriff deputies guarding the paths into the villages." The blame, according to the journalist, was National Prohibition and how it had brought city bootleggers to the country looking for spirits. It explained the desperation of the wild new moonshiner class: "They are independent, clannish, living an isolated existence, and brook no interference. Rather than be lodged in jail they would put a bullet in their own heads, there are several instances of this." While these mountain desperados didn't seem to mind taking their own life, according to the paper, they also didn't mind snuffing out the life of those trying to bring them down. "The moonshiner still slings a rifle and can pick off a revenuer at three hundred yards with deadly accuracy." But no longer were revenuers the only target—informers were in more danger.[752]

National Prohibition had truly created a Wild West scenario. The question in Tennesseans' minds was, would the federal government learn how to enforce the law by looking at their example, or was Prohibition doomed to fail?

Death Watch

Through all of this madness, one man had stayed true to his principles and allowed the allure of big money to pass him by. So appreciated was he by his community that if Cal Johnson so much as coughed, it made the news. In March 1920, a notice in the *Knoxville Journal and Tribune* noted "Cal Johnson Ill." It let readers know he had spent two weeks at home under doctor's orders with high blood pressure. In typical temperance-era fashion, they did not mention his saloon. Instead, he was the guy who "sent horses to various parts of the country."[753]

But in early 1925, Cal became seriously ill and a sort of death watch emerged in the daily newspapers. By April 4, the Journal reported "Cal Johnson's End Probably at Hand," noting that he was lapsing in and out of consciousness.[754]

For over eighty years, Cal had defied the odds and made his life an incredible success. When he passed on April 4, the next day's newspaper featured a headshot of the dapper-looking Cal. He was sporting his favorite woolen Frederick Fedora hat, a bow tie, and a bushy mustache that was a throwback to an earlier era. There was also an incredibly detailed obituary about his life.[755]

It brought up many stories that had been missed by earlier biographies. It told of his horse George Condit, who broke the world speed record for horses at the Chicago World's Fair in 1893. It mentioned how, while lacking an education himself, he donated liberally toward the education of Black people. It gave a full accounting of his birth and his full name, Caledonia Fackler Johnson. His parents, Cupid and Harriet Johnson, were mentioned, as was the name of the man who enslaved them all, Colonel Pless McClung. But he had nothing but high praise for his enslaver and his wife, saying traits in his character could be traced back to them. It told of his rags-to-riches story and his desire to run a clean house as a saloon keeper. In fact, it mentioned an anti-saloon drive in 1907 where one speaker noted, "if Knoxville saloons had been operated as Cal Johnson run his place there would have been no fight against the saloons."

He was a man of God and a believer in education, even though he missed out on the opportunity himself. He would say to friends, "he would have given his wealth for a bit of education." Thankful city fathers wanted to reward his contributions to Knoxville, so they opened a park and playground and named them in his honor.[756] That park still exists today.

When his funeral was held that Saturday at the Shiloh Presbyterian Church, those same city leaders were in attendance, most of them white. They remembered the measure of respect Cal gave whenever one of them walked into his saloon or met him at his race track—he would always take off his hat. The moment the pallbearers raised Cal's coffin, these same businessmen in unison took off their hats to honor the great man who had lived his principles and made something extraordinary out of his life.[757]

PART THREE: REVIVAL
THE LONG ROAD BACK

Chapter 26

HOW DRY I AM?

The Great Milking Case

"Mule Sale!" read an advertisement in the *Chattanooga Daily Times*. Several hundred of "the finest and best lot of mules" were being offered for sale by Lem Motlow.[758] While the mule business wasn't Lem's dream, he had resigned himself to a life without Old No. 7 by 1923.

But it wasn't like Lem needed the mule business to survive. He was a millionaire. The few years he spent making whiskey in St. Louis and selling it from Hopkinsville had made him rich. The mule business was a way to keep him active and gave him an excuse to get away from St. Louis, as did his stable of prized Tennessee Walking Horses.

But he never lingered in Lynchburg for too long. Seeing the Jack Daniel's Old Time Distillery sitting there vacant was heartbreaking. Back in April 1917, Lem had watched the last 168 barrels leave the warehouse. Then he said goodbye to the federal gauger Cicero Stone, who was being forced into retirement. It was a symbolic moment, particularly as Stone had started in the business at nearly the same time Lem's uncle Jack put up his stills at the Cave Spring Hollow.[759] Life for Lem after that day seemed to be a continuous journey up and down the L&N, riding in the sleeper car between Tullahoma and St. Louis.

It seemed like eventually Lem was going to have to decide on the future of the company. He couldn't make new whiskey and the stock at his Duncan Avenue warehouse in St. Louis was dwindling. Much of the remaining stock was nearing ten years of age and it wouldn't be long before it was ready to be sold. Once the whiskey was gone, staying in the whiskey business seemed pointless. Never in history had a constitutional amendment ever been repealed. To do it, three-fourths of the states would have to vote the country wet again. And while the country seemed to wet its whistle with greater frequency, at the ballot box, the majority continued to vote dry.

Leaving his uncle Jack's namesake behind seemed unthinkable, until thieves broke into his St. Louis warehouse in December 1922. During the heist, they overwhelmed the government guards and stole 118 cases of Jack Daniel's whiskey as well as sixteen barrels worth. It looked like Lem was going to be on the hook for the taxes due on the stolen spirits.[760] And his warehouse wasn't the only one that was being targeted for theft. In Kentucky, bootleggers like George Remus were using bribes to sneak in and drain whiskey from warehouses. The thieves covered their tracks by adding water and neutral grain spirit to the barrels, hoping the gauger's hydrometers wouldn't give the theft away. Lem knew that with this type of activity going on, whiskey warehouses had become a liability. A sale was definitely on his mind.

In what seemed like a case of serendipity, Lem was contacted by a group of businessmen from Chicago who asked if he'd like to sell out his stocks of whisky at his Duncan Avenue warehouse. At first, he gave them a ridiculously high price, hoping they would bite. Eventually, they worked him down to $122,000. In exchange, they got the whiskey and the certificates that allowed them to sell the contents for medicinal purposes. But they needed a place to store the whiskey, so Lem reluctantly rented out the Duncan Avenue warehouse. To protect himself against the tax man, he requested a $90,000 bond, made out by the Southern Surety Co. The insurer didn't ask for any collateral for the bond, but Lem thought nothing of it.[761]

Weeks later, an onsite government gauger and storekeeper, Charles Barlow, decided it was a good time to do a spot check of some of the barrels at the Duncan Avenue warehouse. To his surprise, the hydrometer showed the contents of the barrel only registered 4% alcohol by volume. He immediately went to the next barrel and found the same result. Barlow wasted no time in contacting his bosses and went back to work, assessing the damage. By the time word reached Collector of the Internal Revenue Arnold Hellmich, Barlow had counted six hundred barrels at 4% ABV water. Hellmich reached out to Roy Haynes in Washington and requested an official investigation. The Internal Revenue immediately seized the warehouse. At a bootlegger street value of over $1,000,000, it was the largest theft of whiskey in revenue department history.

Newspapers pieced together any facts they could find. Apparently, during the summer, the chief of detectives in St. Louis heard rumors of a potential heist at the warehouse and posted two guards to secure it. Just two weeks before the September 10 discovery by Barlow, they pulled the two extra guards from the warehouse.[762] This led journalists to surmise that this had to be a recent crime. They also speculated over who the suspects could be. Of course, anyone associated with the Chicago group was under suspicion. The prime suspect was a St. Louis politician, but there were whispers it might be some eastern millionaire masterminding the whole thing behind the scenes. There were also questions surrounding the night watchman, who would have been present during the milking of the barrels.

When the U.S. Attorney held an inquiry on September 27, he requested Lem turn all of his paperwork over to the government. Lem claimed ignorance in what the newspapers were calling the great "Jack Daniel's milking case."[763]

Over the next three months, Lem made his home on the rails, traveling between St. Louis and Lynchburg. His pacing soon came to a halt when he heard two pieces of bad news. First, he learned that he and sixteen other men were set to be indicted for the milking case. And second, the federal government was looking for their $90,000 tax payment and the Southern Surety Company was refusing to pay.

They set the hearing for March 24, so this gave him a week. Disgusted, Lem planned a trip home to Lynchburg, thinking he'd use familiar surroundings of home to clear his head. Knowing he had some time until the night train departed, he went out to dinner with a few friends to enjoy the evening.

The event that happened next would knock the great Jack Daniel's milking case off the front page. Moments after the L&N train carrying Lem made its way out of Union Station, heading toward the Mississippi River, the sounds of shots rang out. The train came to a halt. Authorities were called in. Passengers watched out the window as they brought a man out on a stretcher. Then two officers came out holding a suspect by the arms. The man who had his two arms bound behind his back was Lem Motlow.

The Trial of American Justice

When America's forefathers created the U.S. judicial system, they knew flaws would be inherent in the system. Nothing humans create is ever perfect. The jury trial is an excellent example of this. While a noble endeavor, it can easily fall prey to manipulation and misinformation.

The tone for American justice was first set in Massachusetts by a young attorney named John Adams. Five years before the War for American Independence, emotions in Boston were set ablaze when a mob at the Custom House began pelting British soldiers with snowballs and oyster shells. A soldier, fearing for his life, discharged his musket. The other soldiers, thinking someone gave the order to fire, discharged their weapons. As the smoke cleared, three civilians were dead. It became known as the Boston Massacre. A sketch by Paul Revere was distributed as propaganda: His work made the event look like a pre-planned execution by the British soldiers. Enter John Adams, a man of principle. Against the advice of those around him, he took on the nearly impossible task of defending the soldiers at trial in a town that wanted to tar and feather them.

John Adams needed a lot of things to go right to get those soldier's acquitted. He needed an open-minded jury that could look at both sides of the argument dispassionately with a goal of honoring the truth during their deliberations. He also needed a judge that was impartial and firm in the law. He needed to overcome the prejudices that were easily leveraged by the prosecutor. The witnesses needed to hold to their oaths of telling the truth, the whole truth, and nothing but the truth. And all of this had to take place in a courtroom where citizens displayed their anger with outbursts from the gallery. He also had to hope against hope that journalists and propagandists wouldn't further taint the proceedings. The odds were not in his favor, but somehow Adams won freedom for the soldiers.

In that 18th-century courtroom, justice appeared to be served. But this is not the case with all trials. And when historians try to get to the heart of less clear-cut trials, a lot of different undocumented factors impede understanding: The energy of the courtroom and the emotions running through it. The body language of the defendant, witness, attorneys, judge, and single jurists that might influence a jury. The impact of an attorney or witness with charisma or some kind of distracting tick. The unknown biases or prejudices in the minds and hearts of the players that get revealed in content that is stricken from the record.

This lack of clear information forces historians to supplement the information with contemporary newspaper accounts, interviews of witnesses who may or may not have an agenda, and the writings of other historians who may create a narrative from their own biases or fill in gaps with speculation.

In December 1924, a trial occurred that would put the judicial system and the credibility of news sources to the test. To get to the truth, each part of the judicial system would have to work properly. To accurately tell the story of the trial, historians would need all the elements not documented by the court to be faithfully retold by an unbiased journalism corps.

The defendant was Lem Motlow, charged with the murder of L&N Railroad Conductor Clarence T. Pullis. Beyond the gun, there was little evidence. In terms of witnesses, only three men knew the truth about the event that led to Pullis' death: Lem Motlow; a porter named Ed Wallis; and the dead conductor himself. Since no one thought to get the conductor's official testimony while he was still alive, it was all going to come down to crime-scene evidence, a couple of questionable witnesses, and the words of Lem and Ed Wallis.

The case opened with Lem's attorneys asking for an acquittal. When the judge denied the motion, he entered a plea of self-defense. As jury selection began, the prosecutors asked each prospective juror if they would have a problem with convicting a man in a capital punishment case. They removed men from the jury who said yes.

The *St. Louis Star and Times* led with a picture of Lem seated with his seven lawyers. Their sub-headline read, the "state will demand death for rich Tennessean who shot and killed Pullman conductor on March 17." The paper said the death penalty wasn't a given, but was likely. Then it gave details of the case, pointing out that Lem originally told detectives he'd "had a lot of drinks and could not remember what happened on the train." Then they questioned why the lawyers changed the plea to self-defense. The paper then revealed what it thought the prosecution's strategy would be, saying the state would "contend that Motlow was an intruder, had no ticket, was drunk and noisy" and who shot at the conductor and porter while they tried to keep him from disturbing the other passengers.[764]

In Tennessee, the *Chattanooga News* put out a headline, "Motlow goes on trial for life." In the first paragraph, the paper was quick to point out "there will be no southerner on the jury that will try Lem Motlow, wealthy Tennessean." The reporter noted the removal of jurors that had disclosed they'd once lived in the south. It surmised this was because the porter who struggled with Motlow was a Black man and that racial prejudice might play a part in the trial. The paper avoided speculating on strategies, but noted that Motlow's friends had come up from Tennessee to support him. They believed the porter attacked Motlow, and he had pulled his gun to defend himself. The conductor, in their eyes, was an unfortunate victim of the struggle.[765]

When the state presented its case, the jury received its first detailed outline of the events. It was the prosecution's assertion that Lem was drunk when he arrived at Union Station. Before he boarded the train, he was told by the porter to go see

Conductor Pullis to get a ticket. Motlow walked toward the table but then got on the train without a ticket. Then Motlow told the porter to make up "Lower 3" and to change the berth around because he didn't enjoy sleeping with his feet toward the engine. Lem gave the porter a quarter, which he accepted and the porter closed the ventilators and returned the ventilator stick to the closet. When the conductor asked for Lem's ticket, Lem became belligerent and threw a fist at the conductor over the porter's shoulder. The conductor told Wallis not to retaliate; it was at this point that Lem pulled a gun and shot the conductor.

The defense disagreed. They said it was true Lem had drinks before arriving at Union Station, but he wasn't drunk. They also didn't deny that Lem was without a ticket, but they claimed this was normal for him. Then they noted that the porter had attacked Lem with the ventilator stick and knocked him down twice. They claimed he fired the gun in self-defense, and it was unfortunate that a bystander took the bullet.[766]

When the wife of the conductor showed up in court, the newspapers played on the emotions of the moment. Some called her stoic and brave, while others said her emotions could be heard throughout the courtroom. Tennessee papers talked of Lem's friends coming to his defense. The *St. Louis Star* posted side-by-side pictures of Lem Motlow and the widow. On her face was a somber look. The photo of Lem showed him wild-eyed, with an uncomfortable glare that strategically pointed in her direction. Above the photos were the words "widow and her husband's slayer" written in capital letters.[767] Followers of the trial were getting a masterclass in emotional manipulation.

The questions raised by ongoing testimony were many. How inebriated was Lem? Did he attack the porter? Did the porter attack him? When did the conductor get involved? Did Lem throw out racial slurs? And if he did, was he yelling at the porter or the conductor who was defending the porter? There was even a suggestion that Lem had stared down the porter before shooting the conductor by mistake.

Nothing was adding up. Because of this, the jury spent more time focused on issues like the death penalty and racial prejudices.

The closing arguments from both sides played heavily on both these elements. With a lack of credible facts, the attorneys acted more like politicians attacking their opponents than attorneys seeking the truth. With the prosecution not being clear whether they were going for the death penalty. The state worked to remove any sympathy for Motlow and said they were only trying to put the millionaire behind bars. The defense used the last few minutes of their closing arguments to let their oldest attorney, Colonel Frank P. Bond, wax poetic about southern virtue while liberally tossing racial slurs and statements of white supremacy across the courtroom.[768]

When Judge Hamilton gave his instructions to the jury, he clarified he wouldn't allow the excuse of an accidental shooting regarding self defense. Then he asked them to consider "elements of premeditation, deliberation and malice aforethought, the degree of provocation and the element of self-defense" and went into detail on what each of these meant. Then he told them they had rights to find Lem guilty of first-degree murder with the choice of death penalty or life imprisonment, second-degree murder, manslaughter, a fine and/or an acquittal. He also said that if the killing of Pullis was in an attempt to kill Wallis, then it is still first-degree murder. But if they believed it was self-defense, then he was not deserving of punishment regarding either man.[769]

The jury left the courtroom for what seemed like minutes before they were ready to render a verdict. They acquitted Lem, but said he was deserving of a fine. But they considered his financial penalty "paid in full." It seems, prior to the trial, Lem had paid the widow of the slain conductor $10,000.[770]

Newspapers worked their narratives. The *Commercial Appeal* said there was no way the Tennessean was drunk "because Lem had always been closely affiliated with church movements."[771] The St. Louis papers interviewed the widow of the conductor who said, "wealth and influence" won the case.[772]

The jurors refused to talk individually about their verdict, but they allowed their foreman to speak on their behalf. He said "We didn't believe the negro. We believed there was a fight and that Motlow was forced to defend himself. This was the opinion of all of us, and there was very little discussion among us." When the reporter asked the foreman about how much the jury was affected by the defense's two attorneys evoking southern virtue and white supremacy, he said, "oh, we didn't pay any attention to the speeches." But then he added, "Col. Bond certainly made an interesting and highly entertaining speech."[773]

The case had everything: class warfare, racial prejudices, conflicting testimony, attorney manipulation, theater, courtroom outbursts, and emotionally clouded closing arguments.

But in no way did this trial live up to the spirit of John Adams. It seemed no one cared about justice and finding the truth. Even the jury foreman was full of contradictions by the end of the trial.

In a perfect world, one hopes that the jury, who witnessed all the proceedings first hand, would render an unbiased and just verdict. But in a trial where emotions were high, attorneys were looking for an edge, and with prejudices on display, finding the truth becomes almost impossible. The two clearest facts from the trial were that a man was dead and American justice had lost its way.

The End of Double Trouble

When attention turned back to the great Jack Daniel's milking case, Lem had to take the stand in his defense. He declared he did not know of the plot to steal the whisky. In his testimony, he told how a St. Louis business broker named R.A. Organ came to him with an offer to buy his whisky stock certificates and warehouse. Lem, who had warehouses in St. Louis, Birmingham, Alabama, and Cincinnati, made an offer of $400,000 for the St. Louis stock and warehouse. When Organ whittled him down to an offer of $125,000 for the whisky alone, Lem declined. They made another offer on June 18 and Lem and Col. Bond, his attorney, went to talk through the deal.

They met with Don Robinson, a Chicago financier, along with Mr. Meininger and their attorney, Mr. Remus. They drew a contract up and carried it out on the 25th. Lem said the men were supposed to pay $500 rent on the building and only purchased the whisky certificates.[774]

When asked if he knew George Remus or the other men, Lem said he'd only met with Remus and his wife Imogene on that one day. It's rather far-fetched to think Lem Motlow didn't know who George Remus was. By the time of their meeting, Remus was known as the "King of the Bootleggers." But maybe Tennessee's disinterest in national Prohibition left the state's journalists disinterested in Remus' exploits. By 1927, even they couldn't avoid his name after George killed his wife in cold blood and then defended himself and won his freedom by pleading insanity.

Lem claimed he didn't know the whisky was gone until he read it in the news. He claimed he was just about to sue the men because they hadn't paid him rent.[775]

The next day, Lem, along with Jack Daniel's company president T.A. Hefferman, were relieved of all charges. A jury eventually found twenty-three guilty in the milking case. The judge sentenced the plotters to time in Leavenworth prison in Kansas.

During testimony, a witness revealed that the thieves were supposed to siphon out only a few gallons of the whisky per barrel and to replace it with neutral grain spirits. Originally the siphoning was supposed to happen over a year, but they got greedy. Soon a year turned into weeks, a few gallons turned into the whole barrel, and neutral grain spirits were dropped in favor of water.

As for Lem's case against the Southern Surety Company, it would be eight more years before a judgment would arrive, and Lem received his $90,000.

Two weeks after filing suit on the surety case, Lem and his son Reagor were on their way to St. Louis on the L&N when they heard terrible news coming out of Lynchburg. A fire had ripped through the Jack Daniel's Old Time Distillery, turning most of the property into charred wood and ashes. So close to the end of Prohibition, it was one last stake in the heart for Lem and a Tennessee whisky industry that had lost so many of its great distilleries.

With most of its records destroyed, the history of Jack Daniel's was left almost entirely to courthouse records, census records, and oral tradition.

Repeal

For as long as anyone could remember, America was the place where drinking alcohol was shameful. So it was hard to deny the country was in the middle of a fundamental change when a poll taking the pulse of people's feelings about repeal found its way into newspapers ahead of the 1932 presidential campaign. The poll was conducted by the *Literary Digest*, who asked readers whether the Eighteenth Amendment should be continued or repealed.

Out of over two million surveyed, the readers voted 488,335 for continued enforcement and 1,574,776 for repeal. Only Kansas seemed determined to keep Prohibition in force. Of the southern states, Tennessee was the closest vote, with 10,070 for enforcement and 11,211 for repeal.[776] It looked like, even if the country voted for repeal, it wouldn't be easy for Tennessee to dump its Bone Dry Law.

By June of '32, as the depression deepened across the country, the Nashville-based *Southern Agriculturists* magazine did a state-by-state survey to see how interested each state would be in repeal. The overall survey showed southern farmers favoring repeal two-to-one, but Tennessee's votes were evenly split.[777]

The summer brought on the Democratic and Republican conventions. All eyes were on Chicago, where the Democrats would choose the man who would face off against Herbert Hoover. Hoover's failure to bring the country out of the Depression left him exposed.

On June 29, the Democratic Convention voted on the party's plank regarding Prohibition. Any "aye" meant staying with the status quo and a "no" meant they favored repeal. As they polled each state, several went as expected. Illinois, Michigan, New York, and Pennsylvania were all unanimous in favoring repeal. The first big shocker was Louisiana, which went seventeen to three for repeal. When North Carolina voted eighteen to eight to keep Prohibition on the plank, it looked like Tennessee would follow suit. But then South Carolina went eighteen-to-zero for repeal. When Tennessee's representative was called upon somewhere, Lem Motlow was smiling. Eighteen for repeal and six for prohibition. Maybe Jack Daniel's was going to be flowing sooner than he thought.

In the general election that fall, Tennesseans voted two to one for Franklin Delano Roosevelt. He won in a landslide nationally, and joined five new "wet" senators and seventy new "wet" House members in Washington, D.C. In Louisiana, voters repealed their dry law and Michigan did away with its Bone Dry Act. Within a day or two, plans were being discussed in the corridors of the Capitol on how to proceed with legalizing beer and wine, and producing repeal legislation.

Three years earlier, the idea of repeal legislation having any kind of chance was only a pipe dream. But on February 20, 1933, the House passed the bill with the two-thirds majority needed, with fifteen votes to spare. Now it was up to three-fourths of the states to ratify.

As the states awaited their opportunity to vote on ratification, the Senate moved forward with the Cullen-Harrison Act. It was legislation that would legalize beer and wine at a limit of 3.2 percent alcohol in states free of their own prohibitions. The House only deliberated for fifteen minutes before passing it. In the Senate, Texas Rep. Blanton complained the bill would bring back the saloon and it would be worse now, because it would push its evils on both boys and girls. But the measure passed and President Roosevelt signed it into law on April 7, 1933. As he finished the deed, he said, "I think this would be a good time for a beer."

One week after the president signed the Cullin-Harrison Bill into law, the Tennessee legislature produced a modification bill for the Bone Dry Law that would allow the sale and manufacture of beer in Tennessee. Free lunches and the word saloon were hotly contested. The bill allowed each community to make up their own rules and ordinances around its sale. The law passed and on May 1, Tennesseans finally had the right to purchase beer.

The next step was to get the state's vote on the repeal amendment.

There were already eighteen states that had ratified the amendment when Tennesseans went to the polls. Wets were encouraged by Alabama and Arkansas voting to repeal the amendment. For the drys, gone were the throngs of women and children singing at the polling places. The WCTU made an effort, but it paled in comparison to campaigns of the past.

It was apparent to anyone that the times were changing. In fact, Roosevelt's Postmaster General Farley told the press corps he and the president believed the country would have repeal by Christmas.

On a July morning in 1933, Tennesseans woke up to the news their state voted for repeal by a slim margin. The passage was thanks again to Memphis and Nashville. The opposition came from the mountains in East Tennessee. It was a razor-thin margin, but history would remember Tennessee as being all in, as the ratification convention in Nashville voted sixty-three to zero for ratification.

Chapter 27

NOT SO FAST!

In a strange twist of fate, the repeal of Prohibition meant nothing to the new owners of the Old Taylor Distillery in Frankfort, Kentucky. When they purchased the property, they did not know the 18th Amendment had a chance of being repealed. So when the American Medicinal Spirits company sold the pride and joy of the late Colonel E H. Taylor, the deed stipulated they couldn't use the plant for the manufacture or storage of liquor for a period of at least twenty years! Oops.

Not everyone was caught unaware. The gamble made by National Distillers' President Seton Porter paid-off big time, as he brought the company out of Prohibition with a huge supply of Kentucky Bourbon along with Maryland and Pennsylvania rye whiskies. While Roosevelt negotiated to bring Canadian whisky south to fill the void and his son and Joe Kennedy brought in Scotch through the port of New York, Seton dished out straight Kentucky Bourbon along with blends mixed with neutral grain spirits to extend his supplies.

As for Tennessee distillers, two men were ready to get their distilleries back up and running. One was Lem Motlow, who was eager despite the loss (due to fire) of his Old Time Jack Daniel's Distillery in Lynchburg. The other was the man who had purchased the White Oak brand from E.R. Betterton.

Yet, while distillers had to wait for law changes, there was one Tennessee industry tied to distilling that was ready and raring to go.

The Forgotten Industry

For centuries, the barrel, specifically tight cooperage for liquids, has been a critical element in the aging of wines and spirits. In Europe, hogsheads and sherry butts became popular storage containers for Irish and Scotch whiskies. The charred oak barrel has been one of the most important flavor enhancers in American whisky.

During the 19th century, Tennessee emerged as a center for barrel production. The tale of Davy Crockett's boat that capsized with thirty thousand barrel staves on board shows an industry in its infancy.

The state's first barrel boomtown grew just north of Nashville. In the mid-1850s, a small community of skilled coopers developed around the mills on the Red River in Robertson County. It became known as Coopertown. Not only did it feed the distillery boom in the county, it also supplied loose cooperage for everything from flour to tobacco barrels. With the addition of a railroad stop in nearby Montgomery County, access opened to Memphis and Louisville. By the 1880s, William Moore of Woodward, Moore & Co. estimated Robertson County distilleries alone spent $125,000 annually on barrels.[778] There is little doubt, Coopertown mills provided a good number of them.

Other areas around the state also thrived. While the Nashville Cooperage Company saw its success shipping along the L&N Railroad, Chattanooga Cooperage Company shipped to points as far away as the Minneapolis flour mills, the Liverpool docks in the UK, and all across the southern United States. By the first decade of the 1900s, they had three sawmills and still couldn't keep up with demand. The addition of several new Chattanooga distilleries only added to their success.

As for Memphis, their industry grew up shortly after the Civil War. The Memphis Cooperage and Manufacturing Company was one of its earliest successes. Memphis became home to some of the largest barrel-stave factories in the country. In total, there were nine plants in the city by 1908, employing several thousand people between them.

By this time, coopers were going through lumber at breakneck speeds. Demand was so high, supplies of white oak, red gum, and cypress trees were running short.

The United States had become a nation of consumers, using barrels on rail cars to transport everything from molasses, lard, and oil to nails, nuts, bolts, flour, sugar, coffee, fruits, and vegetables. Tight cooperage was especially scarce because of the high demand for beer and whisky.

But it was an industry that took a major hit as Prohibition spread across the south and then the entire nation. Losing whisky, wine, and beer hit Tennessee, Missouri, and Arkansas the hardest. For tight coopers, layoffs became the norm, and many companies shut their doors during the lead up to the Volstead Act.

When wets took control of congress in 1933, there was a genuine sense in the cooperage industry that something big was on the horizon. The industry's mouthpiece at the time was the Associated Cooperage Industries of America (ACIA), a trade organization centered in Memphis. Its president, Guy I. Frazier, spent the year readying the cooperage industry for the onslaught of barrel demand. All looked good, except for one caveat. Apparently the new beer bill being sponsored by Rep. Thomas H. Cullen of Brooklyn was rumored to be leaning toward a storage requirement of metal and glass containers over barrels. The organization sent a petition to the congressman and had it entered in the Congressional Record the previous December.[779] Frazier and the ACIA weren't about to take any chances.

Caught with Their Pants Down

The barrel industry seemed to be miles ahead on post-repeal plans. So were the architects who were reinventing the old saloons as fresh, new barrooms. Seton Porter was another example of someone well prepared for the end of Prohibition. His American Medicinal Spirits Company had bought up warehouse after warehouse filled with whisky to sell as soon as the states repealed the 18th Amendment.

The government, on the other hand, appeared to be clueless. President Roosevelt had backed up the prediction of repeal by Christmas, yet he did nothing to prepare for its eventual arrival. When Utah became the thirty-sixth state to ratify the 21st Amendment, the U.S. Congress and the president had no plan or legislation set for legally managing and taxing alcohol. This oversight led to a comedy of errors brought on by a band aid solution by the president.

With Congress out on recess, the president did the only thing in his power. He created an executive order under the authority of the NIRA or the National Industrial Recovery Act. The act regulated prices and wages to help foster competition and create public works projects. It also allowed Roosevelt to legislate from the White House. With this power, he set up rules and divided the liquor industry into six branches: Distilleries, Rectifiers, Brewers, Importers, Wholesalers, and Vintners. It was Roosevelt's hope that with a set of rules focusing on fair trade practices, each branch could police itself.

One rule was a prohibition on any connection between the manufacturer, importer, wholesaler of liquor, or retail operation where liquor was sold or consumed. This was the origin of the modern three-tier system that makes some whiskies impossible to get in certain states. It stopped the pre-Prohibition practice of having breweries like Pabst, Busch, Miller, Schlitz and others from owning bars. It was Roosevelt's belief that it was the direct funding of the saloons that led to most of the problems in the past. Unfortunately, the rules punished distillers and the whisky consumers who rarely took part in this strategy.

The new government agency was called the Federal Alcohol Control Administration (FACA) and its primary job was to issue permits under each branch's codes, giving it ultimate control over the establishment of any liquor, beer, or wine entity. While it covered the importation and distribution ends of the business, it left retail regulations up to the states.

As for taxation, that was to be handled by the Treasury Department with prosecutions handled by the Department of Justice.

What caught Washington and Roosevelt by surprise was the rush into this industry. It seemed like everyone got the same idea at the same time and went for it. In the days before Prohibition, the country had sixty importing houses. In the first six months after repeal, there were nearly two thousand. Where before Prohibition there were one thousand wholesale dealers, after Prohibition there were twenty thousand.[780] It made administration difficult, especially when the government was unprepared for the onslaught.

Fighting Back

Things had happened, just as the ACIA predicted. Except it wasn't Congress legislating them out of business, it was the U.S. Treasury Department under the NIRA. The treasury had decided the best way to stop bootleggers was to forbid the use of bulk containers in the distribution and sale of liquors. To top it off, they were bringing back bad practices by allowing artificial color to be added to whisky, doing away with the practice of aging in wood. It's true. Just a glance at whisky ads from that year shows brands had to reassure customers "No artificial color added."

But color and quality were the least of the industry's worries. This new ruling put an end to the brief boom in barrel demand. Within months, three quarters of the stave mills in Arkansas and Missouri shut down.

The question the ACIA was sending to Washington was, did the glass and metal regulation actually slow bootleggers? Not according to T.L. Gaukel, the Executive Secretary of the ACIA. He wrote a letter titled "Forgotten Industry" and sent it to newspaper editors around the country saying the country had thirteen years of proof that you can't legislate the bootlegger out of business.

Then something happened that no one expected. In June 1935, the U.S. Supreme Court struck down the NIRA, declaring it unconstitutional. It gave the Executive Branch the power to legislate, breaking down the clear divisions of government. The FACA was an example of the overreach. The high court's decision threw the liquor industry back into uncertainty. With the FACA dead, Congress needed a new solution.

As Congress debated bills through the summer of 1935, it looked as if the sale of liquor in bulk was about to make it into law, saving the coopers. But then Congress put forward a new bill creating the Federal Alcohol Administration (FAA).

They placed the new agency under the control of the Treasury Department.[781] This meant the decision about bulk sales would fall to it.

The problem was, the inept people who ran the old organization were brought over to the new organization. They also brought in a New York judge, Franklin C. Hoyt, to head the organization. But he was in over his head. Within weeks, he began complaining that Congress wasn't going to give him any money. The industry was fighting him at every turn. Regulations were slow to develop, whisky quality suffered, and, without the ability to ship in bulk, demand for barrels stayed low.

Then the unexpected happened. At the end of the year, Hoyt stepped down. He said it was for health reasons, but most who knew him personally saw how frustrated the post made him. Within days, Roosevelt picked Assistant Secretary of the Treasury Josephine Roche to hold the post for thirty days until someone could be permanently appointed.

One of the projects Hoyt had been working on was the further defining of the term "straight whisky." He wouldn't move forward because rectifiers and industry leaders pushed back saying it was too soon after Prohibition for an aging rule. Apparently Josephine Roche liked what she saw and on January 22, two weeks after taking the post, she codified the rules straight whiskies live by today. To be called "straight," they must be aged for two years, including rye, Bourbon, wheat, malt, and rye malt whiskies. There would be an exception for corn whiskies that weren't aged in charred oak barrels. As for the meaning of the word "age" she defined that as the period during which the whisky has been kept in new charred oak containers, except in the case of corn whisky.[782]

After all of their lobbying and fighting both Congress and the treasury over their preferential treatment of the glass and metal industries, a single "can-do" administrator who saw a regulation that was good for the industry made a decision that would secure the cooper industry well into the future.

As for the quality of spirits, they solidified the concept of aging as a part of creating a quality American whisky. American distillers embraced the single-use rule. Scotch distillers liked the rule too, because it meant American distillers had plenty of single-use barrels to send them to age their own spirits.

Now the biggest worry of coopers was running out of white oak as the brewing and liquor industries emerged from their cocoon.

Perseverance

When it came to protecting and promoting a whiskey brand, there were few who fought with more veracity than Lem Motlow of Jack Daniel's. After all, it was Lem, not his uncle Jack, that wanted the brand competing for gold medals in St. Louis and Belgium. Once he won them, Lem used every opportunity he could to promote the awards. Lem was also the one that reached out to the Maxwell House Hotel, got an exclusive deal, and elevated the hotel's experience by providing them with an elegant decanter that would impress customers. When Prohibition hit Tennessee, it was Lem and Carl White of J.W. Kelly who tried to get a Memphis attorney to squeeze one more distilling season out of the state. And, in 1911, when he caught wind that a soft-drink stand in Nashville was peddling fake Jack Daniel's, he offered a $500 reward for the person who revealed the counterfeiter.[783] Yes, Lem sold mules and cattle. He bred Tennessee Walking Horses. And he was one of the wealthiest landowners in Tennessee. But his actions showed, in every cell of his body, he was a Jack Daniel's man.

Moving the brand to St. Louis wasn't easy, but it was necessary. Lem did his best to integrate himself into the business community, unsure whether that would be the permanent home of the brand.

When Lem saw a turning tide in Prohibition's political landscape. He wanted to be a part of it. So, in March 1932, he made the decision to run for the lower house of the legislature, representing Lincoln, Moore, and Bedford counties. He wanted to help with national repeal and then to work for the repeal of the Manufacturer's Law that kept him out of the whiskey business. He was also looking to get the pulse of the state and the legislature to see if there was enough support for a renewal of distilling in Lynchburg.

When he won the election, he became a member of the legislature that brought 3.2 percent beer back to the state. But he must have felt the obstacles in Tennessee were too high to bring distilling back. He decided to re-registered the Jack Daniel's Distilling Corporation in Missouri. When his lawyer found three other entities had applied for the use of the name with the securities commissioners' office, he made a deal to have them dissolve their corporation. On July 7, 1933, the company was back in business at a value of $2,000, with Lem holding eighteen of the company's twenty shares.[784] He negotiated for a plant on Duncan Avenue at the site of the old Ames Shovel & Tool Company, renewed his lease on the warehouse, and started planning the distillery. Once he was legal, he quickly ramped up the production of brandy and whiskey.

Apparently, Lem wasn't the only one dissuaded from returning to Tennessee. In 1933, George A. Dickel, & Co. was in search of a new home. While Manny Shwab was still alive, the Cascade brand had spent the rest of its life before national Prohibition living off juice from the A. Ph. Stitzel Distillery in Louisville. With Prohibition ending, Cascade was once again being distilled at Stitzel. The distillery had renewed producing whisky around 1930 after a distiller's holiday was called for by Congress because of a shortage of medicinal whisky stocks. This allowed Cascade to come out of the gate with a 90 proof Kentucky whiskey. They also sold off older stocks of up to seventeen-year-old bonded whiskey. But when the family decided they wanted to find a new home. Eventually, they ended up at the James E. Pepper Distillery in Lexington, Kentucky.

Lem was willing to try anything to get back to Tennessee distilling—even selling to the state. House Speaker Frank Moore suggested Lem was prepared to bottle and label his whisky for the state. to offer the state whisky at 20 cents a pint, bottled and labeled. Lem thought the state could easily make a profit if the state took every drop he made. But the drys weren't about to see their state responsible for whiskey sales.

Lem won a second term in the General Assembly but, instead of liquor laws, he spent his time voting on sales tax and fishing licenses. Disgusted, he quietly walked away and went back to his Tennessee Walking Horses, farming, and St. Louis distillery.

Lem was right to focus on St. Louis. It was 1937 before there were stirrings surrounding the Manufacturer's Law. Finally, Tennessee legislators who were on the fence saw the tax revenue being raised by Kentucky. At first, the concept of state-owned distilleries was floated. But if it was hard for teetotallers to accept the state selling whiskey, it was an even bigger ask to have them approve the state making whiskey.

A better option appeared just days before the close of the May legislative session. Two bills were being rushed through the Assembly. The first called for a mid-summer referendum on the repeal of the Bone Dry Law. The second was a repeal of the Manufacturer's Law. This second bill, authored by Henderson County Rep. Lon Austin, would give Lem Motlow exactly what he needed to bring Jack Daniel's back to Moore County. But if it passed, it had a couple of hitches. First, a petition would need to be signed by ten percent of registered voters in the county, asking for a referendum. Then a vote would be held where citizens could allow or disallow distilling in the county. Of course, no one in Tennessee could buy it. They could only sell it out of state. It was a bill that Lem had nothing to do with, but, as the one man steadfast in his desire to bring distilling back to the state, members of the Assembly started referring to the revised Manufacturing Bill as the "Motlow Bill."

By May 20, one day before the end of the session, the Motlow Bill had the approval of the Senate, but it looked to fail in the House by two votes. Rep. Austin felt confident about the bill's chances. He had the assurance of Governor Browning, a dry, that he would sign the bill if it passed. The debate continued through the afternoon.

The next morning, Lem was sitting in the corner of the chamber when the Motlow Bill came up for a vote. It passed by a fifty to thirty-eight margin. A cheer rose as they completed the roll call and a grin spread across Lem's face. He couldn't wait to share the news. He had a sizable chunk of change to invest in the building of a new distillery in Lynchburg. And he said he'd ask the voters of his county to participate in a referendum within a couple of months, predicting easy victory in Moore County. Lem had all he needed, including the original trademark and his brother Jess, who had distilled before Prohibition, and who was ready to rev up again, making the same whiskey that made Jack Daniel famous.

Meanwhile, the Bone Dry Law referendum passed the Senate and received the governor's signature. But the liquor interests weren't impressed. It wasn't going to change the law. It was only taking the temperature of the electorate on the subject of repeal. The General Assembly scheduled a September vote.

As for Lem, he went right to work on getting petition signatures for the Moore County referendum. He also needed to complete plans for his $100,000 distillery. In Lynchburg, all that remained were a couple of warehouses filled with tobacco. Those warehouses would have to be re-racked. He was hoping to make the new distillery a tourist-friendly stop off. Before Prohibition, visitors to the area would stop off at the Cave Spring to drink water from underneath the arched rock. As for the whiskey, his goal was to shift to a one hundred percent Tennessee product. Yes, he would sell younger charcoal mellowed whiskey, but his goal was to rack the choicest runs for seven years.

But when the participants gathered at the Moore County Courthouse on June 12, the dry forces smelled blood in the water and vowed to fight. They pointed out that this was a bill for one man. If they could cause this vote to fail, they might get rid of the blasted law and turn sentiment in their direction. It was surprising that with such an important vote, Lem was out of town. The person who unexpectedly showed up was Bishop Horace DuBose of the Anti-Saloon League. He preached about the evils of alcohol and asked the court to deny the petition. The vote ended in a tie. Then the magistrates denied the petition. When he heard the news, Lem tried to take it in stride. He thought he had fifteen votes secured. The presence of DuBose was an unexpected turn. He promised it would carry the next time.

The next time was less than a month later on July 5, during the quarterly session of the court. Lem had plenty of signatures and was there to fight. The courthouse was abuzz with activity. Lem and his associates sat on one side of the court and the leaders of the temperance movement sat on the other. The arguments were heated, with no one willing to give an inch. When a vote was called, the drys carried the day eleven votes to ten with two abstaining. This time, Lem was there to hand them the petition personally. The court was duty-bound to approve the referendum. Again, they denied it.

Lem couldn't understand it. This wasn't supposed to be so hard. The legislature and the citizens of Moore County had spoken. Lem conferred with his attorneys about options that would compel the court to follow the rule of law. The best they could get was another vote, set for July 27 at the courthouse.

This time, DuBose and the Tennessee Anti-Saloon League found a new way to frustrate the 68-year-old Lem. They had a Moore County taxpayer, Landry C. Bobo, file a bill attempting to stop the vote by having the Motlow's Law declared unconstitutional. Bishop DuBose presented it to the court and Chancellor Thomas B. Lytle called a halt to the vote so he could review whether the complaint was valid. For the next week, Lem and wet advocates throughout the state held their collective breath.

The judge's verdict was that the law was unconstitutional. Lem immediately filed an appeal and again went back to waiting. His dream of having the Jack Daniel's distillery open by Christmas looked to be dead in the water.

As Moore County held the Motlow Law hostage, all eyes turned toward the September state referendum on the Bone Dry laws. The drys were excited at the prospect of scoring a second victory against the wets. But the liquor interests still saw the referendum as a sham and told wets to stay home in protest. The result was a landslide against repeal. Bishop DuBose called it a victory while the wets tried to dismiss the vote as meaningless.

As for Lem, he was tired of having his emotions tossed around. He took the next few months off to focus on his livestock and show horses. All Lem could do was hope 1938 would usher in a different mood in the state.

Finally, some good news. On January 15, the Tennessee State Supreme Court ruled that the citizens of a county had the right to permit the manufacture of liquor within their borders, thus reversing Chancellor Lytle's ruling.[785] With that action, attention turned back to the Moore County Courthouse. They set the next meeting for January 24. But once again it was an eleven-all deadlock and, again, they refused to call a referendum.

For Lem, that was the last straw. These politicians were denying the will of the people, ignoring the State Supreme Court, and the state attorney general. He asked his attorneys to file a writ of mandamus that would force the court to comply with the law. Unfortunately, to do it, he would have to take it before Chancellor T. B. Lytle in Columbia, the judge who had just had his decision reversed by the high court.

The hearing before Chancellor Lytle was set for March 7. It was the last round of the cage match between Bishop DuBose and Lem Motlow. Lytle granted the writ. Down on the mat, DuBose immediately appealed to the Supreme Court. The decision was to be rendered on April 2. Lem didn't want to be overconfident, but he felt like things might go his way. He took the opportunity of the break to once again throw his hat in the ring for a position in the General Assembly, this time as a State Senator. He realized these types of fights would only be won with all hands on deck. The next big battle would be trying to open the state up for whiskey sales.

When the high court's decision was read, Lem had won again.[786] The next meeting of the Moore County magistrates would be on April 5. Finally, the referendum was approved and scheduled for May 3. It was an incredible fight, but Lem had prevailed.

Then came the cruelest blow of them all. Two days before the vote, a letter to the editor appeared in the *Nashville Tennessean*. It was from Lem's own brother Felix, opposing the distillery.

It was the ultimate stab in the back at the absolute worst time. Lem was confident in the people of Moore County, but the letter sure made the last forty-eight hours tense. In the end, the citizens voted 595 to 411 to allow distilling within the county.

One month later, a permit was issued in St. Louis for a wrecking ball to take out the site of the old St. Louis Arch & Shovel Company on Duncan Avenue. The owner was listed as Lem Motlow of Lynchburg, Tennessee. That wrecking ball was to send a message: From this point forward, every drop of Jack Daniel's Tennessee Whiskey would come from the Hollow.

For most of the next seventy-five years, the Jack Daniel's brand would have the honor of setting the tone for Tennessee whiskey. Others would try to duplicate Lem's entrance into the market, but only a couple would make it through. And none of them dealt with as much adversity as Lem Motlow, who fought the battle almost single-handedly. Sadly, his contributions to preserving and growing the brand are overshadowed by his legendary uncle. But it could be argued that no one in the history of Jack Daniel's did more to elevate the brand and set it on the path to where it is today than Lem Motlow. And not only did he bring back Jack Daniel's––he brought back Tennessee whiskey.

All he had to go through to do it makes him truly the stuff of legend.

Chapter 28

AND THEN THERE WERE TWO

Time for a Drink

When the calendar turned over to 1939, Tennessee was one of only four states still holding onto dry laws. The others included stubborn Kansas along with Mississippi and Oklahoma. It was the hope of the Tennessee Anti-Saloon League that Tennessee continued to be a shining example of dryness and virtue for the rest of the country. But they were quickly losing support in the state legislature.

One thing driving the alcohol question was a lack of funds in the state treasury. Before Prohibition, agriculture, distilleries, tippling houses, and wholesalers brought in a lot of money for the state. Now that money was seeping over the border into wet states like Kentucky, Virginia, Georgia, and Arkansas. The return of Jack Daniel's was a start, but it was only one small distillery. It wouldn't make a dent in the state's revenues.

Once again, Rep. Lon Austin took the lead in crafting an alcohol bill. This one would call for a statewide referendum to legalize spirit sales under government control while providing a local option. Lem Motlow's attorney Seth Walker went to work on writing the Senate bill. Governor Prentice Cooper, a dry, liked this bill only because it allowed citizens to vote on the measure. He threatened to veto anything the legislature produced that didn't give the people a voice. But

Attorney General Roy Beeler shot down the bill, saying the statewide referendum bill would be unconstitutional, since it gave the power of the legislature directly to citizens. It seemed like Gov. Cooper was boxing the legislature into a corner.

Then Senator Lester Doak of McMinnville came up with another idea: Why not skip the statewide referendum and instead allow each individual county to call for its own referendum on alcohol sales? But Rep. Austin thought there was an easier way. The two worked on compromise bills and eventually settled on repealing the Bone Dry Law and allowing for package liquor sales wherever they were approved by county officials.

The bill passed the House fifty-two to forty-two, and the Senate added small amendments to it, before passing it eighteen to fifteen. They reaffirmed it in the House and sent it to the Governor's desk. As expected, Governor Cooper vetoed it. But it didn't matter. The General Assembly just needed a simple majority to override him. On March 2, 1939, the Tennessee Bone Dry Law was dead. It was a surprise to Lem Motlow, who would get to sell his whiskey in-state, years before he expected to.

Immediately, counties throughout the state put in motion plans to hold referendums. Chattanooga's Hamilton County was the first. For them, the influx of liquor across the border from Georgia and dangerous bootleg liquor coming from the mountains needed to be stopped. Davidson and Knox counties announced their petition drives that same day. Hamilton would pass their measure with ease on May 2.

By July, George A. Dickel & Co, which had been sold by the Shwab family to Schenley Industries, celebrated the return of their spirits to store shelves across the state. The advertisement proclaimed, "Back at Last!" It was partially true. Yes, the whiskey was back on the store shelves, but it was now a Kentucky whisky rather than a Tennessee one. That didn't stop them from touting their use of the same old secret formula and the tagline "Mellow as Moonlight."

Lem Motlow was in a celebratory mood as well. At the same time the Tennessee's Bone Dry Law was being put to rest, Lem was preparing to make his reentry into Tennessee distilling. He was in Nashville in March, getting his distillery charter from Secretary of State A.B. Broadbent.[787] It was a proud day for Lem, who tacked his own name onto the new corporation, now officially known as Jack Daniel Distillery Lem Motlow Prop. Inc.

The last step was getting his distilled spirits' plant number. Like the old days, every distillery had to carry a number issued by the federal government. But since the U.S. Internal Revenue no longer served as the primary agency, Jack Daniel's Old-Time Distillery "registered distillery" number 514 was retired. And because the distillery at Cave Spring Hollow was the first in Tennessee to be re-registered under the new FAA, Lem would receive the number DSP-TN-1.

But Jack Daniel's wouldn't be the only historic Tennessee brand to be made at a distillery carrying the number 1. In a historical twist, George A. Dickel & Co.'s acquisition by Schenley meant a change of distilling location for the brand. Cascade was now being produced at Bernheim Distillery, the home of I.W. Harper. When Kentucky came out of prohibition, its distilleries began applying for the new federal plant numbers. Bernheim would be the first in line, making George Dickel's onetime Tennessee Cascade brand a product of DSP-KY-1.

Building a Dynasty

Post-Prohibition brought many changes to the world of Lynchburg distilling. Long gone were the log stills, natural fermentation, and local competition. One of the biggest changes was the shift to a more modern distilling plant with column stills instead of the old pot stills.

Yet Lem wanted to stick with tradition any way he could. He wanted to make sure Jack Daniel's always stayed true to the concept of old time Tennessee whiskey. The best way to do this was by making sure the brand always emphasized its historic roots and achievements.

Coming out of Prohibition, Lem reminded customers of the gold medals the brand had won in St. Louis, Belgium, and London. The early ads spoke of the generations of distilling Daniel's and Motlow's and young Jack, who set up stills at the Hollow in 1866. They assured customers there was continuity between the

Old No. 7 and the new Old. No. 7, thanks to Jack's secret formula being locked up in the company's safe.

For tourists coming to the distillery, Lem wanted them to feel like Uncle Jack was there with them. He had a marble statue of the founder placed in front of Cave Spring Hollow in 1941.

While stories and statues connected people to the past, it was the whiskey that really had to tell the tale. Lem's brother Jess worked quickly to get spirits ready and aged for the market. By Christmas 1940, Jack Daniel's Whiskey at 90 proof was on the market with ads touting their limestone spring water, expensive filtering process, and a new slogan, "Making new friends every day."

In December 1939, just as the distilling train got on the tracks, Lem suffered a stroke. It took a toll on his body that limited his activities around the distillery. Undeterred, he announced his candidacy for the lower branch of the legislature in March 1940, but the strain was too much and his son Reagor took his place as a candidate. Reagor also took over more of the business duties for his father.

Lem wasn't the only connection to the past that was moving out of the spotlight. With the distillery up and functioning, Jess Motlow turned his post of distillery manager over to his nephew, Lem "Big Hyde" Tolley. If his last name sounds familiar, it is because he was the grandson of William Tolley, the patriarch of the Tolley distilling dynasty. It created a fascinating bridge between two legendary Lincoln County distilling families.

A man with an armor-plated demeanor, Big Hyde, was going to need his thick skin to get through some rough years. Months after taking over distilling operations, Big Hyde was told to shut down after the attack on Pearl Harbor brought the U.S. into World War II. Larger distilleries shifted over to distilling industrial alcohol and grain restrictions forced smaller distilleries to close. Things didn't get much better in the early days after the war as grain shortages continued. Lem Motlow's insistence that the distillery use only top-quality grains meant production was severely limited. This put the distillery far behind demand. It would become a regular theme with Old No. 7 over the next couple of decades. But Big Hyde would fight through it and produce some of the most memorable spirits in the company's history, and his juice would soon earn Jack Daniel's a cult-like status among American whiskey drinkers.

Sadly, Lem Motlow wouldn't live to see his nephew's brilliant success with the brand. On September 1, 1947, complaining of a headache, the once-feisty old man laid down to take a nap. He passed away shortly after.

Straight Out of Hollywood

To the people of East Tennessee, fast cars became synonymous with bootleggers, known in the area as moonshine runners. The sound of engines revving and police chases through the streets of Bristol, Johnson City, and along Kingston Pike east of Knoxville was commonplace in the 1930s.

As laws changed and counties opened up to legal liquor sales, runners felt the pinch. But the suspension of legal distilling during World War II helped reignite their activities.

After the war, soldiers came home from Europe and the Pacific and found themselves hard pressed to find jobs. Locals, looking for any way they could to make ends meet, went back to what they knew best––running liquor. With big cities supplied with legal liquors, runners focused on buyers in dry counties around Kentucky, Tennessee, the Carolinas, and Georgia.

If they needed fast cars in the past, now they needed fast and reliable cars to cover these greater distances. Yet they also needed to make sure the law couldn't easily spot these souped-up cars. Runners were soon converting everyday vehicles into super machines. One of the runners' early favorites was the Ford Model A Coupe. The engine was easy to modify and they could easily stiffen suspensions to improve hauling capacity. The best part was, they didn't have to adjust the bodywork of the car, so they looked like they did when they came stock from the factory.

Stock cars became an important part of the moonshiner's life. But runners also benefited from another technological improvement, the U.S. Highway. No longer were cars rattling apart on rough mountain dirt roads. Roads like US 25 and US 11 gave cars long stretches of straight road where they could outrun cops and revenuers.

It wasn't long before these adrenaline junkies got the bright idea to show off what their cars could do. On the east side of the Smokies, the son of a Wilkesboro, North Carolina moonshiner, took his driving talents down to Florida and joined a new organization called the National Association of Stock Car Auto Racing. His name was Robert Glenn Johnson, Jr. but everyone just called him Junior. Junior Johnson quickly became NASCAR's first great superstar.

On the west side of the mountains, Kentucky and Tennessee were trying to work out their own association of stock car drivers. In 1949, the Cherokee Racing Association was born.

Its first season was short. They held the races at the Broadway Speedway near Fountain City on the outskirts of Knoxville. The first race, scheduled for late October, featured fourteen cars. Each race featured a qualifying session at 2:30 and races at 3:30. The plan was to have four tracks by the following year. Within five years, the circuit touted its own batch of stars, including Duck Moore, Toodle Estes, Ken Milligan, and a wildcard moonshine runner from Cocke County, Rufus "Rufe" Gunter.

Racers knew Rufe as a rough-edged talent who showed great potential. Like many of them, he'd spent his youth as a moonshine runner. But when it came to the feds, Rufe seemed to have no luck. It was like he was a magnet for revenuers. Twice in his teens, he was hauled into federal court in Asheville, North Carolina, after being caught with moonshine in his car. In Newport, Tennessee, he met up with Aden Willie Garver, a man with an excellent reputation for 'shine. While the change of scenery improved the quality of his product, it didn't stop the feds from catching up with him.

It wasn't because he was slow. When he joined the Cherokee Racing Association, fans saw him as a diamond in the rough. Each race gave him plenty of opportunities to impress people with his skills and the power of his #47 car.

But life on the Cherokee circuit was anything but lucrative, unless you were good in a variety of categories. While NASCAR established itself as a big purse main event circuit, the Cherokee circuit stayed small and put its focus on giving people their money's worth. Shifting itself into a Saturday night event, the evening featured heat races, fast car dashes, and a trophy dash all leading up to the main event––a twenty-five lap nightcapper.

In his first year, Rufe only raced in a few events at the end of the season. But he started strong the next year, and soon was living up to his potential and challenging for wins in nearly every event. Racing was the 26-year-old moonshine runner's ticket to legitimacy.

But then it all came to a screeching halt. The feds had uncovered a sizable moonshine network with Rufe at the head of the transportation and distribution channel. It seems the Alcohol Tax Unit, formerly the FAA, had been tracking Rufe for the last three years, waiting for an opportunity to strike. They hauled him and twenty-three others into federal court. Garver and Gunter were sentenced to a year and a day in jail. It looked like Rufe's racing career was in jeopardy.

For the next twelve months, Tootle Estes and Duck Moore made headlines winning races while Rufe was nowhere to be seen. There were hopes for a late season return. But the season came to a close without a whisper from Rufe.

With racing, there was time away. But with running likker, there was never an off-season. One of the more exciting chases happened during the wee hours of December 24 when troopers caught sight of three suspicious-looking vehicles heading west on Asheville Highway, east of Knoxville. This was a popular route for moonshine runners, and these cars were moving along at quite a clip. When the drivers saw the troopers behind them, all three put their pedals to the floor.

The first car took a curve too fast and slid off the road into a telephone pole. With one car down, troopers did their best to keep up with the other two vehicles. The cars appeared to be heading to Cocke County, but suddenly one spun off toward Morristown. The two troopers followed it.

To slow the runner down, an officer shot at the back of the vehicle as a warning. The car skidded off on a side road, busted through barbed-wire fences, and slid to a halt at the banks of the Holston River. As the troopers came up behind, they saw the car's driver scurrying his way toward the river. One of the officers jumped out of his patrol car and shot his pistol in the air to keep the man from jumping in the river, but it was no use. A distant splash let them know he'd dived into the Holston.

As they made their way to the edge, they heard a voice downriver yelling out "help!" The troopers called in support. All night long, searchers looked for any evidence of the man's whereabouts but to no avail.

When the troopers searched his car, they found around a hundred jars of moonshine. When they ran the plates, the owner's name was Rufus Gunter.

The search for Gunter hit the major newswires. No one was sure if he'd made it to the other side of the river. For weeks, his family and the authorities dragged the river, hoping to find evidence of his whereabouts. On February 12, 1956, six weeks after he disappeared, searchers found his body two miles downriver, lodged under the roots of a sycamore tree.

Two years later, a Connecticut-born film star, interested in making a film about moonshiners and bootleggers, came to the Great Smokies. After interviewing several locals, he wrote a script and began filming a movie on the east side of the mountains, in and around Asheville, North Carolina.

When his movie *Thunder Road* was released, Robert Mitchem was questioned about whether the movie's lead character, a runner named Lucus Doolin, was based on anyone in particular. The actor said no.

Several people have speculated on whose story inspired Mitchem. The great racer and luckless runner Rufe Gunter is as good a candidate as anyone. The timing of his demise and the creation of the script make him a credible choice, even if the facts don't completely match up.

Thunder Road became a cult-classic and favorite throughout the southeast. The legend of Rufe Gunter faded into obscurity.

Who Speaks for Jack?

When it came to American whiskey in the post-war era, Kentucky dominated the market. The state's friendly attitude toward its historic industry helped it jump out well ahead of its pre-Prohibition rivals in Pennsylvania, Maryland, and Tennessee.

By the start of the 1950s, Tennessee whiskey and Jack Daniel's were only distant memories for some old timers. Tennesseans knew Jack was back, but advertising was mostly regional, with only California and New Jersey targeted beyond the southeast. This was on purpose. The little distillery was having a hard enough time keeping up with demand.

Those who knew about Jack Daniel's were fiercely loyal to it. It didn't matter that it cost twenty to thirty percent more than a James E. Pepper, Old Crow, Four Roses, or Ancient Age. To them, this was a rare gem. A whiskey that was sticking to tradition, making a distinctly Tennessee style.

With Kentucky blending their straight Bourbons to stretch their supplies, a mystique built up around the little Tennessee distillery that wouldn't compromise on quality. And those in the know introduced the old-time sour mash whiskey to their friends. Whether it was the green bottle or a black bottle with an additional year of aging, Old No. 7 was something special. It was soon established as a favorite of the old-time gentlemen's clubs. Its scarcity made people want to go out of their way to find it. Restaurants would charge more for it and customers would gladly pay, just for the status of drinking a Jack Daniel's.

That mystique went mainstream in July 1951 when *Fortune Magazine* ran an article called "Rare Jack Daniel's." The story noted that not only did the vice-president prefer Jack Daniel's, but so did Nobel Prize-winning author William Faulkner. It gave a background on the history of Cave Spring Hollow, a place where it was suggested distilling started during the Revolutionary War. Then it talked of how a twelve-year-old boy named Jack learned the craft of distilling not far from there, and of the limestone-filtered water that the cave delivered at the perfect temperature. Then it introduced the audience to little Lynchburg, a town of 390 people. It emphasized how the distillery did things the old-fashioned way and pointed to Jess Motlow as the connection to that heritage. Then it talked of the leaching process and how the locals suggested it removed the headache from the whiskey and made it great, even with less aging.[788] Newspapers across the state and across the country caught Jack Daniel's fever and reprinted many of the details from the article. It seems everyone was fascinated by the little Lynchburg distillery.

Whoever they interviewed for that article gave away the brand's future advertising strategies. This homespun image would become a mainstay of Jack Daniel's advertising. But the first advertisements released by the Motlow brothers launched ads with a Madison Avenue flair. The ads featured sophisticated gentlemen wearing bow ties and double-breasted suits. Perhaps they were trying to appeal to those gentlemen's clubs. But this advertising would soon shift with the hiring of Winton Smith as their National Sales Manager. He moved the focus of the ads to the laborious charcoal mellowing process that set Jack Daniel's apart.

The *Fortune* exposé had taken the name Jack Daniel's to a national audience for the first time since before Prohibition. This led to another article, written by Emmett Gowen, for a men's magazine called *TRUE*. The November 1954 article built on the mystery and lore surrounding the brand. The brand released advertisements to newspapers with teasers from the article in late October titled "Sippin' Whisky and the Shirtsleeve Brothers." Gowen's writing showed he was a genuine lover of the whiskey. He talked of its longevity, the distillery's focus on quality over quantity, Lynchburg's small-town, traditional values that kept it grounded, and the origins of the charcoal mellowing process.

Jack Daniel's could have spent millions on touting their own brand and would never have achieved what these two trusted secondary sources did for them. The magazines took elements of the brand's mystique and supercharged them.

Something else they did was point out the advantage of focusing on little Lynchburg. While Seagrams and Schenley were buying up Kentucky Bourbon brands left and right, Jack's focus on their hometown kept them grounded in the minds of their fans. In 1955, the brand ditched the bow ties and sophistication in their ads and offered a Christmas greeting card advertisement from Lynchburg, Tennessee, population 399. The population number would become a staple of all future ads and would eventually show up on the bottle.

The advertising was almost too good. As the mystique built, sales rose and production fell far behind demand. The company was boxed into a corner. How do you produce more whiskey, yet not compromise on the leaching process, nor lose that "handmade sour mash" reputation?

From One Family to Another

In the years following Prohibition, the General Assembly introduced a basketful of punitive laws to keep the liquor interests from getting out of hand. Tennessee was one of the more aggressive states in this respect, while Kentucky was lenient from a historical perspective.

But there was one law, unique to Kentucky, that Bourbon distillers weren't pleased about. It was a 5 cents per gallon state tax on all whiskey introduced to the state, whether through import or in-state production. Introduced in 1936, it appeased the Baptists at the expense of the smaller Catholic regions that were making profits off of liquor.

While distillers held their tongues on the bill, that tolerance disappeared in February 1956, when the Kentucky House of Representatives raised the tax from 5 cents to 20 cents per gallon. The outcry was so loud, the Senate amended the bill and only raised it to 10 cents. But to the distillers, that was still a 100% increase in the tax rate.

T.W. Samuels Distillery decided the best way to handle it was to go to court and see if they could have the entire law declared unconstitutional. Other distilleries threatened to leave the state if the tax remained at that level. While some talked, the Brown-Forman Company took action and started looking for distilleries out-of-state that could be a fallback, if they needed one.

What they wanted was another family-owned distillery they could purchase. The perfect one was sitting in Lynchburg, Tennessee. Their timing was right. The Motlow brothers were having trouble strategically and financially. Brown-Forman saw an opportunity to both help themselves while taking the Jack Daniel's Distillery to the next level. Before anyone could catch their breath, arrangements were made and the Brown family bought out the Motlows and their secondary investors. Jack Daniel's joined Kentucky legends Old Forester, Early Times, and King Blended Whiskies as part of the company's portfolio. As part of the $20 million sale agreement, the Motlow brothers would stay on to manage the distillery. The marriage of these two family-owned companies benefited both in ways neither could have imagined.

Mellow As Moonlight

When George Dickel Sour Mash Tennessee Whisky was released to the market in the 1960s, it had been well over half a century since the brand distilled whisky at Cascade Hollow. That put the former customer base well into their 70s. So it's hard to blame Tennesseans for forgetting the brand's history.

Thanks to Tennessee Prohibition, Cascade ended up as a Kentucky Straight Bourbon and a Kentucky blended whisky. Produced at A.Ph. Stitzel in Louisville before Prohibition, the Shwab family considered building a new distillery near Pembroke, Kentucky, just after Prohibition, but they eventually sold the business to Schenley Corp in 1936. Schenley put Cascade back on the market with juice made at the George T. Stagg Distillery, today known as the Buffalo Trace Distillery. Then it moved to Lexington, where it spent time at the James E. Pepper Distillery, before ultimately ending up at the Bernheim Distillery after the war.

The whisky was a shell of its former self, never reaching the quality levels achieved by McLin Davis at Cascade Hollow. Before World War II, Cascade became a blended whisky made with at least 70% neutral grain spirit. The "Mellow as Moonlight" slogan remained, but gone was the cold fermenting and charcoal mellowing. By the early 1950s, Geo. A Dickel's Cascade had become a value brand six- and seven-year-old Straight Kentucky Bourbon.

Then, in 1955, the advertising for Cascade evolved. Schenley placed full-page advertisements in newspapers focusing on a secret 1870's formula and the old master George Dickel who crafted it. It appeared Schenley was contemplating a bigger focus on the brand it was producing in Louisville.

In 1957, Schenley President Louis Rosenstiel made a surprise announcement that George A. Dickel was coming back to Tennessee. Rumors developed, suggesting Schenley had attempted to buy Jack Daniel's before Brown-Forman made their deal. Others thought Schenley might leave Kentucky because of the 10 cent tax being declared constitutional.

The plan was to put a new distillery on the land where the old Cascade Hollow Distillery had once stood. The land had a highly valued water source. So much so that in 1935, the nearby towns like Normandy, Bellbuckle and Wartrace set up a gravity water system to tap it for their own communities. The only thing that might hold the distillery plans back was that Coffee County hadn't passed a referendum to allow distilling. That didn't stop Schenley from purchasing the land.

At first, the feedback in Coffee County was all positive. The Tullahoma Chamber of Commerce talked of the significant benefits the distillery would bring to the community. But after the announcement, religious groups began forming in opposition to the distillery. Advocates pressed ahead and collected the signatures necessary to call for a referendum. Unlike Lem's experience in Moore County, Coffee County's magistrates gave up without a fight and a referendum vote was scheduled for August 7, 1958.

Rosenstiel was understandably nervous. A no vote in the referendum would be a disaster. He was determined to get into Tennessee anyway he could. As a backup plan, he secured a piece of land in Moore County, just east of the Jack Daniel Distillery.

On the day of the vote, the measure passed by just under one thousand votes. Coffee became the second Tennessee county to allow legal distilling. And, just like Moore County, they could make liquor, but the county's citizens couldn't legally buy it. Coffee and Moore counties were dry.

The new distillery construction began about a mile from the old site. During the ribbon cutting, a reporter asked Lewis if they were going to bring down the old Cascade Bourbon from Kentucky. He said no. That was a high rye Bourbon, and he had plans for more of a Tennessee corn whisky with just a hint of rye and malted barley. They would also go back to charcoal mellowing. The brand name would honor the company founder, George Dickel.

Ralph Dupps was brought in to supervise construction and manage the plant. To bring in some revenue, he released a short-aged 100-proof corn whisky called Pride of Tennessee. It was labeled as "Sour Mash Tennessee Mountain Whisky." His promise was not to release George Dickel Tennessee Sour Mash Whisky until it was properly aged. The first bottles didn't hit the market until 1963. To create an inviting atmosphere, George Dickel offered a free official tour of the plant on weekdays.

As the new George Dickel whisky hit the market, Ralph began promoting the things he felt set his whisky apart. Through articles in the paper, he established his own lore surrounding "stubborn" George. The new George Dickel character inherited much of the McLin Davis legacy, including the discovery of cool temperature fermentation by the light of the moon. But he was also perfectly aligned with Ralph's vision for the brand. He correctly noted that Cascade was one of the most sought-after whiskies prior to Prohibition. The rest was all part of remaking Tennessee whisky history for a younger generation, something the makers of Jack and George felt they had carte blanche to do.

For the rest of the 1960s, Dickel built up the founder's legacy story and image with campaigns featuring special powder horn decanters. They also established the Old No. 12 brand toward the end of the decade, promoting that they actually charcoal mellowed before and after placing the spirit in the barrel.

While the Tennessee whisky market was small, it was hard to deny the large competitor down the road in Lynchburg. Dickel embraced their position in the market. In one of their more curious advertisements, they tipped their cap to their competitors. The ad featured several bottles of Jack Daniel's with one bottle of George Dickel standing apart. It asked, "What do you give a Jack Daniel's drinker for Father's Day?" In other words, maybe it was time to give another Tennessee whisky a try.

Allocation

Walk into liquor stores around the world today and there are sure to be several bottles of Jack Daniel's on the shelf. With that large supply, it may be hard to believe that at one time, Jack Daniel's Old No. 7 at 90 proof was a rare and coveted whiskey.

It was all because of the distillery's limited output, fanciful promotion through major magazines, the buzz surrounding it, and a growing mystique. The brand was so revered that a newspaper reporter named Ben A. Green felt compelled to write the book *Jack Daniel's Legacy* about the founder's life. Released in 1967, the biography romanticized the story of young Jack with details coming from the *Fortune* and *TRUE* magazine articles, and oral tradition. The people he interviewed were related to or had friendships with Jack Daniel, Lem Motlow, Dan Call, Bill Hughes, and others. The cover featured the marble statue Lem had erected in 1941 in front of the Cave Spring. For the next 35 years, Green's book was considered the definitive resource for the history of the brand and for Tennessee whiskey. It's an entertaining read and great for marketing, but the lines are fuzzy between what is fact, what is folklore, and what is creative license. Many critical pieces of its timeline don't hold up under the light of scrutiny, which is to be expected in something that hinges so much on oral tradition. Still, it is an eye-opening work. And it shows the power the Jack Daniel's brand had in the 1960s. After all, how many 19th-century distillers have biographies written about them?

The tone of Jack Daniel's advertisements showed their self-confidence. After promoting Lynchburg and charcoal mellowing in the early 1950s, Brown-Forman shifted the ads into an embracing of the distillery's shortcomings. They knew there were fans of the brands who couldn't get their hands on the whiskey because of the limited supply. They scapegoated their charcoal mellowing process but also implied its importance. "We'd rather ask for your patience than lose your respect for Jack Daniel's." They informed readers they were trying to increase capacity, but they couldn't sacrifice quality. They'd turned a perceived issue into a positive. They even asked people to forgive their bartenders for not having Jack

Daniel's on hand--it wasn't their fault. It was a brilliant campaign. It stressed the commitment to quality. It tested people's trust in the brand, but also verified that the trust was genuine.

At the same time, they continued running advertisements featuring that always-included Lynchburg's population of 399. Then in 1960, showing they were keeping up with the census (somewhat loosely), the population dropped to 384. It would be interesting to know how many people called the distillery or asked when they visited what happened to those fifteen people. That connection to the town might have been the reason so many people visited the distillery. They didn't advertise tours: People just stopped by to check the place out. It's amazing to consider this when realizing how far off the beaten path Lynchburg really is.

Until 1964, visitors might have caught a glimpse of distillery manager Lem "Big Hyde" Tolley hard at work. For twenty-three years, he had carried on the tradition of making Jack Daniel's. One man who worked alongside him was Jess C. Gamble. Jess was up in age, but Winton Smith wanted to honor his commitment to the company, so he gave Jess a brief two years to guide the distillery when Big Hyde retired.[789] It wasn't long before another legendary distiller, Frank Bobo, took the reins--he would go on to oversee production for twenty-two years.

As the 1970s progressed, veterans returned from Vietnam, inflation went out of control, there was an oil embargo, and America saw its first president resign. Bourbon and Scotch were falling out of favor and experiencing the early stages of a depression. People were slowly making their way to clear spirits like vodka and gin. Yet the strategy of "always leave them wanting more" was perfectly timed for Jack Daniels. While other distilleries were trying to invent lighter whiskies to compete with clear spirits, Jack Daniel's stayed with the tried and true.

There were attempts to increase production, but every time they did, they found the demand growing even stronger. Between 1977 and 1978, demand skyrocketed, prices jumped, and shortages became national news. All of the spent grain the distillery was producing and selling to farmers caused a cattle boom.

Dickel too was having a hard time keeping up with demand. There were only two distilleries in Tennessee, but for the moment, both were riding high.

Chapter 29

PLAYED TO PERFECTION

The Great Hi-Jacking

It was the perfect setup. There, by the Jack Daniel's Distillery, sat a truck trailer loaded down with more than 1,250 cases of allocated Jack Daniel's Old No. 7. It was the most coveted major label whiskey in the States. To James Ervin and his partner James Burnette, what sat before them was the thieving opportunity of a lifetime. That whiskey was worth a ton of money on the black market.

They were well prepared. James had secured a truck tractor built to haul this kind of 63-foot aluminum trailer. He also had an insider, Robert, who worked as a dispatcher for the trucking company that serviced the distillery. He'd been told the distillery would fill a trailer on Thursday night and a driver would arrive early the next morning to pick it up.

It was July 27, 1972, one day after a full moon, so night vision was good enough to avoid using flashlights. Adrenaline was running high. When they hitched to the trailer, both men pumped a fist in the air in silent celebration. Now all they had to do was quietly get away. The loudest noise was the sound of the truck's air brakes releasing. After that, the sound of the engine humming grew quieter and quieter as the thieves made their way out of Lynchburg and deep into the night.

The next morning, the truck driver shook his head, wondering where his morning pick up was. He checked in with the dispatcher to make sure he had the right instructions. He was told the trailer should be there. But where?

The FBI was called in to search for the missing booze. It wouldn't be easy to find. It wasn't a Jack Daniel's truck, so it didn't have obvious logos on it. Teams were alerted in Georgia, Tennessee, Kentucky, and North Carolina. All day Friday and into Saturday, law enforcement was on high alert.

Then, late in the afternoon on Saturday, Knoxville law enforcement got a tip. There was an abandoned 63-foot aluminum trailer sitting outside of a warehouse on Walker Boulevard. When the police arrived, they had warrants to search the building. When they opened the doors, there sat case after case of Old No. 7.

It took weeks for the federal investigators to gather all the names and sift through all the clues. When they went to make arrests, they talked one conspirator into giving up his friends for a lesser sentence. He gave the authorities all the information he could. Soon, more arrests were made. Twelve were charged, but one man, James Ervin, was already sitting in a Georgia jail charged with an unrelated crime.

Just days before Christmas, the accused heard the guilty verdict. Ten of the conspirators were charged, including James Ervin who was given nine years in prison while James Burnette received eleven. The dispatcher was the only one not given jail time, he got three years probation.

In an era when plane hijacking seemed to be a weekly occurrence, Jack seemed like the perfect name for a stolen whiskey. It also made sense from a value standpoint. Like Pappy Van Winkle today, Jack Daniel's was a revered product. It would be easy to sell on the black market. And 1,250 cases would make for a lot of profit. Unlike the Pappygate scandal of the early 21st century, when a worker slowly relieved a distillery of its prized whiskey, this caper would go down quickly. Thanks to astute law enforcement, the great hi-Jacking was quickly resolved.

Whiskey Music Capital of the World

In the modern whiskey world, there are quite a few celebrities endorsing brands, investing in brands, and building distilleries. Athletes and actors are coming out of the woodwork, taking advantage of the 21st-century whiskey boom. Yet the most natural fit for whiskey has always been music and musicians. And Tennessee's status as both a music center and whiskey center makes it the ideal place for a union between the two.

The first music man in Tennessee to earn a reputation with whiskey was the original country music star, Jimmie Rodgers. A brakeman for the railroad, he took to playing gigs whenever and wherever he could. When his doctor diagnosed him with tuberculosis, he moved to the drier climates around Asheville, North Carolina. There he would pick up whiskey as a medicinal cure. When he heard that Ralph Peer, a well-respected recording engineer from Victor Talking Machine Company, was going to be in Bristol, Tennessee, he tried to talk his band into making a record. But they broke up thanks to an argument over what the band should be called. Jimmie went alone and recorded songs featuring only his voice and guitar. Those recordings would lead to further recordings, and Jimmie became a sensation.

Alcohol became a companion of Jimmie's during Prohibition. In those days, a prescription was required to purchase whiskey. He used his illness to keep a fresh supply of spirits around. Eventually whiskey made it into one of his songs, "Gambling Barroom Blues". But Jimmie drank too much and that hard drinking mixed with his tuberculosis claimed his life at thirty-three.

Jimmie was a tremendous influence on another groundbreaking musician. A young bluesman, Robert Johnson, counted Rodgers' "Waiting on a Train" as one of his all-time favorite songs.

Like Jimmie, Robert had a hard life. Things weren't too bad at first. Although his mother had abandoned him, leaving him with his stepfather, he spent his first few years in a loving home in Memphis. His adopted family encouraged his love for music and he attended one of the best schools in the city. But after his mother remarried, she took Robert from his happy home into the Mississippi Delta with a new stepfather. He went from the energy and vibrance of Memphis to the life of a sharecropper.

Isolated, Robert channeled his energies into music any way he could. His first instrument was a set of strings on the side of a barn. When his sister bought him a guitar, he went to a local juke joint to display his talent. But the music he played was passé and the other performers thought his skills were average.

Frustrated, Robert ran off to Southern Mississippi to search for his real father. There he met a bluesman who helped him hone his skills. Robert took advantage of his abnormally long fingers to develop a revolutionary style that mimicked the boogie-woogie music he used to play on the piano. When he returned home to the Delta, he went back to the juke joint and blew the crowd and other musicians away. The transformation led some to question how such a mediocre talent had become a genius in such a short amount of time. The legend of Robert Johnson selling his soul to the devil at the crossroads was born.

Robert spent hard years working bars and juke joints throughout the south, drinking plenty of whiskey and moonshine along the way. His doctors told him to slow down and to stop drinking because of ulcers. On his next trip, he spent time in Greenville, Mississippi. There was a woman there that he'd become romantically involved with. The only problem was, she was the wife of the owner of a juke joint where he was performing. One night, while preparing for his evening performance, she gave him a bottle of whisky to drink. Unbeknownst to her, it was tainted hooch. Her husband had put a mild poison in the bottle to make Robert sick. But the combination of the ulcer and the poison killed the bluesman. He was only 27.

During his brief life, Robert had a couple of recording sessions that preserved his music. Mostly, however, the world ignored his music. But then British musicians like Keith Richards, Eric Clapton, and Jimmy Page fell under his influence. Much of Robert's influence is still heard today in bluesy hard rock. Rock musicians not only learned from his musical style, many also picked up his hard-drinking ways.

Whiskey has also been an inspiration for instruments and instrumentation. Poor country musicians would find anything they could use to play music. In Memphis, the whiskey jug became a rhythmic and melodic centerpiece of a craze known as jug band music. And, to pay homage to his favorite whiskey, Van Halen's long-time bassist Michael Anthony played a bass guitar shaped like a Jack Daniel's bottle.

Then there were the stage and backstage whiskey influences. Country legend Hank Williams not only sang about "Honky Tonk Blues", he and his friend Ernest Tubb were quite friendly with the bottle on stage and behind it. Like Robert Johnson, whiskey would lead to an untimely demise for Hank.

When rock bands started putting on expensive arena shows, to make sure promoters thoroughly read the contracts, they added interesting and unique backstage requirements. Van Halen requested a certain color M&M's, while the Rolling Stones and several other bands requested bottles of Jack Daniel's Black Label.

Merle Haggard became synonymous with George Dickel after they sponsored his tours. Eventually hard-drinker George Jones would join him on that tour. Merle would also introduce the Dickel brand to Willie Nelson, John Mellencamp and the other musicians supporting FarmAid in 1985. George A. Dickel promoted FarmAid's mission of helping America's farmers and proceeds from Merle's concerts were used to support the organization.

The number of songs written about whiskey or because of whiskey are endless. "White Lightnin'" by George Jones and Steve Earle's "Copperhead Road" are songs about moonshine. "Copperhead Road" became the theme song for the Discovery Channel's reality show *Moonshiners*. The Doors' "Alabama Song (Whisky Bar)", "Whiskey Bent and Hell Bound" by Hank Williams, Jr., Van Halen's "Take Your Whiskey Home", Thin Lizzy's "Whiskey In a Jar", "Whiskey On The Rocks" by AC/DC, "I Drink Alone" by George Thorogood, and Willie Nelson's "Whiskey River" are just a few examples of straight whiskey songs.

The most famous brand in whiskey songs has to be Jack Daniel's. There's "Jack Daniel's Old No. 7" by Jerry Lee Lewis, "Jack Daniel's If You Please" by

David Allan Coe, "Jack Daniel's" by Miranda Lambert and brand superfan Eric Church, "Jack Daniel's You Lied To Me Again" by Ray Stevens, and Ronnie Dunn's "That's Why They Make Jack Daniel's", again just to name a few.

One of the earliest songs about a specific brand of Tennessee whiskey came from the Country Music Hall of Fame songwriting duo of Felice and Boudleaux Bryant. Known for writing the Everly Brothers hits "Bye, Bye, Love," "All I Have To Do Is Dream," and "Wake Up Little Susie," they also penned the song "Rocky Top," which became the University of Tennessee's unofficial fight song in the 1970s. But in 1964, their contribution to the whiskey world was a song about good "Old George Dickel." Recorded by Texan Bob Luman. It promoted the spirit as a fine remedy for your ills. It wasn't a big hit, but it may have inspired songwriters to look to Tennessee spirits for inspiration.

The best-known modern song about spirits from the Volunteer State is the song simply known as "Tennessee Whiskey". Today, music fans are well-acquainted with the country blues version by Chris Stapleton. Released in 2015, it was a remake of a song written in 1981 by Country Music Hall of Famer Dean Dillon and the late Linda Hargrove. Originally, Dean offered the song to George Strait, who was busy working on his first album. When George turned it down, one of the outlaws of country music, David Allen Coe, recorded it instead. Coe's version never cracked the Top 40, but legendary country star George Jones liked it and made it a Top 10 hit. Both of the early versions were uptempo. Stapleton embraced the word "smooth" in his sultry styling of it.

One reason Tennessee whiskey gets so much musical attention is thanks to Nashville's status as Music City U.S.A. It earned that status thanks to the success of the Grand Ole Opry. But Jack Daniel's found its biggest musical influence in a crooner from New Jersey.

The Chairman of the Board

No one knows with one-hundred percent certainty when Frank Sinatra fell in love with Jack Daniel's, but when he did, he fell hard.

He was one of the first advocates of a whiskey brand since Prohibition. And he did it after a long period of whiskey avoidance by big stars. In the 1930s and 1940s, there was still a stigma around whiskey. In fact, whenever whiskey was shown in movies, it was usually associated with organized crime or the town drunk. The safest vice to promote in those days was smoking.

During this time, Sinatra was a young star singing first for the Harry James Orchestra and then Tommy Dorsey's Orchestra. While mostly an equal-opportunity drinker, he grew a fondness for Chivas Regal blended Scotch.

There is speculation that Frank's first dalliance with Jack Daniel's came in the early 1940s. Some credit Jackie Gleason as the man who introduced "Ol' Blue Eyes" to Jack Daniel's in New York. But if he did, Jackie definitely had some inside information, as the brand wasn't advertised in New York until the early 1950s.

The early '50s weren't kind to Sinatra. He was down on his luck. His transition from a young heartthrob to the mainstream wasn't going so well, and his personal life was a mess. After divorcing his first wife Nancy to marry Hollywood sex symbol Ava Gardner, his career hit the skids. He lost his recording and acting contracts. And with Ava constantly on the road, Sinatra was down in the dumps.

After a couple years of self-pity, in 1953, he'd had enough and threw himself into his acting career. He auditioned for the most demanding dramatic role of his career, the part of Maggio in *From Here to Eternity*. His performance won him an Oscar for Best Supporting Actor and put him back in demand. Suddenly, he was in a Hollywood recording studio at Capitol Records, making some of his most iconic music.

As Sinatra integrated with the Hollywood lifestyle, he became the life of the party. He was part of Humphrey Bogart's group of friends that Bogie's wife, Lauren Bacall, referred to as the Rat Pack. In 1957, when Humphrey Bogart died and Ava Gardner divorced him, Sinatra and some of the Rat Pack went off to Las Vegas to work the clubs. Those members included Dean Martin, Sammy Davis, Jr., Joey Bishop and Peter Lawford. For a time, each worked in separate hotels, but in 1960, they started working together at the Sands. By this time, it was rare to see Frank on stage without a Jack Daniel's in his hand. The crowd knew it was Jack Daniel's because he'd talk about it. He was basically an unpaid spokesperson.

One day, Sinatra grew frustrated that he wasn't able to get his beloved Jack Daniels. His assistant Jilly Rizzo told him he had a cousin who knew Angelo Lucchesi, the brand's only salesperson. Sinatra asked for Angelo's number and called him directly. Angelo, a Memphian who had fallen into the job after a chance meeting with Hap Motlow in Nashville, knew that voice on the other end of the line. A bit in shock, he told Sinatra not to worry, he would get him some Old No. 7. From that day forward, no matter how low the reserves were, Sinatra always got his supply. The two became lifelong friends.

Sinatra returned the favor in May 1976 during a performance at the Grand Ole Opry. In between songs, he pulled out a square bottle with a black label and poured whiskey into his glass. With that, he raised the glass to toast the audience and thanked Tennessee for both Andy Jackson and Jack Daniels.

Sinatra remained fiercely loyal to the whiskey to the end and beyond. Jack Daniel's was loyal to him as well. Angelo was at Sinatra's funeral to pay his respects. Upon his request, several items made their way into Sinatra's casket: a Zippo lighter, a roll of dimes in case he needed to call someone, and a bottle of Old No. 7 Jack Daniels.

The Tale of Two Distilleries

While Bourbon languished in the 1980s and 1990s, George Dickel felt sympathy pains as the brand languished under several corporate ownership changes. In 1987, Guinness PLC, which had become a large player in the whisky industry after acquiring brands like Johnnie Walker and Dewars, acquired Schenley Industries, Inc. After being promoted through the association with Merle Haggard, the brand got lost in the shuffle at Guinness.

The one thing that would remain consistent at Dickel was its distilling. Jennings "Dave" Backus took the reins as master distiller in 1978 and produced Dickel's No. 8 and No. 12 "sippin' whisky" for the rest of the century.

Visitors to Cascade Hollow continued to be treated to free tours on weekdays, although neither George nor Jack could provide samples because of their dry county status. They also couldn't sell bottles until Moore and Coffee counties held successful referendums in the fall of 1994. But, for the distillery at Cascade Hollow, the celebration over the law change was short-lived. When Guinness went through another merge in 1997, George Dickel once again was on the move. They would fall under the United Distillers division of the newly formed Diageo. The lack of advertising and support continued, and, in 1999, the distillery closed down its free tours along with its visitor's center and gift shop.

It was a curious time to shut down a visitor's attraction. Jack Daniel's was booming with visitors that year and the Kentucky Distillers Association had just launched the Kentucky Bourbon Trail. Whiskey tourism was just getting started. But supporting the free tour was becoming an expense Diageo couldn't justify.

The free tours in Lynchburg continued, even as the Motlows stepped away from operations. One reason their tours were successful was thanks to the seven-day-a-week schedule, versus Dickel's weekday-only schedule. The tours included a walk around the distillery and a photo-op by the white marble statue of the founder in front of his cave. To make up for not being able to serve whiskey, the distillery offered visitors an ice-cold glass of lemonade.

One thing Jack Daniel's hadn't done since the days of Lem Motlow was release a new whiskey. That changed on the last day of September 1988. At a launch party attended by fans and Lynchburg citizens alike, the brand introduced an elevated whiskey meant to compete with premium spirits. They called it Gentleman Jack, and what made it different was its additional run through sugar maple charcoal and an ABV (40% or 80 proof) that matched international competitors.

It wouldn't be the first time the modern Jack Daniel's would come in a lower proof. Just a year earlier, they had shifted Black Label from 90 to 86 proof. Then, in 1995, Jack Daniel's made a big push into the international market. The world standard was 40% ABV and Jack Daniel's was having to make two proofs of whiskey. In 2004, they dropped Old No. 7 to 80 proof to create a standard. Any outcry fell on deaf ears as the brand expanded across the globe and started to challenge Johnnie Walker as the world's number-one selling whisky brand.

Meanwhile, fans of higher-proof Jack Daniel's were taken care of thanks to Jimmy Bedford, the man who stepped in after the retirement of Frank Bobo in 1988. For his tenth anniversary as master distiller, Bedford went on tour around the country promoting Jack Daniel's new Single Barrel Reserve and Jack Daniel's 1904 Gold Medal Series. They released the Single Barrel Reserve in 1997 and picked up on a trend started by brands like Brown-Forman's own President's Choice and Blanton's Single Barrel. These uniquely individual expressions told the tale of the barrel and gave the consumer a higher 94 proof point for a more robust whiskey-drinking experience. The Gold Medal Series was a series of commemorative bottles released annually in uniquely shaped bottles. They sold this series at the old standard of 90 proof.

It wasn't just the whiskey and marketing that was evolving. In June 2000, Brown-Forman completed a major revamping of the Jack Daniel Visitor's Center. To celebrate the 150th birthday of the founder, they brought the Jack Daniel marble statue that had stood guard in front of the cave for 59 years inside and a bronze lifesize statue of Jack Daniel was placed in front of the cave.

They held a massive free birthday celebration in the September of that year, featuring Jakob Dylan's Wallflowers and Third Eye Blind, who performed a concert for attendees. The show was free, so the company kept the identities of the bands a secret. It was the first time since Prohibition they could legally serve Jack Daniel's at the distillery. Thanks to it being a free private function, each adult guest was provided with two pours of Jack Daniel's.

By the end of the 20th century, Jack Daniel's and George Dickel had masterfully built the history of Tennessee whiskey around their brands. With a new century dawning, this history was bound to be challenged, but by whom and when? The ghosts of Tennessee's whiskey past would have to have some patience. And the future stars of Tennessee whiskey would have a bumpy road to bringing the industry back. A final chapter in the renewal of Tennessee whiskey's legacy was finally at hand.

Chapter 30

BLAZING A NEW TRAIL

False Starts

For decades, no one seemed to question why there were only three counties open to distilling in Tennessee. And even less asked why Lincoln County was open for distilling, but didn't have a distillery. People had become comfortable with Tennessee whiskey just being two brands. So why wasn't there an attempt to open a third distillery?

Truth is, there were several attempts to establish a third distillery in Tennessee and the first one actually succeeded--at least, for a while.

The story of the first attempt at a third distillery goes back to July 1958. That's when Schenley attempted to enter the state by opening a facility at Cascade Hollow. Not willing to lose his opportunity if Coffee County residents balked at the proposal, Lewis Rosenstiel had the company purchase one hundred acres of land along Turkey Creek Road in Moore County. When Coffee County citizens approved the building of a distillery, the need for the Turkey Creek Road property disappeared.

Shortly after the release of George Dickel Sour Mash Tennessee Whisky in October 1964, Lewis thought of another use for the Turkey Creek Road property. It was an age when blended Canadian and Scotch whiskies were overtaking American spirits. Schenley thought the time might be right for a Tennessee blended whisky. In 1966, playing upon the pride the area had for their Tennessee Walking Horses, Schenley built a distillery on Turkey Creek Road and named it the Tennessee Walker Distillery.

They named the spirit Tennessee Walker: Tennessee Walking Horse Brand Blended Whisky. The whisky contained 61.5% neutral grain spirits, and they sold it at 86.6 proof. Whether the facility distilled or just blended sourced spirits is unknown. The box the bottle came in promoted the whisky's use of a unique shale rock "up-hill water" that created a breakthrough in blending and distilling. From there, it's marketing attempted to push it into competition with Irish, Canadian, and Scotch whiskies. Schenley bragged it was Tennessee's first blended whisky and a sticker on the bottle said "Xported from Tennessee." One of the great mysteries presented in the marketing is a disclaimer at the bottom of the box. It said the whisky brand had "no connection to any other distilling company of a similar name." Perhaps the company thought having a brand with the word Walker and blended whisky might confuse Johnnie Walker fans. Then again, maybe that's what they wanted people to do.

Schenley focused whisky sales on two test markets. The first ads hit throughout South Florida in May 1967 and a year later it was picked up by a distributor in San Antonio, Texas. But after that, all traces of the product disappeared.

Two years later, another distillery plan surfaced as Tullahoma realtor and building contractor Earl M. Shahan began restoring an abandoned mill. He filed a charter with the state for Tennessee Sour Mash Whiskey, Inc. and gave an interview to two newspapers talking about Ledford's Mill and his plans for the distillery. But finances were tight in the early 1970s and the distillery never materialized.

In the mid-1970s, a rumor developed that a big player was looking to bring distilling back to legendary Lincoln County. As with Coffee and Moore, the citizens of Lincoln needed to pass a referendum to allow a distillery in their county. But there wasn't a wave of enthusiasm in the area. By the end of 1975, there were enough signatures for a referendum, but it wasn't until August 1976 that the vote was held. By that time, the outside interest had cooled. Then the citizens upset any chance of a distillery being built by voting against it. Undaunted, the business community continued to seek outside interest and pressed on with getting a second referendum. In June 1979, the measure passed. But by that time, outside of Jack Daniel's, the demand for American whiskey was low, so any investment interest waned.

It would take two more decades before Lincoln County drew interest again. But this time, it wasn't from some large corporation looking to leverage the name and waters of the famous whisky county. It was a telecom worker from Memphis who was using his wife's canning pot and a makeshift condenser to see if he could make rum. His distillate received rave reviews, so he started looking for a place to open a distillery. Lincoln County was about to get into the rum business.

And Then There Were Three

When Phil Prichard got into the spirits-making business, it wasn't an overly obvious occupation for him to undertake. Growing up in Memphis, he moved to Colorado in the 1970s and then to Vermont in the early 1980s. There he met his wife Connie, and the two invested in a small Christmas store in Upstate New York. Phil loved horses, and he became a breeder and imported forty Norwegian Fjord horses for his farm in the late 1980s. But in 1993, a downturn in the economy and increasing area taxes sent Phil and Connie back to Shelby County and Memphis. That is when Phil took a job in the telecom industry. He wasn't sure that was the industry he wanted to stay in, so he kept his eyes open for other opportunities.

Then one day, he and his cousin Mack got into a discussion about the possibility of distilling locally grown sorghum molasses and making rum. This was when Phil got out Connie's canning pot and tried his hand at distilling in his kitchen. When Connie came home and found him hard at work, she asked him what he was up to. When she sampled what he was making, the rum impressed her. So Phil put some in a one-gallon barrel to see what would happen. He gave a sample to an old high school friend that was working in the wholesale liquor industry, who told Phil it was some of the best rum he'd tasted. Then he asked Phil when he was going to build a distillery.

As Phil began putting together a business plan, he realized the federal government didn't recognize sorghum spirits as rum. He started researching the history of rum and learned it was the drink of choice of pre-Revolutionary War America. If sorghum was out, then instead he would work to mimic the spirits that were being produced in New England in the 18th century.

As for the location of his distillery, putting it in Shelby County would require him to get signatures from ten percent of the county's registered voters. This was a daunting task for a small micro-distillery. When he put his feelers out, Coffee County seemed interested, but the deal fell through over zoning issues. While a temporary defeat, it turned out to be the best thing Phil could have hoped for. While Coffee County was wooing Phil, they had publicized his plans for a distillery in newspapers across the state. When Coffee was out, several other counties contacted Phil.

The one that stood out was Lincoln County. At one time, Phil had scouted out land there for a horse farm, so he was already familiar with it. What made it the most attractive was its already-passed referendum and a location that sounded like it was perfectly suited for a distillery. Through a contact, he was told about an old 1939 schoolhouse that had also served as the Kelso Community Center. After touring it, Phil realized it had everything he needed for a distillery, including plenty of space for a visitor's center. He made the deal to acquire it, then bought two copper pot stills from a Vermont vodka distillery and ordered molasses from Louisiana. After applying for his license in August 1999, he started off the new millennium with Tennessee's first modern craft distillery.

When Phil's first batches of spirits hit the market in March 2002, there were some odd looks when he said he was selling Tennessee rum, but it soon caught on. Phil spent three years on the road evangelizing about the quality of his rum and its historical significance. Soon he had bottles of Prichard's Tennessee Rum in twenty states. His micro-distillery had beaten the odds, and his success showed future entrepreneurs that Tennessee was no longer just the realm of two big brands——small distillers could make it too.

Following in the path of his five-times great grandfather Benjamin Prichard, Phil soon started distilling up his own style of Tennessee whiskey.

The Great Renewal

The first decade of the 21st century saw a growing interest in craft distilling. Nationally, the growth was slow, with less than one hundred in operation by 2007. Most of those distilleries were making vodka, gin, and brandy, but a few dabbled in single malts, Bourbons, and rye whiskeys. Yet to most Americans, whiskey was something you consumed in cocktails or knocked back, like in old Westerns. Ordering a glass of neat whiskey still seemed like something Grandpa did back in the old days.

Then, during the summer of 2007, the cable network AMC launched a television series called *Mad Men*. Based on the lives of 1950s Madison Avenue advertising executives, each episode featured multiple pours of Scotch and Canadian whisky. The series was an instant hit and suddenly drinking neat whiskey was cool again.

Around this time, a veteran U.S. Army infantry officer and West Point graduate named Paul Tomaszewski returned from tours in the Middle East with the idea of opening a craft distillery in Clarksville, Tennessee. As the economy soured in 2008, Paul decided it was a great time to build his dream while also providing jobs. In the process, he hoped to create something distinctly different from Jack Daniel's.

He started his petition drive in the summer of 2008, but things quickly bogged down on his way to the ten percent of signatures he needed. His desire to bring jobs to the area was bumping up against its religious sensibilities. When the drive for signatures became daunting, Paul set the task aside and looked north to Kentucky for better opportunities.

It turns out Paul was just one of several future distillers that were kicking around the idea of getting Tennessee on the craft-distillery map. Two entrepreneurs, Darek Bell and Andrew Webber, registered Corsair Artisan, LLC with the state in January 2008. Their target for a distillery was Nashville, but the barrier to entry was high and so, like Paul, they went north into Kentucky, setting up shop in Bowling Green. By the end of the year, they established the distillery and began producing rum, gin, and distillate for Bourbon.

During that fateful year, Darek was attending an event with former state Representative Mike Williams. Mike, too, was interested in bringing craft distilling to Tennessee and had been working on a bill to open up distilling in the state. His advantage was being an insider who had experienced the political battles in the General Assembly. The pair was introduced to Heath Clark, a healthcare attorney from Murfreesboro.

Heath had a growing interest in becoming a distiller, but his life was busy and he didn't have the time to fight under the current rules. He decided to try a different approach. When he was introduced to a powerful state senator, Bill Ketron, he told the senator of his desire to open a distillery and the barriers in his way. Intrigued, Ketron asked him what he needed to succeed. Heath talked of the labor-intensive and costly process of getting petitions signed, and how the distillers then had to hope people would come out to vote in the special elections. What he wanted to do was circumvent that system by automatically opening up counties to distilling that had already voted by referendum for package stores and liquor-by-the-drink. Heath argued that if a community was accepting of liquor sales, opening a distillery would benefit the county by adding jobs. Impressed with the idea, the senator put Heath to the task of writing the bill.

Meanwhile, Jim Massey, an entrepreneur with a love for agriculture and a lifelong interest in distilling, was chatting with legendary Senator Thelma Harper of the 19th District when she mentioned Heath Clark's bill. When he approached Heath, Jim learned that Mike Williams was combining forces with Heath on his bill. Jim offered up his lobbying skills, having once worked for Senator Douglas Henry, the chairman of the Senate Finance Ways and Means Committee. His father had also spent twenty-five years as the head of the Tennessee Wine and Spirits Retailers Association. A perfect storm of distilling and political know-how was forming.

There was another storm in play at that time--the Great Recession. It was early 2009 and jobs were growing scarce. By the time the bill was written, Tennessee's unemployment rate had doubled in just a year to 10.1%. The jobs aspect of the bill attracted Rutherford County's State Representative Joe Carr, who jumped on board as the sponsor of the House bill. As a farmer, he saw the positive impact it would have on the state.

As usual, there were objections. The main issue was the bill not allowing the people to have a say in introducing distilling to their county. But those fighting for the bill's approval argued that it should appease religious factions because the local government would still have the final say, thanks to the need for zoning approval. In East Tennessee, there was a concern that legalizing distilling could encourage a rash of illicit moonshine production. And as always, there were the party squabbles. The House sponsor Joe Carr was a polarizing figure. His victory in the last election gave the Republicans control of both houses of the General Assembly for the first time since their pseudo control as part of the Fusionists in the early 1910s. As if channeling the past, objections to the current bills sounded eerily similar to those of that teetotalling bygone era.

Then the bill was put in jeopardy. House Judiciary chairperson Kent Coleman, also from Rutherford County, added an amendment to the House bill to reintroduce the need for a referendum. But the Senate bill without the amendment had already passed nineteen to five. The dispute between the House and Senate versions dragged on for a month. Time was running out. The General Assembly term was quickly coming to a close. But days before the session ended, a joint House and Senate Conference Committee removed the referendum amendment in the House version. The bill passed the House fifty-eight to twenty-six, and the Senate validated it with an eighteen to nine vote for passage. By this point, the only thing that was needed to open up distilling to nearly half of the state was a signature from Democratic Governor Phil Bredesen. There was some concern he would take his frustrations over the loss of the legislature on the bill. But there was a sigh of relief among the future distillers of Tennessee when he signed the bill into law two days later, on June 29, 2009.

It had been 99 ½ years since the dreaded Manufacturer's Bill extinguished the flames of Tennessee distilling. Finally, nearly half the state was once again a land of opportunity for distillers. Forty-one new counties immediately became eligible.

Part of the compromise of the bill was to allow counties to opt themselves out. One of the counties that took advantage was Hamilton. This left Chattanooga as the only major municipality in the state where distilling was still illegal.

Ready. Set. Go!

Weeks after the governor signed the new manufacturing bill into law, Heath, Darek, Andrew, and Mike turned their attention to business planning and began scouting for land. They were joined by Jim Massey.

Of all the players, Darek and Andrew's Corsair Artisan held the greatest advantage. They had already gone through the federal permitting process for their Bowling Green, Kentucky facility. They struck a deal to take over the Yazoo Brewing Tap Room at the historic Marathon Motor Works building on the edge of downtown. The Corsair facility opened in May 2010, becoming Nashville's first legal distillery since Prohibition and the fourth in the state.

It was an important milestone in the development of the craft-distilling industry in Tennessee. Not only did Corsair introduce their own unique styles of whiskey to the state, they soon lent their space out to other distillers wanting to get in on the action. Mike Williams' Tennessee Distilling Company started distilling his Collier & McKeel Tennessee Whiskey there not long after the facility opened, followed by Jim Massey's Fugitive Spirits. After this head start, Mike later established his own facility in Columbia, Tennessee, in 2014. He would pay it forward to many future distillers when he began contract distilling for startups. Heath Clark would eventually get planning approval for a distillery at Thompson Station, south of Nashville. His H. Clark Distillery was in operation by 2014, specializing in making Tennessee gin and a four-grain Tennessee Bourbon on a small flame-fired Portuguese still.

As for the ties to Kentucky, Corsair kept their facility in Bowling Green for several years, finally moving out in 2018. Paul Tomaszewski stayed in the Bluegrass State. In his hunt for property, he found an Amish farm that was up for sale south of Pembroke, in Christian County, Kentucky. It was an area close to where the Shwabs had once considered moving George Dickel just before they sold out to Schenley. After almost a year getting federal permits and state licenses, Paul opened the doors of the distillery and began distilling white dog, which is another name for new make spirit, and what he called black dog, which used corn that was fired in a tobacco barn. Knowing his name would be difficult to pronounce, he named the distillery after his wife, Merry Beth. By November 2009, M.B. Roland was producing spirits and Paul was giving tours to visitors. In 2019, he reconnected with the state of Tennessee when he joined the Old Glory Distillery in Clarksville and Casey Jones Distillery in Kentucky as members of a mini-distillery trail they called the Stateline Tour.

Crafting Tennessee whiskey wasn't the only thing on the minds of the state's future distillers. East Tennessee was abuzz with talks of moonshine.

The illicit spirit came into focus in 2007, when a Cocke County and Maggie Valley, North Carolina moonshiner Marvin "Popcorn" Sutton, was arrested by local authorities after a fire at his home led to the discovery of hundreds of gallons of moonshine. Placed on probation, Popcorn would soon appear in two separate documentaries, one produced by the History Channel, the other by PBS-TV. Popcorn wasn't shy about attention. He'd written an autobiography years before. His recent arrest and elevated persona drew the attention of the federal authorities. Once again, he was arrested and this time by the ATF after trying to sell white lightning to an undercover agent. When he appeared in court, he pled guilty and the judge sentenced him to eighteen months in prison. Just prior to his incarceration, he was found dead by apparent suicide. The events only increased the buzz around East Tennessee's history with illicit moonshine.

For attorney Joe Baker, distilling moonshine was a family tradition. He had heard the stories all his life and understood the culture. Having grown up around the tourist towns of Gatlinburg and Pigeon Forge, Joe saw an opportunity to give visitors to the Great Smoky Mountains a taste of moonshine culture. With the passage of the new manufacturing law, he and his wife Jessi, who was also an attorney, agreed it was time to set up a distillery. Joe formed a partnership with Tony Breeden and Cory Cottongim and started working on a business plan. Being their first attempt at building a distillery, the group reached out to whisky industry veterans Rob Sherman of Vendome Copper and Brass in Louisville, Kentucky, and Dave Pickerell, who had left Maker's Mark after fourteen years to start his own distillery consulting business. They set up their distillery in Gatlinburg and opened Ole Smoky for visitors in June 2010. Being within a short proximity of the nation's most visited national park didn't hurt. Suddenly, they were having a hard time finding enough jars for their moonshine.

It wasn't long before more distilleries dotted the Tennessee landscape. In Cannon County, Billy Kaufman, a farmer who owned a historic farm with its own moonshining history, decided it was time to go the old route and got the signatures he needed to get a referendum. When the vote opened the county to distilling, Billy built out Short Mountain Distillery, looking to give visitors more of the country feel of a distillery from his organic farm, while also providing a top-quality dining experience at his restaurant. The distillery opened in March 2012. That year turned out to be a busy one. It saw Southern Pride Distillery take advantage of Lincoln County's long since passed referendum to open without delay in Fayetteville, while in West Nashville, Jeff Pennington and his wife Jenny founded SPEAKeasy Spirits and built Pennington Distilling Co's distillery. Initially, the Penningtons focused on producing their Whisper Creek Tennessee Sipping Cream with spirits provided by Mike Williams. Once their Tennessee whiskey was ready for the market, they branded it as Davidson Reserve. By the end of their first year, they were offering tours of the distillery.

While these new upstarts were lining up to get into the industry, Jack Daniel's said goodbye to Jimmy Bedford with Jeff Arnett taking over as the company's new master distiller. A native of Jackson, Tennessee, Jeff started his business life working for Procter & Gamble in his hometown and spent time as a taster and blender for Folgers Coffee in New Orleans. After ten years with the company, he started looking for opportunities in the automotive industry. Nissan had a plant just south of Nashville and Jeff worked with a headhunter to get him an interview. It was then he was told about a quality-control position available at an area beverage company. He agreed to take an interview with the company, then asked who it was. They told him it was Jack Daniel's.

Jeff was a huge fan of the brand and was also a Tennessee Squire—an invitation-only club for the friends of Jack Daniel's. He jumped at the opportunity.

To that point, Brown-Forman had been content to keep the product line at Jack Daniel's simple. There was Old No. 7, Gentleman Jack, and Single Barrel Select, which joined the lineup in 1997. Jeff's job was to pick barrels for Single Barrel Select. Eventually he worked his way into the job of assistant master distiller under Jimmy Bedford, before being promoted to master distiller in 2008.

When he took the position, Jack Daniel's distribution was well on its way to being in the 170 countries where it is currently sold worldwide. Since the mid-1990s, growth had been the company's focus. Jeff's tenure as master distiller would see the company go from market growth to expanding product offerings. One of his biggest moves was adding rye to the lineup, something Jack Daniel's had never done. During his tenure, the brand expanded from around three labels to at least eleven. Perhaps all the new competition was inspiring the company to try new things.

The growth of the new industry was impressive. By 2012, the lucrative job-creating industry had developed. But the historical legacy of Tennessee spirits remained hidden. What of the long-lost distilleries of Old Lincoln and Old Robertson? Who would remember them? With these new distilleries popping up right and left, it seemed someone was bound to stumble upon one of these old legacies.

Ghosts of Old Robertson

As local parks go, J. Travis Price Park in Springfield has a lot to offer the area's residents. There is a playground where kids can play, fields for baseball and softball, and there are basketball courts. There are also trails for walking and biking, and opportunities for fishing. And on a lazy Sunday, it's an excellent place for a family picnic.

For fans of whiskey history, the park offers another feature, but very few people know about it. In fact, whiskey fans may have stumbled past it hundreds of times, not knowing its historic ties to one of the centers of 19th-century whisky production.

It's the old humble looking two-story cabin that sits in the park. Originally built by Joseph and Nancy Ann Hart in 1796, it became tied to the legacy of Old Robertson when Jordan Stokes and Josephine Brown converted it into the manager's office of the Wartrace Distillery. Purchased by Jordan in 1880, it remained at Wartrace Creek until 1995. A group of local volunteers who saw a need to preserve the historic structure saved it from demolition that year. They moved it two and a half miles northeast to J. Travis Price Park, bordering Sulphur Fork Creek so more people could enjoy it.

While the names Woodard, Brown, Johnson, and Draughon still linger in the area, the memories of Old Robertson's flourishing distilleries and wholesale houses faded with the 1903 Adams Law and the subsequent Manufacturing Bill. Only local historian Kay Baker Gaston, a descendant of the Woodards, took the time to research and write about the area's whisky history. But in 2006 an event occurred that brought Robertson County and its whisky legacy into focus. It started during a family's trip to pick up meat from the family butcher. While stopped to fuel up the car, brothers Andy and Charlie Nelson noticed a historical sign with their last name on it.

The sign sits by a gasoline station in Greenbrier, Tennessee. It tells of Charles Nelson and the distillery he opened nearby in 1870. It touts his standing as the largest producer of sour mash whiskey and fruit brandy in Robertson County's history. Andy and Charlie were curious and wanted to know how they were related to Charles and how big this mysterious distillery really was. Their parents said Charles was their great, great, great, grandfather, but beyond that, they knew little. They realized the butcher they were going to see lived near where the sign said the distillery used to be. When they arrived at his house, they asked him if he knew where the old distillery was. He raised his arm and pointed across the street. There sat an old metal warehouse. They all walked down and noticed there was an old spring house behind the creek and a building up on the hill. It definitely seemed like the remnants of a distillery.

The butcher told them they could learn more if they made their way to the Greenbrier Historical Society. When they arrived, they asked the woman working in the library about the distillery and told them their last name was Nelson. She walked them over to a room that was dedicated to the history of the distillery. There they found two old bottles of Greenbrier Tennessee Whiskey with the original labels on them. They immediately thought, "We should bring this back!"

There were several obstacles in their way. First, this was three years before the changes in the state's manufacturing law, so Robertson County wasn't open to distilling. Second, they needed a lot of money to start a distillery and they were only twenty-two and twenty-six years old, and their college degrees were in philosophy. While searching for money and hearing a lot of "noes," they continued to research the family heritage. Then, they stumbled into a solution. It seems that after Charles Nelson ended his partnership with John Sperry, the latter asked Nelson if he'd help with the branding for his Belle Meade Distillery. The brothers felt like they'd just received permission from their ancestor to source whiskey using that brand. By sourcing, they could raise the money they needed, use the experience to learn about the industry, and prove their worthiness to investors.

Leaning on the advice of Dave Pickerell, they made an agreement with MGP Ingredients of Lawrenceburg, Indiana and used the whiskey they received to blend Belle Meade Bourbon. They released their first batch in March 2012.

Eventually they made enough money to build out their own distillery, and they laid down their first barrel in August 2014. The brothers went with a wheated mashbill, creating a distinct character that would separate them from Dickel's and Daniel's. They released their first bottles of Nelson's Greenbrier Tennessee Whiskey in the fall of 2019. It was the first time in almost 110 years a whiskey bore that name. They kept the family tradition by mimicking the original 20th-century label design and adjusted it to fit modern regulations. They also honored the memory of Louisa Nelson by naming their pot still after her, making a cream liqueur in her name, and creating the Louisa Nelson Award to honor female leaders in Nashville.

The largest producer from the Old Robertson tradition was back in the spotlight. Soon, whiskey fans were asking, "Was Charles Nelson's operation really bigger than Jack Daniel's and George Dickel's in the 19th century?" The reemergence of the brand helped them learn about a legacy that started way back in 1850, when a candle and soap maker left Germany with his family, hoping to find prosperity in America. Not only would his son become Tennessee's largest distiller in the 19th century, Johann Phillip Nelson's great, great, great, great grandsons would be on the forefront of that same industry's resurgence in the 21st century.

Why Not Us?

What seemed like one of the strangest occurrences in Tennessee whiskey's history was the 2009 move by Hamilton County to exclude itself from allowing distilleries within its borders. It was Hamilton County, after all, that was the first to approve package store liquor sales when the Bone Dry Law was put to rest. It was also the only county with massive growth in distilling during the decade before Tennessee prohibition. But in 1939, weeks after Lem Motlow received his distillery charter for the Jack Daniel Distillery, a second planned distillery received their charter. The company Signal Mountain Distilleries planned to establish a distillery in Hamilton County, but a petition and court action doomed the project. And now, almost 75 years later, the decision to opt out of the new law was about to open up another can of worms.

It all started when two college buddies, Joe Ledbetter and Tim Piersant, posted a question on a Facebook group. They asked the community, "Would you drink Chattanooga whiskey?" What came back was an energetic yes. So they established Chattanooga Whiskey Co. with a goal of bringing distilling back to the city. Like the Nelson brothers, they reached out to MGP Ingredients in Indiana to source aged whiskey until they could produce their own.

Joe and Tim sold out of their first shipment within weeks and were looking to add more. But not everyone was happy with an Indiana whiskey being labeled as Chattanooga 1816. The genius of the move was it started conversations. The partners gave interviews and reassured customers they weren't trying to pull the wool over their eyes. They clearly marked the bottles as "Made in Indiana." Whenever anyone asked why they did this, they reminded people that Hamilton County opted out of the new law, and because Chattanooga was beholden to their rules, the company couldn't legally build a distillery in the town. Then they urged people to help them get the law changed. Their openness continued to win them fans. After almost two years, however, there was little movement in Hamilton County.

Once again, Rutherford County legislators Senator Ketron and Representative Carr came to the rescue. A House bill sponsored by Rep. Carr sought to allow city governments to okay distilleries within their borders if they already allowed liquor by the drink and package stores––even if the county they were in denied it. Once again, the debate was heated and shot off fireworks in a way no one expected.

As written, the bill superseded rules in cities and towns with approved distilling. A law meant to help Chattanooga hit Gatlinburg like a ton of bricks. Thanks to the incredible success of Ole Smoky Moonshine Distillery, Joe Baker's wife Jessi put together a team of investors and built a second distillery called Gatlinburg Barrelhouse's Davy Crockett Tennessee Whiskey. It was located just a thousand feet away from Ole Smoky on the main strip known as The Parkway. Soon, a third moonshine business called Sugarlands looked to move in right next door to Ole Smoky's original location. Worried that the family centered town was going to fill up with distilleries and get a reputation, the city commissioners in

Gatlinburg voted to limit the town to four distilleries that had to be at least a thousand feet apart. It allowed them to refuse to grant permission to Sugarlands for their proposed location. But the new state law, as written, overruled the local ordinance.

While no Hatfield's and McCoy's, it did kick up quite a scuffle in the General Assembly. Accusations flew and arguments ensued. As the drama played out, Tim and Joe in Chattanooga were stuck wondering how things had gone so wrong.

Eventually, the sponsor Bill Ketron helped get the bill past the Senate. When it reached the House floor, old wounds festered, creating a heated session, but in the end, the representatives voted to pass it. Finally, Chattanooga Whiskey Co. had the right to get zoning approval and Federal permits. Meanwhile, Ole Smoky got a new neighbor.

Getting a distillery site would prove to be a little more difficult than Chattanooga planned for, but they finally settled into a location directly across from the famed Chattanooga Choo-Choo train station. The plan was to create their own whiskey and eventually drop the Chattanooga 1816 brand. They hired former Samuel Adams brewer Grant McCracken as their head distiller. Using his brewing expertise, the company began its focus on both creating uniquely high malt Bourbons and experimental whiskeys. When the whiskey reached maturity, Tim Piersant took the bold step of ending his relationship with MGP and going all-in on his new whiskey. It was a risk launching such a unique Bourbon and hoping the customers would like it. Tim and Grant's belief in the product was well placed. Fans embraced Chattanooga Whiskey as their own.

Ole Smoky's success led to an explosion of legal moonshine and whiskey distilleries in East Tennessee. The small town of Hartford, along the North Carolina border, saw the establishment of Bootleggers Distillery. Established by Darrell Miller, he brought his family's way of making spirits into the legal world. One of his unique approaches was to single distill, rather than double distill. As his grandfather used to say, if you have to double distill, you're doing something wrong. His small fifty-gallon copper still, lined with wood, is a throwback to an earlier time. And while he barrels his whisky, he also uses an old moonshiner's trick of putting oak staves into bottles to age his other spirits. Bootleggers revealed the unique nature of Tennessee's distilling past, creating an experience that differed from Jack and George and the distilleries of Kentucky.

Sugarlands Distilling Company officially opened its location in March 2014 and soon brought national attention to the area through its association with the Discovery Channel's television show *Moonshiners*.

Meanwhile, Cocke County, who initially opted out, finally opened to distilling, and the Popcorn Sutton brand built a distillery in Newport. For their distilling team, they added John Lunn, the master distiller that replaced Dave Backus at George Dickel after his retirement. He was replaced at Dickel by Allisa Henley. Soon after, Allisa followed John to the Newport distillery, which was eventually purchased by Sazerac. In 2018, George Dickel's Cascade Hollow brought in Nicole Austin as distiller and general manager after a stint at Tullamore Dew, in Ireland. Meanwhile, Sazerac would leave Newport with eyes centered on building a facility in Murfreesboro.

The summer of 2014 brought distilling to Pigeon Forge when Old Forge Distillery established their location next to The Old Mill. Its head distiller Keener Shanton partnered with the old 1830s mill to grind its grain.

Before the year was out, three more moonshine distilleries arrived, including Doc Collier's in Gatlinburg, Thunder Road in Kodak (now Old Tennessee Distilling Co.), and Cocke County Distillery in Newport. Tennessee Legend arrived the following year.

It seems the Gatlinburg City Commissioners were right to see a coming explosion of moonshine distilleries and brands. But Gatlinburg and Pigeon Forge have kept their family atmosphere, thanks to its association with Dolly Parton and the Great Smoky Mountains. The number of moonshine establishments and whiskey distilleries is large, but there seems to be enough business to go around for all of them. Ole Smoky found enough business to support four locations. Today, Ole Smoky's original "Hollar" location alone entertains 2.3 million visitors a year, beating both Kentucky and Scotland.[790]

Knowing History

July 1, 2013, was a landmark day in the history of Tennessee whiskey, although few people outside the industry knew about it. With the General Assembly's passage of House Bill No. 1084, for the first time, labeling something as Tennessee whiskey meant it had to fit a strict standard.

To put it in simple terms, the law elevated the spirit from the basic standards of whiskey to something akin to Bourbon. To be labeled as "Tennessee Whiskey", "Tennessee Whisky", "Tennessee Sour Mash Whiskey" or "Tennessee Sour Mash Whisky, the spirit has to be:

1. Manufactured in Tennessee;

2. Made of a grain mixture that is at least fifty-one percent (51%) corn;

3. Distilled to no more than 160 proof or eighty percent (80%) alcohol by volume;

4. Aged in new, charred oak barrels in Tennessee;

5. Filtered through maple charcoal prior to aging;

6. Placed in the barrel at no more than 125 proof or sixty-two and one-half percent (62.5 %) alcohol by volume; and

7. Bottled at not less than 80 proof or forty percent (40%) alcohol by volume.

The crucial difference beyond the state of manufacture was the addition of the leaching process outlined in item number five--often referred to as the Lincoln County Process.

While being a leap forward for what the words Tennessee whiskey mean, the definition didn't please everyone. It's the reason the bill also included an amendment to item five. It states that the charcoal mellowing rule:

> "shall not apply to intoxicating liquor manufactured at a distillery located in a county that authorized the manufacturing process by referendum after January 1, 1979, and prior to January 1, 1980; provided, however, that any such distillery was first licensed by the state alcoholic beverage commission after January 1, 2000, and before January 1, 2001."[791]

If that rule seems to be a little vague and specific at the same time, that was on purpose. The Tennessee Constitution doesn't allow laws to be written to benefit any single person or company. Legislators learned the best way around this was to create a framework that could only encompass the single entity. Prichard's Distillery in Kelso was excluded from the law so Phil didn't have to change how he was already making his whiskey.

Mainstream media sources ignored the rule change at first. That all changed during the 2014 legislative session, when opponents pushed for changes or the repeal of the law. Suddenly the question of "what is Tennessee whiskey" was playing out in the press and the General Assembly.

Diageo, who owned the George Dickel brand, suggested the rules should allow the use of used barrels. Phil Prichard and a start-up in West Tennessee called Full Throttle called for a repeal, due to it codifying the rules of one company as the state style.

What the dustup proved was that no one really knew the heritage of Tennessee whiskey. The reason for this lack of knowledge was clear. For over a century, Prohibition and decades of marketing at the expense of accuracy had buried its genuine history. This led to unnecessary squabbles that did nothing to advance the well-deserved legacy of Tennessee whiskey.

After a year of heated debate, the opponents of the law withdrew their repeal measure. In a strange twist, when Phil Prichard opened a new distillery location in Nashville, the exemption did not include his new facility. To this day, his Kelso distillery is the only distillery in the state that isn't required to charcoal mellow its Tennessee whiskey.

Just a year after the heat died down on the arguments over the rules for Tennessee whiskey, history was back on a collision course with marketing.

The year 2016 started as a year of celebration for the Jack Daniel's brand. The company was touting its 150th anniversary, with a year of special releases, culminating in a shindig in September. All went according to plan until a *New York Times* article surfaced in June. It questioned why the company only recently began giving credit to "a slave" named Nearis [sic] Green as the man who taught Jack Daniel how to distill. It credited the 1967 *Jack Daniel's Legacy* book for a portion of its research.[792] In a year filled with racial strife, the story went viral across the nation's news sources.

Halfway around the world, a real estate investor and *New York Times* best-selling author Fawn Weaver was sitting in a hotel room looking to kill some time while her husband Keith was in a business meeting. She picked up a copy of the New York Times International Edition and began reading the article about Nearest Green. As she read, she realized there was something peculiar about the photo that accompanied the text. It featured a Black man in the middle of the picture, surrounded by white distillery workers. The photo was clearly from the late 19th century or early 20th century. Within this odd juxtaposition, something didn't jibe.

Fawn immediately got online and started researching Jack and Nearest. She was amazed to find a severe lack of information about Nearest Green. To her, the idea of an enslaved man being the foundation of the world's largest whiskey brand was intriguing. She ordered a copy of *Jack Daniel's Legacy* and read it cover-to-cover. Expecting only brief mentions of Nearest, it amazed her how much of the book focused on Nearest and his sons. He came across as the area's most celebrated distiller. Wanting to know more, she boarded a plane for Nashville, rented a car, and drove to Lynchburg.

By this time, the little community was on edge. Fawn knew any outsider was going to be looked at suspiciously. Especially one who was a New York Times best-selling author. But Fawn immediately cooled nerves when she met a member of the Daniel family in the library. She told them she wasn't there to do a hit piece. Thanks to the photo, she thought there might be a richer, more positive story beyond the headlines.

Over the next year, she went through local, state, and national archives. She interviewed members of the Green, Daniel, Motlow, and Call families, and then married together records with oral tradition. What she was finding was a story of friendship and one that ran counter to the racially charged articles making the rounds.

She was also finding serendipitous moments everywhere she turned. In one of her interviews, she received quite the surprise. She met a 107-year-old woman who was raised by the man in the old distillery photo. It was George Green, Nearest's son. Then, out of the blue, she was told the farm where Nearest worked for Daniel & Call was up for sale. As she talked to her real estate agent, she learned she was talking to Sherrie Moore, the retired Director of Whiskey Operations for Jack Daniel's. Sherrie offered to come out of retirement to honor Nearest with a commemorative bottle of whiskey. Fawn decided to take it a step further. She wanted to create a whiskey brand centered on the legacy of Uncle Nearest and eventually build a distillery.

By this time, she had built a relationship with Jack Daniel's. They were relieved to have a third party working on Nearest Green's history. She received their blessing to use the name of their first distiller under a separate brand. Soon, Fawn was honoring the distiller with scholarships under the Nearest Green Foundation. Then she started work on the Uncle Nearest whiskey brand and distillery. Her two high-priority hires were Sherrie Moore, who became Director of Whiskey Production, and Victoria Eady Butler, as the brand's Master Blender. Creating a tie back to the distillery's namesake, Victoria is the great-great-granddaughter of Nearest Green. In June 2020, she joined Jack Daniel's in creating the Nearest & Jack Advancement Initiative, with a goal of bringing more diversity to distilling.

In the end, what could have been a painful chapter became a moment of rediscovery of a long-lost Tennessee whiskey legacy. For a nation in turmoil it was a moment of healing. It was also an opportunity to remind the world of the countless people who worked in the industry, whose names or deeds will never be known. Some who were paid, some who were enslaved, and some whose great achievements went undocumented.

Today, Uncle Nearest whiskeys are winning awards and Fawn is doing all she can to spread Nearest Green's name around the world. The Nearest Green Distillery in Shelbyville stands like a shrine to the exploits of the long-forgotten distiller. Meanwhile, Jack Daniel's added the Nearest Green story to its visitor's center and its tours. Apparently, sometime after the Motlows left, his story faded from the company's history. But he was never forgotten in Lynchburg. There was always a member of the Green family hard at work in the distillery, all the way up into the 21st century. It was a hard way to pull the story forward again. But it finally was, and thanks to the grace and curiosity of Fawn Weaver.

Bringing it all Together

In just five short years and two law changes, Tennessee had grown from just three distilleries to twenty-five. The Great Recession was slowly fading and Tennessee was helping to spark the nation's craft whiskey boom.

This fast growth led to the formation of the Tennessee Distillers Guild in 2014. Starting as a thirteen-member organization, the guild focused on promotion, advocacy, and building a network between distilleries. Billy Kaufman of Short Mountain Distillery took the helm as the organization's first president. The coup was bringing large distilleries like Jack Daniel's and George Dickel's Cascade Hollow and having them at equal voting weight with the other members.

The first challenge they faced was a whiskey shortage. The nationwide boom caught everyone off guard. Part of the problem was a lack of barrels, but there was also an unanticipated level of demand for aging spirits. Unfortunately, it is almost impossible for an industry to predict the future. Overproduction and underproduction are unavoidable side effects.

Tennessee's solution? Build more distilleries. The year 2014 saw the emergence of nine new facilities, including TennSouth Distillery (now Big Machine Distillery) in Lynnville. In 2015, four more distilleries joined the fold. Then, in 2016, another four distilleries arrived, including Tennessee Hills in Jonesborough, Nashville Craft in the city, and Leiper's Fork south of Nashville. None of these distilleries were cookie cutter: Tennessee Hills was built by Stephen and Jessica Callahan in a pre-Civil War salt house; Leiper's Fork was built in a two-century-old log home; and Nashville Craft leaned on the scientific expertise of Bruce Boeko. Meanwhile, Jack Daniel's added new warehouses and capacity in a $140 million upgrade. George Dickel was adding warehouse capacity, too. And deep in one of their warehouses, Allisa Henley stumbled into seventeen-year-old whiskies, unheard of for Dickel. The distillery celebrated by releasing them as Distillery Reserve offerings. It was still early, but it wouldn't be long before the increased interest in whiskey had more distilleries doing these kinds of exclusive offerings.

With a fast-growing distillery landscape, the guild celebrated Tennessee whiskey with an end of the year festival in 2016. They held the Grains and Grits Festival in the small East Tennessee town of Townsend. With Jack and George at the event, along with twenty-two other guild members, the event was a great success. It was a chance for whiskey fans to finally see the growth of the industry firsthand.

One of the historic brands returning to the scene as part of that festival was Old Dominick. After Prohibition killed off the brand, the family went into the development of food and products. When the beer laws were loosened after Prohibition, D. Canale and Co., became a major distributor for Anheuser-Busch of St. Louis. In 2013, Domenico Canale's great, great grandsons Alex and Chris Canale discovered a historic, unopened bottle of Dominick Toddy. The two agreed it was time to get the family back into the whiskey business. They found a building on Front Street in Downtown Memphis, near to Domenico's location and began a major renovation. They went north of the border to Kentucky and brought on Alex Castle as their head distiller. She had experience at both Alltech in Lexington and Wild Turkey. The company sourced whiskey until they could release their first Tennessee whiskey in 2022. It also embraced the brand's original icon, the Dominicker rooster, which is proudly displayed in neon atop their distillery.

June 2017 brought something else new to the state: the Tennessee Whiskey Trail. With twenty-five member distilleries, the time was right. The guild produced a passport and maps, and distilleries opened their doors from Old Dominick in Memphis to Bootleggers in Hartford. The guild celebrated the start of the trail with events in Franklin, Memphis, and culminating in the second annual Grains and Grits Festival in Townsend.

By the end of 2017, the plan for a Nearest Green Distillery was revealed and Nelson's Green Brier released their first bottles of Tennessee Whiskey with their Nelson's First 108 limited release. The year also saw the development of a second Knoxville distillery, as PostModern Spirits took the state into the world of American single malt.

Over the next few years, the state continued to expand to an impressive number of distilleries. Not all would join or remain with the guild, so not all have been listed as part of the official trail and some have joined or dropped from the trail at various points in time. The following dates are the estimated years they opened.:

- B.R. Distilling in Memphis (Originally 2014 as a vodka distillery)

- Smith Creek Moonshine in Nashville and Pigeon Forge (2016)

- Leatherwood Distillery in Pleasant View (2018)

- Lost State Distilling in Bristol (2018)

- King's Family Distillery in Pigeon Forge (2018)

- Brushy Mountain Distillery at the State Penitentiary (2018)

- Gate 11 Distillery in Chattanooga (2018)

- Gobbler Springs near Lawrenceburg (2018)
- Gutter Bound in Humphrey County (2019)
- Junction 35 Spirits in Pigeon Forge (2019)
- Nashville Barrel Company (2021)
- Mossback Distilling Company in Jefferson City (2021)
- Dam Whiskey Corp. in Guild (2022)
- Company Distilling in Townsend (2022) with Heath Clark, Jeff Arnett, and Kris Tatum (formerly of Old Forge)

By 2022, the growth of Tennessee whiskey had been nothing short of stunning. An industry that once thrived in the early 19th century had finally returned stronger than ever.

EPILOGUE: FINDING HISTORY

Five years ago, a web developer from South Carolina took off on a journey across Kentucky, exploring distilleries and reveling in their histories and myths. That journey moved on to Scotland, where more stories awaited his arrival. After a second trip to Scotland, he knew he had to share those stories and so he started the *Whiskey Lore* podcast.

Yes, that is the story of my journey into the world of studying whiskey history and creating stories for my podcast. It started simply as seeking the truth beyond the lore.

At that time, I was like most people. I only saw whiskey history as a fun, frivolous endeavor---fodder for coffee-table books, trivia, and barroom discussions. I didn't see it as real scholarship. My first two seasons of the *Whiskey Lore* podcast are proof of that. Beyond the Bottled-in-Bond episode, most episodes are lighthearted and my research was easily handled through internet searches, books, and interviews.

Season three is when it all changed. The country was going through a pandemic and with international travel shut down, I was left to travel close to home. Suddenly I was making trips into Tennessee, learning about the history of Charles Nelson and elements of the Jack Daniel story I'd never heard. But the real eye opener was the Uncle Nearest story.

With all the tension in the world, here was a story about an unexpected friendship. After interviewing Fawn Weaver, I saw how taking a closer look at a whiskey story not only revealed some unexpected surprises, it changed lives and attitudes. It was the first time the words "question everything" went through my mind.

This human problem solving side of history got me thinking back to my western history professor Arthur Smith. On the first day of class, he told us not to worry about names and dates. What he cared about was us correlating historical events to issues we may be dealing with today. To him, history wasn't just for trivia and academic pursuits, it was a window into ourselves and our very nature. I was seeing that coming true.

After that, I couldn't go back to my old frivolous attitude. Yes, these stories were entertaining, but they also held deeper lessons for us as humans. I realized that I needed to stop being so hyper-focused on first and biggest claims and instead search for impact and things that relate to our everyday struggles. My stories shifted to things like the Pattison Crash in Scotland in the 1890s where greed and speculation created a boom and bust in the whisky industry. My Whiskey Rebellion episodes dispelled the narrative that Western Pennsylvania farmers didn't want to be taxed. The deeper story was in Alexander Hamilton's use of the government as a vehicle to pick winners and losers by favoring industry over cashless farmers. While telling the tale of dusty pre-Prohibition bottles discovered in California, I found the story of how whiskey helped establish industry in Los Angeles. And, in the sixth season, about Irish whiskey, I showed how the drink played a central role in the evolution of Ireland's tax system, industry and strife. Whiskey's impact on the human experience was so much more than I ever imagined.

Without that evolution in my storytelling, this book would have been very different. Like most other whiskey writers, I would have stuck strictly to distillers and the industry. But you can't truly know the history of whiskey without knowing the history of the people involved, their struggles, and what they had to cope with. Whiskey is nothing without the people who make it, buy it, distribute it, drink it, and ban it.

As I worked through my research, I realized I needed to tune out of the modern narratives and really get to know my 18th- and 19th-century subjects. For four months, I lived almost exclusively in the newspapers, books, and documents from those eras. I wanted to know what these people valued, their biases, how they were being influenced, and their motivations. What I found caused me to take a deeper look at myself and take stock of my own beliefs and motivations. It was a powerful process, but it also challenged me in ways I couldn't have imagined.

Then came the hard decision of what voice to use in my writing. I actually started this book five different times. At first it sounded like a textbook. Then I started injecting my own voice and personalizing things too much. I realized I had to tell stories, just like I do in my podcasts and I needed to immerse the reader in the same world I was immersing myself in. I also knew the best book would come from someone laying out the facts so the reader could judge for themselves and have the same moments of self-reflection I was having. After all, history is best when it makes you think, not when it preaches to you or tries to sway you.

Things went well at first. But soon, I hit a roadblock. I kept wanting to judge the people I was reading about. I had to bring back two virtues I had lost touch with in the modern world: grace and forgiveness. There were literally moments where I got angry and moments where I wanted to cry after reading certain articles. I couldn't believe people could be so cruel. But I had to remind myself that people are complex animals, and they are shaped by what they are fed. I couldn't excuse their deeds, but I had to forgive them for their ignorance or I wouldn't have made it through this book without railing against humanity.

The two people who held me up through this entire experience were Cal Johnson and Robert Renfro. Through their stories, both men exemplified forgiveness and grace. How else could you explain how they overcame the oppression and prejudice that was present in their societies? These men not only succeeded beyond anyone's wildest expectations, they changed the hearts and minds of people around them. If I'm proud of anything in this book, it is that I got to amplify their stories. They were such a big help to me and they drove me to finish this book so I could share their stories. And because of them, I look at the modern world in a whole different light. If only this world could tap into a fraction of their spirit and positive energy.

Something else I'm proud of with this book is getting the names Old Robertson, Old Lincoln, Evan Shelby, Frederick Stump, the Woodards, Tolleys, and Eatons joining Jack, George, and Charles in the history of Tennessee whiskey. Hopefully they find their way into more books about American whiskey history.

Their names have been so close to me over the last few months, I couldn't help but wonder what led to having these great whiskey names stricken from the record?

The long drought of Tennessee's elongated prohibition had something to do with it. It gave Kentucky Bourbon time to win hearts and minds. Then in 1964, an act of Congress made Bourbon a distinct product of the United States. The revival of craft distilling embraced this idea and soon a Kentucky county name became synonymous with "American spirits." In fact, ask most people overseas and they will likely call Jack Daniel's a Bourbon. Technically it is by today's rules. It's one of the drawbacks in the 2013 law. Following the rules of Bourbon "with one extra step of charcoal mellowing" was meant to legitimize Tennessee whiskey as a high quality product. But it also minimizes the need to dig into Tennessee's history, if all it is, is Bourbon that goes through an extra step. So no one went looking for all of those long lost Tennessee distilling names. What was the point, if Bourbon had the grander legacy?

I must say, the more I researched, the closer I became to Tennessee whiskey's legends and the more I wanted to defend them. And then, I'd hear someone say, "oh it's just Bourbon that goes through an extra step." I could help but think, how this phrase marginalizes the work of all of those great Tennessee distillers of the past. And then worse, hearing someone trying to convince another person Jack Daniel's is Bourbon. I think, why would Jack Daniel's want to be called Bourbon? Nothing against Bourbon. It truly deserves its spot as "America's spirit." But, if you asked Jack what the difference was between his whiskey and Bourbon, it wouldn't have been just charcoal mellowing and he definitely wouldn't call it Bourbon. Tennessee saw Kentucky as industrial and sweet mash focused. In the eyes of Jack Daniel, they were taking shortcuts. He was still making whiskey the slow, traditional way. There were smaller Kentucky distillers that lived by the same rules Jack did, but overall, the theory was, Tennessee whiskey's strength was quality over quantity. That belief continued on, even into Lem and Reagor Motlow's years. It's the reason Jack Daniel's was stuck in allocation. They weren't completely ready to let go of tradition. I doubt Reagor would have been happy having his whiskey called Bourbon. He even went as far as to argue that Tennessee whiskey should be spelled with an "e" when Brown-Forman, who didn't use the "e," purchased them. They may have been owned by a Kentucky family, but there was still a heartbeat of competition with the Tennesseans.

I'm sorry. Two years digging hard into Tennessee whiskey history and its hard not to become a little passionate about it!

You might expect me to call for the 2013 rules to be overturned and the log stills and five day fermentations to be mandated. No, nobody would agree to that. At some point you have to advance. Even Jack Daniel and McLin Davis moved past the log stills. But I do think its worth discussing how Tennessee can stand on its own, like it once did, without using Bourbon as a crutch.

At the very least, hopefully Tennessee distilleries can start finding localized stories to start telling during their distillery tours. There's no reason to lean on Kentucky's history anymore. Tennessee has an amazingly rich distilling history that actually predates Kentucky Bourbon. How does that statement feel, Tennessee distillery tour guides? It would also be great to see the term "Lincoln County Process" retired in favor of terms like the more historically accurate Old Lincoln and Old Robertson. They are names to be proud of—just like Kentucky is proud of its famous county. It's time to let visitors to Tennessee get a dose of Tennessee history. If they want Kentucky's, it's not far away.

As I close this project, it should be noted that in no way do I see this as the end of research into the history of Tennessee whiskey. Tennessee whiskey history is rich with opportunity, not least because I left a lot of stories on the cutting-room floor. Plus, I am humble enough to know some of these stories will evolve as additional evidence comes to light. I look forward to that.

We need to keep challenging history. Question everything, I say. Losing Tennessee's whiskey history should be evidence enough that we don't know all we need to know about whiskey history. Let's keep getting closer to the truth.

There is a new breed of whiskey history writers just starting to make noise. These are people who love finding the truth behind the lore and who aren't afraid to dig into original documentation to find the richer stories beneath. Carol Roberts is one of those people. Without her amazing research into the story of Nancy Patterson, her life story would still be hidden in the Bedford County and Tennessee state archives. Her book on distilleries around Moore, Coffee, Bedford and other counties proves there is still a lot of Tennessee whiskey history left to explore. Andrew Braunberg's amazing work on his Texas whiskey history book takes that state's distilling history back to long before the Revolutionary War. His details on rectifying and the connection between Texas and Tennessee make a great companion to this book. And Laura Fields in Pennsylvania and Alan Bishop in Indiana inspire with their dedication to uncovering the lost whisky histories of their own states.

It's time for more people to follow their lead and take whiskey history scholarship to another level. After all, as we've discovered together through Tennessee, whiskey history is the story of us. Digging into our history is no frivolous endeavor: the loss of Tennessee whiskey history is all the evidence you need.

ACKNOWLEDGEMENTS

A book of this magnitude could not be completed without the dedication and support of others.

Thank you to all of the founders, owners, distillers, blenders, brand ambassadors, and tour guides who gave me a first hand introduction to Tennessee's modern spirits.

Thanks to the following for one-on-one interviews and in-depth offline conversation time: Nelson Eddy and Minh Le of FINN Partners, Fawn Weaver of Uncle Nearest, Andy and Charlie Nelson of Nelson's Green Brier, Steve Bashore of the George Washington Distillery, Dr. Jim Ambuske and Jeanette Patrick of the Washington Library, McCauley Williams of B.R. Distilling, Shelby County Historian Jimmy Rout, Jim Massey of Fugitive Spirits, Jeff Pennington of SPEAKeasy Spirits, John Hatcher of Gobbler Springs Distillery, Ed Kohl and Leslie Sampson of J.W. Kelly and Keeper's Question Brands, Tim Piersant of Chattanooga Whiskey, Phil Prichard of Prichard's Distillery, Old Dominick's Alex and Chris Canale, and Alex Castle, Clay Risen of the New York Times, Jeff Arnett, Heath Clark, Jenna Wagner, and Kevin Smith of Company Distilling, Nicole Austin of George Dickel, Chris Fletcher of Jack Daniel's, Joe and Johnny Baker of Ole Smoky, Keener Shanton of Old Forge Distillery, Chris Poynter, Chris Morris, and Tim Holz of Brown-Forman, Laura Fields of the Delaware Valley Fields Foundation and the SeedSpark™ Project, Alan Bishop of Spirits of French Lick, Andrew Braunberg of Still Austin Distillery, Jason and Jeanne

Queen of Cooks Mill Bourbon, Stephen Callahan of Tennessee Hills Distillery, Joe and Nick Bianchi of Lost State Distillery, Aaron Brost, Kyle Harder of Grain and Barrel Spirits, Clayton Cutter of Big Machine Distillery, Billy Kaufman of Short Mountain Distillery, Darrel Miller of Bootleggers Distillery, author Chuck Cowdery, Ron Grazioso of PostModern Spirits, Paul Tomaszewski of M.B. Roland Distillery, and Arlon Jones and Peg Hayes of Casey Jones Distillery. I know I missed a few, but it doesn't lessen how important your help was in this process.

Also, this book wouldn't be as complete without the help of some amazingly dedicated archivists. Thank you to Judy Phillips (Coffee County), Christine Pyrdom (Moore County), Carol Roberts and Kathryn Hopkins (Bedford County), Sherrie Tomerlin and Byron "Butch" Carter (Lincoln County), and Tonya and Jailyn (Robertson County). Also thanks to Kelley Sirko, the Metro Archives Librarian at the Nashville Library for finding some gems, and to Kevin Cason, Ph.D. and rest of the staff at the Tennessee State Library and Archives for going above and beyond. Also thank you to Lara Szypszak in the Manuscript Division of the Library of Congress for your genuine enthusiasm and help in trying to track down the origins of Tennessee distilling. Thanks to the Reference Staff at the Missouri State Archives for the help and speedy responses. And thanks to the number of unnamed writers whose documenting of facts and figures in newspapers throughout Tennessee and the country helped me verify or dispel stories that I collected through oral tradition.

Thank you to my *Whiskey Lore* family, especially those fiercely loyal Patreon members who have been here from the beginning. I treasure your friendship and support. Thank you Fernando Rivera, Mike Hanson, Todd Ritter, Matt Kirkpatrick, Robert Dixon, Ron Montgomery, Matthew King, Nick Streeter, Dean Dowsett, and David Levine.

Thank you to all of the amazing friends, family, and followers who support me on social media and the *Whiskey Lore* podcast. And thank you for ignoring my absences when I really had to get down to business working on this book.

And to Emma Gibbs, thank you again for the yeoman's job you did in brushing up my text, removing inconsistencies, and providing helpful suggestions along the way. It is always a pleasure working with you.

To all – cheers and slàinte mhath,
Drew Hannush

BIBLIOGRAPHY

Barnette, Charlie. "Bristol, Tenn-Va Whiskey Distillers."

Bassett, John Spencer. *The Life of Andrew Jackson* (Garden City and New York: Doubleday, Page & Company, 1911)

Batchelor, Bob. *The Bourbon King: The Life and Crimes of George Remus, Prohibition's Evil Genius* (Diversion Books, 2019)

Bolton, Charles Knowles. *Scotch Irish Pioneers in Ulster and America*. Boston: Bacon and Brown, 1910.

Braunberg, Andrew. *Fires, Floods, Explosions, and Bloodshed: A History of Texas Whiskey* (State House Press, 2023).

Conforth, Bruce and Gayle Dean Wardlow, *Up Jumped the Devil: The Real Life of Robert Johnson* (Chicago Review Press, 2019).

Crockett, David. *Narrative of the Life of David Crockett, of the State of Tennessee*, Sixth (Philadelphia and Baltimore: Carey, Hart & Co., 1834), https://www.gutenberg.org/files/37925/37925-h/37925-h.htm.

Davis, Burke. *Old Hickory: A Life of Andrew Jackson* (New York: The Dial Press, 1977).

Del Papa, Eugene M. "The Royal Proclamation of 1763: Its Effect upon Virginia Land Companies." *The Virginia Magazine of History and Biography* 83, no. 4 (1975): 406–11. .

Dixon, Kelly J. *Boomtown Saloons: Archaeology, and History in Virginia City* (University of Nevada Press, 2005).

Ellis, Larry Michael. *Spizzerinctum: The Life and Legend of Robert "Black Bob" Renfro* (Bloomington, IN: AuthorHouse, 2004).

Federal Distillery Tax Book for Tennessee, 1796-1801, Overton, John, 1796-1801, Jacob McGavock Dickinson Papers, 42918, Tennessee State Library and Archives, Tennessee Virtual Archive,

Federal Distillery Tax Books for the First, Second, Fourth, and Fifth Districts, Internal Revenue. National Archives Atlanta, Georgia.

Green, Ben A. *Jack Daniel's Legacy* (Shelbyville, TN: Ben A. Green, 1967).

Guice, Julia Cook. *Frederick Stump: The Rest of the Story.* Tennessee State Library and Archives (United States: J.C. Guice, 1991).

Hamer, Phillip M. *Tennessee a History 1673-1932*, vol. 1 (New York: The American Historical Society, Inc., 1933), 25.

Henderson, Archibald. Dr. Thomas Walker and the Loyal Company of Virginia. Worcester, Mass.: Virginia Historical Society, 1931

Hogeland, William. *The Whiskey Rebellion: George Washington, Alexander Hamilton, and the Frontier Rebels Who Challenged America's Newfound Sovereignty* (Simon and Schuster, 2006).

Isaac, Paul E. *Prohibition and Politics: Turbulent Decades in Tennessee 1885-1920* (Knoxville, TN: The University of Tennessee Press in Cooperation with the Tennessee Historical Commission, 1965).

Jackson, Andrew. The Papers of Andrew Jackson: Volume I, 1770-1803. Edited by Sam B. Smith and Harriet Chappell Owsley.(Knoxville: University of Tennessee Press, 1980).

Jackson Andrew. The Papers of Andrew Jackson, V. II, 1804-1813. Edited by Harold D. Moser and Sharon Macpherson. (Knoxville: University of Tennessee Press, 1984).

Kennedy, Billy. *The Scots-Irish in the Hills of Tennessee* (Emerald House Group Incorporated, 1995).

Killebrew, J.B. and J.M. Safford PhD, *Introduction to the Resources of Tennessee*, Website: Google Books (Nashville: Tavel, Eastman, and Howell,

1874), https://www.google.com/books/edition/First_and_Second_Reports_of_the_Bureau_o/xgBkWsGFM9MC.

Land, Robert H. "The Shelby Family Papers." *Quarterly Journal of Current Acquisitions* 11, no. 3 (1954): 140–53. http://www.jstor.org/stable/29780743.

Longueville, Thomas. *The Life of Sir Kenelm Digby* (1896; repr., Hansebooks, 2017).

Minnick, Fred. *Whiskey Women* (Potomac Books, Inc., 2013).

Mooney, James. *Myths of the Cherokee* (Washington, DC: Washington Printing Office, 1902), 242–49, https://archive.org/details/mythsofcherokee00moon/page/n5/mode/2up.

Murdock Collection of John Overton Papers 1797-1820 (THS Collection) Microfilm. State of Tennessee Department of State. Tennessee State Library and Archives.

Okrent, Daniel. *Last Call:* The Rise and Fall of Prohibition (Scribner, 2011).

Roberts, Carol. *A Dozen Tennessee Distilleries and "Old Sport": Pre-Prohibition Distilleries of Bedford County Region*, 2023.

Shelby, Evan, and Isaac Shelby. Shelby Family Papers. Library of Congress.

Stephens, T.E. ed., *Prohibition in Kansas* (Topeka, KS: T.E. Stephens, 1901), https://www.google.com/books/edition/Prohibition_in_Kansas/Xx0yAQAAMAAJ.

Waggoner, Burnice Dorris. *My Menees Family Line*, Binder: Robertson County Archives, n.d.

Young, John Preston and A.R. Young, *Standard History of Memphis: From a Study of Original Sources* (Knoxville, TN: H.W. Crew & Co., 1912), https://lccn.loc.gov/13001493.

Zoeller, Chester. *Bourbon in Kentucky: A History of Distilleries in Kentucky* (Louisville, KY: Butler Books, 2009).

Websites

- Ancestry.com
- Dramdevotees.com
- FamilySearch.org
- Library of Congress
- Newspapers.com by Ancestry
- Tennesseeencyclopedia.net

ENDNOTES

1. "Northern Boundary of Tennessee." *The American Historical Magazine* 6, no. 1 (1901): 19. http://www.jstor.org/stable/42657520.

2. P.M. Hamer. "Fort Loudoun in the Cherokee War 1758-1761." *The North Carolina Historical Review* 2, no. 4 (1925): 443. http://www.jstor.org/stable/23526648.

3. Ibid, 450

4. "To the Officer Commanding Fort Prince George," *South Carolina Gazette*, September 13, 1760, 2.

5. "1768 Boundary Line Treaty of Fort Stanwix (U.S. National Park Service)," n.d., https://www.nps.gov/articles/000/1768-boundary-line-treaty-of-fort-stanwix.htm.

6. "To Be Sold by the Subscriber," Newspapers.com. *Pennsylvania Gazette*, June 28, 1770, 6. All but a handful of newspaper references in this book are courtesy of searches on Newspapers.com by Ancestry.

7. Robert H. Land. "The Shelby Family Papers." *Quarterly Journal of Current Acquisitions* 11, no. 3 (1954): 143. http://www.jstor.org/stable/29780743.

8. "Evan Shelby, Pictured as a Man, Fighter, Strategist," *Bristol Herald Courier*, June 13, 1925, 24.

9. Evan Shelby, "Agreement Between Evan Shelby and Pierce Wall to Manufacture Rye Whiskey SC263_FF1_001," Kentucky Historical Society Digital Collection, February 19, 1780, accessed October 28, 2023, https://www.kyhistory.com/digital/collection/MS/id/25849/rec/3.

10. James Mooney, *Myths of the Cherokee* (Washington, DC: Washington Printing Office, 1902), 242–47, https://archive.org/details/mythsofcherokee00moon/page/n5/mode/2up. A paraphrasing and dramatization of the story.

11. "*Aurora General Advertiser,* February 18, 1802, 3."

12. Frank Eshleman, *Lancaster County Indians*, Library of Congress (H. Frank Eshleman, Esq., 1908), 229–30, https://archive.org/details/lancastercount00eshl/page/229/mode/2up.

13. Israel Daniel Rupp, *The History and Topography of Dauphin, Cumberland, Franklin, Bedford, Adams, and Perry Counties [Pennsylvania]*, Library of Congress (Lancaster, PA: Gilbert Hills, 1846), 175, https://archive.org/details/historytopograph00rup/page/n5/mode/2up.

14. Ibid., 176.

15. *The Pennsylvania Gazette,* February 11, 1768, 3." Extract of a Letter from Carlisle, Containing a Full Account of the Taking and Rescue of Frederick Stump.

16. Theodore Roosevelt, *The Winning of the West*, Website, New Knickerbocker Edition (New York-London: G. P. Putnam's Sons, 1896), 242, https://www.google.com/books/edition/The_Winning_of_the_West/hbY-AAAAYAAJ.

17. *Draper Manuscript Collection: Draper's Notes*, Source: Wisconsin Historical Society Library-Archives, Mss S 31 58-59, n.d. Interview of John Stump, son of Frederick Stump by Lyman C. Draper in 1844.

18. *Draper Manuscript Collection: Draper's Notes*, Source: Wisconsin Historical Society Library-Archives, Mss S 1 74-75, n.d. Interview of Thomas Eaton, son of Amos Eaton by Lyman C. Draper on September 22, 1844.

19. *Draper Manuscripts*, Mss S 31 59.

20. *History of Tennessee from the Earliest Time to the Present: Together with an Historical and a Biographical Sketch of Montgomery, Robertson, Humphreys, Stewart, Dickson, Cheatham and Houston Counties* (Goodspeed Publishing Co., 1886), 828–29, https://archive.org/details/historyoftenness00good_1/page/n893/mode/2up. Based on an article written in the Springfield Record by Dr. J.S. Mulloy.

21. "Cumberland Compact," Tennessee Virtual Archive: Tennessee State Library and Archives, May 1, 1780, accessed October 28, 2023, https://teva.contentdm.oclc.org/digital/collection/tfd/id/457.

22. "Early North Carolina / Tennessee Land Grants at the Tennessee State Library and Archives," n.d., https://sos.tn.gov/tsla/guides/early-north-carolina-tennessee-land-grants-at-the-tennessee-state-library-and-archives.

23. *Draper Manuscripts*, Mss S 31 63-64.

24. Evelyn Yates Carpenter, *Thomas Kilgore, Sr. and His Proven Descendants to 1991*, Robertson County Archives (Nashville, TN: Evelyn Yates Carpenter, 1991), 11.

25. John Haywood, *The Civil and Political History of the State of Tennessee: From Its Earliest Settlement up to the Year 1796* (1823; repr., John Haywood, 1891), 247, https://www.google.com/books/edition/Civil_and_Political_History_of_Tennessee/R1ERD9cyR3QC.

26. Elijah Embree Hoss and William B. Reese, *History of Nashville, Tenn.* (Charles Elder Bookseller, 1890), 79-80, https://www.google.com/books/edition/History_of_Nashville_Tenn/bsIlAAAAMAAJ. Tradition has it that Charlotte Robertson set the dogs free.

27. Hoss and Reese, *History of Nashville, Tenn.*, 72.

28. *History of Tennessee from the Earliest Time to the Present: Together with an Historical and a Biographical Sketch of Montgomery, Robertson, Humphreys, Stewart, Dickson, Cheatham and Houston Counties*, 830.

29. Jay Guy Cisco, *Historic Sumner County, Tennessee*, Website (Folk-Keelin Printing Company, 1909), 101, https://www.google.com/books/edition/Historic_Sumner_County_Tennessee/EIltFS hmmekCr.

30. *Frederick Stump License For Bond: Tennessee Historical Society Miscellaneous Files: T-100 Box 14 S-161*, January 10, 1789, Tennessee State Library and Archives.

31. *The Tennessee Gazette*, June 11, 1800, 3.

32. "Domestic Articles," *The Philadelphia Inquirer*, December 1, 1792, 4

33. Hoss and Reese, *History of Nashville, Tenn.*, 61–70.

34. Haywood, *The Civil and Political History of the State of Tennessee*, 127.

35. "Mystery of the Spanish Milled Dollar," *Nashville Union and American*, May 15, 1859, 1.

36. "Davidson County Court Minute Books," *Microfilm: Tennessee State Library and Archives*, n.d., 90, accessed November 15, 2023.

37. Edward Scott, *Laws of the State of Tennessee Including Those of North Carolina Now In Force In This State from the Year 1715 to the Year 1820 Inclusive*, vol. II, Google Books (Knoxville, TN: Heiskell & Brown, 1821), 182–83, https://www.google.com/books/edition/Laws_of_the_State_of_Tennessee/_340AQAAMAAJ.

38. Haywood, *The Civil and Political History of the State of Tennessee*, 127.

39. *Tennessee Records of Davidson County: Minutes of Superior Court of North Carolina Including Mero District 1788-1803: Part I, 1788-1798*, Book: Tennessee State Library and Archives (Works Progress Administration, 1938), 188.

40. Ibid., 189.

41. *Tennessee Records of Davidson County: Minutes of Superior Court of North Carolina Including Mero District 1788-1803: Part II, 1798-1803*, Book: Tennessee State Library and Archives (Works Progress Administration, 1938), 37–38. The State v Andersen Lavender.

42. House of Representatives Petition 20-1-1801-1. On file at the Tennessee State Library and Archives.

43. *Journal of the House of Representatives at the First Session of the Fourth General Assembly of the State of Tennessee*, Book: Tennessee State Library and Archives (Knoxville, TN, 1801), 43, 48.

44. "Robert Rentfro," *The Impartial Review and Cumberland Repository*, February 15, 1806, 3.

45. "Notice," *The Clarion*, October 18, 1808, 3

46. "Samuel Hutchinson," *The Tennessee Gazette and Metro-District Advertiser*, October 24, 1804, 4.

47. "Entertainment," *The Democratic Clarion and Tennessee Gazette*, September 16, 1812, 4.

48. "Fire!" *The Democratic Clarion and Tennessee Gazette*, December 22, 1812, 2.

49. "Notice," *Nashville Whig*, January 20, 1813, 4.

50. "Robert Rentfro," *Nashville Banner and Nashville Whig*, March 23, 1814, 3.

51. Oliver Taylor, *Historic Sullivan: A History of Sullivan County, Tennessee with Brief Biographies of the Makers of History*, Google Books (Bristol, TN: King Printing Company, 1909), 116. https://www.google.com/books/edition/Historic_Sullivan/8fITAAAAYAAJ.

52. William Laurence Saunders and Stephen Beauregard Weeks. *The State Records of North Carolina, Volume XXII*. United States: Nash brothers, printers, 1907, 705-708. https://www.google.com/books/edition/The_State_Records_of_North_Carolina/zgUMAAAAYAAJ

53. George Neville and Andrew Jackson. Andrew Jackson to George Neville. 1796. Library of Congress: Manuscript/Mixed Material. https://www.loc.gov/item/maj000285/.

54. Homer T. Fort and Drucilla Stovall Jones, *A Family Called Fort: The Descendants of Elias Fort of Virginia*, Book: Tennessee State Archives (Midland, Texas, 1970), 343.

55. "Research Guides: This Month in Business History: The Whiskey Rebellion," Library of Congress, accessed October 29, 2023, https://guides.loc.gov/this-month-in-business-history/august/whiskey-rebellion.

56. Andrew Jackson and George W Deaderick. *George W. Deaderick to Andrew Jackson*, January 2. January 2, 1800. Library of Congress: Manuscript/Mixed Material. https://www.loc.gov/item/maj024840/.

57. "Petition of Andrew Jackson," US House of Representatives: History, Art & Archives, accessed October 29, 2023, https://history.house.gov/Records-and-Research/Listing/pm_014/.

58. Thomas Hutchings and Andrew Jackson. *Andrew Jackson to Thomas Hutchings*, January 3. January 3, 1801. Library of Congress: Manuscript/Mixed Material. https://www.loc.gov/item/maj000494/.

59. Andrew Jackson and Thomas Watson. *Thomas Watson to Andrew Jackson*. 1802. Library of Congress: Manuscript/Mixed Material. https://www.loc.gov/item/maj000553/.

60. Andrew Jackson, *The Papers of Andrew Jackson: 1770-1803*, ed. Sam B. Smith and Harriet Chappell Owsley, vol. 1 (Knoxville, TN: University of Tennessee Press, 1980), 319.

61. Andrew Jackson and Thomas Watson. *Thomas Watson to Andrew Jackson*, August 6. August 6, 1803. Library of Congress: Manuscript/Mixed Material. https://www.loc.gov/item/maj000650/.

62. Andrew Jackson, *Correspondence of Andrew Jackson*, Book: Tennessee State Library and Archives, ed. John Spencer Bassett, vol. 1 (Washington, D.C.: Carnegie Institution of Washington, 1926), 122.

63. James Parton, *Life of Andrew Jackson*, vol. 1, Google Books (Mason Brothers, 1860), 292, https://www.google.com/books/edition/Life_of_Andrew_Jackson/KrwpAQAAIAAJ.

64. Ibid., 298-299, 304.

65. "Thirty Dollars Reward," *Nashville Whig*, October 26, 1813, 4.

66. *The Tennessee Gazette*, November 28, 1804, 3.

67. "Round About the Town," *Nashville American*, October 22, 1885, 4.

68. "More Particulars Respecting the Fall of the Alamo," *The National Banner and Nashville Whig*, April 20, 1836, 3.

69. John Preston Young and A.R. Young, *Standard History of Memphis: From a Study of Original Sources*, Library of Congress (Knoxville, TN: H.W. Crew & Co., 1912), 62, https://www.loc.gov/item/13001493/.

70. Ibid, *63*.

71. "Old Times and Old Memories," *Memphis Daily Appeal*, November 26, 1867, 3.

72. Young and Young, *Standard History of Memphis*, 69.

73. Andrew Jackson, *The Papers of Andrew Jackson: 1816-1820*, ed. Harold D. Moser, David R. Hoth, and George H. Hoemann, vol. IV (Knoxville, TN: University of Tennessee Press, 1994), 259.

74. Ibid.

75. "Old Times and Old Memories," *Memphis Daily Appeal*, November 26, 1867, 3.

76. Ibid.

77. Ibid.

78. James D. Davis, *The History of Memphis,* University of Pittsburgh (Memphis, TN: Hite, Crumpton & Kelly, 1873), 125, https://archive.org/details/historyofmemph00davi/page/n7/mode/2up.

79. "Forthcoming Work," *Litchfield Enquirer*, February 12, 1835. 4.

80. "Politics of the Day," *National Banner and Nashville Whig*, January 16, 1835, 3.

81. Davis, *The History of Memphis*, 146-147.

82. Ibid., 110-111.

83. Ibid., 139-144.

84. "Col. Crockett," *Alexandria Gazette*, 2.

85. *History of Tennessee from the Earliest Time to the Present: Together with an Historical and a Biographical Sketch of Montgomery, Robertson, Humphreys, Stewart, Dickson, Cheatham and Houston Counties*, 831. Based on an article written in the Springfield Record by Dr. J.S. Mulloy.

86. "FamilySearch.Org," n.d., https://ancestors.familysearch.org/en/KL6S-CSC/benjamin-menees-sr.-1743-1811.

87. Overton's tax records

88. A.W. Putnam, *History of Middle Tennessee: Or the Life and Times of James Robertson,* Harvard College Library (Nashville, TN: A.W. Putnam, 1859), 299–300, https://www.google.com/books/edition/History_of_Middle_Tennessee/9DjMSsxUR_UC.

89. Robertson County Will Book 1:266, 267, Robertson County Archive (Benjamin Menees Will).

90. Cave Johnson, *Record of the Johnson Family, Prepared for C. J. Couts, by His Uncle Cave Johnson,* (Robertson County Archives: Johnson folder, 1858, 1-2.

91. Ibid., 3.

92. Robertson County, TN, Deed Book A: 15, Robertson County Archives (Mathew Johnson to Thomas Johnson, July 27, 1796)

93. Cave Johnson, *Record of the Johnson Family.*

94. NC Land Grant Patent Book 63: 201 (Thomas Woodard, assignee of Redick Smith, Military Warrant Number 1231, September 15, 1787. https://www.nclandgrants.com/grant/?mars=12.14.2.589&qid=926893&rn=4

95. *History of Tennessee from the Earliest Time to the Present: Together with an Historical and a Biographical Sketch of Montgomery, Robertson, Humphreys, Stewart, Dickson, Cheatham and Houston Counties,* 831.

96. Robertson County, TN, Deed Book B: 119, Robertson County Archives (John Caffrey to Arthur Pitt, April 16, 1798)

97. NC Land Grant Patent Book 81: 34 (William Fort, assignee of John Gibson, Guard Warrant Number 496, April 27, 1793). https://www.nclandgrants.com/grant/?mars=12.14.2.589&qid=926893&rn=4

98. "Federal Distillery Tax Book for Tennessee, 1796-1801," Overton, John, 1796-1801, 12.

99. Wells Robert Draughon, *Descendants of James Draughon of Edgecombe County North Carolina* (Durham, NC, 1974), 252.

100. Robertson County, TN, Deed Book J: 395, Robertson County Archives (Joseph Barnes to Johnathan Derden, July 21, 1796)

101. NC Land Grant Patent Book 77: 336 (Andrew Irvin, assignee of Andrew Letchworth, Military Warrant Number 2521, December 20, 1791).

102. Robertson County, TN, Deed Book A: 50, Robertson County Archives (John Couts to James Appleton, March 10, 1797)

103. Robertson County, TN, Deed Book A: 321, Robertson County Archives (Thomas Woodard to John Couts, July 19, 1800)

104. "Three Farms For Lease," *The Clarion and Tennessee State Gazette*, October 21, 1817.

105. "Notice," *Wilson's Knoxville Gazette*, October 18, 1813

106. "To Distillers and All Interested in Distilling," *Nashville Whig*, August 14, 1819

107. "Patent Rights," *Nashville Whig*, October 12, 1813.

108. "Auction," *National Banner and Nashville Whig*, June 28, 1837.

109. "To Coopers & Distillers," *The Clarion and Tennessee State Gazette*, November 30, 1813

110. "Stills," *Nashville Whig*, September 27, 1814.

111. *History of Tennessee, from the Earliest Time to the Present: Together with an Historical and a Biographical Sketch of Giles, Lincoln, Franklin and Moore Counties*, Library of Congress (Nashville, TN: Goodspeed Publishing Company, 1886), https://lccn.loc.gov/10012992.

112. Ibid.

113. Ibid., *770*.

114. Ibid., *771*.

115. Ibid., 769.

116. Ibid., 778, 782.

117. Ibid., 807.

118. "Land! Land!" *Fayetteville Observer*, December 7, 1865.

119. Lincoln County, TN, Deed Book H-1:600, Lincoln County Register of Deeds (Andrew Hamilton to Middleton Fanning, August 1, 1829)

120. "Land! Land!" *Fayetteville Observer*, December 7, 1865.

121. Lincoln County, TN, Deed Tax Ledger 1829, 41. Lincoln County Archives. Part of Captain Thomas L. Parks' Company.

122. "Lynchburg Academy," *Fayetteville Observer*, January 22, 1857, 3.

123. Lincoln County, TN, Deed Book C-1:259, Lincoln County Register of Deeds (Thomas Eastland to John Eaton, August 8, 1812)

124. Lincoln County, TN, Deed Book K-1:541, Lincoln County Register of Deeds (John Eaton to Calloway Daniel, December 13, 1836)

125. "New Goods," *The Impartial Review and Cumberland Repository*, September 8, 1808, 1.

126. "Stout & Adams," *(Advertisement) Paris (KY) Western Citizen*, May 1, 1821.

127. "The Subscriber," *Charleston Daily Courier*, October 29, 1824, 3.

128. *A Book of Scotish Pasquils: 1568-1715* (Edinburgh: William Paterson, 1868), 404, https://www.google.com/books/edition/A_Book_of_Scotish_Pasquils_1568_1715/klMCAAAAQAAJ.

129. "Joseph Wood's Commission Store," *The Clarion and Tennessee Gazette*, 5.

130. Ambrose Cooper, *The Complete Distiller*, Website: Google Books (London, 1787), 90–96, https://www.google.com/books/edition/The_complete_distiller/rfAHAAAAQAAJ.

131. Samuel McHarry, *The Practical Distiller* (Harrisburg, PA: John Wyeth, 1809), 67.

132. Ibid., 73.

133. Harrison Hall, *Hall's Distiller*, Website: Google Books (Philadelphia: John Bioren, 1813), 171, https://www.google.com/books/edition/Hall_s_Distiller/DflAAQAAMAAJ. Hall suggests Allison started using the process as far back as 1786.

134. "John Quincy Adams Diary," Massachusetts Historical Society, December 27, 1804, accessed October 30, 2023, https://www.masshist.org/publications/jqadiaries/index.php/document/jqadiaries-v27-1804-12-27-p112.

135. "Robertson County Tennessee: and its Capital," *Louisville Courier-Journal*, April 19, 1896, 26.

136. "Old White Oak Whiskey (Advertisement)," *The Chattanooga News*, November 21, 1905, 10.

137. "Tennessee Whiskies: The Genuine and the Spurious Liquors and How They are Made," *Nashville Banner*, December 14, 1889.

138. "A Word About Green-Brier," *Nashville American*, February 9, 1896, 5.

139. "Inquire at Deacon Giles' Distillery," *Tennessee Baptist*, February 10, 1855, 4.

140. "Trial of Rev. Mr. George Cheever," *Fall River Monitor*, July 4, 1835, 1.

141. Bruce I. Bustard, "National Archives," *Spirited Republic*, 2013, 15, https://www.archives.gov/publications/ebooks/spirited-republic.html.

142. Alexis De Tocqueville, *Democracy in America*, trans. Henry Reeve, Library of Congress (New York, United States of America: J & H.G. Langley's Astor House, 1845), 231, https://lccn.loc.gov/28029589.

143. Thomas Franklin Waters, *A Sketch of the Life of John Winthrop, the Younger, Founder of Ipswich, Massachusetts, in 1633* (Cambridge, United States of America: University Press, 1899), 56, https://lccn.loc.gov/04019526.

144. *History of Tennessee, from the Earliest Time to the Present: Together with an Historical and a Biographical Sketch of Giles, Lincoln, Franklin and Moore Counties.*, 277.

145. "Temperance," *National Banner and Nashville Whig*, August 29, 1829, 2.

146. *The Democratic Clarion and Tennessee Gazette*, Mar 30, 1810, 2.

147. "A Good Inscription," *Knoxville Register*, June 10, 1825, 1.

148. Scott, *Laws of the State of Tennessee Including Those of North Carolina Now In Force In This State from the Year 1715 to the Year 1820 Inclusive*, II:70.

149. "An Ordinance," *Knoxville Register*, January 12, 1819, 3.

150. "Another Warning!" *The Enquirer*, March 28, 1827, 3.

151. *National Banner and Nashville Daily Advertiser*, October 16, 1832, 2.

152. "Senate," *The Tri-Weekly Nashville Union*, November 23, 1837, 3.

153. "Of the Causes of the Abuse of Ardent Spirits," *National Banner and Daily Advertiser*, January 27, 1834, 1.

154. "Report," *Republican Banner*, November 18, 1837, 2.

155. *Acts Passed By The First Session of the Twenty-Second General Assembly of the State of Tennessee, 1837-8*, Book: Tennessee State Library and Archives (Authority, 1838), 186–87.

156. "The Tippling Law," *Tri-Weekly Memphis Enquirer*, February 3, 1846, 2.

157. Benjamin Franklin Clark, *Prohibition of the Sale of Intoxicating Liquors Impracticable: The Maine Law a Failure,* Harvard College Library (Lowell, MA: Stone & Huse, 1864), 8-10 https://www.google.com/books/edition/Prohibition_of_the_Sale_of_Intoxicating/egopAAAAYAAJ.

158. Ibid., 13.

159. Henry S. Clubb, *The Maine Liquor Law: Origin, History, and Result*, Harvard College Library (New York: Fowler and Wells, 1854),18-19 https://archive.org/details/maineliquorlawi00goog/page/n2/mode/2up.

160. "Maine Public Documents 1851-1852," Maine State Legislature, 1851, accessed October 31, 2023, https://www.maine.gov/legis/lawlib/lldl/pubdocs/1851_52.html.

161. Clubb, *The Maine Liquor Law: Origin, History, and Result*, 35-40.

162. "Governor Johnson's Answer," *Nashville Union and American*, April 28, 1855, 2.

163. "Mr. Cavitt on the Liquor Traffic," *Nashville Union and American*, January 19, 1856, 2.

164. Legislative Petitions Roll 20 Date 1853-1859 TSA Bethel College 48-1853-1 Petition from Bethel College.

165. *Senate Journal: The First Session of the Thirtieth General Assembly of the State of Tennessee*, Book: Tennessee State Library and Archives, vol. 1853, 1854, 284.

166. "McMinnville and Manchester Railroad," *Republican Banner*, November 22, 1852, 2.

167. *History of Tennessee from the Earliest Time to the Present: Together with an Historical and a Biographical Sketch of Montgomery, Robertson, Humphreys, Stewart, Dickson, Cheatham and Houston Counties*, 1203.

168. Gaston, "Robertson County Distilleries, 1796-1909," 52. Based on notes in Wiley Woodard's Distillery Account Book: 1837-1859.

169. "The Louisville and Nashville Railroad Charter," *Nashville Union*, January 1, 1852, 2.

170. The National Archives in Washington D.C.; Record Group: *Records of the Bureau of the Census*; Record Group Number: *29*; Series Number: *M653*; Residence Date: *1860*; Home in 1860: *District 10, Robertson, Tennessee*; Roll: *M653_1270*; Page: *296*; Family History Library Film: *805270* (Ancestry.com)

171. Gaston, "Robertson County Distilleries, 1796-1909," 53. From Wiley Woodard's Distillery Account Book: 1837-1859.

172. "For Sale on Commission," *The Democratic Clarion and Tennessee Gazette*, July 14, 1812, 8.

173. "Fairintosh Whisky," *The Edinburgh Advertiser*, June 15, 1779, 6.

174. "Crow's Whiskey," *Vicksburg Weekly Sentinel*, January 6, 1846, 4.

175. "Whisky," *Nashville Union*, May 5, 1851, 2.

176. "Fresh Arrivals," *Nashville Union*, December 18, 1852, 3.

177. "Lincoln County Whisky," *Republican Banner*, February 20, 1861, 3.

178. "A Caution to Brandy and Wine Drinkers," *Republican Banner*, Aug 16, 1857, 3.

179. "New Goods," *Republican Banner*, September 19, 1851, 3.

180. "Burge & Allen," *(Advertisement) Nashville Union and American*, February 7, 1856, 3.

181. "Whisky! Whisky!" *(Advertisement) The Memphis Daily Avalanche*, April 23, 1859, 4.

182. James H. Shackland, ed., *Public Statutes of the State of Tennessee: Since the Year 1858, Being in the Nature of a Supplement to the Code*, University of Michigan, Second (Nashville: Paul & Tavel, 1872), 99, https://www.google.com/books/edition/Public_Statutes_of_the_State_of_Tennesse/HH80AQAAMAAJ.

183. *Nashville Union and American*, August 20, 1852, 2.

184. "Unfortunate Affray," *Nashville Union and American*, August 21, 1852, 2.

185. Paul Leicester Ford, ed., *The Federalist,* Leland Stanford Jr. University (New York: Henry Holt and Company, 1898), 718–20, https://www.google.com/books/edition/The_Federalist/dI2RzQEACAAJ.

186. "Whig Convention," *Nashville American*, April 11, 1855, 2.

187. "Meeting of the Opposition of Robertson County," *Republican Banner*, February 18, 1859, 2.

188. "The Union Feeling and the Union Ticket in Tennessee," *Daily Nashville Patriot*, June 11, 1860, 2.

189. "Where Does Abraham Lincoln Stand?" *Republican Banner*, November 10, 1860, 2.

190. J.L. Morphis "Reminiscences of Eventful Session of the Legislature," *Nashville Banner*, April 5, 1913, 27.

191. *Daily Nashville Patriot*, March 2, 1861, 3.

192. "Robertson," *Daily Nashville Patriot*, April 4, 1861, 2.

193. Morphis, "Reminiscences of Eventful Session of the Legislature," 27.

194. "Battle of Fishing Creek!" *Nashville Patriot*, January 24, 1862, 2.

195. "Attempted Murder," *Daily Nashville Patriot*, May 12, 1861, 3.

196. "Whisky," *The Memphis Daily Avalanche*, February 7, 1862, 1.

197. "The Curse of Whisky," *The Athens Post*, February 21, 1862, 2.

198. *The Nashville Daily Union*, September 11, 1862, 3.

199. Gayoso House, "The Effect of Opening the Whisky Shops in Memphis," *Memphis Daily Appeal*, August 26, 1862, 1.

200. "A Century of Lawmaking for a New Nation: U.S. Congressional Documents and Debates: 1774-1875," Library of Congress, 432, 446–56, accessed October 31, 2023, http://memory.loc.gov/ammem/amlaw/lawhome.html.

201. "By Authority," *The Knoxville Daily Register*, May 21, 1863.

202. "Temperance Reform," *Brownlow's Knoxville Whig*, October 11, 1865, 3.

203. "Liquor Selling Near Colleges, *Memphis Daily Post*, October 8, 1867, 1.

204. "A Heavy Northern Tax Necessary," *Memphis Daily Appeal*, February 5, 1864, 1.

205. Office Of Communications, "TTBGOV - Historical Tax Rates," n.d., https://www.ttb.gov/tax-audit/historical-tax-rates.

206. "Statutory Pillage," *Memphis Daily Appeal*, February 22, 1867, 2.

207. "What Becomes of the Whisky?" *Nashville Union and Dispatch*, December 29, 1866, 2.

208. "Statutory Pillage."

209. "SOI Tax Stats Archive - 1863 to 1999 Annual Reports and IRS Data Books | Internal Revenue Service," n.d., 1865 PDF, 277. https://www.irs.gov/statistics/soi-tax-stats-archive-1863-to-1999-annual-reports-and-irs-data-books.

210. "To the Public," *Republican Banner*, November 17, 1865, 2.

211. "Retort to Circular," *Nashville Union*, November 16, 1865, 3.

212. "Internal Revenue Decisions," *Nashville Union and American*, August 6, 1868, 1.

213. "Whisky Frauds," *Chicago Evening Post*, April 26, 1867, 1.

214. "US63964A - I. P. Tice Spirit Meter," U.S. Patent Office, April 16, 1867, accessed November 1, 2023, https://patents.google.com/patent/US63964A/

215. "Closing of Distilleries," *Nashville Union and American*, May 31, 1867, 3.

216. "SOI Tax Stats Archive - 1863 to 1999 Annual Reports and IRS Data Books | Internal Revenue Service," n.d., 1867 PDF, 85. https://www.irs.gov/statistics/soi-tax-stats-archive-1863-to-1999-annual-reports-and-irs-data-books.

217. "Robertson County Whiskey–How the B'hoys are Humbuged," Knoxville Daily Free Press, July 16, 1867, 3.

218. "Old Robertson County," *Republican Banner*, December 21, 1867, 2.

219. The New Tax Law," *Republican Banner*, April 4, 1868, 1.

220. "Whisky," *Nashville Union and American*, May 4, 1870.

221. Goodspeed Publishing Company, *History of Tennessee: Containing Historical and Biographical Sketches of Thirty East Tennessee Counties*, Website: Family Search (The Goodspeed Publishing, Co., 1887), 848, https://www.familysearch.org/library/books/viewer/87512.

222. Ibid., 849

223. "Rum and Radicalism," *Nashville American*, March 15, 1868, 1.

224. "Dangers of the Whisky Tax," *Nashville Union and American*, Mar 11, 1868, 3.

225. "Closing Scene of the Whisky Rebellion in East Tennessee," *Memphis Public Ledger*, March 13, 1868, 1.

226. "Distilleries," *Nashville Union and American*, May 27, 1870, 4.

227. "Washington," *Public Ledger*, December 27, 1867, 2.

228. "SOI Tax Stats Archive - 1863 to 1999 Annual Reports and IRS Data Books | Internal Revenue Service," n.d., 1868 PDF, 73. https://www.irs.gov/statistics/soi-tax-stats-archive-1863-to-1999-annual-reports-and-irs-data-books.

229. "Digest of the New Liquor Law," *The Fayetteville Observer*, August 20, 1868, 1.

230. J.G. Mattingly & Bro., "Low Wines," *Republican Banner*, October 9, 1868, 1.

231. "General Market," *Republican Banner*, October 16, 1868, 4.

232. "Whisky Meter," *Nashville American*, February 19, 1869, 4

233. "A Complicated Business," *Press and Messenger*, September 1, 1869, 3.

234. C. Delano, "Important to Distillers," *Nashville American*, March 19, 1870, 3.

235. "SOI Tax Stats Archive - 1863 to 1999 Annual Reports and IRS Data Books | Internal Revenue Service," n.d., 1870 PDF, 32. https://www.irs.gov/statistics/soi-tax-stats-archive-1863-to-1999-annual-reports-and-irs-data-books.

236. "SOI Tax Stats Archive - 1863 to 1999 Annual Reports and IRS Data Books | Internal Revenue Service," n.d., 1871 PDF, 12. https://www.irs.gov/statistics/soi-tax-stats-archive-1863-to-1999-annual-reports-and-irs-data-books.

237. "SOI Tax Stats Archive - 1863 to 1999 Annual Reports and IRS Data Books | Internal Revenue Service," n.d., 1874 PDF, 21. https://www.irs.gov/statistics/soi-tax-stats-archive-1863-to-1999-annual-reports-and-irs-data-books.

238. *Fayetteville Observer*, January 12, 1871, 3.

239. Lincoln County, TN, Deed Book 1: 98, Lincoln County Register of Deeds (C.H. and W.R. Call to Hughes & Tolley Distillery Site Lease, March 25, 1869)

240. Lincoln County, TN, Deed Book E2: 293, Lincoln County Register of Deeds (Alfred Eaton to Holt, Hiles & Berry, May 21, 1869)

241. "Whisky Making," *Nashville American*, June 27, 1872, 4.

242. "Tice Meter," *The Ottawa (IL) Free Trader*, June 17, 1871, 4.

243. *Nashville Union and American*, June 16, 1871, 1.

244. "Distilleries in Tennessee," *Nashville American*, December 24, 1871.

245. "SOI Tax Stats Archive - 1863 to 1999 Annual Reports and IRS Data Books | Internal Revenue Service," n.d., 1873 PDF, 12. https://www.irs.gov/statistics/soi-tax-stats-archive-1863-to-1999-annual-reports-and-irs-data-books.

246. *Morristown Gazette*, May 28, 1873, 1.

247. Lynchburg Pioneer, *Fayetteville Observer*, May 15, 1873, 2.

248. "Reverend Daniel Houston Call," Geni_Family_Tree, May 1, 1836, accessed November 1, 2023, https://www.geni.com/people/Reverend-Daniel-Call/6000000064632640828. Several sources were used including U.S. Census records and FamilySearch.org to verify dates of Dan Call's family events.

249. Ben A. Green, *Jack Daniel's Legacy* (Shelbyville, TN: Ben A. Green, 1967), 28.

250. U.S. Census, 1870 Lincoln County First District, June 10, 1870.

251. This is one of the great mysteries in Tennessee whisky. No birth records survive for Jasper Newton Daniel, so we are left to census records. I arrive at August as it is used in the 1900 U.S. Census for Moore County. That is the first census where birth months are listed. The date is still a mystery. The August time frame and 1849 year also work with the ages noted in the 1850, 1870, and 1880 census records–taking into account the month the survey was completed. It, however, doesn't match with his death certificate which would conclude he was born in 1850–which would be impossible, since his mother died in January of that year. The 1860 census has him at 9 years old, which again would be impossible. The 1890 census records are not available.

252. U.S. Mortality Census, For the year ending June 1850 in Lincoln County, TN, 474. Lucinda Daniel, age 44, died in January of Typhoid Fever and was sick for 7 days.

253. Lincoln County Probate Records from FamilySearch.org. Samuel Rutledge Admin. Of Calaway Daniel Deed. Number 402. Property sold at auction on April 29, 1864

254. Lincoln County Probate Records from FamilySearch.org. Matilda Daniel Petition for Dower, November 20, 1865. William Tolley and Felix Waggoner were appointed commissioners to lay off and set apart the dowry.

255. "Married!" *Fayetteville Observer,* February 15, 1866.

256. Lincoln County Guardianship Document for Jasper N. Daniel. March 28, 1886.

257. U.S. Census 1870, Lincoln County, 118.

258. "Water-Spouts," *Nashville American*, March 17, 1875, 4.

259. *Herald and Mail*, March 26, 1875, 2.

260. Moore County, TN, Deed Book 1 (Daniel H. Call lease of distillery No. 16, September 1877), 257.

261. "The Sour Mash Distillers," *The Winchester Home Journal*, June 21, 1877, 3.

262. Ibid.

263. Moore County, TN, Deed Book 1 (Daniel H. Call lease of distillery No. 16, September 1877)

264. House of Representatives Congressional Record (H.R.No. 685) For the Relief of Tolley & Eaton, 2229. https://www.govinfo.gov/content/pkg/GPO-CRECB-1880-pt3-v10/pdf/GPO-CRECB-1880-pt3-v10-7.pdf

265. "Who Made the Whisky," *Nashville American*, September 24, 1883, 5.

266. Moore County, TN, Deed Book 3: 130-131 (Wilburn Hiles and Berry to Jack Daniel, Just 17, 1884).

267. "Loss of the Helena Sloman," *New York Tribune*, December 6, 1850, 5.

268. "Death of Chas. Nelson," *Nashville Banner*, December 14, 1891, 8.

269. Ibid.

270. Ibid.

271. The Church of Jesus Christ of Latter-day Saints, "Ancestral File," database, FamilySearch (https://familysearch.org/ark:/61903/2:1:MWKY-TQS : accessed 2023-11-01), entry for Louise Brengleman (1GSQ-DMH); submitted by cmiller1796007

272. "Prof. Nelson's Inheritance," *Hamilton Evening Journal*, November 29, 1892, 3.

273. "Death of Chas. Nelson"

274. Wikipedia contributors, "Nashville, Tennessee," Wikipedia, October 25, 2023, https://en.wikipedia.org/wiki/Nashville,_Tennessee#Demographics.

275. E. Doug King, *Nashville Business Directory*, Microfiche SR NO: S 3A-Reel 1: Tennessee State Library & Archives, 1st ed. (Nashville, TN: R.H. Singleton, 1861), 48.

276. "Just Received by Nelson & Pfeifer," *(Advertisement) Nashville Daily Union*, May 5, 1863, 2.

277. King, *Nashville Business Directory*.

278. "Nelson & Co.," *(Advertisement) Nashville Daily Union*, May 11, 1865, 4.

279. "Corn & Rye," *(Advertisement) Republican Banner*, October 18, 1844, 3.

280. "Building Lime," *(Advertisement) Nashville Daily Union*, January 20, 1866, 4.

281. E. Doug King, *King's Nashville Business Directory*, Hardback: Tennessee State Library & Archives, 1st ed. (Nashville, TN: E. Doug King, 1867), 229.

282. "Wanted," *Republican Banner*, January 24, 1869.

283. "Dissolution," *Nashville Union and American*, September 21, 1867, 2.

284. "Rectifiers and Distillers," *Nashville American*, April 4, 1869, 4.

285. "Fire," *Republican Banner*, August 26, 1869, 4.

286. Robertson County, TN, Deed Book 14: 452, Robertson County Archives (James A. White and Henry White to Travis Winham, August 2, 1869).

287. Ibid.

288. Robertson County, TN, Deed Book 15: 128-9, Robertson County Archives (Travis Winham to Charles Nelson, October 20, 1870).

289. Robertson County, TN, Deed Book 15: 352, Robertson County Archives (Henry H. Kirk to Charles Nelson, April 18, 1871).

290. "Dissolution," *Republican Banner*, November 3, 1867, 4.

291. "Destructive Conflagration," *Nashville American*, November 22, 1868, 4.

292. "Notice," *Republican Banner*, September 28, 1869, 3.

293. "A Big Concern," *Republican Banner*, September 17, 1871, 4.

294. *Memphis Public Ledger*, January 10, 1872, 2.

295. "A Word About Green Brier," *Nashville American*, February 9, 1896, 5.

296. "$8,765.50," *Memphis Daily Appeal*, January 28, 1872, 4.

297. "A Pleasant Day in the Country," *Nashville American*, May 26, 1878.

298. "Great Belle Meade Distillery," *Memphis Daily Appeal*, December 10, 1880, 4.

299. "A Revenue Officer Cut in the Head," *Nashville American*, September 3, 1881, 4.

300. "Fined for Assault," *Nashville Daily American*, September 3, 1878, 4.

301. "Swept by Fire," *Nashville American*, August 30, 1885, 5.

302. "Robertson County Fair," *Nashville Union and American*, October 12, 1871, 3.

303. "Death of Chas. Nelson," *Nashville American*, December 14, 1891, 5.

304. "The Barbecue," *Memphis Public Ledger*, June 3, 1879, 4.

305. "S.T. Suit Kentucky Salt River Bourbon Whisky Distilleries," *Buffalo Courier*, October 10, 1860, 1.

306. Joseph S. Miller, *Report of the Commissioner of Internal Revenue for the Fiscal Year Ended June 30, 1895*, Website: IRS (Washington, DC: Government Printing Office, 1895), 135, https://www.irs.gov/statistics/soi-tax-stats-archive-1863-to-1999-annual-reports-and-irs-data-books.

307. "Export it in Bottles," *Nashville American*, March 29, 1896, 7.

308. Michael J Owens, "US766768A - Glass-Shaping Machine," Google Patents, April 13, 1903, accessed November 2, 2023, https://patents.google.com/patent/US766768A/en.

309. Kay Baker Gaston, *Tennessee Historical Quarterly: Robertson County Distilleries, 1796-1908.*, Book: Tennessee State Archives, vol. XLIII (Tennessee Historical Society, 1984), 59. Noted as having come from miscellaneous records at the Robertson County Archives. Location in the facility is currently unknown.

310. Tonya Blades and D. Lorne McWatters, "National Register of Historic Places Registration Form" (United States Department of the Interior: National Park Service, April 2, 2008), 7:1-5.

311. "Looking Backward in Robertson Co," *Springfield Herald*, October 16, 1975. Said to be based on J.B. Killebrew's *Middle Tennessee*.

312. "Reminiscence of Eventful Session of the Legislature."

313. "Death's Harvest," *Columbia Herald and Mail*, May 22, 1903, 5.

314. "Andrew Johnson's Habits," *Knoxville Sentinel*, January 8, 1913, 4.

315. Robertson County, TN, Will and Estate Book 20:1, Robertson County Archives (John Woodard Admin June 1878 Term).

316. "Robertson County Fair," *Nashville Union and American*, October 13, 1870, 1.

317. "Business Changes at Springfield," *Clarksville Leaf-Chronicle*, January 11, 1871, 3.

318. "Woodard & Moore," *(Advertisement) Nashville Union and American*, May 29, 1873, 2. December 19, 1874, 4.

319. "Woodard & Moore," *(Advertisement) Nashville American*, November 18, 1879, 1.

320. *Annual Report of the Commissioner of Patents for the Year 1896*, Website: Google Books, vol. 2 (Government Printing Office, 1871), https://www.google.com/books/edition/Commissioner_of_Patents_Annual_Report/BAEXAQAAIAAJ.

321. "Wiley Woodard," *(Advertisement) Clarksville Leaf-Chronicle*, December 14, 1870, 4.

322. "Middle Tennessee," *Republican Banner*, August 25, 1871, 3.

323. Robertson County, TN, Deed Book 16: 534, Robertson County Archives (John R. Bridges to Hopkins and Lawrence, February 16, 1874)

324. Tennessee. Bureau Of Agriculture and Joseph Buckner Killebrew, *First and Second Reports of the Bureau of Agriculture for the State of Tennessee: Introduction to the Resources of Tennessee* (Nashville, TN: Tavel, Eastman, & Howell, 1874), 897, https://archive.org/details/firstsecondrepor00tenn/page/n7/mode/2up.

325. "Robertson County," *Nashville Union and American*, July 25, 1872, 1.

326. Agriculture and Killebrew, *First and Second Reports of the Bureau of Agriculture for the State of Tennessee: Introduction to the Resources of Tennessee*, 898.

327. *History of Tennessee, from the Earliest Time to the Present: Together with an Historical and a Biographical Sketch of Giles, Lincoln, Franklin and Moore Counties*, 1203.

328. "Distilleries in Robertson County–Three Soon in Operation," *Nashville Union and American*, February 19, 1871, 1.

329. "Personal," *Clarksville Tobacco Leaf*, November 12,1873, 1.

330. *History of Tennessee, from the Earliest Time to the Present: Together with an Historical and a Biographical Sketch of Giles, Lincoln, Franklin and Moore Counties*, 1203.

331. Robertson County, TN, Deed Book 21: 68, Robertson County Archives (Elbert Duncan to Jordan Brown, August 14, 1880).

332. Agriculture and Killebrew, *First and Second Reports of the Bureau of Agriculture for the State of Tennessee: Introduction to the Resources of Tennessee*, 897.

333. "Personal," *Memphis Daily Appeal*, October 31, 1877, 4.

334. "Death of Mr. Wilson Pitt," *Clarksville Tobacco Leaf*, April 30, 1880, 3.

335. "Death's Harvest."

336. "Trust Sale," *Nashville Daily American*, July 21, 1871, 2.

337. Robertson County, TN, Chancery Court Case 1536, Robertson County Archives (B.G. Hilliard vs Jo C. Stark).

338. "Whisky Making in Robertson County," *Clarksville Tobacco Leaf*, May 1, 1872, 1.

339. Gov. John C. Brown. "Bargain and Sale," *Nashville Union and American*, August 17, 1873, 3.

340. *Acts of the State of Tennessee: Passed by the Fortieth General Assembly 1877*, Book: Tennessee State Library and Archives (Authority, 1877), 37.

341. *The Morristown Gazette*, April 9, 1879, 3.

342. "State v Elizabeth Rouscher," Tennessee Supreme Court Case File, Tennessee State Library and Archives (October 25, 1878), ET Box 99.

343. "Vote of Kansas," *Ottawa Daily Republic*, November 9, 1880, 1.

344. "Rum Ridden Kansas," *Newton Republican*, April 15, 1889, 2.

345. "Whisky Men," *Chattanooga Daily Times*, September 22, 1882, 4.

346. "Liquor Dealers," *The Daily Memphis Avalanche*, October 19, 1882, 1.

347. "Prohibitionists," *Nashville American*, May 23, 1884, 5.

348. "Sumptuary Legislation," *Nashville American*, September 10, 1885, 7.

349. "Untrue Report," *Nashville American*, June 4, 1887, 2.

350. Ibid.

351. John Vertrees "An Address," *Nashville American*, August 13, 1887, 2.

352. "No Prohibition," *Chattanooga Daily Times*, September 30, 1887, 1.

353. "Third Ward," Chattanooga Daily Times, September 30, 1887, 4.

354. "Wet and Dry," *Daily American*, September 30, 1887, 1.

355. "Late News Items," *Maryville Times*, November 2, 1887, 2.

356. "No Prohibition."

357. "Wet and Dry."

358. "Mr. G.A. Dickel Dead," *Nashville Banner*, June 11, 1894, 1.

359. U.S. Census Year: *1870*; Census Place: *District 18, Davidson, Tennessee*; Roll: *M593_1522*; Page: *75B* (Ancestry.com)

360. "Mr. G.A. Dickel Dead."

361. *The Knoxville Register*, October 20, 1847, 2.

362. "Firemen's Grand Annual Parade," *Nashville Daily Union*, May 12, 1849, 2.

363. "Mr. G.A. Dickel Dead."

364. "Programme of the Procession," *Nashville Daily Union*, July 12, 1847, 2.

365. "Confectionary Store," *Nashville Union*, December 31, 1840, 3.

366. *Nashville Business Directory 1855-1856*, 36. Tennessee State Library and Archives.

367. National Archives and Records Administration (NARA); Washington D.C.; NARA Series: *Passport Applications, 1795-1905*; Roll #: *193*; Volume #: *Roll 193 - 25 Apr 1873-08 May 1873* (Ancestry.com)

368. The National Archives and Records Administration; Washington, D.C.; *Passenger and Crew Lists of Vessels Arriving at and Departing from Ogdensburg, New York, 5/27/1948 - 11/28/1972*; Microfilm Serial or NAID: *M237, 1820-1897* (Ancestry.com)

369. "Liquors and Cigars at Wholesale," *The Southern Citizen*, January 21, 1858, 4.

370. "Clothing, Wholesale and Retail," *The Southern Citizen*, June 3, 1858, 4.

371. Tennessee State Library and Archives; Nashville, TN, USA; *Tennessee State Marriages, 1780-2002* (Ancestry.com)

372. John Fitch, *Annals of the Army of the Cumberland*, Website: Library of Congress, 5th ed. (Philadelphia, PA: J.B. Lippincott & Co., 1864), 495, https://lccn.loc.gov/02011200

373. Ibid., 493-497.

374. National Archives at Washington DC; Washington, DC. USA; *War Department Collection of Confederate Records*; NARA film publicaton #:: *M598*; Record Group: *War Department Collection of Confederate Records*; Record Group Number: *109* (Ancestry.com)

375. Davidson County Chancery Court, Case File 3570-1964. Metro Archives Nashville Library.

376. King, *Nashville Business Directory 1865*, Tennessee State Library and Archives, 173.

377. King, *Nashville Business Directory 1866*, Tennessee State Library and Archives, 149.

378. "Meeting of German Citizens," *Nashville Union and American*, May 30, 1871, 1.

379. "Notice to Show Cause–In Bankruptcy," *Nashville American*, September 26, 1868, 3.

380. "United States vs George A. Dickel," *Nashville American and Union*, May 15, 1867, 3.

381. "Victor E. Shwab Bank and Public Service Head Dies," *The Tennessean*, November 3, 1924, 1.

382. "Annoyances of the New York Custom House Officials," *Nashville Union and American*, February 11, 1874, 3.

383. "Destructive Fire," *Republican Banner*, August 14, 1874, 4.

384. "Wholesale Liquor Trade," *Nashville Union and American*, March 14, 18875, 5.

385. "Southern Kentucky News," *Daily American*, November 25, 1877, 3.

386. "Yesterday's Fire," *The Daily American*, May 18, 1881, 4.

387. "Circuit Court," *The Daily American*, October 3, 1886, 8.

388. "The Climax Saloon Sold," *Nashville Banner*, January 11, 1887, 4.

389. "Capt. Clack to Dr. Kelley," *Nashville Banner*, June 14, 1893, 2.

390. *History of Tennessee: From the Earliest Time to the Present; Together with an Historical and a Biographical Sketch of Maury, Williamson, Rutherford, Wilson, Bedford and Marshall Counties*, vol. 2 Allen County Public Library (Goodspeed Publishing Co., 1886), 864, https://archive.org/details/historyoftenness02good/page/n5/mode/2up.

391. "Whisky in Bond," *Daily American*, January 22, 1884, 8.

392. "Victor E. Shwab versus Ewin L. Davis, et al, 1013," 5. *Coffee County Chancery Court Records, Coffee County Archives*. Records show R.J. King transaction is in Book "T" page 241 in the Register's office of Coffee County.

393. "Victor E. Shwab versus Ewin L. Davis, et al, 1013," 2. The Shwab land deed sale with M.B. Sims and the Davis' is located in the Register's office of Coffee County in Book W on pages 265 and 267.

394. "Violation of Revenue Laws," *Nashville Banner*, April 2, 1909, 7.

395. "How Tennessee Whisky Is Made," *Nashville Banner*, December 14, 1889, 4.

396. Ibid.

397. Ibid.

398. "Cascade Distillery," *(Advertisement) Nashville Banner*, May 8, 1892, 7.

399. "Old Cascade Whisky," *Daily American*, June 19, 1892, 3.

400. "Deaths and Births," *Daily American*, August 9, 1891, 10.

401. "Mr. G.A. Dickel Dead."

402. "James W. Kelly," *The Chattanooga Star*, March 11, 1907, 7.

403. Ibid.

404. King, *King's Nashville Business Directory 1866*, Tennessee State Library and Archives, *210*.

405. "Death Claims James W. Kelly," *Chattanooga News*, March 11, 1907

406. "Long Years Ago," *Chattanooga Daily Times*, August 12, 1892, 5.

407. Ibid.

408. "*Terrible Conflagration*," *Nashville Union and American*, September 22, 1867, 1.

409. "National," *Knoxville Daily Herald*, December 6, 1867, 1.

410. "Kelly & Webb," *(Advertisement) The Daily Republican*, February 7, 1896, 4.

411. "Personal," *Daily Press and Herald*, August 11, 1869, 4.

412. "Long Years Ago."

413. "Death Claims James W. Kelly."

414. *The Sweetwater Enterprise*, March 10, 1870, 2.

415. "James W. Kelly."

416. "Jno. G. Webb's," *Chattanooga Evening Mail,* December 18, 1872, 4.

417. "Long Years Ago."

418. "Faulkner Is Himself Again," *Gazette and Advertiser*, Jan 25, 1862, 3.

419. "Chancery Sale at Chattanooga," *The Daily Republican*, August 11, 1869, 4.

420. "Notice," *The Daily Republican*, July 14, 1869, 2.

421. "Dissolved," *Chattanooga Daily Times*, April 14, 1873, 4.

422. "E.R. Betterton," *Chattanooga Daily Times*, April 14, 1897, 3.

423. "Betterton's Distillery Burned," *Knoxville Daily Press and Herald*, April 23, 1875, 4.

424. "J.W. Kelly," *(Advertisement) Chattanooga Daily Times*, August 1, 1875, 1.

425. "Dissolution," *Chattanooga Daily Times*, January 6, 1876, 2.

426. "E.R. Betterton," *(Advertisement) Chattanooga Daily Commercial*, February 26, 1876, 1.

427. "E.B. Edwards," *Chattanooga Daily Times*, February 6, 1879, 3.

428. "The Liquor Men," *The Daily American*, July 10, 1887, 3.

429. "Big Money in Whiskey," *Chattanooga Daily Times*, June 4, 1890, 8.

430. "Business Change," *Chattanooga Daily Times*, July 1, 1890, 3.

431. "Read House Bar Lease," *Chattanooga Daily Times*, September 24, 1890, 4.

432. "Wanted," *Chattanooga Daily Times*, July 13, 1876, 1.

433. "For Sale," *Chattanooga Daily Times*, January 22, 1880, 3.

434. "Geo. W. Cureton," *Chattanooga Daily Times*, May 14, 1886, 2.

435. *Chattanooga Republican*, August 10, 1890, 8.

436. "New Brewery," *Chattanooga Republican*, February 22, 1891, 1.

437. "The Oldest House," *(Advertisement) Chattanooga Daily Times*, September 18, 1895, 5.

438. "Jack Daniel's," *Lawrence Democrat*, February 22, 1895, 4.

439. "Fred Fox Appointed," *Chattanooga Daily Times*, July 15, 1893, 8.

440. "Tennessee Whiskey," *(Advertisement) Chattanooga Daily Times*, June 22, 1898, 5.

441. "White Oak," *(Advertisement) Chattanooga Daily Times*, December 19, 1898, 5.

442. "Lookout Distillery," *Chattanooga Daily Times*, November 18, 1897, 8.

443. "Two Stuffed Goats," *Chattanooga Daily Times*, March 19, 1898, 5.

444. "All Whisky," *(Advertisement) Chattanooga Daily Times*, June 10, 1898, 5.

445. "The Great Street Fair," *Chattanooga Daily Times*, May 9, 1900, 10.

446. "Distillery," *Clarksville Tobacco Leaf*, December 29, 1900, 2.

447. "White Oak Distillery in Operation," *Chattanooga News*, October 25, 1902, 9.

448. "To Make Whiskey," *Chattanooga News*, November 3, 1902, 2.

449. "Old Tennessee Club," *(Advertisement) Chattanooga News*, December 4, 1903, 2.

450. "Work on Distillery," *Chattanooga Daily Times*, September 23, 1904, 5.

451. "Kelly Distillery," *Chattanooga News*, January 2, 1905, 7. The newspaper suggests they had capacity to make 5,000 barrels of whisky a day. It had to be a misprint. Gallons makes much more sense.

452. "Distillery Changes Hands," *Chattanooga News*, August 19, 1903, 7.

453. "New Still House," *Chattanooga News*, June 27, 1905, 10.

454. "Quit Business," *Chattanooga Daily Times*, August 23, 1906, 5.

455. "Revenue Increases in the Chattanooga District," *Chattanooga News*, November 23, 1905, 5.

456. "Death Claims James W. Kelly."

457. "Death of Mrs. J.W. Kelly," *Chattanooga Daily Times*, November 7, 1907, 3.

458. "A Marshal's Luck," *Memphis Avalanche*, July 12, 1888, 4.

459. "Among the Moonshiners," *Nashville Banner*, September 1, 1888, 4.

460. "A Wild-Cat Distillery," *Knoxville Daily Journal*, April 15, 1890, 2.

461. "Cold Blooded Murder," *Morristown Gazette*, June 11, 1890, 3.

462. "A Big Still Destroyed," *Nashville Banner*, September 1, 1890, 6.

463. "The Moonshiner's Way," *The Daily American*, March 12, 1892, 3.

464. "Decoyed to Death," *Chattanooga Sunday Times*, October, 9, 1892, 2.

465. Ibid.

466. "Shot Down," *Nashville Banner*, October 7, 1892, 1.

467. "After the Assassins," *Chattanooga Sunday Times*, October 9, 1892, 2.

468. "Decoyed to Death."

469. "Lincoln County Murder," *Clarksville Tobacco Leaf*, October 27, 1892, 1.

470. "After Many Days," *Nashville Banner*, October 28, 1892, 1.

471. "Well Under Way," *Daily American*, May 24, 1893, 1.

472. "Not Guilty," *Daily American*, June 4, 1893, 5.

473. "Miscellaneous," *Bolivar Bulletin*, May 4, 1894, 1.

474. "A Wildcat Distillery," *Nashville Banner*, June 6, 1895, 1

475. "Mountain Dew in Tennessee," *The Commercial Appeal*, October 28, 1894, 18.

476. "Wildcat Whisky," *Republican Banner*, October 19, 1871, 1.

477. "Mountain Dew in Tennessee."

478. Ibid.

479. "A Raid on East Tennessee Illicit Distillers," *Republican Banner*, January 22, 1871, 1.

480. *Fayetteville Observer*, June 13, 1872, 3.

481. "Moonshiner's Barbecue," *Memphis Avalanche*, August 28, 1877, 4.

482. "Illicit Distilling," *Nashville Union and American*, January 6, 1870, 4.

483. "Seized All the Outfit," *Knoxville Tribune*, December 13, 1894, 4.

484. "A Famous Woman Moonshiner," *Sacramento Daily Union*, August 25, 1873. Website: Center for Bibliographical Studies and Research https://cdnc.ucr.edu/?a=d&d=DT18940707.2.12

485. "The Second Waterloo," *Daily American*, August 28, 1878, 4.

486. Ibid.

487. Ibid.

488. "The Revenue Raiders," *Daily American*, November 14, 1878, 2.

489. "W. Campbell Morgan," *Daily American*, April 27, 1879, 27.

490. "Wm. Campbell Morgan," *Daily American*, August 15, 1888, 5.

491. "Deputy Davis," *Chattanooga Daily Times*, March 15, 1882, 3.

492. "Woman with an Unusual History Dies; Aged 100," *Nashville Banner*, July 18, 1920, 1.

493. *History of Tennessee from the Earliest Time to the Present: Together with an Historical and a Biographical Sketch of Montgomery, Robertson, Humphreys, Stewart, Dickson, Cheatham and Houston Counties*, 1134.

494. "Another Disastrous Fire at Springfield," *Clarksville Tobacco Leaf*, March 4, 1882, 2.

495. Robertson County, TN, Deed Book 21: 68 (Elbert Duncan to Jordan Brown, August 14, 1880).

496. "For Sale," *(Want Ad) Daily American*, May 4, 1886, 3.

497. "Corn Is Too High," *Daily American*, September 23, 1890, 5.

498. "Closed for Repairs," *Nashville Banner*, July 24, 1890, 4.

499. "Fire at Springfield," *Daily American*, September 18, 1890, 1.

500. "The Death Record," *Daily American*, October 15, 1890, 5.

501. "Mrs. Brown Dies at Springfield," *The Tennessean*, February 11, 1940, 40.

502. "Death of Chas. Nelson."

503. "Noble Woman Passes Away," *The Tennessean*, February 21, 1918, 1.

504. "A Will Probated," *Nashville Banner*, June 21, 1894, 7.

505. "Real Estate Transfers," *Nashville Tennessean and Nashville American*, November 10, 1912, 46.

506. *Minden City Herald*, June 27, 1919, 3.

507. The National Archives in Washington D.C.; Record Group: *Records of the Bureau of the Census*; Record Group Number: *29*; Series Number: *M653*; Residence Date: *1860*; Home in 1860: *District 25, Bedford, Tennessee*; Roll: *M653_1239*; Page: *172*; Family History Library Film: *805239*

508. "D.G. McCarthy, Wife Mollie, et al vs. Nancy Patterson, MT 1171," *Tennessee Supreme Court Collection: Tennessee State Library and Archives*, n.d., 34.

509. United States Census, 1870", , *FamilySearch* (https://www.familysearch.org/ark:/61903/1:1:MD8F-N7L : Fri Oct 06 01:01:34 UTC 2023), Entry for Parry Patterson and Nancy Patterson, 1870

510. Federal Tax Books, Fourth District. December 1872.

511. "Distillery Seized," *Public Ledger*, November 18, 1885, 2.

512. "Tullahoma," *Daily American*, October 25, 1879, 3.

513. "D.G. McCarthy, Wife Mollie, et al vs. Nancy Patterson, MT 1171," 29, 38, 41, 46. Testimony from several witnesses.

514. "Distillery Seized."

515. "Tullahoma," *Daily American*, October 22, 1886, 1.

516. Bedford County TN Title Deed Book QQQ: 431-432 Tennessee State Library and Archives (Barney Patterson to Nancy Patterson). Roll 131.

517. Bedford County TN Will Book 1: 735 Tennessee State Library and Archives (Barney Patterson Will Filed in Robert Singleton's Office). Roll 96.

518. "D.G. McCarthy, Wife Mollie, et al vs. Nancy Patterson, MT 1171," 12-13, 16.

519. Ibid., 12, 16-19.

520. Ibid., 5-6, 22-31.

521. Ibid., 32-50.

522. "United States Census, 1900", , *FamilySearch* (https://www.familysearch.org/ark:/61903/1:1:MSZ5-Y6V : Fri Oct 06 00:00:27 UTC 2023), Entry for Nancy Patterson and Tinis Liles, 1900.

523. Moore County TN Title Deeds Book 3: 180, Moore County Archives (Jasper N. Daniel to Tolley & Eaton, October 11, 1884).

524. Green. *Jack Daniel's Legacy*, 78.

525. "Palatable Whiskies," *(Advertisement) Chicago Tribune*, January 16, 1898, 8.

526. "Announcement" *(Advertisement) Nashville Banner*, June 23, 1904, 3.

527. "Tullahoma Blaze," *Chattanooga Daily Times*, June 28, 1887, 1.

528. "Fire at Cleveland," *Daily American*, November 28, 1891, 4.

529. "A Distillery Burned," *Daily American*, December 5, 1891, 5.

530. "Distillery Burned Near Newport," *Knoxville Tribune*, April 26, 1894, 5.

531. "Work of an Incendiary," *Knoxville Tribune*, July 23, 1895, 3.

532. "Fiery Liquid Sure Enough," *Knoxville Tribune*, May 12, 1898, 2.

533. "Destroyed By Fire," *Nashville Banner*, June 1, 1898, 2.

534. "Whisky Warehouse Burned," *Chattanooga Daily Times*, June 2, 1898, 3.

535. "Reversal Secured," *Daily American*, December 22, 1899, 2.

536. "Goes to Chattanooga," *Daily American*, November 13, 1897, 1.

537. R.A. Halley, "Stories of the Town," *Nashville Banner*, July 15, 1899, 8.

538. Enters the Race," *Nashville Banner*, January 21, 1902, 4.

539. "Distillery to be Sold," *Daily American*, April 27, 1901, 3.

540. "Federal Court," *Knoxville Daily Journal*, January 13, 1887, 5.

541. "Make 'Ole Lincoln'," *Chattanooga Daily Times*, June 5, 1897, 1.

542. "Has Never Suspended," *Daily American*, March 8, 1896, 18.

543. "Jack Daniel's Famous Distillery," *Daily American*, March 8, 1896, 18.

544. Jack Daniel's Plant Seized," *Nashville Banner*, February 25, 1898, 1.

545. Mt. Pleasant Joyful," *Columbia Herald*, April 21, 1899, 5.

546. "Allensville Local Items," *Clarksville Tobacco Leaf*, August 19, 1874, 3.

547. King Booze Victorious," *Nashville Baptist and Reflector*, February 14, 1901, 8-9.

548. "Whisky Fund," *Knoxville Sentinel*, February 22, 1901, 7.

549. "Current Topics," *Nashville Baptist and Reflector,* March 21, 1901, 1.

550. "The Adams Bill," *Johnson City Comet*, January 29, 1903, 2.

551. "The Election at Springfield," *Chattanooga News*, March 14, 1903, 12.

552. Lincoln County Expiration Register, 64-120. Lincoln County Archives.

553. "Saloons are Going," *Morristown Republican*, April 11, 1903, 3.

554. "Senator Edward Ward Carmack," *Nashville Baptist and Reflector,* November 19, 1908, 8.

555. "Sober Thoughts," *Union City Commercial*, May 11, 1906, 4.

556. "Tollett Road Bill Passes," *Nashville Banner*, April 12, 1907, 4.

557. "Saloons are Going."

558. "Repeal of Jamestown Appropriation Asked," *Nashville Banner*, April 6, 1907, 1.

559. Edward Ward Carmack "Saloon Must Be Destroyed," *Nashville Banner*, September 19, 1906, 3.

560. "Carrie Nation Says Knoxville Is Wicked," *Nashville American*, November 29, 1906, 3.

561. "Pat's Barn," *Knoxville Sentinel*, June 17, 1899, 12.

562. "Shooting Scrape," *Knoxville Daily Chronicle*, April 23, 1873, 4.

563. "Cal Johnson to Quit Gay Street Business," *Knoxville Sentinel*, August 20, 1913, 6.

564. Ibid.

565. "Popular Voice," *Knoxville Daily Chronicle*, August 12, 1885, 5.

566. "County Court Proceedings," *Knoxville Daily Chronicle*, December 5, 1882, 4.

567. "Cal Johnson For Alderman," *Knoxville Daily Tribune*, January 13, 1883, 1.

568. "Why Not Have Horse Races in Knoxville This Fall?" *Knoxville Sentinel*, August 20, 1902, 8.

569. "Cal Johnson to Quit Gay Street Business,"

570. "Prohibition Cause Wins Almost Two to One," *Knoxville Sentinel*, March 12, 1907, 1.

571. "Cal Johnson Has Bought Lincoln Theater," *Knoxville Sentinel*, March 12, 1908, 3.

572. "Cal Johnson to Quit Gay Street Business."

573. "Won First Race 30 Years Ago," *Knoxville Sentinel*, June 13, 1907, 12.

574. "Speeches Made For Red Wolf," *Memphis Commercial Appeal*, June 24, 1908, 4.

575. "Hot Reply to Carmack," *Chattanooga Daily Times*, April 25, 1908, 4.

576. "Mr. Carmack Hits Saloons," *Chattanooga Daily Times*, March 18, 1908, 3.

577. "Whisky Men Posting City," *Nashville Banner*, March 4, 1908, 7.

578. "Carmack's Platform," *Knoxville Sentinel*, April 11, 1908, 1.

579. "Who Killed Margaret Lear?" *Chattanooga Star*, May 28, 1908, 4.

580. "That Gin Matter," *Nashville Banner*, June 17, 1908, 7.

581. "Lee Levy's Vile Gin," *Chattanooga Star*, June 19, 1908, 1.

582. "Only One Is Guilty," *Chattanooga Daily Times*, June 26, 1908, 5.

583. "With Carmack as Editor," *Nashville American*, August 24, 1908, 1.

584. "The Carmack Folly," *Chattanooga News*, October 8, 1908, 4.

585. "Conference of Monday Proceeding the Tragedy," *Knoxville Daily Journal and Tribune*, November 10, 1908, 2.

586. "Ex-Senator Carmack Killed," *Chattanooga Daily Times*, November 10, 1908, 1-2.

587. "Ex-Senator Carmack Killed."

588. "Enormous Crowd Honors Dead Man," *Nashville American*, November 16, 1908, 10.

589. "Shall Hate and Hysteria Ruin the State While Betraying the Democracy?" *Memphis Commercial Appeal*, January 5, 1909, 6.

590. "State-widers Bolt Caucus in the House," *Memphis Commercial Appeal*, January 5, 1909, 1, 3.

591. "Against State-wideism," *Memphis Commercial Appeal*, April 17, 1908, 14.

592. "Some of the Striking Sentences in Gov. Patterson's Veto Message," *Memphis Commercial Appeal*, January 20, 1909, 1.

593. "Afraid of Delay," *Nashville American*, January 16, 1909, 2.

594. "Free Speech Denied to Local Option," *Memphis Commercial Appeal*, January 12, 1909, 1, 3.

595. "State-wide Prohibition Bill Passes," *Memphis Commercial Appeal*, January 13, 1909, 1.

596. "Is Confiscation Legal?" *Memphis Commercial Appeal*, January 20, 1909, 6.

597. "Shot Through Like a Comet," *Memphis Commercial Appeal*, January 20, 1909, 1.

598. "Leased Wire Into Sentinel Office," *Knoxville Sentinel*, Jan 19, 1909, 1.

599. "Politics Enters Cooper Trial," *Chattanooga Daily News*, February 4, 1909, 3.

600. "Dramatic Scenes in Cooper-Sharp Trial," *Knoxville Sentinel*, February 17, 1909, 8.

601. "Fight on Prohibition Carmack's Greatest Irritant," *Chattanooga Daily Times*, March 20, 1909, 2.

602. "Judge Hart Declines to Accept Verdict of Disagreement," *Chattanooga Daily Times*, March 20, 1909, 1.

603. "Coopers Convicted of Murder," *Clarksville Leaf-Chronicle*, March 20, 1909, 3.

604. "Motion is Filed in Cooper Case," *Nashville American*, April 16, 1909, 5.

605. "Errors in Charge and Rulings of Lower Court," *Nashville Banner*, April 13, 1910, 11.

606. "Final Act in a Political Drama Has Taken Place," *Richmond Palladium and Sun*, November 14, 1910, 1, 11.

607. "Murdered at Nashville," *Crossville Chronicle*, September 3, 1919, 1.

608. "Serious Case," *Chattanooga Star*, July 1, 1908, 2.

609. "M.H. Davis, Tullahoma, Tenn," *Chattanooga Daily Times*, April 1, 1898, 3.

610. Kay Baker Gaston, "George Dickel Tennessee Sour Mash Whiskey: The Story Behind the Label," *Tennessee Historical Quarterly* Volume LVII Fall 1998 No. 2: 160. Based on Gaston's interview with McLin's son Thurman Davis in 1983.

611. One-Half Million Gallons Cascade in Seizure," *Columbia Herald*, April 9, 1909, 9.

612. "In Miladi's Realm," *Nashville American*, December 17, 1909, 7.

613. "Survey of Large Brandy Distillery," *Chattanooga Daily Times*, July 29, 1906, 13.

614. "The Standard Whiskey," *(Advertisement) Chattanooga News*, December 12, 1908, 16.

615. "E.R. Betterton & Co,." *(Advertisement) Chattanooga Daily Times*, July 16, 1909, 5.

616. "Liquor Test a Certainty," *Chattanooga Daily Times*, January 15, 1910, 5.

617. "Drink Manufacturers To Be Closed Today," *Knoxville Sentinel*, December 31, 1909, 10.

618. "An Interstate Liquor Shipment Law to be Passed," *Nashville Baptist and Reflector*, February 11, 1909, 4.

619. "Fight Against Prohibition," *Nashville Tennessean and Nashville American*, June 11, 1911, 4.

620. "Bristol Distillery Busy," *Chattanooga Daily Times*, September 29, 1909, 2.

621. "As to the Kelly Case," *Johnson City Comet*, December 1, 1910, 4.

622. "Rectifying Whisky," *The Roanoke Times*, December 19, 1909,

623. "Local Briefs," *Chattanooga Daily Times*, May 21, 1910, 5.

624. "Cascade Pure Whisky," *(Advertisement) Chattanooga Daily Times*, December 8, 1909, 7.

625. "At Least One Saloon Out of Law's Reach," *Chattanooga Daily Times*, August 14, 1909, 1.

626. "Mountain Saloon Burned To Ground," *Chattanooga News*, September 29, 1909, 1.

627. "Cal F. Johnson's Gift to Y.M.C.A.," *Knoxville Sentinel*, November 27, 1908, 4.

628. "Colored Y.M.C.A. Work Encouraged," *Knoxville Sentinel*, November 27, 1908, 4.

629. "Cal Johnson's "Dan" Has Crossed Over River," *Knoxville Sentinel*, February 12, 1910, 12.

630. "Cal Johnson to Quit Gay Street Business,"

631. "Cal Johnson to Quit Gay Street Business,"

632. *The Nashville Issue*, September 17, 1891.

633. "Ledger Lines," *Memphis Public Ledger*, November 26, 1876, 4.

634. "Ledger Lines," *Memphis Public Ledger*, December 7, 1876, 3.

635. "$500 Reward," *Memphis Daily Appeal*, September 5, 1858, 5.

636. "Fine Liquors," *Memphis Bulletin*, April 25, 1865, 3.

637. "The Whisky Pool," *Memphis Daily Appeal*, September 18, 1886, 4.

638. "A. Vaccaro Dead," *Memphis Commercial Appeal*, Aug 8, 1899, 5.

639. "Prominent Business Man Dies at Ripe Old Age, *Memphis Commercial Appeal*, January 13, 1919, 5.

640. "A. Vaccaro & Co.," *Memphis Daily Appeal*, November 18, 1865, 1.

641. T.M. Halpin, ed., *Memphis City Directory 1866,* Tennessee State Library and Archives (Memphis, TN: Bingham, Williams & Co., 1866), 95.

642. *Edwards' Memphis Directory 1868-9*, Tennessee State Library and Archives (Memphis, TN: Southern Publishing Co., 1868), 57.

643. *Edwards' Annual Director to the Inhabitants, Institutions, Incorporated Companies, Etc.: In the City of Memphis for 1870.* Tennessee State Library and Archives (Memphis, TN: Southern Publishing Co., 1870), 69.

644. "Dissolution," *Memphis Daily Appeal*, September 7, 1873, 1.

645. *Memphis Public Ledger*, August 26, 1876, 3.

646. "Removal," *Memphis Daily Appeal*, September 5, 1880, 6.

647. "A. Vaccaro Dead."

648. "Miscellaneous," *Memphis Commercial Appeal,* June 6, 1903, 11.

649. "All Smart Men Know," *Memphis Commercial Appeal*, March 3, 1907, 14.

650. "Like Old Rips Van Winkle," (Advertisement) *Memphis Commercial Appeal*, October 8, 1906, 5.

651. "Much Damage to Factories," *Memphis Commercial Appeal*, February 3, 1907, 11.

652. "Crashed Through Whisky Barrel," *Nashville Banner*, August 24, 1909, 3.

653. Bill of sales procured from Chris and Alex Canale from their own private records at Old Dominick.

654. "'Old Dominick' Whiskey" *(Advertisement) Memphis Commercial Appeal*, November 23, 1911, 11.

655. "Liquors," *(Advertisement) Memphis Commercial Appeal*, March 12, 1914, 10.

656. Dr. R.B. Maury, "Reasons Why Crump Should Be Elected," *Memphis Commercial Appeal*, October 29, 1909, 10.

657. "People Coming and Going," *Chattanooga Daily Times*, March 28, 1910, 4.

658. "After Soft Drink Dealers," *Clarksville Leaf-Chronicle*, January 3, 1910, 4.

659. "Investigation of Grand Jury," *Nashville American*, February 10, 1910, 5.

660. "Injunctions Against Saloons Dissolved," *Memphis Commercial Appeal*, October 29, 1910, 1.

661. "Gov. Patterson Announces Candidacy For Governor," *Nashville Banner*, April 19, 1910, 10.

662. "Littleton and Hooper," *Chattanooga Daily Times*, December 24, 1912, 4.

663. "Message to Legislature," *Nashville Banner*, January 28, 1913, 6.

664. "Crump Brands Stahlman and Hooper 'Liars,'" *Knoxville Sentinel*, March 15, 1913, 2.

665. "Democracy United; Hoopers Plans Awry," *Memphis Commercial Appeal*, March 18, 1913, 1.

666. "Hegina to Other States is Now On," *Chattanooga News*, March 31, 1913, 5.

667. "Road Roller Runs Roughly," *Nashville Banner*, April 30, 1913, 4.

668. "In Torrid Message Governor Says Grafters Oppose Law Enforcement," *Nashville Banner*, September 9, 1913, 1, 6.

669. "Law Enforcement People Ready to Shoot Their Way out of Legislative Halls," *Chattanooga Daily Times*, September 24, 1913, 1.

670. "Praise for M'Reynolds," *Chattanooga News*, September 27, 1913, 4.

671. Many Liquor Licenses Have Been Turned In," *Knoxville Journal and Tribune,*" October 2, 1913, 5.

672. "How the Battle for Law Was Won," *Chattanooga News*, October 17, 1913, 15.

673. "Nashville Dry as the Sahara," *Knoxville Journal and Tribune*, December 10, 1913, 5.

674. "A Dry Town," *Memphis Commercial Appeal*, March 3, 1914, 6.

675. "Too Busy For Boating," *Memphis Commercial Appeal*, March 19, 1914, 4.

676. "Will Test Nuisance Act," *Nashville Banner*, March 10, 1914, 1.

677. "Nuisance Act Valid Says Supreme Court," *The Parisian*, June 19, 1914, 1.

678. "Nashville Saloonmen to Rockpile," *Clarksville Leaf-Chronicle*, March 17, 1914, 7.

679. "Makes Road Builders of Two Saloon Men," *Memphis Commercial Appeal*, March 17, 1914, 18.

680. "'Pie Hunters Control Democrats' - Hooper," *Memphis Commercial Appeal*, June 2, 1914, 18.

681. "Anti Saloon Leader Resigns Position," *Memphis Commercial Appeal*, October 6, 1914, 14.

682. "Rye's Majority Will Go Beyond 20,000," *Memphis Commercial Appeal*, November 5, 1914, 4.

683. "Democratic Control," *Knoxville Sentinel*, January 19, 1915, 4.

684. "That Ouster Law," *Memphis Commercial Appeal*, Jan 31, 1915, 6.

685. "Text of State's New Ouster Law," *Nashville Banner*, January 30, 1915, 2.

686. *Public Acts of the State of Tennessee: Passed by the Fifty-Ninth General Assembly 1915* Tennessee State Library and Archives (Authority, 1915), 20–26, 77–81, 142–43, 187–90, 386.

687. "Democracy of Moore County," *Knoxville Journal and Tribune*, November 12, 1915, 5.

688. Mayor Crump Believes Liquor Bills Doomed-Substitute Bills Ready," *Nashville Banner*, December 10, 1915, 10.

689. "Crump Again Is In Power," *Chattanooga Daily Times*, February 13, 1916, 1.

690. "Crump Resigns Office of Mayor," *Nashville Banner*, February 22, 1916, 1.

691. "Text of the Famous "Bone Dry" Law Which Will Be Effective March 1," *Chattanooga Daily Times*, February 5, 1917, 8.

692. "Crump Indorses the Ouster Law," *Memphis Commercial Appeal*, May 18, 1916, 8.

693. "Police Arrest 26 In Lottery Game Raid," *Memphis Commercial Appeal*, February 25, 1916, 10.

694. "Patrolman Is Dismissed," *Memphis Commercial Appeal*, April 9, 1916, 5.

695. "Policemen Suspended," *Memphis Commercial Appeal*, May 30, 1916, 5.

696. "White Woman Goes Free," *Memphis Commercial Appeal*, April 18, 1916, 7.

697. "Goldklang Gets Off," *Memphis Commercial Appeal*, May 9, 1916, 8.

698. "Hid Booze in Safe," *Memphis Commercial Appeal*, June 6, 1916, 6.

699. "The Boys Made Hay While Lid Was Off," *Memphis Commercial Appeal*, June 28, 1916, 10.

700. "City Runs Blind Tiger to Catch Liquor Men," *Memphis Commercial Appeal*, September 6, 1916, 4.

701. "Revenue Violations," *Chattanooga Daily News*, September 23, 1898, 6.

702. "U.S. Revenue Laws May Trip Up Couch," *Memphis Commercials Appeal*, September 7, 1916, 1.

703. "Passing of Couch's AntiLiquor Squad," *Memphis Commercial*, January 1, 1917, 5.

704. "These Officers, " *(Photo) Memphis Commercial Appeal*, January 11, 1917, 8.

705. "T.C. Betterton Under Arrest," *Chattanooga News*, October 2, 1915, 1.

706. "Chattanooga Coffin Factory," *Chattanooga Daily Times*, June 7, 1889, 4.

707. "Betterton on Stand," *Chattanooga Daily Times*, November 20, 1915, 9.

708. "Wholesale Liquor Men Sign Binding Pledge," *Chattanooga News*, October 15, 1913, 8.

709. "Acquittal of Betterman," *Chattanooga Daily Times*, November 24, 1915, 5.

710. "Secret Service Man Principal Witness, *Chattanooga News*, November 18, 1915, 5.

711. "Statement by Betterton Detailing Facts Surrounding Investigation, *Chattanooga Daily Times*, October 3, 1915, 5.

712. "Coffin Company Guilty; Betterton Not Guilty," *Chattanooga News*, November 23, 1915, 1.

713. "Bitterness of Lawyers," *Chattanooga Daily Times*, November 23, 1915, 8.

714. "Judge Sanford Fixes Fines in Coffin Company Case," *Chattanooga News*, November 27, 1915, 5.

715. "Loving Cup Given to Mr. Betterton by Men in Ranks," *Chattanooga Daily Times*, December 18, 1915, 7.

716. "Gouge's Distillery to Begin Operation," *Bristol Herald Courier*, February 9, 1910, 6.

717. "Lost Heavily on His Hogs, *Bristol Evening News*, January 17, 1911, 4.

718. "Distillery Resumes," *Memphis Commercial Appeal*, July 13, 1911, 3.

719. "Gouge Company Found Not Guilty on Charge of Defrauding Uncle Sam," *Bristol Herald Courier*, May 21, 1912, 3.

720. "Officers Seize Stock of E. Gouge and Company," *Bristol Herald Courier*, December 28, 1916, 6.

721. "'Gouging' Gouge & Co.," *Knoxville Journal and Tribune*, Feb 28, 1917, 5.

722. "Liquor Property Sold," *Memphis Commercial Appeal*, April 24, 1917, 9.

723. Robert Loving. "Whisky Was Prescribed in Big Flu Epidemic, *Bristol Herald Courier*, July 31, 1960, 8.

724. "Terms of Compromise in Gouge Case Agreed Upon," *Bristol Herald Courier*, December 28, 1919, 3.

725. "Flames Destroy Big Distilling Plant," *Bristol Herald Courier*, June 4, 1919, 2.

726. "Whiskey Is Shipped Away From Bristol," *Bristol Herald Courier*, July 24, 1920, 3.

727. "Carl White Buys Interest in Distillery," *Chattanooga News*, February 2, 1911, 2.

728. "A Misunderstanding," *(Advertisement) Knoxville Journal and Tribune*, February 5, 1911, 15.

729. "Jack Daniel's No. 7 Still Flourishes," *Nashville Banner*, April 30, 1909, 15.

730. "Fire!" *(Advertisement) Chattanooga Daily Times*, November 1, 1914, 25.

731. "Wanted-Female Help," *Louisville Courier Journal*, April 29, 1917, 47.

732. "Notice," (Advertisement) *Louisville Courier Journal*, December 18, 1919.

733. "V.E. Shwab Died Sunday," *Nashville Banner*, November 3, 1924, 1, 7.

734. "Walker Votes Aye, Will Move to Reconsider," *Chattanooga Daily Times*, August 19, 1920, 1.

735. G.F. Milton "Proud of Opportunity to Free American Women from Political Slavery," *Chattanooga News*, August 19, 1920, 1.

736. G.F. Milton, "Burn's Vote Was Influenced by His Mother's Views," *Chattanooga News*, August 19, 1920, 1.

737. "Booze and Bolshevism," *Chattanooga News*, January 17, 1920, 8.

738. "How Thirsty are Supplied in Hamilton County," *Chattanooga Daily Times*, Sept 28, 1921, 12.

739. "Ibid.

740. "Holiday Raid on 5th Avenue Nets 200 Gallons of Rum," *Nashville Tennessean*, December 24, 1926, 1.

741. "Moonshiners Most Active in the Summer," *Memphis Commercial Appeal (New York Herald)*, April 9, 1922, 60.

742. "Moonshiners Most Active in the Summer."

743. "Death Grins When Thirsty Drink 'Pizen,'" *Chattanooga Daily Times (New York Times)*, December 28, 1925, 5.

744. "How Thirsty are Supplied in Hamilton County."

745. "Death Grins When Thirsty Drink 'Pizen.'"

746. "James Pierce Cruelly Slain by Bootlegger," *Chattanooga Daily Times*, August 5, 1921, 5.

747. "Two Condemned Men Subnormal," *Nashville Banner*, February 16, 1922, 1.

748. "Attempt to Saw Way to Freedom," *Chattanooga News*, November 17, 1921, 5.

749. "Costs Millions to Enforce Law," *Knoxville Journal and Tribune*, May 5, 1920, 3.

750. Thomas Crain, "Modern Moonshiner Desperate Criminal, Unlike Distiller of Pre-Volstead Days," *Chattanooga Daily Times*, April 22, 1923, 18.

751. Ibid.

752. "The Harvest of Gold and Death in the Moonshine Belt," *Chattanooga News*, April 1, 1922, 15.

753. "Cal Johnson Ill," *Knoxville Journal and Tribune*, March 15, 1920, 8.

754. "Cal Johnson's End Probably at Hand," *Knoxville Journal*, April 4, 1925, 8.

755. "Benefactor For Negro Race Dies," *Knoxville Journal*, April 8, 1925, 4.

756. Ibid.

757. "White Men Will Take Off Hats to Cal F. Johnson," *Knoxville News*, April 9, 1925, 5.

758. "Mule Sale!" *(Advertisement) Chattanooga Daily Times*, January 12, 1923, 3.

759. "Passing of Jack Daniel's Plant," *Nashville Banner*, April 19, 1917, 15.

760. "16 Barrels, 118 Cases of Whisky Stolen in Robbery at Warehouse," *St. Louis Post Dispatch*, December 9, 1922, 1.

761. "Lem Motlow Takes the Stand," *Nashville Banner*, December 7, 1925, 9.

762. "Removal Revealed on Sept. 10," *St. Louis Star*, September 21, 1923, 1-2.

763. "Witnesses Called in Distillery Inquiry," *St. Louis Post Dispatch*, September 27, 1923, 14.

764. "Jurors Picked, Motlow Trail Waits One Day," *St. Louis Star*, December 3, 1924, 1.

765. "Motlow Goes on Trial for Life," *Chattanooga News*, December 3, 1924, 1.

766. "White Witness Agrees," *St. Louis Star*, December 5, 1924, 1.

767. "Widow and Her Husband's Slayer," (Photo) *St. Louis Star*, December 4, 1924, 2.

768. "Arguments Given in Motlow's Trial in Pullis Killing," *St. Louis Post Dispatch*, December 10, 1924, 1-2.

769. "Instructions of Court to Motlow Jury," *St. Louis Post Dispatch*, December 10, 1924, 1-2.

770. "'Just Forget Me' Widow of Pullis Requests Public," *St. Louis Star*, December 13, 1924, 3.

771. "Ave Lem Salutamus!" *Memphis Commercial Appeal*, Dec 12, 1924, 6.

772. "'Just Forget Me' Widow of Pullis Requests Public," *St. Louis Star and Times*, December 13, 1924, 3.

773. "Lem Motlow Free on Plea He Acted to Defend Himself," *St. Louis Post Dispatch*, December 11, 1924, 1.

774. "Lem Motlow Takes the Stand," *Nashville Banner*, December 7, 1925, 9.

775. Ibid.

776. "Wets Hold 3 to 1 Lead in Literary Digest's Poll as 38 States Return Votes," *Belleville Daily Advocate*, March 11, 1932, 2. Sample of the March 12, 1932 poll tracked in newspapers across the country.

777. "Rural Districts For Repeal, Poll Indicates," *Nashville Banner,* June 16, 1932, 16.

778. Agriculture and Killebrew, *First and Second Reports of the Bureau of Agriculture for the State of Tennessee: Introduction to the Resources of Tennessee*, 897.

779. Joe Early. "Around the Town," *Brooklyn Times Union*, December 11, 1932, 6. Referencing the 1932 U.S. Congressional House Record 8560 "Petition of the Associated Cooperage Industries of America".

780. Frederic J. Haskin. "Federal Alcohol Control Administration," *St. Joseph News-Press*, October 5, 1934, 22.

781. Office Of Communications, "TTBGOV - Federal Alcohol Administration Act Historical Background," n.d., https://www.ttb.gov/trade-practices/federal-alcohol-administration-act-historical-background.

782. "Standards of Identity for Distilled Spirits, Title 27 Code of Federal Regulations, Pt. 5.22(1)(Iii)," *Government Publishing Office*, n.d., accessed November 7, 2023. https://www.govinfo.gov/content/pkg/CFR-2008-title27-vol1/pdf/CFR-2008-title27-vol1-sec5-22.pdf

783. "Motlow Offers Reward of $500." *Nashville Banner*, September 30, 1911, 13.

784. "Jack Daniel Firm Again in Hands of Lem Motlow," *St. Louis Star and Times*, August 31, 1933, 8.

785. "Clark et al. v. State Ext Rel. Bobo, 172 Tenn. 429, 113 S.W.2d 374," *Case Text*, January 15, 1938, accessed November 7, 2023, https://casetext.com/case/clark-et-al-v-state-ex-rel-bobo.

786. "State Ex Rel. Motlow v. Clark et al 173 Tenn. 81 114 S.W.2d 800," *Case Text*, April 2, 1938, accessed November 7, 2023, https://casetext.com/case/state-ex-rel-v-clark-7.

787. Charter of Incorporation Record Group 42. Jack Daniel's Distillery Vol 18:81. Tennessee State Library and Archives (March 11, 1939).

788. "Rare Jack Daniel's," *Fortune Magazine*, July 1951.

789. MikeandJack, "Jess Gamble - MD #4," *Maxwells House Forum*, August 27, 2012, accessed December 2, 2023, https://maxwellshouse.co.uk/forum/index.php?/topic/18218-jess-gamble-md-4/.

790. "Ole Smoky Again Named the Most Visited Distillery in the World In 2022," February 14, 2023, https://olesmoky.com/blogs/news/ole-smoky-again-named-the-most-visited-distillery-in-the-world-in-2022.

791. "Tennessee General Assembly Legislation," n.d., https://wapp.capitol.tn.gov/apps/Billinfo/default.aspx?BillNumber=HB1084&ga=108.

792. Clay Risen, "Jack Daniel's Embraces a Hidden Ingredient: Help From a Slave," *New York Times*, June 25, 2016, accessed November 8, 2023, https://www.nytimes.com/2016/06/26/dining/jack-daniels-whiskey-nearis-green-slave.html.

Thank You For Reading My Book!

CAN YOU DO ME A FAVOR?

Your feedback on my books is important to me. Please leave me an honest review on Amazon, letting me know what you thought of the book. Thanks so much! *Cheers and slàinte mhath!*
Drew Hannush

INDEX AND COMMUNITY

Full Index On-Line

For a detailed index of this book, please visit **whiskey-lore.com/tennesseeindex**

Join the Whiskey Lore Community

If you love whiskey history and can't get enough. Keep up with Drew's travels and stories, and learn about future book releases. Join the Whiskey Lore Community at **whiskey-lore.com/community**

www.ingramcontent.com/pod-product-compliance
Lightning Source LLC
Chambersburg PA
CBHW050223100526
44585CB00017BA/1760